ABHANDLUNGEN
DER RHEINISCH-WESTFÄLISCHEN AKADEMIE DER WISSENSCHAFTEN

Sonderreihe
PAPYROLOGICA COLONIENSIA
Herausgegeben von der
Rheinisch-Westfälischen Akademie der Wissenschaften
in Verbindung mit der Universität zu Köln
Vol. XVI. 2

PAPYROLOGICA COLONIENSIA · Vol. XVI. 2

Supplementum Magicum

Vol. II

(Suppl. Mag. II)

edited with translations and notes by
Robert W. Daniel and Franco Maltomini

WESTDEUTSCHER VERLAG

In Zusammenarbeit mit der Arbeitsstelle für Papyrusforschung im Institut für Altertumskunde
der Universität zu Köln
Leiter: Professor Dr. Reinhold Merkelbach

Das Manuskript
wurde von der Klasse für Geisteswissenschaften
am 19. Juni 1991
in die Sonderreihe der Abhandlungen aufgenommen.

Die Deutsche Bibliothek – CIP-Einheitsaufnahme

Supplementum magicum : (Suppl. mag.) / ed. with transl. and notes by
Robert W. Daniel and Franco Maltomini. [In Zusammenarbeit mit der Arbeitsstelle
für Papyrusforschung im Institut für Altertumskunde
der Universität zu Köln]. – Opladen: Westd. Verlag
(Abhandlungen der Rheinisch-Westfälischen Akademie der Wissenschaften:
Sonderreihe Papyrologica Coloniensia; Vol. 16)
NE: Daniel, Robert W. [Hrsg.]; Suppl. mag.; Rheinisch-Westfälische Akademie
der Wissenschaften <Düsseldorf>: Abhandlungen der Rheinisch-Westfälischen
Akademie der Wissenschaften / Sonderreihe Papyrologica Coloniensia
Vol. 2. Ed. with transl. and notes by Robert W. Daniel and
Franco Maltomini. – 1992
ISBN 3-531-09933-7
NE: Daniel, Robert W. [Hrsg.]

Der Westdeutsche Verlag ist ein Unternehmen
der Verlagsgruppe Bertelsmann International.

© 1992 by Westdeutscher Verlag GmbH, Opladen
Druck und buchbinderische Verarbeitung: Boss-Druck, Kleve
Printed in Germany
ISSN 0078-9410
ISBN 3-531-09933-7

CONTENTS

Contents

INTRODUCTION

Also in the course of preparing this second volume, all transcriptions were controlled against photographs, and when possible we checked the originals ourselves.[1] Some readings were kindly checked for us by others on the originals, namely by A.Blanchard (**54, 57**), R.A.Coles (**58, 88, 89, 90, 94, 99, 100**), G.B.D'Alessio (**58, 83**), C.Gallazzi (**67**), H.Maehler (**83**), P.J.Parsons (**94**), and J.R.Rea (**85, 89**). W.Brashear confirmed some new readings resulting from our autopsy of **72**. We would like to extend our thanks to all of these scholars and also, for assistance of more general nature, to G.Bastianini, G.Petzl, R.Kotansky, A.Kwiecinski, G.Messeri and J. Quaegebeur. Those mentioned in the preface to Vol. I continued to be of help, and we repeat our thanks to them here.

We are grateful to the Rheinisch-Westfälische Akademie der Wissenschaften for including the two volumes in the present series and for a subsidy towards the cost of printing. Our indebtedness to the Alexander von Humboldt Foundation, of course, remains. Maltomini wishes to thank once again the Consiglio Nazionale delle Ricerche and the Ministero dell'Università e della Ricerca Scientifica e Tecnologica.

Soon after the completion of Vol. I, it became possible for both editors to use the computer-readable disks of the Thesaurus Linguae Graecae[2] and the Duke Data Bank of Documentary Papyri[3], and so parts of the commentaries in Vol. II could be provided with fuller documentation.

In yet another respect, the preparation of the present volume has differed from our former procedure when both editors could collaborate daily and in person in Cologne. This time communication was confined to the post between Cologne and Pisa. Although each editor profited from the remarks of the other, for practical purposes each assumed significantly greater editorial autonomy than in the first volume. Consequently, Daniel claims

---

[1] This applies to **52, 53, 55, 61, 64, 65, 66, 71, 72, 73, 74, 75, 77, 78, 81, 82, 86, 87, 91, 92, 95, 96, 97, 98**.

[2] Thesaurus Linguae Graecae Pilot CD ROM # C (1987).

[3] Packard Humanities Institute Demonstration CD ROM # 2 (1988); CD ROM # 6 (1991) came out too late for us to make any use of it.

complete responsibility for **52, 54, 55, 56, 57, 59, 60, 61, 62, 63, 64, 65, 67, 68, 69, 70, 79, 84, 85, 87, 89, 90, 99, 100,** Maltomini the same for **53, 58, 66, 71, 72, 73, 74, 75, 76, 77, 78, 80, 81, 82, 83, 86, 88, 91, 92, 93, 94, 95, 96, 97, 98.** Indexes I-IV, VII-IX, XI.B and XIII were organized and compiled by Daniel, indexes V, VI, X, XI.A and XII by Maltomini. The surveys and concordances were compiled jointly.

The texts reproduced in the plates have been selected by the same criteria as in Vol. I. This time exceptions have been made for **53, 55, 67** and **68,** of which our photographs were not of publishable quality, and for **72,** which is reproduced in an exhibition catalogue that is not generally available.

Cologne - Pisa, January 1992   R.W.Daniel - F.Maltomini

TABLE OF TEXTS

Curse, Pagan

Curses, Christian

Charms to Win Favor

Divinatory Charms

Charms of Uncertain Nature

Formularies

BIBLIOGRAPHY: SUPPLEMENT TO VOL. I

Bell, H.I., Nock, A.D., and Thompson, H., "Magical Texts from a Bilingual Papyrus in the British Museum," *PBA* 17 (1931) 235-287.

Betz, H.D., "The Formation of Authoritative Tradition in the Greek Magical Papyri," in: B.F.Meyer-E.P.Sanders (edd.), *Jewish and Christian Self-Definition. III: Self-Definition in the Graeco-Roman World* (London 1982), pp. 161-170 (= H.D. Betz, *Hellenismus und Urchristentum*, Tübingen 1990, pp. 173-183).

Björck, G., *Der Fluch des Christen Sabinus. Papyrus Upsaliensis 8* (Arbeten utgivna med understöd av Vilhelm Ekmans Universitetsfond, Uppsala 47, Uppsala 1938).

Brashear, W.M., *Magica varia* (Papyrologica Bruxellensia 25, Brussels 1991).

Daniel, R.W., *Two Greek Magical Papyri in the National Museum of Antiquities in Leiden. A Photographic Edition of J 384 and J 395 (= PGM XII and XIII)* (Papyrologica Coloniensia XIX, Opladen 1991).

Deissmann, A., *Bibelstudien. Beiträge, zumeist aus den Papyri und Inschriften, zur Geschichte der Sprache, des Schrifttums und der Religion des hellenistischen Judentums und des Urchristentums* (Marburg 1895).

DGE = Diccionario Griego-Español, red. bajo la dirección de F.R.Adrados (Madrid 1980-).

DGE Supl. = Diccionario Griego-Español. Suplemento al volumen I, in: *DGE* II, pp. 3*-6*.

Dodds, E.R., *The Greeks and the Irrational* (Sather Classical Lectures 25, Berkeley-Los Angeles 1951).

Eitrem, S., *Some Notes on the Demonology in the New Testament* (Symbolae Osloenses Suppl. 20, Oslo 1966).

Erman, A., and Grapow, H., *Wörterbuch der ägyptischen Sprache* (5 Bände und Beleg-stellen. Leipzig 1925-1953).

Faraone, C.A., and Obbink, D., (edd.), *Magika Hiera. Ancient Greek Magic and Religion* (New York-Oxford 1991).

Gazza, V., "Prescrizioni mediche nei papiri dell'Egitto greco-romano" in two parts: (I) *Aegyptus* 35 (1955) 86-110 and (II) *Aegyptus* 36 (1956) 73-114.

Handwörterbuch des deutschen Aberglaubens, hrsg. von H.Bächtold-Stäubli unter Mit-wirkung von E.Hoffmann-Krayer, I-X (Leipzig-Berlin 1927-1942).

Hatzidakis, G.N., *Einleitung in die neugriechische Grammatik* (Bibliothek indogermani-scher Grammatiken 5, Leipzig 1892).

Hopfner, Th., *Der Tierkult der alten Ägypter* (Denkschr. Kais. Akad. Wiss. Wien, phil.-hist. Klasse, 57.2, Vienna 1913).

Hopfner, Th., *Fontes historiae religionis Aegyptiacae* I-V (Bonn 1922-1925).

Hopfner, Th., *Offenbarungszauber*, II.2 (veränderter Nachdruck, Amsterdam 1990).

LIMC = *Lexicon Iconographicum Mythologiae Classicae* (Zurich und Munich 1981-).

Martinez, D.G., *P.Michigan XVI. A Greek Love Charm from Egypt (P.Mich. 757)* (ASP 30, Atlanta 1991).

McNamee, K., *Abbreviations in Greek Literary Papyri and Ostraca* (BASP Suppl. 3, 1981).

Merkelbach, R., and Totti, M., *Abrasax. Ausgewählte Papyri religiösen und magischen Inhalts* I, II (Papyrologica Coloniensia XVII.1, 2, Opladen 1990-1991).

Mouterde, R., "Le Glaive de Dardanos. Objets et inscriptions magiques de Syrie," *Mélanges de l'Université Saint-Joseph* 15 (1930) 53-137.

Naveh, J., and Shaked, S., *Amulets and Magic Bowls. Aramaic Incantations of Late Antiquity* (Jerusalem-Leiden 1985).

Preisendanz, K., *Akephalos. Der kopflose Gott* (Beihefte zum Alten Orient 8, Leipzig 1926).

Radermacher, L., *Neutestamentliche Grammatik* (Handbuch zum Neuen Testament 1, zweite, erweiterte Auflage, Tübingen 1925).

Reinhold, H., *De Graecitate patrum apostolicorum librorumque apocryphorum Novi Testamenti quaestiones grammaticae* (Diss. phil. Halenses XIV.1, 1901).

Ritner, R.H., "Horus on the Crocodiles: a Juncture of Religion and Magic in Late Dynastic Egypt," in: J.P.Allen *et al.* (edd.), *Religion and Philosophy in Ancient Egypt* (Yale Egyptological Studies 3, New Haven 1989), pp. 103-116.

Roberts, C.H., *Greek Literary Hands. 350 B.C.—A.D. 400* (Oxford 1955).

Schubart, W., *Papyri Graecae Berolinenses* (Bonn 1911).

Stegemann, V., *Die koptischen Zaubertexte der Sammlung Papyrus Erzherzog Rainer in Wien* (Sitzb. Heid. Akad. Wiss., phil.-hist. Klasse, 1933/1934, 2. Abh., Heidelberg 1934).

Till, W.C., *Die Arzneikunde der Kopten* (Berlin 1951).

Totti, M., *Ausgewählte Texte der Isis- und Sarapis-Religion* (Subsidia Epigraphica 12, Hildesheim 1985).

Turner, E.G., *The Typology of the Early Codex* (University of Pennsylvania Press 1977).

Wessely, K., *Neue griechische Zauberpapyri* (Denkschr. Kais. Akad. Wiss. Wien, phil.-hist. Klasse, 42, Vienna 1893).

Wünsch, *DTA = Defixionum tabellae Atticae* [*Corpus Inscriptionum Atticarum (Inscriptiones Graecae III.3). Appendix continens defixionum tabellas in Attica regione repertas*], ed. R.Wünsch (Berlin 1897).

ADDENDA AND CORRIGENDA TO VOL. I

p. xv. Add to the list: P.Köln inv. 8001 verso. The recto bears a fragment of Demosth., *Or*. 34 published as P.Köln IV 184, where it is stated that the verso contains magic. This is apparently correct, but next to nothing can be made out except perhaps αβραϲαξ, two ring-stars and part of another.

p. xvi. P.Wash. Univ. inv. 181+221 has now been republished as P.Wash. Univ. II 73.

p. xx. Marganne, "Compléments" appeared in *ZPE* 65 (1986), not (1968).

All references to Martinez, Diss., (referred to in quite a few places, esp. in **46-51**; cf. below on **48** in specific) should be replaced by the more recent Martinez, *P.Mich. 757*. The pertinent pages can be located easily through its indexes.

1, p. 5, note 10: Cf. also Marcell. Emp. XIV 52, and see E.S.McCartney, "Verbal Homeopathy and the Etymological Story," *AJP* 48 (1927) 326-343, esp. p. 328.

2, 17: καταϲβέ- should be changed to καταϲβε-.

14, app.cr.: "11" should be changed to "10."

16 has been republished as P.Wash. Univ. II 75. We indicated the provenance as unknown, but it is from Oxyrhynchos like all Washington University papyri (see P.Wash. Univ. I, p. ii).

32, 7 comm. on ἡμίκρανον: the word has the meaning 'migraine' also in PGM LXV 4.

38, 12 comm.: to the examples of the polyptoton, add Theocr. 2, 140 χρὼϲ ἐπὶ χρωτί.

42, 11 comm.: "**2**, 2-4 comm." should be changed to "**4**, 2-4 comm."

42, 14 comm.: for γενοῦ βαλάνιϲϲα, cf. PGM XII 494 as revised by Daniel, *Two Greek Magical Papyri*, p. xxii f.

43, 8 comm.: that "Eve" may be an allonym for the unknown name of a real mother gains futher support from lines 24 and 28 of the magical lamella from Bostra in Arabia, ed. R.Kotansky, *ZPE* 88 (1991) 41-60 (see p. 51 comm. on line 28).

44, 15 comm.: "'soul of darkness', 'son of darkness'" should be changed to "'soul of darkness, son of darkness'."

48: the ed.pr. (Martinez, Diss.) has been republished as Martinez, *P.Mich. 757* (see above).

49, 72 app.cr.: κεϲτῶ should be changed to κεϲτῷ.

LIST OF PLATES

APPLIED MAGIC:

CURSES, PAGAN

52

Provenance
unknown[1]

I AD[2]

T.Louvre inv. AF 6716.

ED.PR.: B.Boyaval, "Une malediction pour viol de sepulture," *ZPE* 14 (1974) 71-73.

REPUBL.: SB XII 11247; Horsley, *New Documents* 2, no. 13.

COMM.: ed.pr.; Horsley, *loc.cit.*

TRANSL.: ed.pr.; Horsley, *loc.cit.*

PHOTO: ed.pr., plate III a and b.

DESCR.: wooden tablet; 5.5 × 13.5 × 0.5 cm. Inscribed on both sides. Traces of some washed out writing are visible above line 1.

LOC.: Musée du Louvre, Département des Antiquités égyptiennes, Paris.

The spirit of a male[3] corpse is adjured to cry out to the gods against the woman Senblynpnos, because she has neglected his burial: lines 13-15 τὴν ταφήν cου ἀπεcτέρηκε. This is paralleled by the curse UPZ I 1 (= PGM XL) in which Artemisia prays to Oserapis against the father of her dead daughter for similar reasons: lines 2-3 he (the father) [αὐτὴν (the daughter) τ]ῶ[ν] κτ[ερ]έων ἀπεcτέρηcε καὶ τῆc θήκηc (see UPZ I, p. 99 f. for various interpretations). Probably in both texts the persons are cursed not because they actually deprived the deceased of their tombs, but because they failed to continue to pay the fees owed to undertakers for the maintenance of the graves and for the performance of religious liturgies for the dead (see P.W.Pestman, *The Archive of the Theban Choachytes*, § 22 [forthcoming in the series P.Lugd. Bat.]).

---

[1] The first editor stated that the provenance of the tablet is unknown, but he noted, "Au Louvre il se trouvait dans un lot issu des fouilles de Mariette et pourrait venir de Saqqarah."

[2] For the handwriting, cf. e.g. British Museum Facsimiles II 12 of AD 15 and O.Montevecchi, *La Papirologia*, (Milan 1988[2]), Tav. 35 of AD 13. The first editor compared the hand to Schubart, *Griechische Palaeographie*, Abb. 96 of the first half of the fourth century, which is certainly too late.

[3] The sex of the corpse is determined by line 22 ἀγύναιοc.

Front   **Back**

1   cαοραυινιενουτι῾ο῾,   16   μὴ ἀφῇς τοὺς
    ἐζορκίζω cε τοὺς   θεοὺς καθεύδιν·
    θεοὺς τοὺς ἐνδά-   εἰcακούcι cε
4   {α}θι καὶ τοὺς cαρα-   ὁ Οὔcιρις, ὅτι
    φάκουc καὶ τοὺ῾c῾   20   ἄω{ο}ρος καὶ
    θ⟨ε⟩ούc cου [[π]] τοὺς   ἄτεκνος καὶ
    κατ' Ἄδου περὶ   ἀγύναιc καὶ
8   Cενβλυνπνῶτο῾c῾·   αχαβιccοc.
    κρᾶξον εἰc τὸν
    Ἄδην, μὴ ἀφῇc   24   κϛ
    τοὺς ἐν Ἄδῳ τού-
12 c θεοὺς καθεύδι-
    ν. τὴν ταφήν
    cου ἀπεcτέ-
    ρηκε τὸ λοιπόν.

2 ἐξορκίζω   3-4 ἐνθάδε   4-5 cαρκοφάγουc   7 καθ' Ἄιδου
8 cενβλυνπνωτος: υ ex ο   10 Ἄιδην   11 Ἄιδου   12-13 καθεύδειν
17 καθεύδειν   18 εἰcακούcει   22 ἀγύναιος   23 ἀχάριcτοc?

Saorauinienoutio, I adjure you by the gods who are here [4] and those who eat flesh and your gods in Hades concerning [8] Senblynpnos. Cry out to Hades, do not allow the gods in Hades [12] to sleep. She has deprived you of burial already. [16] Do not allow the gods to sleep. Osiris will listen to you, for [20] you suffered an untimely death and you are childless and wifeless and disgraced (?). [24] The 26th.

1 cαορ: the first editor suggested Egyptian 'daughter of Horos' and compared PGM IV 1215 cαηcι 'daughter of Isis'.

At the end of 1, perhaps one may isolate νουτι ο, Egyptian 'great god'; cf. Westendorf, p. 127 *s.v.* ⲚⲞⲨⲦⲈ and p. 139 *s.v.* ⲟ.

2-3 ἐξορκίζω (ⲅ. ἐξορκίζω) cε τοὺς | θεούς: the ed.pr. supplied ⟨καὶ⟩ between cε and τοὺς θεούς, but, as Horsley noted, ἐξορκίζω is here constructed with double accusative. Cf. **32**, 2 comm. on ὁρκίζω; also **45**,

20-21 comm.; **71** fr. 14, 3 comm.; **75**, 18 comm.; PGM XV 10 f. ὁρκίζω ὑμᾶς δαίμονες τὴν cυνέχουcαν ὑμᾶς βίαν καὶ ἀ[νά]γκην; NT Marc. 5, 7 ὁρκίζω cε τὸν θεόν, μή με βαcανίcῃς; Act. Apost. 19, 13 ὁρκίζω ὑμᾶς τὸν Ἰηcοῦν Audollent, *DT*, 271, 1-3, 8, 10 f., etc.; *Test. Sal.*, p. 40*, 11 McCown. Further references: Bauer, *Wörterbuch*, *s.v.* ὁρκίζω; Brashear, *Magica varia*, p. 51. Discussions: Bell-Nock-Thompson, "Magical Texts from a Bilingual Papyrus," p. 34; Brashear, *loc.cit.*

3-4 ἐνδάl{α}θι: r. ἐνθάδε rather than the Attic ἐνθαδί with the first editor. In a text so clumsily spelled, one should assume an example of ι written for ε, not a rarely attested Atticism.

4 καὶ : {καὶ} ed.pr. Three categories of gods are indicated.

4-5 τοὺc cαραlφάκουc (r. cαρκοφάγουc): the 'flesh-eating' gods; cf. PGM IV 2865-67 καρδιόδαιτε, cαρκοφάγε καὶ ἀωροβόρε, of Hekate; 1444 f. ὠμοφάγοι χθόνιοι; cf. also καρδιο⟨δαί⟩τα of Hekate in the lead curse tablet from the Athenian Agora, inv. IL 493, line 19 (ed. G.W.Elderkin, *Hesperia* 6, 1937, 389-395; = Jordan, "Survey," no. 21). On the daemons of the Greek underworld who devour the corpses of the dead, see A.Dieterich, *Nekyia. Beiträge zur Erklärung der neuentdeckten Petrus-apokalypse* (Leipzig-Berlin 1913²), pp. 46-54, esp. 52 f. The interpretation proposed by Horsley, "the (gods of the ?) coffins," is probably to be rejected for linguistic reasons (or r. cαρκοφάγων ?). It may also be noted that purpose of the Egyptian mummy coffin was to *preserve* the body (an allegorical name for the mummy coffin was 'lord of life' (see *Lexikon der Ägyptologie* V, col. 471 [E.Brovarski]), and hence the term cαρκοφάγοc does not seem appropriate for it.

8 Cενβλυνπνῶc: *addendum onomasticis.*

9 κράξον: like βοᾶν 'cry out in accusation', probably with a juridical nuance; cf. (ἐκ)βοᾶν καὶ κράζειν repeated several times in the petition P.Oxy. IV 717 (I BC); ἔκραξεν in the complaint P.Lond. I (p. 224) 113, 11(b), 2; κατακράζω in P.Fouad 87, 11 f. and P.Münch. III 122, 10; also Men., *Sam.* 580 Ni. ἰὼ 'νθρωποι. De. κέκραχθι (cf. D.Bain, *ZPE* 44, 1981, 169-171); and see W.Schulze, *Kleine Schriften*, p. 184 n. 2 on κραυγή, κραυγάζειν. On καταβοή in the curse of Artemisia, see UPZ I 1, 6 comm. Publicizing an accusation by crying out is evidenced in the Ptolemaic papyri and other Hellenistic sources; see D.Bain, *art.cit.*; W. Schubart, *APF* 12 (1937) 16; W.Ameling, "Ein Hilferuf bei Polybios," *ZPE* 70 (1987) 157 f. with note 4. Cf. also καταβοᾶν in the legal code P.Oxy.

XLVI 3285, 3, 5, 7, etc., and, for the demotic phrases in the legal code of Hermoupolis that καταβοᾶν renders, see P.Lugd. Bat. XXIII, pp. 116-143, esp. p. 118. Further literature and later influence: E.H.Kantorowicz, "Friederich II. und das Königsbild des Hellenismus,"*Varia Variorum. Festausgabe für K.Reinhardt* (Münster-Köln 1952), pp. 169-193 (repr. in *Stupor Mundi. Zur Geschichte Friedrichs II. von Hohenstaufen*, hrsg. von G.Wolf [Wege der Forschung 101, 1966] pp. 296-330), esp. pp. 174-178.

9-10 κρᾶξον εἰς τὸν | Ἅιδην - - - 18-19 εἰσακούcει cε | ὁ Οὔcιρις: the linguistic pattern that establishes the relationship between supplicant and god can be paralleled in the Septuagint, especially in Psalms; cf. e.g. Exod. 22, 22 ἐὰν δὲ κακίᾳ κακώcητε αὐτοὺς καὶ κεκράξαντεc καταβοήcωcι πρόc με, ἀκοῇ εἰcακούcομαι τῆc φωνῆc αὐτῶν; Job 30, 20 κέκραγα δὲ πρὸc cὲ καὶ οὐκ εἰcακούειc μου; Ps. 3, 5 φωνῇ μου πρὸc κύριον ἐκέκραξα, καὶ ἐπήκουέν μου; 4, 4; 16, 6; 17, 7; 26, 7; 33, 7, 18; 54, 17 etc.; see Hatch-Redpath, *s.v.* κράζω, and Kittel, *Theol. Wt.* III, p. 899 f.

10-13 μὴ ἀφῇc | τοὺς ἐν Ἅδω (r. Ἅιδου) τοὺ|c θεοὺc καθεύδιν: cf. 16-17 μὴ ἀφῇc τοὺc θεοὺc καθεύδιν. On the nightly sleep of the Egyptian gods, see *Lexikon der Ägyptologie* V, *s.v.* Schlaf, col. 643 (R.Schlichting). If the great gods are kept from sleeping on account of Senblynpnos, they will not be kindly disposed towards her.

11-12 τοὺc ἐν Ἅδω τοὺc θεού|c: the first editor normalized by deleting the article before θεούc, probably correctly. The modern Greek construction ὁ καλὸc ὁ ἄνδραc can be traced back to the Byzantine papyri (see Ljungvik, *Beiträge*, pp. 1-3), but the present text is probably too early for the construction here to be regarded as a true precursor.

13-15 τὴν ταφήν | cου ἀπεcτέ|ρηκε: for the construction ἀποcτερεῖν τί τινοc rather than the normal ἀποcτερεῖν τινά τινοc, cf. LXX Sir. 4, 1; 34, 21; Hermae Past., *Vis.* III 9, 9 αἱ διχοcταcίαι αὐταὶ ὑμῶν ἀποcτερήcουcιν τὴν ζωὴν ὑμῶν. If the line of interpretation proposed in the introduction is correct, ταφή in the present text and θήκη in UPZ I 1, 2 do not refer to actual burial, but to proper burial. One might alternatively understand τὴν ταφήν cου ἀπεcτήρεκε in the present text as 'he has withheld payment for your burial'; cf. LSJ *s.v.* ἀποcτερέω I 4 and *s.v.* ἀποcτέρηcιc II.

15 τὸ λοιπόν: 'for the future' in classical Greek, but afterwards the phrase can also mean 'now', 'already', 'afterall', 'once'; see A.Cavallin, "(τὸ) λοιπόν. Eine bedeutungsgeschichtliche Untersuchung," *Eranos* 39 (1941) 121-144; Tabachovitz, *Études sur le Grec*, p. 32.

18 εἰcακούcει: for the future active form, see Mandilaras, *Verb*, § 367; Gignac, *Grammar* II, p. 321.

18-19 εἰcακούcει cε | ὁ Οὔcιρις: see above on 9-10 for parallels in the Septuagint. Also the Egyptian gods directly give ear to individual supplicants, an aspect of the personal relationship between god and man stressed by later Egyptian religion; see *Lexikon der Ägyptologie* II, *s.v.* Hören, coll. 1233-35 (R.Schlichting). For the traditional quasi-juridical appeal to Osiris against evil-doers, see UPZ I 1 intr., esp. p. 101.

19 Οὔcιρις: for the spelling, see **44**, 8-9 comm.

Understand ὅτι ⟨εἶ⟩.

23 αχαβιccοc: L.Koenen (see ed.pr.) provided ἄβιος as a diagnostic conjecture, comparing CIG 3915, 46 ἄτεκνος καὶ ἄβιος. Perhaps something closer to the reading of the tablet is preferable: a miscopying of ἀχάριστος? The deadman might be described as 'unthanked' or 'disgraced' because Senblynpnos has ceased to pay for the traditional servicing of his mummy.

24 $\overline{κς}$: probably the day of the month (cf. **45**, 37 comm. and, for other examples, see Audollent, *DT*, Index XI B, pp. 556-558) rather than the age of the deceased (Horsley).

Oxyrhynchos   III AD[1]

T.Köln inv. 4.

ED.PR.: D.Wortmann, "Neue magische Texte. Nr. 12: Schadenzauber gegen zwei Athleten,"
    Bonner Jahrb. 168 (1968) 108 f.

COMM.: ed.pr.

TRANSL.: ed.pr.

REF.: Jordan, "Survey," no. 157.

DESCR.: lead tablet consisting of a large fragment (8 × 13 cm) and several smaller ones that
    cannot be placed securely. The tablet was rolled and folded, and it is now cracked and
    corroded. Inscribed on one side only.

LOC.: Institut für Altertumskunde, Universität zu Köln.

To date this is the only known applied spell of Egyptian provenance
directed against athletes: the persons cursed are foot-racers (δρομεῖς).[2]
Charms of agonistic content from formularies are PGM III 1-164 (cf. 19 f.,
41, 162 f.); IV 2159-63; VII 390-393, 919-924; XXVII. A list of curse tablets
against athletes is to be found in D.R.Jordan, *Hesperia* 54 (1985) 214.[3]

Because of the tablet's poor and fragmentary state of preservation, the
first editor gave only a partial transcription of the text (here lines 1-6 left, 1
right, 9 *fin.*, 12 *fin.*-20 *init.*, 21 *init.*, 22 *init.*, 23-25, 29).

The first 10 lines of the text were written in sections side by side: permutations of Ευλαμω in a column on the left side of 1-6, an invocation and the
χυχβαχυχ logos on the right side of 1-10.

Diaeresis on iota in 17.

---

[1] IV AD according to the first editor.

[2] Another probable instance of curse against a foot-racer is Jordan, "Survey," no. 29
(from the Athenian agora); for an unpublished curse from Isthmia, see idem, *Hesperia* 54
(1985) 214.

[3] Add the two defixiones against charioteers from Apamea published by W.van Rengen
in: *Apamée de Syrie. Actes du colloque tenu à Bruxelles les 29, 30, 31 mai 1980* (ed.
J.Balty, Paris 1984), pp. 213-233.

1 ευλαμω [ἐπι]καλοῦμαι ἐπιτελ[
   υλαμωε [   ] αν ὑπὸ γῆν
   λαμωευ [   ] τονυολ υνπα
4 αμωευλ [   ] νϲα
   μωευλα [   ] ιτατη του
   ωευλαμ [   ] ϲτρο ϲα
   π ρ [   ]αχυχ βαχυχ βακα
8 κ[   ]βαχυχ[ ]χυ
   αιωνα [   ]χυχβαζαχυχ
   τον ου[   ]χ [βα]δητοφωθι
   βαψι βιβιωθ αρλ[c. 10   ]φιλχαλωχακον
12 κοχλωκον οχλωιο[ ] λ [ ]ακ κιαβ· δῆϲον, κα-
   τάδηϲον τὰ ν[εῦ]ρα, τὰ μέλη, τὸν νοῦν, τὰς φρένας,
   τὴν διάνοιαν, τὰ τριακόϲια ἑξήκοντα πέ[ν-]
   τε μέλη καὶ νεῦρα τῶν περὶ τὸν [ὃν]
16 ἔ⟦ν⟧τεκεν Ταειάϲ, καὶ ᾽Αφοῦν, ὃν ἔτεκεν [Ταεῖϲ,]
   τῶν ἀθλητῶν δρομέων, ἵνα μὴ [c. 8]
   μιν μηδὲ εὐρωϲτῆϲαι, ἀλλὰ ἀγρυ[πνείτωϲαν]
   δι᾽ ὅλης νυκτὸς καὶ ἀποβαλ[έ]τωϲαν [πᾶϲαν]
20 τροφὴν ἐπὶ κακῶϲι καὶ νου [c. 7]
   ϲι ν αὐτῶν, ἵνα μὴ ἰϲχύ[ϲωϲι δρα-]
   μῖν, ἀλλὰ ὑϲτερίτωϲαν ὑϲτε[c. 7]
   καὶ κατάϲχες αὐτῶν τῶν περὶ [τὸν c. 5]
24 ὃν ἔτεκεν [Τ]α[ειάϲ,] κ[αὶ ᾽Αφοῦν, ὃν ἔτε-]
   κεν Ταεῖϲ, [c. 20]
   ὑπ[ὸ] πάντω[ν] υ[c. 10]
   κρανειον ν[ ] ν κώλυϲο[ν c. 10]
28 καὶ ἀμαύρωϲον αὐτῶν τοὺς [ὀφθαλμούϲ,]
   ἵνα μὴ ἰϲχύϲωϲιν τραμῖν [c. 10]
   καὶ ἐνεάδιν, ἀμαυρου [c. 7]
   τῆϲ ϲῆϲ δυνάμεωϲ, κύριε [c. 7]
32 Αβραϲαξ [

17 ἵνα Pap.   20 κακώϲει   21-22 δραμεῖν   22 ὑϲτερείτωϲαν
27 κρανίον?   29 δραμεῖν   30 ἐνεάζειν?

Fragments.

A

1   ] . . . [
    ]cου   voι
    Aβ]ρασαξ
4   ]ρεν[.] . . . .

B

1   ]o . [
    ] λ . . ουδ[
    ]λλατ . [
4   ] . . . [

C

1   ] . χαρα[
    ] . αι [

D

1   ]ινα[
    ]δεμ . [

E

1   ] . . . [
    ] . αραη . . . [
    ]αραβα . . [

(Lines 1-6 left) *Eulamô ulamôe lamôeu* |⁴ *amôeul môeula ôeulam.* (1-10 right) - - - I call upon you, fulfill (?) - - - under the earth - - - *achych bachych baka - - -bachych- - - chy- - -chychbazachych- - - ch badêtophôthi.* (11 ff.) *bapsi bibiôth arl- - - philchalôchakon* |¹² *kochlôkon ochlôio- - -ak kiab,* bind, bind down the sinews, the limbs, the mind, the wits, the intellect, the three hundred and sixty-five limbs and sinews of - - -, whom |¹⁶ Taeias bore, and of Aphous, whom Taeis bore, and company, foot-racing athletes, so that they cannot run (?) nor have strength, but let them be sleepless through the entire night and let them throw up all |²⁰ food to their distress and - - - of them, so that they do not have the strength to run, but let them come in behind, let them come in behind (?) - - - and restrain - - -, |²⁴ whom Taeias bore, and Aphous, whom Taeis bore, and company - - - by all - - - the head (?) - - - hinder - - - |²⁸ and dim their eyes so that they do not have the strength to run - - - and be bewildered, dimmed - - - by your power, lord - - - |³² *Abrasax* - - -.

    (Fr. A) - - - *Abrasax* - - -.

1-6 left ευλαμω - - - ωευλαμ: for this name in the same arrangement, cf. **57**, 8-13; Audollent, *DT*, 172, 6-12; 243, 1-6; 252, 13-18; 253, 22-27 (in the last three places it occurs next to the χυχβαχυχ logos, likewise arranged in a column). On the name Ευλαμω, see **44**, 17 comm.

In 1 the first editor read ευ[λαμω.

1-8 right (in 8, βαχυχ only; the following χυ belongs to the main piece) are contained on a now independent fragment from the right side of the tablet. Apparently, there is no longer an exact physical join with 9 ff., but one can hardly doubt where the fragment should be placed.

1 right. Perhaps ἐπιτέλ[ει] or ἐπιτέλ[ε]ι[cον.

3-6 right and 7-10 left could be either Greek or magical words.

7-10 right. Parallels for the χυχβαχυχ logos in PGM, Vol. 3 (Index), p. 242 f. (for βαχυχ, cf. p. 218). Ch.Harrauer, *Meliouchos*, p. 47 n. 50, suggests that the syllables in χυχβαχυχ, like those in the name Βαιν-χωωωχ (see **15**, 3-4 comm.), may have their origin in the Egyptian words *b3* 'soul' and *kkw* 'darkness' (cf. also βακαξιχυχ, for which see **44**, 15 comm.). For other interpretations of the word, see Preisendanz, *Akephalos*, p. 37 n. 2.

11 βιβιωθ: cf. Βιβιου, on which see **44**, 3-4 comm.

]φιλχαλωχακον: part of the sequence recalls PGM III 505 ἀλούχα-κον, an otherwise unattested name of a bird.

12 κοχλωκον: cf. PGM IV 3262 κοκλοτομ; LVIII 27 κοχλωτα.

12-13 δῆcον, κα|τάδηcον : δῆcον, [κα]|τάδηcον ed.pr. For the intensifying combination of simplex and compound, cf. **57**, 34 f.; Audollent, *DT*, 187, 56; van Rengen, cit. (above footnote 3), p. 215, lines 1-2; Youtie-Bonner, "Two Curse Tablets from Beisan," p. 54, line 2; also Audollent, *DT*, 15, 19 δήcατε, cυνδήcατε, 4, 7, 9, 14 λύcατε, ἀναλύcατε. On the phenomenon in literature, see R.Renehan, *Studies in Greek Texts* (Hypomnemata 43, Göttingen 1976), pp. 22-27.

14-15 τὰ τριακόcια ἑξήκοντα πέ[ν]|τε μέλη καὶ νεῦρα: cf. PGM IV 149 f. (Coptic) "I will bewitch her heart, I will bewitch the heart of her, I will bewitch her breath, I will bewitch her 365 members" (transl. by M.W. Meyer in Betz, *Translation*, p. 40; see also idem, "The Love Spell of PGM IV 94-153: Introduction and Structure," in: *Acts of the 2nd Intern. Congress of Coptic Studies. Rome 22-26 Sept. 1980*, Rome 1985, p. 197); Ziebarth, *Sitzungsb. Berlin* (1934) 1042-45, no. 24, fr. III 5; fr. IV 3-6 ἔλθατε - - - εἰc τὴν κ[αρδίαν] κὲ εἰc τὰ τριακόcια ἑξήκο[ντα πέντε μέλη] Γαμετῆc;

Reitzenstein, *Poimandres*, p. 295 (*Cod. Par.* 2316, fol. 316r) ὁρκίζω ϲε, Βαϲκανία, - - - ἵνα ἐξάρηϲ ἀπ' αὐτοῦ (the wearer of the amulet) πᾶν ἄλγοϲ καὶ πόνον καὶ μετώπων καὶ ὀφθαλμῶν, κἂν ϲτόμα, κἂν τράχηλον, κἂν ὦμον, κἂν χεῖρα κτλ. (mention of many other parts of the body) καὶ ἀπὸ τῶν τριακοϲίων ἐξήκοντα πέντε ἀρμῶν κτλ.; Delatte, *Anecdota Atheniensia*, pp. 246, 15-17 φεῦγε, δαιμόνιον πονηρόν, μὴ ἀδικήϲηϲ τὸν δοῦλον τοῦ Θεοῦ ὁδεῖνα· φεῦξαι καὶ ἀναχώρηϲον ἀπὸ τῶν τριακοϲίων ἐξήκοντα πέντε ἁρμονιῶν αὐτοῦ; 90, 16 δήνω τοὺϲ τξε΄ ἁρμούϲ; also 429, 15. According to Epiphanius, *Panar.* 24, 7, 4 (GCS 1, p. 264, 9-18), the Basilidian gnostics, who worshipped Abrasax (this name in Greek numeral-letters makes 365), maintained that accordingly the universe was composed of 365 heavens, the year of 365 days, and the human body of 365 parts, ὡϲ ἑκάϲτη τῶν δυνάμεων ἀπονέμεϲθαι ἓν μέλοϲ. *Pistis Sophia* 132 (p. 224, 16-18 Schmidt-Till) states that the 365 *leitourgoi* built the 365 parts of the human body, and *Apocryphon Johannis* says the same of the 365 angels; see M.Krause-P.Labib, *Die drei Versionen des Apokryphon des Johannes im Koptischen Museum zu Alt-Kairo* (Wiesbaden 1962), esp. p. 159 f. (19, 2-6). The 365 limbs of the body, of course, correspond to the deities who presided over the 365 days of the year. For other *melothesiai* (36 decans ~ 36 members; 12 signs of the zodiac ~ 12 members, etc.), see *RE* X A, *s.v.* Zodiakos, coll. 579-582 (H.Gundel); XX.2, *s.v.* Planeten, col. 2155 f. (W. and H.Gundel); P.Oslo I 1, pp. 41 f. and 140. (In some medieval exorcistic texts, the number of the limbs adds up to 362; see *Handwörterbuch des deutschen Aberglaubens* III, *s.v.* Glieder, col. 866.)

15-17 τῶν περὶ τὸν - - - τῶν ἀθλητῶν δρομέων: it is difficult to decide whether the expression οἱ περὶ + acc. *nominis proprii* (on which see S.L. Radt, *ZPE* 38, 1980, 47-56 and 71, 1988, 35-38) is to be taken here in the sense of 'X and his associates, attendants, family, companions etc.', or simply as a periphrasis for X alone. Both meanings occur in the papyri; see H.C.Youtie, *TAPA* 89 (1958) 395 f. (= *Scriptiunculae* I, p. 305 f.). If 'NN, Aphous and company' is what the writer intended, then the expression will indicate the two athletes with other contestants, or the two athletes with their staff (trainer etc.), or the like. One may compare the defixio edited by D. R.Jordan, *Hesperia* 54 (1985) 214, no. 1 (= Jordan, "Survey," no. 24 = SEG XXXV 213), line 4, where a wrestler is cursed and "those with him" (καὶ τ[ο]ὺϲ ϲὺν αὐτῷ); cf. also the related tablets nos. 2, 3, 5, 6 (= Jordan, "Survey," nos. 25, 26, 28, 29 = SEG XXXV 214, 215, 217, 218).

16 Ταειάc : Ταcίαc ed.pr. For Ταειάc, cf. P.Bon. 39, fr. a verso, 11; P.Cair. Isid. 9, 91; cf. also Ταϊάc in SB I 3852; XIV 12190, 5; P.Oxy. XLI 2977, 9; XLVI 3295, 11.

᾿Αφοῦν : ᾿Εφοῦν (unattested) ed.pr.

16 and 25 Ταεῖc: not registered in the onomastica.

17 ἀθλητῶν : ἀθλητέων ed.pr.

17-18 ἵνα μὴ . [c. 8]|μιν : ἵνα μὴ ἔχ[ειν αὐτοὺc δύνα]|μιν ed.pr. Where Wortmann gave εχ[we see minimal traces, but can read nothing. The text might have run ἵνα μὴ δυ[νηθῶcι δρα]|μῖν; cf. Audollent, DT, 234, 18-20, 44-46; 235, 12-14, 30-33, etc.

18-20 ἀλλὰ ἀγρυ[πνείτωcαν] - - - τροφήν: cf. Audollent, DT, 289, 16 auferas illis dulce somnum, of race-horses; van Rengen, cit. (above, footnote 3), p. 215, lines 6-7 μὴ φάγωcι, μὴ πίωcιν, μὴ κοιμηθῶcιν, of charioteers.

18 ἀγρυ[πνείτωcαν] : ἔγει[ρον αὐτοὺc] ed.pr.

19-20 ἀποβαλ[έ]τωcαν [πᾶcαν] | τροφὴν : κατά[cχεc πᾶ]cαν [αὐτῶν] | τροφὴν ed.pr. The expression τὴν τροφὴν ἀποβάλλειν can be paralleled by Diosc., Eupor. II 8 (III 244, 23 Wellmann) πρὸc δὲ τοὺc τὴν τροφὴν ἀποβάλλονταc ἐπιτιθέμενοc ὠφελεῖ cπόγγοc, and P.Oslo III 152, 4 f. (a letter) πεπυρέχειν ἀποβαλὼν τὴν τροφήν; cf. also Macarius, Serm. 15, 1, 9 (GCS 1, p. 174, 23 f.) πᾶν ὃ ἐὰν προcενέγκηc αὐτῷ βρωτὸν ἢ ποτὸν ἥδιcτον, βδελύccεται καὶ ἀποβάλλεται, and Dittenberger, Syll.³ 1171 (= I.Cret. I, XVII 17), 5-7 cάρκαc ἐνπύου[c καὶ] ἠμαγμέναc - - - ἀ[πο]βάλλειν. These passages show that the phrase indicates not merely a refusal of food due to lack of appetite, but rather 'throw up', 'vomit'. This meaning of ἀποβάλλω is not registered in the lexica.

20 ἐπὶ κακώcι (r. κακώcει): 'to their distress' with final sense is preferable to causal 'because of a condition of distress'. The phrase has final sense also in LXX 2 Ma. 3, 39; Joseph., A.J. IV 294; Sozom. Salam., Hist. eccl. VI 16, 2 (GCS, p. 256, 24); Eust., Il. 23, 212 (IV 606, 16 f. van der Valk). The word κάκωcιc occurs in another curse tablet (from Hebron); see B.Lifshitz, Revue Biblique 77 (1970) 81 f. (= Jordan, "Survey," no. 163), lines 1-3 ἐξορκίζω ὑμᾶc χαρακτῆρα[c κατα]κλῖνε (r. -ῖναι) ἐπὶ κάκωcιν κτλ.; lines 5-6 κατακλίνατ[ε αὐ]τὸν ἐπὶ κάκωcι⟨ν⟩ καὶ θάν[ατον (so Jordan; κακώcι καὶ θαν[άτῳ Lifshitz) κτλ.

21-22 ἵνα μὴ ἰcχύ[cωcι δρα]|μῖν (r. -μεῖν): the restoration seems guaranteed by 29. Cf. lines 20-21 of the Athenian curse tablet against a wrestler edited by D.R.Jordan, *Hesperia* 54 (1985) 218, no. 4 (= Jordan, "Survey," no. 27 = SEG XXXV 216) καὶ μὴ ἰςχυέτω πρώτως [παλαί]ειν (also lines 26-27 μὴ ἰςχύων ὅλως μηδέν); cf. also ibid., p. 252 (= "Survey," no. 38 = SEG XXXV 227, possibly a love charm), lines 26-27 ἵνα μὴ ἰςχύςῃ μηκέτι ἀναςτῆναι, μὴ περιπατῆςαι, κτλ.

22 ὑςτερίτωςαν (r. ὑςτερείτωςαν) ὑςτε[*c.* 7] : ὑςτερὶν ed.pr. Cf. Xen., *Mem.* 3, 5, 13 ἀθληταί τινες - - - ὑςτερίζουςι τῶν ἀντιπάλων.

ὑςτε[*c.* 7]: perhaps once again ὑςτε[ρείτωςαν], an emphatic repetition.

23 κατάςχες: probably an accusative is lost in the lacuna in 25 (cf. PGM IV 372 f. κατάςχες αὐτῆς τὴν βρῶςιν καὶ τὴν πόςιν and the parallels **46**, 20 f.; **47**, 20 f.; **50**, 55-57), though one cannot rule out that κατέχω is here constructed with the genitive object (see LSJ, *s.v.* I 2).

τῶν περὶ [: πᾶν [ed.pr.

24-25 [Τ]α[ειάς,] κ[αὶ 'Αφοῦν, ὃν ἔτε]ικεν : Τ[αςίας καὶ περὶ τὸν 'Εφοῦν, ὃν ἔτε]ικεν ed.pr.

25 [: ἔχει [ed.pr. Perhaps τ[ῶν ἀθλητῶν δρομέων (cf. 17), but the trace is elusive. It is possible, however, that the tablet has suffered damage here since the first edition.

27 κρανειον: perhaps κρανίον; or ἡμι]κράνειον (r. -ιον) 'headache'.

28 ἀμαύρωςον αὐτῶν τοὺς [ὀφθαλμούς]: cf. Audollent, *DT*, 241, 13 f. ἀμαύρωςον αὐτῶν τὰ ὄμματα ἵνα μὴ βλέπωςιν, of a charioteer and his horses; cf. also 252, 30 with app.cr. For the sense, cf. 234, 58-61 ἄφελε αὐτῶν - - - τὴν ὅραςιν ἵνα μὴ δυναςθῶςιν βλέπειν; 242, 57 f. ἀπόκνιςον αὐτῶν τὰ ὄμματα ἵνα μὴ βλέπωςιν.

29 τραμὶν (r. δραμεῖν) : πα ed.pr.

30 ἐνεάδιν: probably for ἐνεάζειν. For the verb, cf. Bekker, *Anecd. Gr.*, p. 251, 27-29 and *Etym. M.*, p. 340, 50, where, as opposed to LSJ *s.v.* ("strike dumb, astonish"), it appears to be intransitive. It is intransitive also in Palladius, *Hist. Laus.* 1, 3 (p. 15, 24 Butler). The syntax, however, is not clear; perhaps something like [ποίηςον αὐτοὺς] stood at the end of 29.

ἀμαυρου [*c.* 7]: first μ or ν; then indecipherable traces. Certainly a form of ἀμαυρόω, probably ἀμαυρουμέν[ους.

30-31. Probably ὑπὸ] | τῆς ςῆς δυνάμεως; cf. Audollent, *DT*, 187, 62.

Alexandria   Plate I   II-III AD[1]

Audollent, *DT*, 38.

ED.PR.: F.Lenormant, "De tabulis devotionis plumbeis Alexandrinis," *Rhein. Mus.* 9
    (1854) 369-382.

REPUBL.: C.Wachsmuth, *Rhein. Mus.* 18 (1863) 563; J.Zündel, *Rhein. Mus.* 19 (1864)
    483-496; Wessely, *Ephesia Grammata,* no. 244; E.Babelon and J.-A.Blanchet, *Cata-
    logue des bronzes antiques de la Bibliothèque Nationale* (Paris 1895), pp. 701-703, no.
    2296; Wünsch, *DTA*, pp. 50-52; Audollent, *DT*, 38.

COMM.: ed.pr.; Zündel, *loc.cit.*; E.Kuhnert, *Rhein. Mus.* 49 (1894) 37-38; Wünsch, *loc.
    cit.*; Audollent, *loc.cit.*; K.Preisendanz in *RAC* VIII, col. 13 f.; Moraux, *Une
    défixion judiciaire*, p. 48 n. 1.

TRANSL.: ed.pr.

REF.: Preisendanz, "Zaubertafeln," p. 147.

DESCR.: lead tablet; 16 × 15 cm. Inscribed on one side only.

LOC.: Bibliothèque Nationale, Cabinet des Médailles, Paris. Inv. C 3844.

Ionikos curses Annianos for reasons that are not immediately obvious.
Audollent stated that Ionikos wished to protect himself from being harmed by
Annianos, and on p. 473 of his index "Defixionum genera et causae" he
included the curse in the category "Causa defixionis obscura." On the basis
of lines 9-10, Moraux suspected the text to be a love charm, and both E.G.
Kagarow (*Griechische Fluchtafeln* [Eus Suppl. 4, Leopoli 1929], p. 51 f.)
and D.R.Jordan (*Hesperia* 54, 1985, 223 n. 16) included it in lists of erotic
defixiones. Preisendanz, on the other hand, regarded the text as a possibly
juridical curse: "Das ... Exemplar ... sollte ... einen Annianos durch
Fluchwirkung seinem Gegner (vor Gericht ?) unterwerfen ..." Perhaps these
seemingly disparate analyses are not incompatible with each other.

---

[1] III AD according to previous editors.

So that the reader can form his own impression about the nature of the text, its telling passages are printed here with normalized spellings and without brackets and dots:

(A) 9-10 ἐπιλάθοιτο Ἀννιανὸς τῆς ἰδίας μνήμης καὶ Ἰωνικοῦ μόνου μνημονευέτω

(B) 19-23 cυνέχετέ μοι τῷ Ἰωνικῷ Ἀννιανοῦ τὴν ἰcχύν, τὴν δύναμιν, ἵνα cυλλάβηcθε αὐτὸν καὶ παραδῶτε ἀώροιc, ἵνα κατατήξητε αὐτοῦ τὰc cάρκαc, τὰ νεῦρα, τὰ μέλη, τὴν ψυχήν

(C) 23-26 ἵνα μὴ δυνηθῇ Ἰωνικῷ ἀντίοc ἐλθεῖν μηδὲ κατ' ἐμοῦ ἀκοῦcαί τι κακόν μηδὲ βλέψαι, ἔτι δὲ καὶ ὑποπεπτωκώc μου ὑπὸ τοὺc πόδαc ἕωc νικηθῇ

(D) 37-38 κατάcχετε τὴν φιλίαν Ἀννιανοῦ πρὸc Ἠωνικόν, πρώτιcτον, ἀδιαλύτωc

Much if not all of (A), (B) and (D) can be regarded as reminiscent of the *defixiones amatoriae*, and if one regards the text as exclusively erotic in nature, then (C) could be interpreted as a metaphor of erotic subjugation.

On the other hand (C), to the extent that it can be paralleled in magical texts, is reminiscent rather of a juridical curse (see comm.). Something similar is not to be found in other preserved love charms. Also because amatory vocabulary is limited only to the word φιλία in 37 and because there is no single reference to sexual acts, the present spell stands apart from conventional love charms.

Perhaps we are dealing with formulas drawn from various kinds of spells and then combined so as to suit a special situation. On the basis of (C) one could suppose that Ionikos fears legal action against him on the part of Annianos, whereas Ionikos is planning to proceed against Annianos. The reason for the use of the formulas from the erotic *defixiones*, then, will not have been love and desire on the part of Ionikos for Annianos (of which there is no indication in the text). They may rather have been intended to disarm and mollify Annianos with feelings of love for a false friend. In such a state (and bewitched with loss of memory) Annianos will not be able to proceed against Ionikos, and he will be rendered entirely helpless if and when Ionikos proceeds against him. Probably the charm should establish or re-establish a relationship between Annianos as *erastes* and Ionikos as unyielding *erome-*

nos.[2] If so, Ionikos may think that this situation will influence a legal decision in his favor,[3] for example in a dispute as to whether valuables were given by Annianos to Ionikos, or whether Ionikos had acquired them dishonestly from Annianos.

If such an analysis is correct, the text may be characterized as a combination of a love spell, the purpose of which is to mollify an opponent, and a charm for victory at court (νικητικόν). Conceivably the writer of the present charm had as a model a θυμοκάτοχον καὶ νικητικόν, which he altered by replacing the wrath-restraining formulae with phrases drawn from the love-charms; see the commentary on 37 κα]τάσχετε [τὴ]ν φιλί[αν].

1　ε[ρη]κισιθφηα{μ}ραχαραραηφ[θισι]κηρε χ ̣ ̣ σεω· παράλαβε 'Αννι-
　αν[όν,]
　['Ε]ρμῆ χθόνιε αρχεδαμα Φωχενσεψευ σαρερταθου μισονκα[ι]κ[τ]
　κ[α]ὶ Πλούτων Υεσεμμιγαδων μααρχαμα καὶ Κόρη Ερεσχιγ[α]λ
　ζ[α-]
4　[βαρ]βαθουχ καὶ Φερσεφόνη [ζα]υδαχθουμαρ· ὁρκίζω σε κ[α-]
　[τ]ὰ τοῦ ὀνόματος τῆς Γῆ[ς] κευημορι μωριθαρχωθ κα[ὶ]
　'Ερμῆ χθόνιε αρχεδαμα Φωχενσεψευ σαρερταθου μισον-
　καικτ καὶ Πλούτων Υεσε[μμι]γαδων μααρχαμα καὶ Κόρη
8　Ερεσχιγαλ ζαβαρβαθουχ [κ]αὶ Φερσεφόνη ζαυδαχθουμαρ·
　ἐπιλάθοιτο 'Αννιανὸς τῆς ἰ[δ]ίας μνήμης καὶ 'Ηωνικοῦ μό-
　νου μνημονευέτω. ἐπικαλοῦμαί σε, τὴν πάντων ἀνθρώ-
　πων δυνάστειραν, παμφόρβα, ῥηξίχθων, ἡ καὶ ἀνενεγ-
12　καμένη τὰ τοῦ Μελιού[χ]ου μέλη καὶ αὐτὸν τὸν Με-
　λιοῦχον, Ερεσχιγαλ, Νεβουτοσουαληθ, ἐρεβεννή,
　ἄρκυια, νέκυι', 'Εκάτη, 'Εκάτη ἀληθῆ, ἔλθετε καὶ τε-
　λειώσατέ μοι τὴν πραγματείαν ταύτην. 'Ερμῆ χθό-
16　νιε, αρχεδαμα Φωχενσεψευ σαρερταθου μισονκαικτ
　καὶ Πλούτων Υεσεμμιγ[α]δων μααρχαμα καὶ Κόρη

9 'Ιωνικοῦ

[2] See **42** intr. on homosexual love charms.
[3] See K.J.Dover, *Greek Homosexuality* (London 1978), esp. p. 23 f.

Ερεσχιγαλ ζαβαρβαθουχ καὶ Φερσεφόνη ζαυδαχθουμαρ καὶ δαίμονες, οἳ ἐν [τ]ούτῳ τῷ τόπῳ ἐστέ, συν-
20 έχετέ μοι τῷ Ἠωνι[κ]ῷ Ἀννιανοῦ τὴν ἰςχύν
{τὴν ἰςχύν}, τὴν δύναμιν, ἵνα ςυλλάβηςτε αὐτὸν καὶ παραδοῖτε ἀώροις, ἵνα κατατήξητε αὐτοῦ τὰς ςάρκες, τὰ νεῦρα, τὰ μέλη, τὴν ψυχήν, ἵνα
24 μὴ δυνηθῇ Ἠωνικῷ ἀντίος ἐλθεῖν μηδὲ κατ' ἐμοῦ
ἀκοῦςαί τι κακὸν μηδὲ βλέψαι, ἔτι δὲ καὶ ὑποπε-
πτωκώς μου ὑπὸ τοὺς πόδες ἕως νεικηθῇ. ἐπέκλω`ςε´
[γ]ὰρ αὐτῷ ταῦτα ἡ πανδυνάςτειρα ἄναςςα Μαςκελλει
28 Μα[ς]κελλω Φνουκενταβαω ορεοβαζαγρα ῥηξίχθων
ἱππόχθων πυριπηγανυξ πότνια Γῆ χθονία μευηρι
μοριθαρχωθ. ὁρκίζω ςε κατὰ coῦ ὀνόματος ποιῆςαι
τὴν πρᾶξιν ταύτην καὶ τηρῆςαί μοι τὸν κατάδεςμον
32 τοῦτον καὶ ποιῆςαι αὐτὸν ἐνεργῆ. Ἑρμῆ αρχεδαμα
Φωχενςεψευ ςαρερταθου μιςονκαικτ καὶ Πλούτων
[Υ]εςεμμιγαδων μααρχαμα καὶ Κόρη Ερεςχιγαλ
[ζα]βαρβαθου⟨χ⟩ καὶ Φερςεφόνη ζαυδαχθουμαρ καὶ δ[αί-]
36 [μον]ες οἱ ἐν τῷ τόπῳ τού[τῳ] φοιτῶντες τελ[ειώ-]
[ςατε τὴν] πρᾶξιν ταύτη[ν· κα]τάςχετε [τὴ]ν φιλί[αν]
[Ἀννιανο]ῦ πρὸς Ἠωνικ[όν, πρ]ώτιςτον, [ἀ]διαλύ[τως,]
[ἀπὸ τῆς c]ήμερον ἡμ[έρας . . . .]εθητο[. . .]ματο[. . .]

20 Ἰωνικῷ   21 ςυλλάβηςθε   22 παραδῶτε   23 ςάρκας
24 Ἰωνικῷ   26 πόδας   νικηθῇ   38 Ἰωνικόν

Erêkisithphêarachararaêphthisikêre ch . . seô; take hold of Annianos, chthonic Hermes, *archedama Phôchensepseu sarertathou misonkaikt* and Pluto *Yesemmigadôn maarchama* and Kore Ereschigal |⁴ *zabarbathouch* and Persephone *zaudachthoumar*. I adjure you by the name of Gê, *keuêmori môritharchôth* and chthonic Hermes *archedama Phôchensepseu sarertathou misonkaikt* and Pluto *Yesemmigadôn maarchama* and Kore |⁸ Ereschigal *zabarbathouch* and Persephone *zaudachthoumar*. May Annianos lose his own power of recollection, and let him remember Ionikos only. I call upon you, the mistress of all men, all-devouring (?), *rêxichthôn*, you who also gathered up |¹² the limbs of Meliouchos and Meliouchos himself, Ereschigal, *Neboutosoualêth*, gloomy, she of the nets (?), she of the dead (?),

Hekate, true (?) Hekate, come and fulfill this magical operation for me. Chthonic Hermes, |16 *archedama Phôchensepseu sarertathou misonkaikt* and Pluto *Yesemmigadôn maarchama* and Kore Ereschigal *zabarbathouch* and Persephone *zaudachthoumar* and daemons who are in this place, possess |20 for me, Ionikos, the strength and the might of Annianos, so that you seize him and deliver him to the untimely dead, so that you melt his flesh, sinews, limbs, soul, so that |24 he not be able to proceed against Ionikos and neither hear nor see any evil to my disadvantage, moreover prostrate under my feet until he is defeated. For this destiny was assigned to him by the all-powerful queen, *Maskellei* |28 *Maskellô Phnoukentabaô oreobazagra rêxichthôn hippochthôn pyripêganyx*, chthonic mistress Gê *meuêri moritharchôth*. I adjure you by your name to perform this magical operation and to watch over this binding charm for me |32 and to make it effective. Hermes *archedama phôchensepseu sarertathou misonkaikt* and Pluto *Yesemmigadôn maarchama* and Kore Ereschigal *zabarbathou* and Persephone *zaudachthoumar* and daemons |36 who frequent this place, fulfill this magical operation. Control the love of Annianos for Ionikos before everything else, indissolubly, from the present day - - -.

1 ε[ρη]κιϲιθφηα{μ}ραχαραραηφ[θιϲι]κηρε: a frequently occurring palindrome; see PGM, Vol. 3 (Index), p. 279 f. It occurs in *Schwinde-schema* in **55**, 1-19 and **57**, 16-31 middle (cf. 39). Noteworthy is the use of most of this palindrome in the following two hexameters: PGM II 100 (= *hymn.* 11, 29, to Apollo-Helios) χαῖρε, πυρὸς μεδέων, αραραχχαρα ηφθιϲικηρε (ἢ φθιϲίκηρε R.Merkelbach, *ZPE* 47, 1982, 172, understanding 'destroyer of the fate of death') and IV 2849 f. (= *hymn.* 18, 43, to Hekate) cὺ δὲ χάουϲ μεδέειϲ, αραραχαραρα {η} φθιϲίκηρε (see E.Rohde, *Psyche* II [Freiburg i.B. 1898²], p. 81, note 2, equating κῆρεϲ with ψυχαί). In light of the former passage, the latter should rather be emended as follows: αραρᾶχαρα{ρα} (or double the χ) ἢ φθιϲίκηρε. Certainly in both hexameters ἢ φθιϲίκηρε should be regarded as Greek, and so it could be that at least part of the palindrome is of Greek origin. It is also possible that ἢ φθιϲίκηρε was a Greek interpretation of something originally foreign.

ε[ρη]κιϲιθφη : θ̣[ρη]κιϲιθφη Audollent, though in his index VII (p. 504) he gave ε[ρη]κιϲιθφη.

ηφ[θιϲι]κηρε with Wünsch : ηφοιϲκηρε Audollent. Babelon and Blanchet, who did not know what ought to be read, gave the following diplomatic transcription of this word ΓΦΟΙϹ‖ΚΗΡΕ.

χ̣ ̣ϲεω Audollent : λ̣ ̣ϲεω Wünsch.

2 Φωχενσεψευ σαρερταθου μισονκα[ι]κ[τ]: PGM, Vol. 3 (Index), p. 242 refers to this as the Φωκενγεψ logos, but most of the examples cited by him have a sigma rather than a gamma; cf. here lines 6, 16, 33; **47**, 2 f.; **48** J 3; **49**, 9 f.

3 Υεσεμμιγαδων (with variants) is commonly attested; see Index VII; PGM, Vol. 3 (Index), pp. 232, 242. To date the name has not been convincingly explained; for various suggestions that have been made, see Martinez, *P.Mich. 757*, pp. 37-40.

3-4 ζ[αβαρ]βαθουχ: cf. PGM VIII 96 and X 6 Ζαβαρβαθιαω.

5 Γῆ[c] κευημορι μωριθαρχωθ: see below on 29-30.

7 Υεσε[μμι]γαδων Wünsch : υεσε[μμ]ιγαδων Audollent.

9-10 ἐπιλάθοιτο - - - μνημονευέτω: optative of wish used side by side with imperative; cf. PGM V 323 and XIII 293-296.

ἐπιλάθοιτο ᾿Αννιανὸς τῆς ἰ[δ]ίας μνήμης καὶ ᾿Ηωνικοῦ μόλνου μνημονευέτω: probably drawn from an erotic *defixio*; cf. **72** ii 15 comm.; also PGM IV 2757-63 ληθομένη τέκνων συνηθείης τε τοκήων καὶ στυγέουσα τὸ πᾶν ἀνδρῶν γένος ἠδὲ γυναικῶν ἐκτὸς ἐμοῦ, τοῦ δεῖνα, μόνον με δ᾿ ἔχουσα παρέcτω, ἐν φρεσὶ δαμνομένη κρατερῆς ὑπ᾿ ἔρωτος ἀνάγκης; XV 4 f. ἐπιλήσῃ γονέων, τέκνων, φίλων; XIXa 52-54 μὴ ἐάσῃς αὐτὴν - - - μὴ [ἰδίῳ] ἀνδρὶ μνημονεύειν, μὴ τέκνου, μὴ ποτοῦ, μὴ βρωτοῦ, ἀλλὰ ἔλ[θη τη]κομένη τῷ ἔρωτι καὶ τῇ φιλίᾳ καὶ συνουσίᾳ, πλείστω⟨c⟩ ποθου[μ]ένη πρὸς τὴν συνουσίαν τοῦ ᾿Απαλῶς; LXI 28-30 ἵνα - - - ἐπιλάθηται πατρὸς καὶ μητ[ρό]c, ἀδελφῶν, ἀνδρός, φίλου, π[λ]ὴν ἐμοῦ μόνου τούτων πάν[τ]ων ἐπιλάθηται; Audollent, *DT*, 266, 15-19 *ut obliviscatur patris et matris - - - solum me in mente habeat* (also 268, 1-3). All of these passages, which come from conventional *defixiones amatoriae*, differ from the present one in that they are quite explicitly erotic.

A loss-of-memory formula, even if drawn from an erotic *defixio*, is perfectly at home in what may be essentially a juridical curse. The present passage may be compared especially with Moraux, *Une défixion judiciaire*, p. 12, lines 4-13 ποιήσατε ᾿Ακείλιον Φαυστεῖνον καὶ Cτέφανον, τοὺς ἀντιδίκους μου, περὶ τῶν cωμάτων καὶ περὶ τῶν κτημάτων καὶ περὶ τῶν γραμμάτων [ὧ]ν ἄν μοι ἐνκαλῶcιν, περὶ τούτων δὲ τ[ῶ]ν πραγμάτων μήτε φροντίζειν μήτε μνημονεύειν. Cf. Cicero on Curio's defense of his feeble memory: *Brut. 217 subito totam causam oblitus est idque veneficiis et cantionibus Titiniae factum esse dicebat*; *Or. 129 nobis privata in causa magna et gravi cum coepisset Curio pater respondere, subito assedit, cum sibi venenis ereptam memoriam diceret*; and similarly Libanius, *Or.* 1, 71 ἰλιγγιάσας ἐξενήνεκτο τῆς μνήμης καὶ ἐβόα μηδὲ τότε πεπαῦςθαι τὸν γόητα ἐμέ. The μνήμη of opponents is occasionally cursed in other juridical *defixiones*. On this and various other ways that legal adversaries might be cursed (especially inability to speak), see C.A.Faraone, *TAPA* 119 (1989) 149-160.

9 Ἠωνικός = Ἰωνικός: not listed in the papyrological onomastica, but Ἰωνικός and Ἰωνική are well known from inscriptions of the Imperial period; see L.Robert, *Gnomon* 31 (1959) 667; Solin, *Die griechischen Personennamen in Rom* I, p. 576 f.

10-14 ἐπικαλοῦμαι - - - ἀληθῆ: cf. PGM III 43-48 ἐπικαλοῦμαί ce, τῶν πάντω[ν] ἀνθρ[ώπ]ων γ]ενέτειρα, τὴν cυναναγκαcαμέν[η]⟨ν⟩ τὰ μέλ[η το]ῦ Μελιούχου καὶ αὐτὸν Μελιοῦχον οροβαcτρια [Νε]-βουτοcουαληθ, ἄρκυια, νέκυια, Ἑ[ρ]μῆ, Ἑκάτ[η, Ἑρμῆ, Ἑρμε]κάτη ληθ.

11 δυνάcτειραν: listed in LSJ only for the present text; cf. 27 πανδυνάcτειρα.

παμφόρβα with Wünsch (παμ[φόρ]βα) : παμφοβέρα Audollent. LSJ, *s.v.* παμφόβεροc, cite only the present passage and a gloss (CGL II 199, 40). The first of these must be deleted. For παμφόρβα of Hekate, cf. PGM IV 1261, 2749. Preisendanz translated "alles Fressende." Another possibility is 'all-nourishing'; cf. LSJ *s.v.* πάμφορβοc.

ρηξίχθων: commonly found in the Maskelli-logos (see below on 27-29).

11-13 ἢ καὶ ἀνενεγ\καμένη τὰ τοῦ Μελιού[χ]ου μέλη καὶ αὐτὸν τὸν Μελιοῦχον: see **42**, 57 comm.

13 Νεβουτοcουαληθ: also in **49**, 45. Occasionally used of the moon-goddess, this magical name of uncertain etymology is often associated with Hekate, Ereschigal and Aktiophis; cf. PGM, Vol. 3 (Index), p. 227. For discussion, see *RE* XVI.2, *s.v.* Nebutosualeth, coll. 2158-60 (K.Preisendanz); Youtie-Bonner, "Two Curse Tablets from Beisan," p. 68; W.E.Crum, *JEA* 28 (1942) 31; Bonner, *SMA*, p. 197 f.

14 ἄρκυια: cf. PGM III 46 f. (cited above, 10-14 comm.); possibly also PGM IV 2277 (αρκηϊ Pap.) and 2780 (αλκυια Pap.). As to the word's meaning: "dub. sens., epith. of Hekate" LSJ; "abwehrende" Preisendanz; "die Netze stellende" K.F.W.Schmidt, *GGA* 193 (1931) 449; "on ne sait que faire de ἄρκυια épithète d'Hécate," Chantraine, *Dictionnaire étymologique,*

s.v. ἄρκυс. The epithet of Artemis δίκτυννα may lend support to Schmidt's suggestion; according to R.K.Ritner in Betz, *Translation,* p. 19 n. 11, "the netter" is an Egyptian underworld daemon.

νέκυια: cf. PGM III 47 (cited above on 10-14); IV 2781.

ἀληθῆ: for the vocative ending -ῆ, cf. **42**, 2 comm. Although one can compare PGM XII 318 τὸ ἱερὸν Οὔφωρ, τὸ ἀληθέc and **45**, 28 Ὠρίων ἀληθινέ, the epithet 'truthful, honest' does not appear to be appropriate for Hekate. The seemingly Greek word may have arisen from miscopying. Already Wünsch remarked, "quid cognominis hic lateat nescio: Ἀλθαία? ἀλήτη ?" The latter conjecture is appealing in light of Hekate's nocturnal wanderings. Another possibility is that αληθη had its origin in a magical word; cf. ληθ in PGM III 48 (cited above, 10-14 comm.); also PGM XIXa 45 left βλαθαθ αληθ βηιγαμα.

21 cυλλάβηcτε: r. cυλλάβηcθε. For cθ > cτ, Gignac, *Grammar* I, p. 87. On the vogue of the middle voice in late antiquity (cf. **61**, 4 comm.), see Blass-Debrunner-Funk, *Grammar,* § 316; Hatzidakis, *Einleitung,* pp. 194-200; L.Robert, *Comptes rendus Acad. Inscr.* 1978, p. 255 (= *Opera Minora Selecta* V, p. 711). Audollent's proposal of cυλλάβη{c}τε does not seem necessary.

21-22 ἵνα cυλλάβηcθε αὐ|τὸν καὶ παραδοῖτε: similar wording is used in orders for arrest and delivery in the documentary papyri, e.g. P.Hib. I 54, 20-22 καὶ τὸ cῶμα δὲ εἰ cυνείληφαc παράδοc [[αυτο]] Cεμφθεῖ, and P.Abinn. 51, 15 f. δέομαί cου τῆc φιλανθρωπίαc, κύριε, τούτουc cυνλαβέcθαι καὶ παραπέμψ[αι] αὐτοὺc τῷ κυρίῳ μου δουκί.

22 παραδοῖτε: if not an instance of ω > οι, then an extension into the plural of singular subjunctive δοῖc, δοῖ (discussed by Gignac, *Grammar* II, p. 388 f., where no instance of the plural of such forms is cited).

22-23 κατατήξητε αὐ|τοῦ τὰc cάρκεc (r. cάρκαc), τὰ νεῦρα, τὰ μέλη, τὴν ψυχήν: drawn from a love charm. Cf. **48**, 36; the formula ποίηcον φθείνειν καὶ κατατήκεcθαι Cαραπίωνα ἐπὶ τῷ ἔρωτι Διοcκοροῦτοc - - - ἔκτηξον that is repeated nine times in PGM XVI; further, PGM XIXa 53 τη]κομένη τῷ ἔρωτι καὶ τῇ φιλίᾳ καὶ cυνουcίᾳ; XVIIa 10 f. [ἐρ]ωτικῇ ἐπιθυμίᾳ τηκομένην; IV 2931 f. φιλότητι τακῆναι; Theocr., 2, 28 f.; Verg., *Ecl.* 8, 80 f.

24 ἀντίοc ἐλθεῖν: especially this phrase characterizes the curse as juridically motivated. Similar phrases are found in other juridical curses; cf. Audollent, *DT,* 14 A, 1-5 γράφω πά[ν]τ[α]c τοὺc ἐμοὶ ἀντία π[ο]ιοῦν-

τας μετὰ τῶν [ἀ]ώρων (cf. line 16 f. Ὀνήςιμον τὸν ἀντίον); 13, 1-4 [ἀνατίθημι] - - - τοὺς ἐπ᾽ ἐμὲ ἐλ[θόντ]ας; Wünsch, *DTA*, 35, 15-19 πάντες ὅςοι ἐμοὶ ἐχθρὰ ἢ [ἐ]ν[αντία] [πράττουςι]; 65 b καὶ ε⟨ἴ⟩ τις ἐναντί⟨α⟩ ε⟨ἰ⟩ τὰ τούτων ἐς⟨τ⟩ι ἄλλος πράττ{ι}ει ἐμοί (which Wünsch interprets as καὶ εἴ τις ἄλλος τούτων ἐςτί, ὃς ἐναντία πράττει ἐμοί); 83 a 4-5 [ἐ]ναντία γίγνε[ςθαι]; b 3-4 τοῖς τὰ ἐναντία πρ[άτ]τουςιν; 158, 3 ἐναντί⟨α⟩ ἐκ[είνοις. For ὁ ἀντίος as 'legal adversary', cf. Preisigke, *Wörterbuch*, *s.v.* See also **79**, 29-30 comm. on ἐ[ναντι]ιώθητε.

25-26 ἔτι δὲ καὶ ὑποπεῖπτωκώς μου ὑπὸ τοὺς πόδες (r. πόδας): prostration under the feet is a metaphor of subjugation occasionally used in the love charms; cf. **45**, 6 f.; PGM XVIIIa 8 f. ἄξον δ[έ μ]οι αὐτὴν ὑπὸ τοὺς ἐμοὺς πόδας. Such turns of phrase, however, are more frequently found in charms for victory and in restrainers of wrath; cf. PGM VII 966-968 (part of a θυμοκάτοχον καὶ ὑποτάκτικον) φίμωςον, ὑπόταξον, καταδούλωςον τὸν δεῖνα τῷ δεῖνα καὶ ποίηςον αὐτόν, ὑπὸ τοὺς πόδας μου ἔλθῃ; and the similar IX 4-7 καθυπόταξον, φίμωςον, καταδούλωςον πᾶν γένος ἀνθρώπων, ἀρρένων τε καὶ θηλυκῶν, παντοίων θυμῶν, τοὺς ὑπὸ τὴν κτίςιν ὑπὸ τοὺς πόδας τοῦ δεῖνα, μάλιστα τόνδε - - - [ὑ]φιεῖ[ς] γὰρ ὑπὸ τοὺς πόδας μου, ὡς περιβόλαιόν μου; cf. also **99** recto i 1-2 comm. PGM VII 925-939 is a νικητικὸν καὶ ὑποτακτικόν that is to be inscribed on a lead tablet and worn under the sole of the left foot (927 f. θὲς ὑπὸ τὸ πέλμα cου τοῦ εὐωνύμου ποδός); likewise PGM X 36-50 is a θυμοκάτοχον and ὑποτακτικόν that prescribes writing the following formula on a lead tablet that is to be worn under the right foot in one's sandal: (40 f.) ὡς ταῦτα τὰ ἅγια ὀνόματα πατεῖται, οὕτως καὶ ὁ δεῖνα κτλ. Cf. also Diod. Sic. XVII 100, 8 ριφέντος δ᾽ ἐπὶ γῆν ἐπιβὰς ἐπὶ τὸν τράχηλον τῷ ποδί καὶ τὸ ῥόπαλον ἀνατεινάμενος ἀνέβλεψεν πρὸς τοὺς θεωμένους; LXX Ps. 109, 1 κάθου ἐκ δεξιῶν μου, ἕως ἂν θῶ τοὺς ἐχθρούς cου ὑποπόδιον τῶν ποδῶν cου and parallels in NT (Matth. 22, 44 etc.); other references in Bauer, *Wörterbuch*, *s.v.* πούς b; much related material in C.Sittl, *Die Gebärden der Griechen und Römer* (Leipzig 1890), pp. 106-108.

26 ἕως νεικηθῇ (r. νικηθῇ): on the possible final sense of ἕως, see **40**, 17 comm. The words νίκη and νικάω are not attested in the magical papyri with reference to amatory conquest. Especially in light of 24 ἀντίος ἐλθεῖν, it seems that the verb refers here to success in legal proceedings; cf. **79**, 26

ἐπὶ ἀ[ν]᾽τι᾽δίκο[υ] νεικητικ[όν]; PGM XXVI 35 (cited above, intr.) and 40 καὶ νικήςεις; the juridical curse edited by F.K.Dörner, *Wiener Jahreshefte* 32 (1940) 65-72, lines 33-36 ποιήςατέ μοι κατάδικον Μακρῖνον ἡττώμενον νεικώμενον and 45-47 ἵνα ποιήςατε νεικηθῆναι Μακρεῖνον. One finds νίκη and νικάω used of success in legal proceedings frequently elsewhere; cf. LSJ, *s.vv.* νίκη I.3, νικάω I.5; Preisigke, *Wörterbuch, s.v.* νικάω d); Dittenberger, Syll.³, vol. 4, p. 458, *s.v.* νικάω 1 b).

27 πανδυνάςτειρα: listed in LSJ only for the present text; cf. 11 δυνάςτειραν.

27-29 Μαςκελλει | Μα[ς]κελλω Φνουκενταβαω ορεοβαζαγρα ῥηξίχθων | ἱππόχθων πυριπηγανυξ: the third element is usually spelled Φνουκενταβαωθ. Earlier literature on this logos can be traced through Ritoók's discussion cited in **12**, 3-5 comm. See now the remarks of H.J. Thissen in: *Religion und Philosophie im alten Ägypten. Festgabe für Philippe Derchain zu seinem 65. Geburtstag am 24. Juli 1991* (Orientalia Lovaniensia Analecta 39, 1991), p. 297 f. Here a brief summary: Μαςκελλι Μαςκελλω may come from Hebrew *mškyl* 'hymn', and the phrase can be translated 'my hymn, your hymn'. (Alternative derivations from Hebrew *šql* proposed by I. Kottsieper *apud* Thissen: 'he who weighs me weighs you' or 'the weigher weighs him'). Φνουκενταβαωθ is probably 'Nun, first of the fathers', which is comparable to the earlier epithet of Nun 'father of the gods'; Φνουκενταβαωθ may be based on Egyptian 'Nun' preceded by the definite article + Egyptian *ḫntj* 'first' + Hebrew *aboth* 'fathers'.

29 ἱππόχθων πυριπηγανυξ with Wünsch : ἱππόχθωνι πυριπηγά-[ζο]υ[ςα] Audollent.

μευηρι: the word is from Egyptian *m ḥ.t - wr.t* 'primal flood' (see Griffiths, *Plutarch's de Iside et Osiride*, p. 512), and because the primal flood was conceived of as a cow, the epithet was also applied to Hathor, as was already pointed out by Zündel, *loc.cit.*, 492-495 (H.J.Thissen).

29-30 Γῆ χθονία μευηρι | μοριθαρχωθ: a variant or variation of 5 Γῆ[ς] κευημορι μωριθαρχωθ.

30 κατὰ coῦ ὀνόματος: standard Greek would require κατὰ ⟨τοῦ⟩ coῦ ὀνόματος or κατά coυ ⟨τοῦ⟩ ὀνόματος.

32 ἐνεργῆ: cf. PGM XII 202 f. δακτυλίδιον πρὸς πᾶcαν πρᾶξιν καὶ ἐπιτυχίαν μ[ετίαcιν] βαcιλεῖc καὶ ἡγεμόνεc. λίαν ἐνεργέc; IV 2976 ἐνεργεcτέραν, of a magical herb.

35 [ζα]βαρβαθου⟨χ⟩: apparently, at least part of initial ζα- was intact when read by Audollent and Wünsch.

37 ταύτη[ν· κα]τάςχετε : ταύτη[ν καὶ κα]τάςχετε Audollent and, similarly, Wünsch. There is not enough room for καί.

κα]τάςχετε [τὴ]ν φιλί[αν]: though κατέχειν means 'check' or 'restrain', here the context requires 'maintain' or 'control'. The unexpected presence of this verb can perhaps be explained by the fact that the writer might have based this charm on a θυμοκάτοχον καὶ νικητικόν, in which he replaced the wrath-restraining formulae with phrases from an erotic *defixio* (see intr.). If so, his model had κατάςχετε τὸν θυμὸν τοῦ δεῖνα πρὸς δεῖνα, which he altered by merely changing τὸν θυμόν to τὴν φιλίαν.

[τὴ]ν φιλί[αν] : [τὴ?]ν φιλί[αν?]Audollent :   ּ ּν φιλ ּ ּ ּ Wünsch.

38 ['Αννιανο]ῦ πρὸς : ּ ּ ּ ּ ּ υπιος Audollent : ּ ּ ּ ּ ּ ὕπνουϲ Wünsch.

'Ηωνικ[όν, πρ]ώτιϲτον, [ἀ]διαλύ[τωϲ] : 'Ηωνικ ּ ּ ּ ּ ּ ὅτι ϲτο ּ ּ ּ ּ διαλυ Audollent and similarly Wünsch.

39 [ἀπὸ τῆϲ ϲ]ήμερον ἡμ[έραϲ : ּ ּ ּ ּ ּ ּν μερινηχ ּ ּ ּ ּ Audollent and similarly Wünsch.

]ε̣θ̣ητο[or]ε̣θ̣ητω[.

Oxyrhynchos   III AD

T.Cairo Mus. JdE 36059.

ED.PR.: O.Guéraud, "Charme de haine, sur tablette de plomb," in: *Mélanges Maspero* II
     (1934-1937), pp. 206-212.

COMM.: ed.pr.

TRANSL.: ed.pr.

REF.: Jordan, "Survey," no. 154.

DESCR.: lead tablet; 19 × 15 cm. Inscribed on one side only.

LOC.: Egyptian Museum, Cairo.

Chichoeis is to be rendered speechless in the presence of Herakles and
Hermias, and he is to become the object of their hate. Although the use of
disjunctive charms was frequently motivated by erotic jealousy (see **95** intr.),
the present one clearly was not. One may compare especially PGM LXVI,
which also establishes strife between one male and two others: εἴϲβαλε τὸν
Φιλόξενον τὸν ψάλτην μετὰ Γενναδίου φ⟨ί⟩λον εἰϲ μάχην. εἴϲβαλε
τὸν Πελάγιον τὸν πρεϲβύτερον εἰϲ μάχην μετὰ Φιλοξένου τὸν ψάλτην.[1] Explicitly or implicitly indifferent to sex are the following passages
from disjunctive charms in the formularies: PGM XII 372-374 δότε τῷ δεῖνα
τῆϲ δεῖνα μάχην, πόλεμον, καί τῷ δεῖνα τῆϲ δεῖνα ἀηδίαν, ἔχθραν, ὡϲ
εἶχον Τυφῶν καὶ Ὄϲιρις (εἰ δὲ ἀνήρ ἐϲτιν καὶ γυνή· 'ὡϲ εἶχον Τυφῶν
καὶ Ἰϲιϲ'); 458 f. ποίηϲον τὸν δεῖνα διαχωριϲθῆναι ἀπὸ τοῦ δεῖνα; 463
διάκοψον [τ]ὸν δεῖνα ἀπὸ τοῦ δεῖνα; also PDM xii 50-61 and 62-75
(Betz, *Translation*, pp. 169-170); Kropp, *Koptische Zaubertexte* I, M, 82-84
(transl. II, p. 46); VBP V 123, 7-24.

The reasons that led to the use of non-erotically motivated separative
charms can vary greatly. The present one, for example, might have been

---

[1] The three names and titles 'cantor' and 'presbyter' show that the setting of this spell is
Christian; see R.W.Daniel, *ZPE* 89 (1991) 119 f. As to its motivation, see L.Koenen, *ZPE*
8 (1971) 199 note 1, and Daniel, *loc. cit.*

written by someone who hoped to replace Chichoeis in business dealings with or employment under Herakles and Hermias. Another possibility is that the spell was juridically motivated: Chichoeis may be cursed with muteness so that he cannot speak out against his opponents in court (see **58**, 8-9 comm.); and when it is said that they should "hate him with great hate" (13-14) and "not wish to see him at all" (16) this may mean that they should proceed against him with strong enmity and disdain. Given either of these hypothetical situations, it is noteworthy that Chichoeis and his mother bear Egyptian names, the two other parties and their mothers Greek names.

Even when disjunctive charms are directed against man and woman, the reason need not *always* have been erotic desire for one of the parties. On occasion the explanation may simply be malice, witness the divisive character of Iago in Shakespeare's *Othello*. On the other hand, a concerned parent, believing that his son or daughter has fallen in love with the "wrong" person, might also resort to a disjunctive charm.

A diplomatic transcription is given to illustrate the layout of the text by sections. A normalized transcription of sections D-G follows.

A

```
              ερεικεισειφθηαραραχαραραπηφθεισεικειρε
               ρεικεισειφθηαραραχαραραπηφθεισεικειρε
                εικεισειφθηαραραχαραραπηφθεισεικει
         ε          ικεισειφθηαραραχαραραπηφθεισεικε        C
         ει          κεισειφθηαραραχαραραπηφθεισεικ      ι
         ειρ         εισειφθηαραραχαραραπηφθεισει        ει
         ειρα         ιειφθηαραραχαραραπηφθεισε         ρει
         ειραμ         ειφθηαραραχαραραπηφθεις          αρει
         ειραμμ         ιφθηαραραχαραραπηφθει           μαρει
         ειραμμα         φθηαραραχαραραπηφθε           αμαρει
         ειραμμαχ         θηαραραχαραραπηφθ           χαμαρει
         ειραμμαχα         ηαραραχαραραπηφ          αχαμαρει
         ειραμμαχαμ         αραραχαραραπη          μαχαμαρει
         ειραμμαχαμμ         ραραχαραρα           μμαχαμαρει
         ειραμμαχαμμα         αραχαραρ           αμμαχαμαρει
         ειραμμαχαμμαρ         ραχαρα            ραμμαχαμαρει
         ειραμμαχαμμαρκ         αχαρ             κραμμαχαμαρει
         ειραμμαχαμμαρκα         χα             ακραμμαχαμαρει
                                 χ
```

```
μισιτοερμιασονε          κατεναντι
τεκενδιδυμητον          ηρακληουονετε
χιχωεινονετεκεν         κενηρακλεια
ταχωεισμυρικωσα         μισιτωσαναυ
τεαυτωνχιχωειν          τοντωμεγαμισημα      F
```

E

D
ειδυμησιστοσαγχχων
καικετεναντιερημουουονετεκεν
ναυτιμηρακουονετεκενηρακλεια
μηηρικοσονγχχοεμονετεκεντανχοεισκατε

B

G

ταχοταχυ
καιμηθελησουσιαυτονβλεψεολαος
τονομηρικοσονατοντονχιχοειν

ιριραμεαρδαπιλισηεμα
εναταλματαρδαπιλισηεμα
οραιρινδιμρο

Sections D-G

<table>
<tr><td>1</td><td>μυρίκοσον Χιχόει⟨ν⟩, ὃν ἔτεκεν Ταχόεις, κατέ-
ναντι Ἡρακλ⟨ή⟩ου, ὃν ἔτεκεν Ἡράκλεια,
καὶ κατέναντι Ἑρμίου, ὃν ἔτεκεν</td></tr>
<tr><td>4</td><td>Διδύμης· μιcίτοcαν Χιχώειν.</td></tr>
<tr><td></td><td>μιcίτο Ἑρμίαc, ὃν ἔ-
τεκεν Διδύμη, τὸν
Χιχώειν, ὃν ἔτεκεν</td></tr>
<tr><td>8</td><td>Ταχώειc· μυρικώcα-
τε αὐτὼν Χιχώειν</td></tr>
<tr><td></td><td>κατέναντι
Ἡρακλήου, ὃν ἔτε-</td></tr>
<tr><td>12</td><td>κεν Ἡράκλεια·
μιcίτωcαν αὐ-
τὸν τὼ μέγα μίcημα</td></tr>
<tr><td></td><td>{ταχὺ ταχύ}</td></tr>
<tr><td>16</td><td>καὶ μὴ θελήcουcι αὐτὸν βλέψε ὅλοc.
τονομυρίκοcον αὐτόν, τὸν Χιχώειν,
ἐν τῇ cήμερον ἡμέρᾳ, ἐν τῇ ἄρτι
ὅρᾳ, ἤδη ἤδη, ⟨ταχὺ ταχύ⟩.</td></tr>
</table>

1 μυρίκωcον	4 Διδύμη· μιcείτωcαν	5 μιcείτω	9 αὐτὸν
13 μιcείτωcαν	14 τὸ	16 θελήcωcι	βλέψαι ὅλωc	17 τονο-
μυρίκωcον	19 ὥρᾳ			

(A) *ereikeiseiphthêararachararaêphtheiseikeire* (etc.). (B) *eirammachammarka* (etc.).
(C) *akrammachamarei* (etc.). (D-G) Make Chichoeis, whom Tachoeis bore, mute over
against Herakles, whom Herakleia bore, and over against Hermias, whom |[4] Didyme bore.
Let them hate Chichoeis. Let Hermias, whom Didyme bore, hate Chichoeis, whom Tacho-
eis |[8] bore. Cause him, Chichoeis, to be mute over against Herakles, whom |[12] Herakleia
bore. Let them hate him with great hate, |[16] and may they not wish to see him at all.
Cause him, Chichoeis, to be mute in voice, on the present day, in this very hour, now
now, quickly quickly.

Section A ερεικεισειφθηαραραχαραραηφθεισεικειρε in Schwinde-schema: on the palindrome see **54**, 1 comm.

Sections B and C ακραμμαχαμαρει spelled backwards and forwards in wing-shaped formations. On the magical name, see **10**, 1 comm.

Sections D-G

1 μυρίκοσον (r. μυρίκωσον): cf. 8-9 μυρικώσατε and 17 τονομυρί-κοσον; on the vacillation between singular and plural, see **44**, 10 comm. Both μυρικόω and τονομυρικόω are *addenda lexicis.* Cf. Hesychius, *s.vv.* μυρικᾶς· ἄφωνος, ἐν ἑαυτῷ ἔχων ὃ μέλλει πράττειν, and μύρκος· ὁ καθόλου μὴ δυνάμενος λαλεῖν. Cυρακούσιοι. ἐνεός. ἄφωνος. On the basis of these passages, Guéraud suggested that the basic meaning of μυρι-κόω is 'to make mute'. He pointed out that the same verb is to be recognized in PGM XIII 239 f. ἐάν τινα θέλῃς μυρικῶσαι πρὸς ἄνδρα γυναῖκα ἢ ἄνδρα πρὸς γυναῖκα (cf. 242 διακόπτω τὸν δεῖνα ἀπὸ τοῦ δεῖνα). Cf. also **95** → 4 for a probable occurrence of a form of μυρικόω in a diakopos. For the general sense Guéraud compared Audollent, *DT*, 139, 1-14 *Quomodo mortuos qui istic supultus est nec loqui nec sermonare potest, seic Rhodine apud M. Licinium Faustum mortua sit nec loqui nec sermonare possit. Ita uti mortuos nec ad deos nec ad homines acceptus est, seic Rhodine aput M. Licinium accepta sit et tantum valeat quantum ille mortuos quei istic supultus est. Dite pater, Rhodine tibei commendo, uti semper odio sit M. Licinio Fausto.* Guéraud concluded that in the *diakopoi* persons are cursed with muteness so that they appear stupid and contemptible.

2 Ἡρακλ⟨ή⟩ου: cf. 11. On the name Ἡρακλῆς variously declined, see Gignac, *Grammar* II, p. 71 f.

14 μίσημα: a poetic word elsewhere attested only in the classical trage-dians (see LSJ, *s.v.*); Soph., *El.* 289 was used by Aristophanes (see Kassel-Austin, *PCG* III.2, Fr. 175).

15 ταχὺ ταχύ: the writer added these words here when he found that there was no space available for them after ἤδη ἤδη in 19.

16 ὅλος (r. ὅλως): suggested by Guéraud in his commentary.

17 τονομυρίκοσον (r. -ωσον) : τονο. Μυρίκοσον Guéraud (p. 210). Because μυρικόω apparently means 'to make mute', one should in all likeli-hood recognize a new compound, the first element of which is from τόνος. The sense must be 'make mute the volume of the voice'.

56

Oxyrhynchos   III/IV AD

P.Oxy. inv. 50.4B 23/J (1-3) b.

ED.PR.: E.G.Turner, "The Marrow of Hermes," in: *Images of Man in Ancient and Medieval
   Thought: Studia G.Verbeke ab amicis et collegis dicata* (Louvain 1976), pp. 169-173.

REPUBL.: G.Giangrande, *Anc. Soc.* 9 (1978) 101-116 (= *Scripta Minora Alexandrina* 2, pp.
   573-588); P.Gorissen, *ZPE* 37 (1980) 199 f.; C.A.Faraone, *ZPE* 72 (1988) 279-286;
   H.S.Versnel, *ZPE* 72 (1988) 287-292.

COMM.: J.Gw.Griffiths, *ZPE* 26 (1977) 287 f.; Giangrande, *loc.cit.* and *Mus. Philol.
   Lond.* 7 (1986) 39-42; Gorissen, *loc.cit.*; Faraone, *loc.cit.*; Versnel, *loc.cit.*

TRANSL.: ed.pr.; Giangrande, *Anc. Soc.* 9, p. 102; Betz, *Translation*, no. CIX; Faraone,
   loc.cit., p. 285.

PHOTO: ed.pr.

DESCR.: papyrus; 8 × 8 cm. Written in a crude hand along the fibers. The back is blank.
   The text seems to be complete, for there is blank space above the first line of writing.
   Below the text, space of 3 cm.

LOC.: Ashmolean Museum, Oxford.

   The nature of the simile magic at work in this charm was first recognized
by Faraone: as a part of a mill turns and as an object is ground by a millstone,
so Zetous also called Kalemera is to be forced to have a change of heart and
mind.[1] As to the motivation of the charm, Turner and others suspected that it
was erotic.[2] Turner compared the metaphor of 'turning' to Theocr. 2, 30 f.

---

   [1] German folklore knows of similar uses of a mill: runaway servants or departed lovers
return, and thieves bring back stolen objects, if a piece of their clothing is placed under a
millstone (see *Handwörterbuch des deutschen Aberglaubens* VI, col. 607).

   [2] Turner proposed the following normalized transcription and translation: ὥσπερ στρέ-
φεται ὁ Ἑρμῆς τοῦ μυελοῦ καὶ ἀληθεῖται τοῦτο τὸ πιττάκιον, οὕτως στρέψον τὸν ἐγκέφαλον καὶ τὴν καρδίαν καὶ πᾶσαν διάνοιαν ζητεῖν ⟨τ⟩ῆ⟨ς⟩ ἐπικαλουμένη⟨ς⟩
Καλημέρας. ἤδη ἤδη ταχὺ ταχύ. "As Hermes turns in his marrow and vouches for the
truth (?) of this chit, so turn the brain and heart and search out all the mind of her who is
called Kalemera. Instantly instantly quick quick." Also Giangrande and Griffiths suspected
that the charm was erotically motivated; since their suggestions are based on now rejected
readings and interpretation, they are not taken into consideration here. (Griffiths' article,

χὼς δινεῖθ' ὅδε ῥόμβος ὁ χάλκεος ἐξ 'Αφροδίτας, / ὡς τῆνος δινοῖτο ποθ' ἁμετέραισι θύραισιν. That the brain and the heart of Zetous are to be influenced can also be paralleled in love charms, as e.g. **45**, 7-9 ἔδησα γὰρ αὐτῆς τὸν ἐγκέφαλον καὶ τὰς χῖρας καὶ τὰ ὑποχόνδρια καὶ τὴν φύσιν καὶ τὴν καρδίαν πρὸς φιλίαν ἐμοῦ Θέωνος.[3] The present text, however, stands apart from the *defixiones amatoriae*, among other reasons, because it lacks explicit mention of love and sexual acts.

An essentially different background is suggested in the first place by a close parallel that is most easily consulted in Heim, *Incantamenta*, no. 221: *Ad fugitivos. In charta scribit dominus manu sua sive domina manu sua sinistra nomen fugitivi et de manu dextra scribat haec nomina 'pallachata* παλλακατα σαπρα' *et ea⟨n⟩dem charta⟨m⟩ mittes in mola⟨m⟩ frumentaria⟨m⟩ et ibi teratur.*[4] The present spell, then, was most likely used by a master against the slave Zetous-Kalemera, who was probably fugitive or suspected of planning to run away.[5] Already Turner pointed out that Kale-

---

nevertheless, remains valuable for its observations on Egyptian religious and biological conceptions about marrow). Versnel and Faraone dealt only with the nature of the simile magic and did not not remark on its motivation. Versnel proposed what he himself called "an alternative, not a superior interpretation" to Faraone's, namely that a figurine of the god Hermes, perhaps made of marrow or fat, was twisted and bruised so as to influence Zetous.

[3] The brain of the beloved is mention also in two other love charms (PGM IV 1543; XXXVIII 11), the heart of course dozens of times (see PGM, Vol. 3 [Index], p. 115, *s.v.* καρδία). The διάνοια of the beloved is not mentioned in the love charms preserved in the papyri.

[4] From the sixth century Codex Vossianus L. Q. 9, ed. J.Piechotta, "Ein Anecdotum latinum," no. 189 (in *Jahres-Bericht des Königlichen katholischen Gymnasiums zu Leobschütz über das Schuljahr 1886/87*, hrsg. K.Hansel, Leobschütz 1887, p. xii).

[5] For prayers against fugitive slaves recited by the Vestal Virgins, cf. Plin., *N.H.* XXVIII 3 *Vestales nostras hodie credimus nondum egressa urbe mancipia fugitiva retinere in loco precatione*; Dio Cass. XLVIII 19, 4 τοσοῦτοι γὰρ δὴ ηὐτομόλουν ὥστε καὶ τὰς ἀειπαρθένους καθ' ἱερῶν εὔξασθαι ἐπιςχεθῆναί ςφων τὰς αὐτομολίας. For Byzantine charms to force a fugitive slave to return, cf. Delatte, *Anecdota Atheniensia*, pp. 12, 1-5 εἰς φυγὴν ἀνθρώπου. ἐὰν φύγῃ τινὰς ἄνθρωπος καὶ θέλῃς νὰ τὸν ἐπιςτρέψῃς, γράψον ἀνάποδα τὸ ὄνομαν τοῦ ἀνθρώπου ὁποῦ ἔφυγεν εἰς καινούργιον κεραμίδιν ἀποκάτω καὶ τὰς χαρακτῆρας· καὶ βάλε το ἀπάνω εἰς μίαν πυροςτιὰν νὰ καῇ· καὶ γυρίζει ὀπίςω; 114, 15-19 (cited here in intr.). Astrological prognoses as to when and how fugitive slaves will return or as to when and where their masters can find them were composed by a Demetrius (*Cat. Cod. Astr. Gr.* I, pp. 104-106), Protagoras of Nicaea (*op.cit.* IV, p. 150 f.), and Maximus Astrologus (pp. 26-36 Ludwich; cf. the epitome on pp. 90-92). For numerological prognoses with the same concern, cf. Delatte, *Anecdota Atheniensia*, pp. 143, 12-18; 151, 1-22; 453, 10-19; 455, 4-6. For a charm to cause a slave to run away, cf. Delatte, *Anecdota Atheniensia*, p. 615, 13-16. A spell to make a fugitive slave indetectable: PGM IV 2145-54 τρίστιχος 'Ομήρου πάρεδρος· - - - (Homeric verses) τούτους τοὺς στίχους ἐάν τις ἀποδράσας φορῇ ἐν σιδηρᾷ λάμνῃ, οὐδέποτε εὑρεθήσεται. A curse against someone who has caused another's slaves to run away is the lead tablet from

mera was a typical slave's name (see here lines 6-7 comm.), and Gorissen thought it probable that this was her status for another reason: the name of her mother is not given, which could mean that Zetous-Kalemera was a purchased slave of unknown descent. The use of the verb cτρέφειν in lines 1 and 3 may also be an indication that the charm was directed against a fugitive slave; cf. Delatte, *Anecdota Atheniensia*, p. 114, 15-19 περὶ τοῦ φυγεῖν ἄνθρωπον. γράψον εἰς ἀγέννητον χαρτὶ 'ξαναστροφῆ· 'Αβραὰμ εἶχεν δοῦλον καὶ ἔφυγεν· 'Ισαὰκ ἐζήτηcεν αὐτόν· γενηθήτω ἡ ὁδὸc αὐτοῦ cκότοc καὶ ὀλίcθημα καί, ἄγγελοc, ἐκδίωξον αὐτόν, 'Αβραάμ, φθάcον αὐτὸν καί, ὁ ἅγιοc Θεόδωροc, cτρέψον αὐτόν.[6]

The slip of papyrus is in a relatively good state of preservation. Surely it has not passed through the works of a mill. It may be an exemplar of a text that was to be recopied and then used.

ωcπερ cτρεφετε ο ερμηc	1	ὥcπερ cτρέφεται ὁ ἑρμῆc
του μυελου και αληθητε του		τοῦ μυλαίου καὶ ἀλήθεταί τοῦ-
το το πιτακιον ουτοc cτρεψον		το τὸ πιττάκιον, οὕτωc cτρέψον
τον ενκεφαλον και την	4	τὸν ἐγκέφαλον καὶ τὴν
καιδιαν και παcαν δια		καρδίαν καὶ πᾶcαν διά-
νοιαν ζητουν η επικα		νοιαν Ζητοῦν τῆc ἐπικα-
λουμενη καλημεραc		λουμένηc Καλημέραc,
ηδη ηδη ταχυ ταχυ	8	ἤδη ἤδη, ταχὺ ταχύ.

Amorgos published by Th.Homolle, *BCH* 25 (1901) 412-430 (= IG XII 7, p. 1 = Jordan, "Survey," no. 60; see now H. Versnel, *ZPE* 58, 1985, 252-255).

For certain or possible references to slaves in the curse tablets, see F.Bömer, *Untersuchungen über die Religion der Sklaven in Griechenland und Rom* (Akad. Wiss. und Lit. Mainz, Abhandl. geistes- und sozialwiss. Kl., Jhrg. 1963, Nr. 10), pp. 121-138. Like many others in recent generations, Bömer believed that magic was resorted to chiefly by the lowest social classes — a view that is gradually losing ground, and rightly so in our opinion. One should, therefore, not necessarily assume with Bömer that when a slave is the object of a curse, the operator will have been a fellow slave rather than the owner or another free man (see e.g. Bömer, *op.cit.*, pp. 124, 126 f., 134). Although a slave might have been cursed by another slave for various reasons, the person most likely to want to alter a slave's behavior and intentions is the slave's owner or someone acting on his behalf.

[6] Cf. the use of ἐπιcτρέφειν in Delatte, *Anecdota Atheniensia*, p. 12, 1-5 (cited above, note 5). Cf. also PGM XII 61 f. (as revised by Daniel, *Two Greek Magical Papyri*, p. 16 f.) ποίηcον cτρέφεcθ[αι πάντ]αc ἀνθρώπουc τε καὶ πάcαc γυναῖκαc εὐπειθῶc μου (εὐπηθῶc μου Pap.; ἐπὶ [ἔ]ρωτά μου Preisendanz).

As the Hermes-stone (?) of the mill turns and as this chit is ground, so turn the brain and the heart and the entire mind of Zetous also called Kalemera, now now, quickly quickly.

1-3 ὥσπερ cτρέφεται - - - οὕτωc cτρέψον: for the *similia similibus* construction (ὥσπερ - - - οὕτωc), cf. **58**, 8-11 and see Audollent, *DT*, Index VI E (p. 491 f.). As to the verb cτρέφειν and the function of the charm as a whole, see intr.

1 ὁ ἑρμῆc: a rotating part of a mill, probably the millstone itself – to judge both from what one expects of the magical procedure and from the meaning that can be expected of words based on ἑρμ-. The cult of Hermes was connected with piles of stones and stone pillars, and the name of the god is etymologically related with words that have the basic meaning of 'stone' or 'pile of stones' – ἕρμα, ἕρμαξ (cf. the roughly synonymous λίθαξ and μύλαξ), ἑρμαῖον, etc. See M.P.Nilsson, *Geschichte der griechischen Religion* I (Munich 1955²), pp. 503-505; Chantraine, *Dictionnaire étymologique*, p. 373 f., *s. vv.* ἕρμα and Ἑρμῆc; further literature in *Der Kleine Pauly* 2, p. 1069 f. Cf. also the proverbial ἐν τῷ λίθῳ Ἑρμῆc transmitted by Arist., *Metaph.* 1002ᵃ 22 and 1017ᵇ 7.

2 μυλαίου: proposed by L.Koenen (see Faraone, p. 284 n. 13).

ἀλήθεται (Faraone): on this verb, which occurs also in PGM IV 3088, 3097, 3110, and P.Oxy. VI 908, 26, 34, see Gignac, *Grammar* II, p. 280.

6-7 Ζητοῦν τῆc ἐπικαλλουμένηc Καλημέραc: Gorissen first recognized the name Ζητοῦc, an *addendum onomasticis*.

Καλημέρα: read by H.M.Cockle (*apud* ed.pr.); attested elsewhere in the papyri only in a contract of sale of a slave (*c.* AD 300), SB V 8007, 4 δούλην Α[ἰλα]νοῦν ὀνόματι Καλημέραν. Cf. *TLL Onomasticon* II, col. 77, *s.v. Calemerus*: "nom. maxime servorum et servarum." Of the sixteen women named Calemera in Solin, *Die griechischen Personennamen in Rom* I, p. 96 f., two belong to the category of slaves or freedwomen, fourteen are of uncertain status. A slave named Καλήμεροc who lived in Palestine under the reign of Honorius and Theodosius II is mentioned by Sozom. Salam., *Hist. eccl.* IX 17, 3 (GCS, p. 407, 19). Καλημέρα is a name of good omen comparable to Καλόκαιροc; see J.&L.Robert, *Hellenica* 9 (1950) 64-66.

Provenance   IV AD[1]
unknown

P.Reinach II 88.

ED.PR.: P.Collart, "Une nouvelle tabella defixionis d'Égypte," *Rev. Phil.* 56 (1930) 248-
    256.

REPUBL.: P.Reinach II 88 (P.Collart).

COMM.: Collart, *locc.citt.*;   (line 1) Bonner, *SMA*, p. 169 f. (see also p. 104 for a general
    description of the text);   (lines 4, 30 left, 32 right, etc.) H.C.Youtie, *ZPE* 21 (1976)
    194 f. (= *Scriptiunculae Post.* I, p. 308 f.).

TRANSL.: Collart, *locc.citt.*

PHOTO: ed.pr., between pp. 250 and 251.

REF.: Jordan, "Survey," no. 162.

DESCR.: lead tablet; 16 × 20 cm (not 19 × 25 cm as indicated by Collart). Inscribed on one
    side only. A horizontal break at line 14 and at least four other creases show that the
    sheet of lead was folded five or more times. There are three holes in the lead: two at the
    left edge by lines 24-25 and 41-43, one at the right edge by 38-40. In the ed.pr. they are
    said to be nail holes, but their diameters (between 1 and 2 cm) appear to be too large for
    this.

LOC.: Institut de Papyrologie, Université de Paris - Sorbonne. Inv. 2063.

The present text is a θυμοκάτοχον or 'restrainer of wrath', a spell that
is occasionally combined with charms for victory (νικητικά), subjugation
(ὑποτακτικά) or silencing (φιμωτικά). The best study of such texts is by
Th.Hopfner, "*Ein neues* ΘΥΜΟΚΑΤΟΧΟΝ," *Archiv Orientální* 10 (1938) 128-
148; see also the discussion by Bonner, *SMA*, pp. 103-106.

Other applied θυμοκάτοχα are **58**; PGM O 1; Bonner, *SMA* D. 149;
and the gem edited by Mouterde, "Le glaive de Dardanos," pp. 77-80

---

[1] V AD according to Collart's ed.pr., IV-V AD according to his republication. For
comparable handwriting in a document dated to AD 372, cf. Cavallo-Maehler, *Greek Bookhands*, pl. 6b = Schubart, *Pap. Gr. Berol.*, Taf. 39.

(described by Bonner, *SMA*, p. 105 f.). The θυμοκάτοχα are represented with greater frequency in the formularies: cf. **79**, 19-25; PGM IV 467 f. (= **831** f.); VII 925-939, 940-968; IX; X 24-35, 36-50; XII 179-181 (cf. 278); XIII 250-252; XXXVI 35-68, 161-177, 211-230; LXXIX-LXXX (= now P.Prag. I 4-5). A wrath-restraining formula occurs regularly in the juridical curse tablets from Kourion on Cyprus: παραλάβετε τοῦ δεῖνα τὸν θυμὸν τὸν πρὸς ἐμὲ ἔχει τὸν δεῖνα καὶ τὴν ὀργήν.[2] **54** might be based on a θυμοκάτοχον καὶ νικητικόν (see intr. and line 37 comm.).

The present 'wrath-restrainer' is the only surviving example written on lead. Cf., from the formularies mentioned above, PGM VII 925 f. λαβὼν λεπίδα μολιβῆν ἀπὸ ζυγοῦ μούλων καὶ γράψον κτλ. and X 36 f. λαβὼν λάμναν ⟨ἢ πέταλον⟩ μολιβοῦν ἀπὸ ἡμιόνων γράφε κτλ.

Perhaps the most interesting detail in the text are the phrases in 36-37 that describe the deity in terms reminiscent of late ancient Platonism.

1   ὁρκίζω ϲε, νεκυδαίμων, ὅϲτιϲ ποτὲ εἶ, κατὰ τῆϲ κυρίαϲ Βριμὼ προκύνη Βαυβώ, νυκτοδρόμα, βιαϲάνδρα, καλεϲάνδρα, κατανικάνδρα, λακι λακιμου Μαϲκελλει Μαϲκελλω Φνουκενταβαωθ ορεοβαζαγρα ρηξίχθων ἱππόχθων

4   πυριπηγανυξ, κατάϲχεται τὴν ὀργήν, τὸν θυμὸν Παωμίου, ὃν ἔτεκεν [ἡ Τ]ιϲᾶται, ἤδη ἤδη, ταχὺ ταχύ.

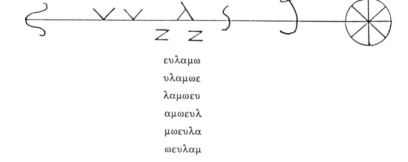

8   ευλαμω
                      υλαμωε
                      λαμωευ
                      αμωευλ
12   μωευλα
                      ωευλαμ

3 ορεοβαζαγρα: γ ex ρ   4 κατάϲχετε

---

[2] These texts are best consulted as a group in Audollent, *DT*, 22-37, or in Mitford, Inscr. Kourion, nos. 127-142. For the specific passages, see Audollent, *DT*, Index VI D, p. 487, *s.vv.* ὁ θυμός, οἱ θυμοί, ἡ ὀργή, αἱ ὀργαί, or Mitford, Inscr. Kourion, p. 418 f., *s.vv.* θυμός, ὀργή.

ναί, κύριε, cιcιcρω cιcι φερμου Χνουωρ Αβραcαξ Φνουνοβοηλ
         οχλοβαζαρω

16   διὰ τὸ ἅγιον   ερηκιcιθφηαραραχαραρανφθιcικηρε
    ὄνομα Ιωβεζεβυθ   ρηκιcιθφηαραραχαραρανφθιcικηρ
    βύθιε Ζεῦ   ηκιcιθφηαραραχαραρανφθιcικη
    ιωβαριαμβω   κιcιθφηαραραχαραρανφθιcικ   οπλομυρτιλοπλη[ξ]

20   μερμεριου Αβραcαξ   ιcιθφηαραραχαραρανφθιcι   εξανακερων[ιθα]
    ευλαμω   cικηρεαραραχαραρανφθιc   λαμψαμερω
    ευλαμ   ωμαλυε   ικηρεαραραχαραρανφθι   λαμψαμαζων
    ευλα   μαλυ   ευλαμω   κηρεαραραχαραρανφθ   βαcυμ Ιαω [?

24   [ευ]λ   αλ   υλαμω   φηαραραχαραρανφ   οπλομυρτιλοπληξ
    [ε]υ   α   λαμω   ηαραραχαραραη   αναχαζα
    ε   αμω   αραραχαραρα   εξανακερωνιθα
                μω   ραραχαραρα   αναξαρναξα

28   ω   αραχαραρρ   κεραcφακερωναc
    κατάcχεται τὸν θυμόν, τὴν   αχαρα   φαμεταθαcμαξαρανα
    ὀργὴν Παωμίου, ὃν ἔτεκεν   ρχαρ   βαcυμ Ιαω ιακινθου
    ἡ Τιcᾶτε, ἤδη ἤδη,   α   κατάcχεται τὴν ὀργήν, τὸν

32   ταχὺ ταχύ.   θυμὸν Παώμιτος, ὃν ἔτεκεν
                              ἡ Τιcᾶτε, ἤδη ἤδη, ταχὺ ταχύ.

βελιαc βελιωαc αρουηου Ἀρουηλ Χμουχ Χμουχ· δῆcον, κατά-
δηcον τὴν ὀργήν, τὸν θυμὸν Παώμιτος, ὃν ἔτεκεν ἡ Τιcᾶτε·

36   ὅτι cὲ ἐπικαλοῦμαι τὸν μέγαν cωματοειδῆ ἀcώματον,
    [τ]ὸν τὸ φῶc καταcπῶντα, τὸν κύριον τῆc πρώτηc γενέcεωc,
    ιαωηιωιαιεου Ιαβορ Cαβαωθ λενταμαουθ[?
    [ε]ρηκιcιθφηαραραχαραρανφθιcικηρε Ιωβεζεβυθ [?

40   μερμεριου Αβραcαξ ιαηιαηε· κατάcχεται τὴν ὀργήν, τὸ[ν]
    θυμὸν Παώμιτος, ὃν ἔτεκεν ἡ Τιcᾶτε, τὸν νοῦν, τὰc φρέναc
    ὅπωc μὴ ἀντίπῃ ἡμῖν, ἐμοὶ τ⟨ῷ⟩ Ὠριγένι, ὃν ἔτεκεν Ἰούλλη ἡ καὶ
    Θεοδώρα, ἀλλὰ εὐήκοοc ἡμῶν γένηται, ἤδη ἤδη, ταχὺ ταχύ.

I adjure you, corpse-daemon, whoever you are, by the mistress *Brimo, dog-leader* (?), *Baubo, night-roamer, subduer of men, summoner of men, conqueror of men, laki lakimou Maskellei Maskellô Phnoukentabaôth oreobazagra rêxichthôn hippochthôn* |[4] *pyripêganyx,* restrain the anger, the wrath of Paomios, whom Tisatai bore, now now, quickly quickly. (Drawing with mag. signs). |[8] *eulamô ulamôe lamôeu amôeul* |[12] *môeula ôeulam.* Aye, lord, *sisisrô, sisi phermou Chnouôr Abrasax Phnounoboêl ochlobazarô.*

(16-32 left) Through the holy name *iôbezebyth, Zeus of the depths of the sea, iôbariambô* |[20] *mermeriou Abrasax eulamô* (etc.). |[29] Restrain the wrath, the anger of Paomios, whom Tisate bore, now now, |[32] quickly quickly.

(16-31 middle) *erêkisithphêararachararaêphthisikêre* (etc.).

(19-33 right) *Hoplomyrtiloplêx* |[20] *exanakerônitha lampsamerô lampsamazôn basym Iaô* |[24] *hoplomyrtiloplêx anachaza exanakerônitha anaxarnaxa* |[28] *kerasphakerônas phameta-thasmaxarana basym Iaô iakinthou.* Restrain the anger, the |[32] wrath of Paomis, whom Tisate bore, now now, quickly quickly.'

(34-43) *Belias beliôas arouêou Harouêl Chmouch Chmouch,* bind, bind down the anger, the wrath of Paomis, whom Tisate bore. |[36] For I call upon you, the great apparently corporeal incorporeal one, you who bring down the light, the lord of the first creation, *iaôêiô-iaieou Iabor Sabaôth lentamaouth erêkisithphêararachararaêphthisikêre iôbezebyth* |[40] *mermeriou Abrasax iaêiaêe.* Restrain the anger, the wrath of Paomis, whom Tisate bore, and his mind and wits, so that he not speak against us, against me Horigenes, whom Ioulle also called Theodora bore, but so that he be obedient to us, now now, quickly quickly.

1 προκύνη Βαυβώ : προκυνητε Collart, suggesting in the ed.pr. a form of προσκυνητός (cf. P.Reinach II 88 "vénérable (?)"). Bonner correctly rejected this, and he pointed out that the reference to the present passage in LSJ, *s.v.* προσκυνητός should be deleted (the same applies to LSJ, *s.v.* προκύνητος, which refers to the present passage only). The new reading was confirmed for us on the original by A.Blanchard (a certain first β followed by faint traces of four letters, of which the third is tall and broad enough to be another β). Cf. PGM VII 692 Βριμώ, ῥηξίχθων: προκύνη Βαυβώ, 885 f. προκύνη Βαυβώ; Bonner, *SMA,* D. 63 βρειμὼ προκύνη ῥηξίχθνων. As was pointed out by Bonner (*SMA,* p. 169 f.), προκύνη is probably an epithet of Hekate. For the possible meaning of the compound, cf. Poll. 5, 65 προκυνεῖν τὸ προϋλακτεῖν πρὶν ἢ τὸ θηρίον ἀνευρεῖν; *Anth. Pal.* 11, 322 (Antiphanes) = Gow-Page, *The Garland of Philip* I, line 774 (cf. II *ad loc.)* ξηροὶ Καλλιμάχου πρόκυνες; and the name of the

lesser Dog Star Προκύων. For the word under consideration, see Bonner: "As Προκύων is the star that goes before Sirius, Προκύνη is Hecate as leader of her pack of hellhounds ... ; or else it is a noun strangely formed on the analogy of Προκύων and calls Hecate herself 'hound'." The epithet of Hecate in PGM IV 2722 f. σκυλακάγεια supports the former possibility, those in PGM IV 1434 κύων μέλαινα and 2251 ἰσοπάρθενος κύων the latter.

2 βιασάνδρα, καλεσάνδρα, κατανικάνδρα: see **42**, 30 comm.

λακι λακιμου: cf. PGM VII 302 f. καὶ κατὰ ⟨τῶν ἐπὶ⟩ τῶν Τιμοριῶν τεταγμένων λακι λικιω λακιμου; XXXVI 345 f. καὶ κατὰ τῆς τούτου 'Ανάγκης λακι λακιω λακιω[υδ] λακιωυδα. Both of these passages follow the Maskelli-logos; in the present passage the situation is reversed. K.Fr.W.Schmidt's suggested that λακι be equated with Egyptian *njk* "der Strafende" (see *GGA* 196, 1934, 172); this not convincing for linguistic reasons (H.J.Thissen).

3-4 Μασκελλει Μασκελλω - - - πυριπηγανυξ: see **54**, 27-29 comm.

4 Παωμίου: the same genitive in 30 left, but Παώμιτος in 32 right, 35 and 41. The same man was called both Παώμιος and Παῶμις, as was pointed out by Youtie (*loc.cit.*) with reference to other such instances, e.g. ῟Ωρος = 'Ωρίων, Θέων = Θεωνᾶς, and Θερμοῦθις = Θερμούθιον.

5 Τισᾶται (spelled Τισᾶτε in 31 left, 33, 35 and 41): a new by-form of the well-attested name Τισᾶτις.

8-13. For the permutations of ευλαμω, see **53**, 1-6 left with comm.

14 ναί, κύριε: see **42**, 35 comm.; add to the parallels PGM XII 106 να[ί, κύρι]ε as restored by Daniel, *Two Greek Magical Papyri*, p. xvii.

14-15 cicicρω cici φερμου Χνουωρ Αβρασαξ Φνουνοβοηλ Ι οχλοβαζαρω: cf. **42**, 49-50 with comm. For the last word in the sequence, cf. PGM XII 167 οχλοβαραχω.

16 middle + 17-20 left ερηκισιθφηαραραχαραρανηφθισικηρε + Ιωβεζεβυθ Ι βύθιε Ζεῦ Ι ιωβαριαμβω Ι μερμεριου (repeated in part in 39-40): cf. PGM IV 1797-1801 ερηκισιθφη αραραχαραρα ηφθισικηρε Ιαβεζεβυθ ἰὼ βύθιε· βεριαμβω βεριαμβεβω· πελάγιε μερμεργου.

16-31 middle ερηκισιθφηαραραχαραρανηφθισικηρε. There are irregularities in the Schwindeschema in lines 21-23 and 27-31. On the palindrome, see **54**, 1 comm.

17 left Ιωβεζεβυθ: a variant of Ιαβεζεβυθ. The latter, like Ιωβεζεβυθ here, follows the ερηκισιθφη-palindrome in PGM IV 1798, 1999; VII 419;

LXVII 14 f.; Audollent, *DT*, 198, 7 f.; it follows after some unread letters in PGM III 448. Adducing evidence for the presence of Samaritans in Ptolemaic and Roman Egypt, Deissmann convincingly argued that Ιαβεζεβυθ reflects the Samaritan pronunciation of Hebrew *Yaweh Sabaoth*, which was usually transcribed as Ιαω Cαβαωθ (see Deissmann, *Bibelstudien*, pp. 13-20; cf. Hopfner, *Offenbarungszauber* I, § 742).

18 left βύθιε Ζεῦ : βυθιεζευ Collart, but βύθιε - - - πελάγιε in PGM IV 1799 f. (cited above on 16 middle + 17-20 left) guarantees the articulation. Cf. *Orph. hymn.* 63, 16 πόντιος εἰνάλιος Ζεὑς; Aesch., Fr. 46a, 10 Radt Πόcειδον Ζεῦ τ' ἐνά[λιε with the parallels adduced *ad loc*. 'Zeus of the depths of the sea' in the present syncretistic text can be regarded as Zeus-Helios and thus as the Egyptian sun god who was born out of the depths of the primeval ocean; see the note on PGM XII 229 ὁ ἐκπεφυκὼς ἐκ τοῦ βυθοῦ in Merkelbach-Totti, *Abrasax* I, p. 172 f.

19 right οπλομυρτιλοπλη[ξ]: also in 24 right. The elsewhere unattested magical word appears to be based on Greek elements. It is reminiscent of the more common νιχαροπληξ, on which see Bonner, *SMA*, p. 201.

20 left μερμεριου: quite possibly based on or related to Μαρμαραωθ, on which see **42**, 52 comm. Cf. also **96 A** 1 μαρμαριθϊ μαρμαρϊθε; **96 F** fr. B 3 right μαρμουρ[; PGM IV 1801 μερμεργου; VII 482 μεριουτ μερμεριουτ, 487 f. μαρμαριουτι, 533 μερμερεω.

21 right λαμψαμερω and 22 right λαμψαμαζων: for λαμψ- and λαμπ- at the beginning of magical words and names, cf. PGM, Vol. 3 (Index), p. 225 f., *s.v.* Λαμψουρη (cf. here **38**, 7 comm.), p. 260, *s.vv.* λαμπηαψ, λαμπιπυρcι, λαμφθεν, λαμψει, λαμψουωρ, λαμψρη etc. The element -λαμ(ψ) also comes at the end of magical names; cf. e.g. **10**, 4-5 Cεμεcιλαμ (see comm.) and **42**, 41 Cεμεcειλαμψ. Cf. also Λαμψουηρ Λαμηηρ Λαμφορη in lines 4-6 of the protective amulet inscribed on a silver lamella from Boraea in Macedonia published by D.M.Robinson in: L.W. Jones (ed.), *Classical and Mediæval Studies in Honor of E.K.Rand* (New York 1938), pp. 245-253, discussed with parallels and reference to various etymologies proposed; see also P.Warren 21, 27 comm.

23 right βαcυμ Ιαω: also in 30 right. For βαcυμ(μ) and βαcημμ, often coupled with Ιαω, cf. PGM, Vol. 3 (Index), p. 218; βαcυμ also occurs in the Αωθ logos in **87**, 10-11. The word is probably in origin Hebrew *bašem* 'in the name of'. Apparently it also came to be regarded as a divine name; see W.Fauth, *Oriens Christianus* 67 (1983) 70.

30 right ιακινθου: it may be pure coincidence that one can recognize the mythological name Ἰακίνθου = Ὑακίνθου (cf. *RE* IX.1, col. 7 f. [S.Eitrem] for the spelling with initial iota), for here ιακινθου follows the Hebrew elements Βαϲυμ Ιαω, and Hyakinthos is not attested elsewhere in Greek magical texts. In the Christian alphabetic *onomasticon sacrum* PGM P 14, 19 Ἱ]ακιν is glossed Ἰάω ἀνάϲταϲιϲ. Possibly, then, for the present passage: Ἴακιν θ⟨ε⟩οῦ. For the element Ια-, cf. Hieron., *Ep*. 25, 3 (CSEL 54, p. 219, 11 f.) on the ten Hebrew names for god: *octavum ia, quod in deo tantum ponitur et in alleluiae quoque extrema syllaba sonat*. Substantially the same in Hieron., *Tractatus de psalmis*, Ps. 146 (CC 78, p. 329, 10-14), and in a fragment attributed to Euagrius, ed. P. de Lagarde, *Onomastica Sacra* (Göttingen 1887), p. 229.

34 αρουηου: in light of the following name, one might consider Ἀρουη⟨ρ⟩ου or Ἀρουη⟨ρ⟩ ου.

Ἀρουηλ = Ἀρουηρ, on whom see **42**, 49 comm.

Χμουχ: since this follows Ἀρουηρ, it must be a variant of the name of Chnum; cf. PGM IV 1576 Ἀρουηρ Χνουφ. On Chnum-Horos, see **42**, 49 comm.

34-35 δῆϲον, κατάλδηϲον: cf. **53**, 12-13 with comm.

36-37 τὸν μέγαν ϲωματοειδῆ ἀϲώματον, | [τ]ὸν τὸ φῶϲ καταϲπῶντα, τὸν κύριον τῆϲ πρώτηϲ γενέϲεωϲ: these phrases appear to reflect late ancient Platonic conceptions about the deity and creation. On points of contact between Neoplatonism and the magical papyri, see S.Eitrem, "La théurgie chez les Néo-Platoniciens et dans les papyrus magiques," *Symb. Osl.* 22 (1942) 49-79; E.R.Dodds, "Theurgy and its Relationship to Neoplatonism," *JRS* 37 (1947) 55-69.

36 τὸν μέγαν ϲωματοειδῆ ἀϲώματον: cf. Iambl., *Myst.* 1, 17, which answers Porphyrios' question: πῶϲ γὰρ δὴ ἥλιόϲ τε καὶ ϲελήνη κατὰ τὸν ϲὸν λόγον καὶ οἱ ἐν οὐρανῷ ἐμφανεῖϲ ἔϲονται θεοί, εἰ ἀϲώματοί εἰϲι μόνωϲ οἱ θεοί; Damascius, *De princ.* 132 (II, p. 11, 5-7 Ruelle) καὶ διττὸν εἶναι τὸν κοϲμικὸν θεόν, ὡϲ τὸν ζῳδιάρχην· τὸν μὲν οἷον δεδεμένον τῷ κοϲμικῷ ϲώματι, τὸν δὲ ἀφιέμενον, καὶ ἀϲώματον μέν, προϊϲτάμενον δὲ τῆϲ κοϲμικῆϲ ὅληϲ ζώνηϲ. For the words ϲωματοειδήϲ and ἀϲώματοϲ in antithesis in Damascius, cf. *De princ.* 14 and 16 (I, p. 28, 22 and p. 31, 28 Ruelle). Cf. already Philo, *Opif.* 36 ὁ μὲν οὖν ἀϲώματοϲ κόϲμοϲ ἤδη πέραϲ εἶχεν ἱδρυθεὶϲ ἐν τῷ θείῳ λόγῳ, ὁ δ' αἰϲθητὸϲ πρὸϲ παράδειγμα τούτου ἐτελειογονεῖτο. καὶ πρῶτον αὐτοῦ τῶν μερῶν - - -

ἐποίει τὸν οὐρανὸν ὁ δημιουργός, ὃν ἐτύμως στερέωμα προσηγόρευσεν ἅτε σωματικὸν ὄντα· - - - εἰκότως οὖν ἀντιθεὶς τῷ νοητῷ καὶ ἀσωμάτῳ τὸν αἰσθητὸν καὶ σωματοειδῆ τοῦτον στερέωμα ἐκάλεσεν, which is based in part on Plat., *Tim.* 31B-32C; cf. also *Tim.* 41D-E ξυστήσας δὲ τὸ πᾶν διεῖλε ψυχὰς ἰσαρίθμους τοῖς ἄστροις ἔνειμέ θ' ἑκάστην πρὸς ἕκαστον, καὶ ἐμβιβάσας ὡς ἐς ὄχημα τὴν τοῦ παντὸς φύσιν ἔδειξε, νόμους τε τοὺς εἱμαρμένους εἶπεν αὐταῖς, ὅτι γένεσις πρώτη μὲν ἔσοιτο τεταγμένη μία πᾶσιν κτλ.; *Leg.* 898D-899B, esp. 898D ἡλίου πᾶς ἄνθρωπος σῶμα μὲν ὁρᾷ, ψυχὴν δὲ οὐδείς, and 899B ἄστρων δὲ δὴ πέρι πάντων καὶ σελήνης - - - τίνα ἄλλον λόγον ἐροῦμεν ἢ τὸν αὐτὸν τούτων, ὡς ἐπειδὴ ψυχὴ μὲν ἢ ψυχαὶ πάντων τούτων αἴτιαι ἐφάνησαν, ἀγαθαὶ δὲ πᾶσαν ἀρετήν, θεοὺς αὐτὰς εἶναι φήσομεν κτλ. For the corporeal and incorporeal aspects of the divinity, cf. also PGM XIII 63 f. τὸν πάντα ὁρῶντα καὶ μὴ ὁρώμενον· - - - 69-71 οὗ οὐδεὶς θεῶν δύναται ἰδεῖν τὴν ἀληθινὴν μορφήν. ὁ μεταμορφούμενος εἰς πάντας, ἀόρατος εἶ Αἰὼν Αἰῶνος.

ἀσώματον: cf. ἀσώματε in **65**, 35 and PGM IV 1777.

37 [τ]ὸν τὸ φῶς κατασπῶντα: the verb κατασπᾶν was used by ancient Neoplatonists of 'dragging down' or 'forcing down' something from a higher to a lower realm; cf. Damascius, *In Phaed.* 170 (p. 103 Westerink) καὶ ὁ Προμηθεὺς ἐν νάρθηκι κλέπτει τὸ πῦρ, εἴτε τὸ οὐράνιον φῶς εἰς τὴν γένεσιν κατασπῶν, εἴτε τὴν ψυχὴν εἰς τὸ σῶμα προάγων, εἴτε τὴν θείαν ἔλλαμψιν ὅλην ἀγένητον οὖσαν εἰς τὴν γένεσιν προκαλούμενος; idem, *Vita Isid.*, Fr. 12 (p. 15 Zintzen) εἶναι γὰρ αὐτὴν (sc. τὴν ἁπτικὴν αἴσθησιν) τῷ ὄντι χθονίαν καὶ ἀντίτυπον καὶ κατασπῶσαν τὴν ψυχὴν εἰς τὸν τῆς γενέσεως ἀέναον ὀχετόν; Porph., *De abst.* 4, 13 (p. 250, 15-18 Nauck) φθαρτὰ μὲν εἶναι τὰ σώματα καὶ τὴν ὕλην οὐ μόνιμον αὐτῶν, τὰς δὲ ψυχὰς ἀθανάτους ἀεὶ διαμένειν, καὶ συμπλέκεσθαι μὲν ἐκ τοῦ λεπτοτάτου φοιτώσας αἰθέρος ῥύμῃ φυσικῇ κατασπωμένας. For the verb used similarly by Christian writers, cf. Lampe, *s.v.* 4b.

τὸν κύριον τῆς πρώτης γενέσεως: cf. PGM IV 487 f. γένεσις πρώτη τῆς ἐμῆς γενέσεως αεηιουω, ἀρχὴ τῆς ἐμῆς ἀρχῆς πρώτη πππ κτλ.; also 742 f. Cf. also γένεσις πρώτη in Plat., *Tim.* 41E (cited above, 36 comm.); for Neoplatonic interpretations of this phrase by Iamblichus, an anonymous and Syrianus, see Procl., *In Tim.* 324C-E (III, pp. 277, 31 - 279, 2 Diehl). Cf. also Damascius, *Vita Isid.*, Fr. 174 (p. 149, 1-3 Zintzen) ἦν δὲ αὐτοῦ καὶ ἡ πρώτη γένεϲιϲ τῷ ὄντι μυϲτική. λέγεται γὰρ κατελθεῖν ἀπὸ τῆϲ μητρὸϲ ἐπὶ τοῖϲ χείλεϲιν ἔχων τὸν καταϲιγάζοντα δάκτυλον, οἷον Αἰγύπτιοι μυθολογοῦϲι γενέϲθαι τὸν ῟Ωρον καὶ πρὸ τοῦ ῟Ωρου τὸν ῟Ηλιον. Horos with his finger raised to his mouth is discussed by D.Wortmann, "Kosmogonie und Nilflut," *Bonner Jahrb*. 166 (1966) 68-70.

38 ιαωηιωιαιεου Ιαβορ: the division and capitalization is ours.

Ιαβορ: cf. PGM, Vol. 3 (Index), p. 222, *s.nn*. Ιαβαθ, Ιαβαι, Ιαβαϲ, Ιαβε, Ιαβου, etc. These names are generally explained as deriving from the Samaritan pronunciation of the tetragrammaton (literature and parallels in Merkelbach-Totti, *Abrasax* 2, p. 163 on PGM V 102). Possibly Horos should be recognized in the termination -ορ. If so, Jahweh-Horos syncretized.

39-40 [ε]ρηκιϲιθφηαραραχαραρανφθιϲικηρε Ιωβεζεβυθ̣ [?] | μερμεριου: see above on 16 middle + 17-20 left.

42 ἡμῖν, ἐμοὶ τ⟨ῷ⟩ Ὠριγένι (r. -γένει) : ἡμῖν, ἐμοὶ τῶριγένι Collart. The omitted ω is more easily explained by haplography than by crasis, which in the Koine has become rare and restricted to a few stereotyped phrases; see Gignac, *Grammar* I, pp. 321-324. The writer's exemplar probably had μοι, ἐμοὶ τῷ δεῖνα; cf. PGM XIII 620 f. μὴ ἀποϲτραφῇϲ με, ἐμὲ τὸν δεῖνα; **39**, 12 φιλεῖν με, ἐμὲ τὸν Πτολεμαῖον. On the use of ἡμεῖϲ for ἐγώ (cf. 43 ἡμῶν), see Mayser, *Grammatik* II.1, pp. 40-42. This generalizing plural may indicate that the writer included, e.g., his family, friends, or those who would take his side in a legal controversy.

Ἰούλλη: not in the papyrological onomastica.

43 εὐήκοοϲ: more common is ἐπήκοοϲ with the same sense; cf. **39**, 6; **58**, 11.

58

Thebes   Plate II   IV-V AD

O.Bodl. II 2180 recto.

ED.PR.: J.G.Tait-C.Préaux, *Greek Ostraca in the Bodleian Library at Oxford* II (London 1955), p. 390, no. 2180 recto.

DESCR.: ostracon (ribbed pottery); 16 × 12.8 cm. The magical text is written on the convex side. On the other side, in a different hand, an account of corn and wine (O.Bodl. II 2180 verso).

LOC.: on deposit at the Ashmolean Museum, Oxford. Inv. O.Bodl. 1129.

Another θυμοκάτοχον. For parallels and literature, see **57** intr. Diaeresis on iota in 3 and 7; dicolon after a magical word in 3.

1   θυμοκάθυκων
      καὶ νικητικῶν.
      Ϊαω Ερβηλ ϊω Πακερβηκ:
4   Αβρασαξ πνουβουη
      μεσκουλ κοφεμωλωλ
      θοραξ.
         ⌐Ϊαω Cαβαωθ Αδωναϊ Αβρασαξ,
8   ὡς ὠ λίθως οὗτος ἄφονος
        καὶ ἄλαλος, οὕτω καὶ πάντες
        οἱ κατά μαι ἄφονοι καὶ ἄλαλοι
        καὶ ἐπήκωοί μοι γένωνται.

1 θυμοκαθυκων· Ostr., l. θυμοκάτοχον   2 νικητικόν   3 dicolon in Ostr.
7 L in Pap.   7-11 in eisthesi   8 ὁ λίθος   ἄφωνος   10 κατά με   ἄφωνοι
11 ἐπήκοοί

A restrainer of wrath and victory charm. *Iaô Erbêl iô Pakerbêk* |⁴ *Abrasax pnoubouê meskoul kophemôlôl thorax. Iaô Sabaôth Adônai Abrasax,* |⁸ just as this stone is voiceless and speechless, so let also all who are opposed to me be voiceless and speechless and obedient to me.

1 θυμοκαθυκων·: if not accidental ink, a high stop (unneeded, it seems). It was not recorded in the ed.pr.

. 1-2 θυμοκάθυκων (r. -τοχον) | καὶ νικητικών (r. -κόν): apparently, another case of a prescriptional phrase mistakenly copied in an applied charm (see **32**, 1 comm. and **92** intr.; also K.Preisendanz, *Acme* 1, 1948, 76 f.; idem, *Gnomon* 24, 1952, 344 n. 3; D.R.Jordan, *Hesperia* 54, 1985, 235 n. 20). The same heading occurs in PGM XXXVI 161; cf. also 35 f. θυμοκάτοχον καὶ χαριτήσιον καὶ νικητικὸν δικαστηρίων βέλτιστον and 211 θυμοκάτοχον καὶ νικητικὸν καὶ χαριτήσιον. On such combinations of charms and their social context, see C.A.Faraone, *Phoenix* 44 (1990) 226 f. For another example on gold, see R.Kotansky, *ZPE* 88 (1991) 41-60.

3 Ἴαω Ερβηλ ἴω Πακερβηκ: the beginning of the Typhonic logos (on which see **95** → 8-12 comm.).

Ἴαω Ερβηλ: usually ιω Ερβηθ.

Πακερβηκ : πακερβικ ed.pr. Most of eta is lost in a surface chip, but the new reading is certain. The dicolon after πακερβηκ was not recorded in the ed.pr.

4 πνουβουη: cf. PGM IX 11 φνουνοβοη (in the Μασκελλι-logos), and see PGM, Vol. 3 (Index), p. 273, *s.v.* φνουνεβεη.

5 μεσκουλ: cf. Μασκελλι, on which see **12**, 3-5 comm. and **54**, 27-29 comm.

κοφεμωλωλ: the last letter could also be ν.

7-11. The ∟-shaped sign at the beginning of 7 (not recorded in the ed.pr.) and the indentation of 7-11 seem to mark a new section of the spell.

7 Αδωναϊ : Αδοναϊ ed.pr.

8-9 ὡc - - - οὕτω: see **56**, 1-3 comm.

ὡ λίθωc (r. ὁ λίθοc) οὗτοc: the formulary (see above, 1-2 comm.) prescribed a stone as writing material, but the operator used a potsherd. The connection of 'stone' and 'dumbness' was common; cf. e.g. Theogn. 568 f. λίθος ἄφθογγος; Philo, *Mut.* 211 λίθου κωφῆς, *Ebr.* 157; Liban., *Decl.* XXXVI 35 ἴσα τοῖc λιθίνοιc ἄφωνος; Joh. Chrys., *Expos. in Ps.* 145,

Migne PG 55, 473, line 20 λίθων ἀφωνότεροι (also *Hom. in Genes.* 4, Migne PG 53, 45, line 33; *Serm. in Genes.* 2, Migne PG 54, 587, line 3); *Orac. Sib.* 4, 28, etc. (cf. also the passage from the Delian aretalogy of Sarapis mentioned below). The inscribed material is the first simile here; so also in Wünsch, *DTA*, 105b, 1 f. ὡς οὖ[το]c ὁ μόλυ[βδ]οc ψυχρὸς καὶ ἄ[θ]υμος [οὕτως καὶ τὰ τῶν ἐνταῦθα γεγ]ραμμένων ψυχρ[ὰ καὶ ἄθυμα ἔςτω] κτλ. (cf. also 106b, 1 f. and 107a, 4 f.); Audollent, *DT*, 98, 2 ff.; E.Ziebarth, *Sitzungsb. Berlin* (1934) 1041, no. 23 A, 8-10 (republished with improvements by B.Bravo in: *Poikilia. Études offertes à J.-P.Vernant*, Paris 1987, p. 202); B, 16-21; R.Marichal, *CRAI* 1981, 43, lines 1-4. Similarly, in some Aramaic love charms the heart of the beloved is to burn with love for the petitioner just as a potsherd inscribed with the charm burns in a fire; see Naveh-Shaked, *Amulets and Magic Bowls*, p. 87, lines 4-5 with comm.

αφονοc: here and in 9 παντεc the top stroke of the final sigma is prolonged to fill the line.

ἄφονοc (r. ἄφωνοc) καὶ ἄλαλοc: that the adversary be unable to speak is a frequent request, especially in judiciary curses; cf. e.g. Audollent, *DT*, 25, 16-18 ἀλλὰ ὡς [ὑμῖc ἄταφοι κὲ ἄφω]νοι κὲ ἄλαλοι κὲ ἄγλωccοι, ο[ὕ]τω . . . . κὲ ἀντίδικοι ἤτωcαν ἄλαλοι ἄφ[ωνοι ἄγλωccοι]. Many such examples are gathered by E.G.Kagarow, *Griechische Fluchtafeln* (Eus Supplementa 4, Leopoli 1929), p. 56; P.Moraux, *Une défixion judiciaire*, p. 49 f.; C.A.Faraone, *ZPE* 72 (1988) 281 n. 7; cf. also Jordan, "Survey," no. 25 (= SEG XXXV 214), 15 f. κωφός, ἄλαλοc (and the related curse tablets nos. 27, 25; 29, 31 f.; 31, 17; 32, 18; 33, 10 f.; 34, 22 [= SEG XXXV 216; 218; 220; 221; 222; 223]). Cf. also the Delian aretalogy of Sarapis, lines 84-90: Sarapis tied the tongues of the accusers, and they became rigid and dumb like stones (IG XI.4, 1299 = H.Engelmann, *The Delian Aretalogy of Sarapis* [EPRO 44, Leiden 1964] = Totti, *Texte*, no. 11). See also **54**, 9-19 comm. and **55** intr.

10 κατά μαι: the two dotted letters are badly damaged. An alternative, but apparently inferior reading might be κατ' ἐμοί. If κατά μαι, the writer intended με, where correct Greek would require ἐμοῦ. Monosyllabic forms of the first personal pronoun after preposition are infrequent; see Mayser, *Grammatik* I.2, p. 62 f.; Gignac, *Grammar* II, p. 161 f.; Youtie, *Scriptiunculae* I, pp. 180, 191; II, p. 1002.

11 ἐπήκωοι (r. ἐπήκοοι): cf. **39**, 6; **57**, 43 (εὐήκοος).

γένωνται: for the jussive subjunctive in the papyri and later Greek, see Jannaris, *Grammar*, App. V 16 C (p. 565); Radermacher, *Neutestamentliche Grammatik*, p. 166 f.; R.Ch.Horn, *The Use of the Subjunctive and Optative Moods in the Non-Literary Papyri* (Diss., University of Pennsylvania 1926), pp. 120-123; Mandilaras, *Verb*, §§ 554-561.

APPLIED MAGIC:

CURSES, CHRISTIAN

59-60

These two papyri were composed by the Christian Sabinos. He curses his daughter Severine and a certain Didymos, who may have been her husband. **59**, which is written partly in prose and partly in verse, is cast in the form of a petition to God in his capacity of divine judge. Sabinus probably had himself buried with **59** in his grave. The hexameters in **60**, parts of which repeat those in **59**, 13-18, were to be inscribed on Sabinos' gravestone.

The reader is referred to Björck's exhaustive treatment of the two papyri in the ed.pr. of **59**. It contains the following chapters: I. "Beschreibung und Ausgabe. Der Erhaltungszustand." II. "Der metrische Teil (Z. 13-18) und Pap. Hamb. 22." III. "Einzelbemerkungen zum metrischen Teil." IV. "Beurteilung des metrischen Teiles." V. "Die religionsgeschichtliche Stellung des Papyrus. Nichtchristliche Rachegebete." VI. "Christliche griechische Rachegebete." VII. "Koptische Rachebebete. Der liturgische Einfluss. Die Anwünschung von Krankheiten." VIII. "Das juristische Element." IX. "Einzelbemerkungen zum prosaischen Teil (Z. 1-12 und Verso)." X. "Beurteilung des prosaischen Teiles. Das Rekto als Ganzes. Die Tradition der Rachegebete." XI. "Zweck des Papyrus. Antike Jenseitskorrespondenz. Die Aussenschrift." XII. "Dioskoros von Aphrodito, eine kulturgeschichtliche Parallele."

It is entirely possible, though not completely certain, that both papyri were written by the same hand.

59

Panopolis   VI AD

P.Ups. 8.

ED.PR.: G.Björck, *Der Fluch des Christen Sabinus. Papyrus Upsaliensis 8* (Uppsala 1938).

REPUBL.: M.David and B.A.van Groningen, *Papyrological Primer* (Leiden 1965[4]), no. 71.

COMM.: ed.pr.; (lines 5 and 8) V.Stegemann, *Gnomon* 16 (1940) 87; (line 9) H.I.Bell, *JHS* 59 (1939) 327.

TRANSL.: ed.pr.; P.Collart, *REG* 52 (1939) 249; idem, *Rev. Phil.* 18 (1944) 199.

PHOTO: ed.pr., plates I (recto) and II.2 (detail of verso).

REF.: van Haelst, *Catalogue*, no. 1000.

DESCR.: papyrus; 32.5 × 16 cm. The writing on the recto runs with the fibers. There is a kollesis 5 cm. from the left edge and another after a space of 20.5 cm. The line inscribed on the verso runs with the fibers below what corresponds to the left edge of the recto. The papyrus was folded from the right to the left 12 times; the line of writing on the verso was visible on the last outer panel. Björck stated that the papyrus is a palimpsest, but the faint traces of ink that suggested this to him may rather have been caused by the folding of the papyrus.

LOC.: Universitetsbiblioteket, Uppsala.

1   [c. 18   ] κ[ύ]ρι[ε . . . . .]ο θε[ός . . . . .]ν γνώτ[ωcαν]
     πάντες, ὅτι κύριος ὁ θεὸς ἀντιλήμψεταί μου. κατιδιωχθήτω
     Δίδυμος καὶ Cευηρίνη ἡ ἐμοῦ θυγάτηρ οἱ καταδιώξαντές με
4   πάλαι. καταξηρανθήτω τὸ cῶμα ἐν κλίνοις, ὡς ἐθεάcω κ[αὶ τὸ]
     ἐμὸν παρὰ τῶν καλυψάντων τὴν ἡμετέραν αἰδῶ. κύρ[ι]ε, δε[ῖξον]
     αὐτοῖς ταχεῖαν τὴν δύναμίν cου. τὰς ἐπιβουλὰ[c τ]ῶν κ[αρδ]ι[ῶν]
     αὐτῶν κατὰ τῶν φιλτάτων μου τέκνων ἀπρά[κτου]c π[οίη]cον.]
8   καταλαβέτωcαν τὸ βῆμα, ὁπουδὰν cύ, ὦ κύριε δέc[ποτα, κρίνῃc.]
                    ἐγὼ [Cαβ]εῖνος κλα[ίω]ν καὶ cτέν[ων νυκ]τ[ὸς καὶ]
                    ἡμέρας ἐπιδέδωκ[α] τὰ ἐμὰ θ[εῷ τῷ τῶν ὅλων]
                    δεσπότῃ εἰς ἐκδίκηcιν τῶν κα[κουργιῶν ὧν]
12   πέπονθα παρὰ Cευηρίνης κ[αὶ Διδύμου.] ——
     [υἱ]ὲ θεοῦ μεγάλο[ιο], τὸν οὐδέποτ' ἔδρακεν ἀνήρ,
     [ὅ]c τυφλοῖσιν ἔδωκας [ἰ]δεῖν φάος ἠελίοιο,
     [δ]εῖξον δ' ὡς τὸ πάροιθε θεουδέα θαύματα cεῖο.
16   ἡμετέρων καμ[ά]των μνημήϊα [τ]ῖcον ἀμοιβήν,
     [ο]ὓς κάμον, οὓς ὑπ[έ]με[ι]να μιῆς ἐπίηρα θυγατρός,
     ἐχθροὺς ἡμετέρο[υ]c cτερεαῖς ἐνὶ χερc[ὶ] πατάccων.

V°   ἐκδίκηcον ⳨ ⳨ ⳨   ⳨ ⳨ ⳨   Εμμανουηλ, ἐκδίκηc[ον.]

     2 καταδιωχθήτω   4 κλίναιc   12 fin.: spat. vac. lineola impletur
13 ουδεποτ' Pap.   14 ῖϊδειν Pap.   15 δ' Pap.   16 μνημηϊα Pap.   17
ϋπεμεινα Pap.

- - - lord - - - God - - - let all know that the lord God will assist me. Let Didymos and Severine, my daughter, be pursued, they who pursued me |[4] in the past. Let her body wither up in bed, just as you beheld how mine (withered up) due to them who covered my dignity with dishonor. Lord, show them quickly your might. Nullify the contrivances of their hearts against my dearest children. |[8] Let them come before the tribunal, o lord and master, wherever you judge. I Sabinus, crying and wailing night and day, have submitted my case to God, the master of all, for vindication of the injuries |[12] which I suffered from Severine and Didymos. Son of the great God, whom man never beheld, you who granted the blind to see the light of the sun, show as before your godlike wonders. |[16] Pay memorable compensation for the sufferings which I suffered, which I endured on account of my only daughter, striking down my enemies with your firm hands. Vindicate ☩ ☩ ☩ ☩ ☩ ☩ Emmanuel, vindicate.

5 καλυψάντων: Stegemann, *loc.cit.*, adduced support for the possibility of ⟨ἀπο⟩καλυψάντων.

5 δε[ῖξον] : δ[εῖξον] ed.pr.

8 καταλαβέτωcαν τὸ βῆμα: discussed by Stegemann, *loc.cit.*

9 [Cαβ]εῖνοc ed.pr. : ἐ[λ]εινόc Bell, *loc.cit.* The latter is palaeographically unfounded.

Panopolis   VI AD

P.Hamb. I 22.

ED.PR.: P.M.Meyer, P.Hamb. I 22 (Leipzig-Berlin 1911-1924), pp. 90-92, no. 22.

REPUBL.: Björck, *op.cit.* (**59**), pp. 10-14; K.Wessely, *Les plus anciens monuments du Christianisme écrits sur papyrus* II (Patrologia Orientalis 18.3, Paris 1924), p. 495 f., no.13; W.Crönert in *Raccolta di scritti in onore di G.Lumbroso* (Milan 1925), p. 496 f.; H.Leclercq in *DACL* 13, col. 1405 f.

COMM.: Björck, *op.cit.*; Wessely, *loc.cit.*; Leclercq, *loc.cit.*

PHOTO: Björck, *op.cit.*, plate II.1.

REF.: van Haelst, *Catalogue,* no. 914.

DESCR.: papyrus; 30.5 × 12 cm. Broken away unevenly at the left. Written against the fibers on the recto. The left margin was at least 1 cm., the right one about 6 cm. Above and below the text, free spaces of 2 cm. The verso is blank.

LOC.: Staats- und Universitätsbibliothek, Handschriftenabteilung, Hamburg. Inv. 58.

1   Cτήλη αἰνομόρου πολυπενθέος ἐcτὶ Cαβείνο[υ],
     ὃc κακὰ πόλλ' ὑπέμεινε μιῆc ἐπίηρα θυγατρόc.
     [υ]ἱὲ θεοῦ μεγάλοιο, τὸν οὐδέποτ' ἔδρακεν ἀνήρ,
4   ὃc τυφλοῖcιν ἔδωκαc ἰδεῖν φάοc ἠελίοιο,
     δεῖξον ἐν ἀνθρώποιcι καὶ αὐτίκα τῖcον ἀπάντη
     ⟦ἐχθροὺc ἡμετέρουc ⸢⟦κρατ⟧ δεινη⟧
     ἐχθροὺc ἡμετέρουc cτερεαῖc ἐνὶ χερcὶ πατάccων.

   2 πολλ'ὑπεμεινε Pap.   3]ἵε Pap.   4 ἵδειν Pap.   5 τῖcον Pap.

The stela of ill-fated, miserable Sabinus, who endured many evils on account of his only daughter. Son of the great God, whom man never beheld, you who granted to the blind to see the light of the sun, show among men and straightway punish everywhere my enemies, striking them down with your firm hands.

Provenance   Plate III   VI AD[1]
unknown

P.IFAO s.n.

ED.PR.: L.Barry, "Une adjuration chrétienne," *BIFAO* 6 (1908) 61-63.

REPUBL.: G.Björck, *Der Fluch des Christen Sabinus. Papyrus Upsaliensis 8* (Uppsala 1938), p. 47, no. 25.

COMM.: ed.pr.; Björck, *loc.cit.*

TRANSL.: ed.pr.

REF.: van Haelst, *Catalogue*, no. 739.

DESCR.: papyrus; 31 × 8.5 cm. Six (?) vertical and five horizontal folds. The writing runs against the fibers on the recto, and the back is blank.

LOC.: Institut Français d'Archéologie Orientale, Cairo.

1   † † † ἅγιος ὁ θεός, Καβριηλ, Μηχαηλ, ποίωcαι τὴν ἡκανών μου· μέγα
κύριε ὁ θεός, πατάξιcον Φηραδέλφηc· καὶ τὰ τέκνα αὐτῆc,
κύριε κύριε κύριε ὁ θεὸc θεό⟦ο⟧c, πατάξιcον μετ' αὐτῆc. ὁ ⟦υ⟧
4   ['Ι]ηcοῦ Χρηcτός, ἐλέηcόν μοι καὶ ἀγούου μου, κύριε.

1 Γαβριηλ, Μιχαηλ, ποίηcον τὸ ἱκανόν μοι   2 πάταξον Φιλαδέλφην   3 πάταξον   4 Ἰηcοῦc Χριcτός   με   ἀκούου

     † † † Holy God, Gabriel, Michael, give me satisfaction. Great (?) lord God, strike down Philadelphe; and her children, lord lord lord God God, strike them down with her. Jesus Christ, pity me and hear me, lord.

---

[1] Late IV AD according to the ed.pr.

1. ποίωcαι for ποίηcαι, if not merely a miscopying, may be due to confusion of the classes of contract verbs (see Gignac, *Grammar* II, pp. 363-365). For the imperative active 2nd sing. ending -αι, see Gignac, *Grammar* II, pp. 349-351; cf. also Mandilaras, *Verb*, § 684.

On τὸ ἱκανόν τινι ποιεῖν (originally a Latinism), see Blass-Debrunner-Funk, *Grammar*, § 5.3b; Bauer, *Wörterbuch, s.v.* ἱκανός 1c.

μου· μέγα or μου Μέγα· : μου Μέcα (personal name) ed.pr. If we are not dealing with the epithet μέγαc, we have the personal name Μέγαc in agreement with the preceding pronoun. On undeclined μέγα and Μέγα, see Gignac, *Grammar* II, p. 143; Psaltes, *Grammatik,* p. 151; Reinhold, *De Graecitate patrum apostolicorum*, p. 56; Sophocles, *Greek Lexicon, s.v.* μέγαc (*in fine*, vocative μέγα).

2-4. πατάξιcον Φηραδέλφηc· καὶ τὰ τέκνα αὐτῆc, | κύριε κύριε κύριε ὁ θεὸc θεό[[ο]]c, πατάξιcον μετ᾽ αὐτῆc. ὁ [[υ]] | [᾽Ι]ηcοῦ Χρηcτόc κτλ. The first editor analysed the passage as follows: πατάξιcον Φηραδέλφηc καὶ τὰ τέκνα αὐτῆc. κύριε κύριε κύριε ὁ θεὸc θεὸ⟨c⟩ θ(εό)c, πατάξιcον μετ᾽ αὐτῆc Ου[. . .]cου. Χρηcτόc κτλ.

2 and 3 πατάξιcον: for the morphological abundance, cf. ἀνεγείρεcον in Audollent, *DT*, 299, 1 comm.; ἀνοίξηcεν in *Apoc. Mosis* 21 cod. C (p. 21 Tischendorf); similar examples in Psaltes, *Grammatik,* p. 222 f. For πατάccειν in curses, cf. **59**, 18 (and **60**, 7), and see Björck, *Fluch des Christen Sabinus*, p. 19 f., and his index *s.v.* For the use of the verb in the Old and New Testament, see Kittel, *Theologisches Wörterbuch* 5, p. 939 f.

3 θεὸc θεό[[ο]]c : θεὸc θεὸ⟨c⟩ θ(εό)c ed.pr., but this would be the only instance of an abbreviation in the text, and what the first editor regarded as a third θ is better regarded as a deleted ο.

3-4 ὁ [[υ]] | [᾽Ι]ηcοῦ : Ου|[. . .]cου (personal name) ed.pr. The faintness of the υ at the end of 3 suggests that the writer rubbed it out; if not, οὐ was apparently written for ὁ (cf. Gignac, *Grammar* I, pp. 211-214).

4 ἀγούου (r. ἀκούου): for possible cases of present and aorist middle forms of ἀκούω (and compounds), cf. PSI VI 591, 9 εἰcάκουcαι (see Mayser, *Grammatik* II.1, p. 112); SB XVI 12240, 19 διακ[ου]cά[με]νοc; SB X 10525, 11 ἀκούομαι (r. ἀκού⟨c⟩ομαι ?). On the vogue of the middle in later Greek, see **54**, 21 comm.

Provenance   V-VI AD
unknown

P.Vindob. G 16685.

ED.PR.: H.Harrauer, "Strafaufschub," *ZPE* 30 (1978) 209 f.

REPUBL.: SB XIV 12184; A.Łukaszewicz, *ZPE* 73 (1988) 61 f.

TRANSL.: ed.pr.; H.Harrauer-H.Loebenstein, *Die Papyrussammlung der Österreichischen Nationalbibliothek. Katalog der Sonderausstellung 100 Jahre Papyrus Erzherzog Rainer* (Vienna 1983), p. 22, no. 34; Łukaszewicz, *loc.cit.*

COMM.: ed.pr.; Łukaszewicz, loc.cit.

PHOTO: ed.pr., plate V b.

DESCR.: papyrus; 4.9 × 5.9 cm. Written against the fibers on the verso. On the recto, 6 incomplete lines of a documentary text of uncertain nature (transcription in the ed.pr.).

LOC.: Österreichische Nationalbibliothek, Papyrussamlung, Vienna.

Comparing this text with negative acclamations, Łukaszewicz showed that it is not a notice concerning the postponement of the punishment of a Theodoros, but that it is a kind of curse. Theodoros is supposed to be punished, and the significant word used, κολάcιμοc, recalls κόλαcιc and κολάζειν in juridical curses and prayers.

Written in clumsy block letters typical of a slow writer, the text can be assigned to the 5th or 6th century on the basis of the documentary hand on the recto.

$$
\begin{aligned}
&1 \qquad\qquad ⳨ \\
&\qquad\qquad\quad χμγ \\
&\qquad\qquad\quad πρὸ μὲν πάν\text{-} \\
&4 \qquad\qquad τῶν κακὸc και\text{-} \\
&\qquad\qquad\quad ρὸc τοῦ κολα\text{-} \\
&\qquad\qquad\quad cίμου Θεοδώ\text{-} \\
&\qquad\qquad\quad ρου· κακὸc \\
&8 \qquad\qquad γάρ ἐcτιν.
\end{aligned}
$$

Above all, bad times for punishable Theodoros; for he is bad.

2 χμγ: a common abbreviation in documents and religious texts from the 4th to the 7th century. It appears in the following magical texts: PGM P 3, 1; P 8a verso; P 24 verso (see app.cr.); Youtie-Bonner, "Two Curse Tablets from Beisan," p. 73 (Tab. II A, line 1 = Jordan, "Survey," no. 165). Among the many explanations that have been proposed, the most appealing are (a) Χριστὸν Μαρία γεννᾷ; (b) Χριστὸς μάρτυς γένηται; (c) χειρός μου γραφή; and (d) by isopsephy (643) = θεὸς βοηθός. Recent discussions: Horsley, *New Documents* 2, pp. 177-180 (important also for earlier literature); A.Gostoli, *Stud. Pap.* 22 (1983) 9-14; G.Robinson, "ΚΜΓ and ΘΜΓ for ΧΜΓ," *Tyche* 1 (1986) 175-177; P.Heid. IV 333, 1 comm.; CPR XIV 32, 32 comm.; P.Oxy. LVI 3862, 1 comm.

3-4 πρὸ μὲν πάν|των: common at the beginning of private letters. See F.X.J.Exler, *A Study in Greek Epistolography* (Washington D.C., 1923), pp. 107-111; H.A.Steen, "Les clichés épistolaires," *Classica et Mediaevalia* 1 (1938) 155 f.; H.Koskenniemi, *Studien zur Idee und Phraseologie des griechischen Briefes bis 400 n. Chr.* (Helsinki 1956), p. 149.

4-5 κακὸς και|ρός: Łukaszewicz compared two negative acclamations from the milieu of the circus factions: [κα]κὰ τὰ [ἔ]τ[η] τῶν Πρασίνων (Aphrodisias; in A.Cameron, *Circus Factions: Blues and Greens at Rome and Byzantium* [Oxford 1976], p. 315); νικᾷ ἡ τύχη Εὐτοκίου κὲ Βενέτων· κακὰ τὰ ἔτη τοῦ Λαχανᾶ (Alexandria; ed. Z.Borkowski, *Alexandrie II. Inscriptions des factions à Alexandrie* [Warsaw 1981], p. 87, no. 47). Cf. also Const. Porph., *De Caer.* 318 (II, p. 124, 25-27 Vogt) "τῶν φιλούντων ἡμᾶς πολλὰ τὰ ἔτη" καὶ πάλιν· "τῶν δὲ μισούντων ἡμᾶς κακὰ τὰ ἔτη."

κακὸς καιρὸς with 7-8 κακὸς γάρ ἐστιν (on which, see below): *similia similibus.*

5-7 τοῦ κολα|σίμου Θεοδώρου: cf. the sixth century letter P.Mich. inv. 490, line 8 ὁ κολάσιμος Ἀμμωνᾶς (ed. R.Hübner, *ZPE* 84, 1990, 40-42).

κολάσιμος is to be added to our dictionaries of ancient Greek, though it and related words are attested later in the development of the language; cf. S.A.Kumanudes, Συναγωγὴ νέων λέξεων (Athens 1900), p. 555, *s.vv.* κολάσιμος, κολασιμότης, κολασίμως. In the present papyrus, the adjective has gerundive force, as is so often the case with adjectives in -σιμος.

For such adjectives in the papyri, see Mayser, *Grammatik* I.3, p. 98 f.;
L.R.Palmer, *A Grammar of the Post-Ptolemaic Papyri* I.1 (London 1946),
pp. 26-28; O.Montevecchi, "Note lessicali nei papiri: gli aggettivi in -σιμος,"
in: M.Capasso-G.M.Savorelli-R.Pintaudi (edd.), *Miscellanea papyrologica in
occasione del bicentenario dell'edizione della Charta Borgiana* II (Papyrologica Florentina 19, 1990), pp. 443-449.

For κόλαϲιϲ, κολάζειν in juridical curses, cf. Audollent, *DT*, 3, 13
κολαζόμενοι; 8, 22 πᾶ[ϲ]αν κόλαϲιν; 41b, 10-12 [κατα]γρά[φ]ομεν
[εἰϲ] κολάϲε[ιϲ . .] καὶ [ποι]νὴν καὶ [τι]μ[ωρ]ί[αν]; Wünsch, *DTA*,
100a, 12; T.Genava inv. MAH 20151, 6 f. (ed. Chr.Dunant, *Mus. Helv.* 35,
1978, 242-244). For discussion, see H.S.Versnel, "Beyond Cursing: The
Appeal to Justice in Judicial Prayers," in: Faraone-Obbink (edd.), *Magika
Hiera*, esp. pp. 64-68, 72 f., 95 n. 26.

7-8 κακὸϲ | γάρ ἐϲτιν: *similia similibus* (see 4-5) and, at the same time,
justification of the punishment. For such terms of abuse, cf. e.g. Wünsch,
DTA, 84 a 1-2 Ἀνδροκλείδη καταδῶ τὴν γλῶτ⟨τ⟩αν τὴν κακὴν καὶ
τὸν θυμὸν τὸν κακὸν καὶ τὴν ψυχὴν τὴν κακήν; and see Versnel,
loc.cit., p. 64 with notes 23 and 24.

APPLIED MAGIC:

CHARMS TO WIN FAVOR

63

Provenance
unknown

Early III AD

P.Merton II 58.

ED.PR.: B.R.Rees-H.I.Bell-J.W.B.Barns, P.Merton II (Dublin 1959), pp. 22-24, no. 58.

COMM.: ed.pr.

TRANSL.: R.Kotansky in Betz, *Translation*, no. XCII.

PHOTO: ed.pr., plate VII a.

REF.: van Haelst, *Catalogue*, no. 949, ("chrétien?").

DESCR.: papyrus; 7.9 × 9.6 cm. Complete on all sides. The writing runs along the fibers, and the back is blank. Upper and left margins of 0.7-0.8 cm. Letters at the ends of the lines are abraded, and some have disappeared entirely.

LOC.: Chester Beatty Library and Gallery of Oriental Art, Dublin.

A *charitesion* or charm to win favor,[1] like **64** and possibly **97** ↓ 2-6. The present text as revised here consists of three sentences addressed to Aphrodite (called Kypris in line 9). The first and third of these sentences are conditional: their apodoses consist of demands made upon the goddess; their protases justify the demands.[2]

---

[1] For discussion of this sort of charm with parallels from the magical papyri and from literature, see C.A.Faraone, *Phoenix* 44 (1990) 219-229, esp. 224-227. Cf. also Bonner, *SMA*, pp. 47-49, 120.

[2] Cf. lines 10-12 comm.; PGM VIII 22-27 (a *charitesion* addressed to Hermes) ἐὰν ἐπεκαλέσατό ϲε ᾽Ιϲιϲ, μεγίϲτη τῶν θεῶν ἀπάντων, ἐν πάϲῃ κρίϲει, ἐν πα⟨ν⟩τὶ τόπῳ πρὸϲ θεοὺϲ καὶ ἀνθρώπουϲ καὶ δαίμοναϲ καὶ ἔν⟨υ⟩δρα ζῷα καὶ ἐπί⟨γ⟩εια καὶ ἔϲχεν τὴν χάριν, τὸ νῖκοϲ πρὸϲ θεοὺϲ καὶ ἀνθρώπουϲ κ[α]ὶ ⟨παρὰ⟩ πᾶϲι τοῖϲ ὑπὸ τὸν κόϲμον ζῷοιϲ, οὕτωϲ κἀγώ, ὁ δεῖνα, ἐπικα[λ]οῦμαί ϲε· διὸ δόϲ μοι τὴ⟨ν⟩ χάριν, μορφήν, κάλλοϲ. For similar constructions in Greek hymns, see Keyßner, *Gottesvorstellung*, p. 134.

1 εἰ ἑcοῦ τὸ μέγα ὄνομα χάριν

    cοῦ πάντεc φοβοῦν[τ]αι, τὸ μέ-

    γα c[ο]υ κράτοc, τὰ ἀγαθὰ δόc μοι·

4 τὴν ἰcχὺν τοῦ Ακρυcκυλου,

    τὸν λόγον τοῦ Εὐώνου,

    τὰc αὐγὰc τοῦ Cαλο`μῶν'τοc,

    τὴν φωνὴν τοῦ Αβραcαξ,

8 τὴν χάριν τοῦ ᾿Αδωνίου

    θεοῦ. δεῦρό μοι, Κύπρι⟦c⟧,

    πᾶcαν ἡμέραν ΟΝ2. ε[ἰ]

    ἐχάριcεν τὸ κρυπτόν

12 cου ὄνομα, θοαθοηθα-

    θοουθαεθωυcθοαιθι-

    θηθοινθω, δόc μοι νίκη[ν,]

    δόξαν, εὐμορφίαν πρὸc

16 πάντας καὶ πρὸς πάcαc.

---

4 ἀκ̔ρυcκυλου Pap.   6 αυγαc corr. ex υυγαc   Cαλομῶντοc

If on account of you all beings fear your great name, your great might, give me the good things: the strength of Akryskylos (?), the intelligence of Euonos, the radiance of Solomon, the voice of Abrasax, the grace of the god Adonis (?). Hither to me, Kypris, every day of (my) life. If your hidden name has granted favor, *thoathoêthathoouthae-thôysthoaithithêthointhô*, give me victory, repute, beauty before all men and before all women.

1-3 εἰ ἑcοῦ - - - κράτοc: this passage is dealt with here as if it is correct as it stands, but possibly it contains one or more interpolations and/or omissions. A possible alternative to the translation given above: 'If on account of you all beings fear your great name, give me your great might (and) the good things'.

1 εἰ ἑcοῦ : ειε cου ed.pr. According to Kotansky (*loc.cit.*), the first word could be the preposition εἰc, but the third letter is certainly ε (cf. the ε

before the break in 10). For ἐcοῦ in place of cοῦ, cf. Gignac, *Grammar* II, p. 163 f.; also PGM IV 3165 f.

1-2 ὄνομα - - - φοβοῦν[τ]αι: cf. e.g. PGM IV 356-361 κατὰ τοῦ ὀνόματος τοῦ φοβεροῦ καὶ τρομεροῦ, οὗ ἡ γῆ ἀκούcα[c]α τοῦ ὀνόματος ἀνοιγήcεται, οὗ οἱ δαίμονες ἀκούcαντες τοῦ ὀνόματος ἐνφόβου φοβηθήcονται, οὗ οἱ ποταμοὶ καὶ αἱ πέτραι ἀκούcαντες τὸ ὄνομα ῥήccονται; and the parallels **46**, 12-14; **47**, 12-14; **48** J, 14-16; **49**, 28-32; **50**, 15-16. Discussion of and further parallels for the divine name feared: Martinez, *P.Mich. 757*, pp. 70-74.

χάριν cοῦ: on prepositional, rather than postpositional, χάριν, cf. Bauer, *s.v.* χάριν; LSJ *s.v.* χάρις VI 1; PGM VII 604.

2-3 φοβοῦν[τ]αι, τὸ μέ˙γα c[ο]υ κράτος assuming asyndeton.

3 τὰ ἀγαθά: on ἀγαθά, ἐcθλά, ὄλβια *et sim.* that can be granted by the gods, see Keyßner, *Gottesvorstellung*, pp. 158-166.

4-9 τὴν ἰcχὺν τοῦ Ακρυcκυλου, | τὸν λόγον τοῦ Εὐώνου, | τὰς αὐγὰς τοῦ Caλο˙μόν˙τος, | τὴν φωνὴν τοῦ Αβραcαξ, | τὴν χάριν τοῦ Ἀδωνίου | θεοῦ: cf. PGM VII 1018-21 δός μοι] τὴ[ν ἐξουcίαν] καὶ τὴν δύναμιν τοῦ Caβ[α]ω[θ, τὸ] κρ[άτος τοῦ Ιαω κ]αὶ τὴν ἐπιτυχίαν τοῦ Αβλαναθα[ναλβα] κα[ὶ τὴν ἰcχὺν τοῦ Α]κρα[μ]μαχα[μ]αρει; XXIIa 23-27 ποίη[cόν] με καλὸν παρ' αὐτῇ γενέcθαι ὡς Ιαω, πλούcιον ὡς Caβαωθ, φιληθῆναι ὡς Λαΐλαμ, μέγαν ὡς Βαρβαραν, ἔντιμος ὡς Μιχαηλ, ἔνδοξος ὡς Γαβριηλ, καὶ χαριτώcομαι; also XXXV 19-22 (part of a *charitesion*) διὰ τὴν δύναμιν τοῦ Ιαω καὶ τὴ⟨ν⟩ ἰcχὺν τοῦ Caβαωθ καὶ τὸ ἔνδυμα τ⟨ο⟩ῦ Ελωε καὶ τὸ κράτος τοῦ Αδωναι καὶ τὸν cτέφανον τοῦ Αδωναι. More frequently, as below in lines 14-15 (νίκη[ν,] δόξαν, εὐμορφίαν) and in **64**, 3-5, the good qualities are enumerated without the addition of τοῦ + name; parallels in P.Oslo I 1, 223-225 comm.

4 τὴν ἰcχὺν τοῦ Ακρυcκυλου: above κ in the curious name or epithet is written γ; perhaps Αγρυcκυλου or Αγκρυcκυλου was intended. At the end, the ed.pr. gave [ου ?], but there are sufficient traces for -ου. Like the first editors, we have no suggestions to make as to the significance of this name or word.

5 τὸν λόγον τοῦ Εὐώνου: the reference is probably to Hermes. One should probably follow the first editors in regarding Εὐώνου as a name, however not a misspelling of Εὐήνου nor a mistake for Εὐωνύμου. According to the Suda (II, p. 462, 14 Adler), Εὔωνος can be a proper name.

Meaning 'of good purchase' just like the Greek adjective, it would be a most appropriate name for Hermes, the god of buying and selling (he had the similar epithet κερδῷος). For λόγος as one of his outstanding characteristics, cf. e.g. λόγων ἀρχηγέτα γλώccηc in the hymn to Hermes, PGM V 402 (= *hymn.* 15/16, 2); Plut., *De Iside* 373B τοῦ Ἑρμοῦ, τουτέcτι τοῦ λόγου; Aristid., *Or.* 37, 21 (II, p. 310 Keil) ὅcτιc Ἑρμῆν καλεῖ Λόγιον καὶ Ἀγοραῖον καὶ Ἐμπολαῖον; and see *RE* XIII.1, *s.v.* Logos, coll. 1061-65 (K.Preisendanz); E.Orth, *Logios* (Leipzig 1926), pp. 77-86, 99.

6 τὰc αὐγὰc τοῦ Caλο῾μόν῾τοc: for various spellings of the name and for the fluctuation in declension between -μῶνοc and μῶντοc, see *RE Suppl.* VIII, col. 660. The first editors suggested that αὐγαί might refer to the 'glances' or 'eyes' of Solomon as magician, and they adduced Damascius, *Vita Isidori* 92 (pp. 132-134 Zintzen), where it is said that a sorcerer can be recognized ἀπὸ τῶν ὀφθαλμῶν. But the reference is probably rather to Solomon's personal radiance, perhaps specifically the radiance of his wisdom. As Kotansky pointed out, in *Test. Sal.*, Rec. C, Prol. 1-2 (p. 76*, 8-11 McCown) Solomon's divine illumination is described as follows: (God speaking) "- - - ἔcη βλέπων πᾶcαν τὴν cοφίαν λελευκαcμένην ὡc χιόναν ἐνώπιόν cου καὶ τῶν ὀφθαλμῶν cου." ταῦτα ἀκούcαc (i.e. Solomon) καὶ ὥcπερ ὑπό τινοc αὐγῆc ἐλλαμφθεὶc κτλ. On the radiance of gods, rulers and deified men, see Keyßner, *Gottesvorstellung*, pp. 148-150.

8-9 τὴν χάριν τοῦ Ἀδωνίου | θεοῦ. The meanings of χάριc in the magical papyri are discussed by A.D.Nock in Bell-Nock-Thompson, "Magical Texts from a Bilingual Papyrus," 259-261, where the following categories are given: (1) charm, attractiveness; (2) success, power; (3) favor; (4) thanks.

τοῦ Ἀδωνίου θεοῦ: possibly of Adonis, though a mistake for τοῦ Ἀδωναίου θεοῦ cannot be excluded. The first possibility was proposed by the first editors, adducing Bekker, *Anecd. Gr.* I, p. 346, 1-4 Ἀδώνιοc Φερεκράτηc εἶπεν ἀντὶ τοῦ Ἀδώνιδοc. λέγει δὲ καὶ τὴν αἰτιατικὴν τὸν Ἀδώνιον. οὕτωc δὲ καὶ Πλάτων καὶ Κρατῖνοc, ἀλλὰ καὶ Ἀριcτοφάνηc καὶ ἕτεροι. λέγουcι δὲ καὶ Ἄδωνιν αὐτὸν πολλάκιc. Cf. now Aristoph., fr. 759 (PCG III.2 Kassel-Austin), where reference is made to ὦ τὸν Ἀδώνιον in Poet. Lesb., frag. inc. 24 (p. 296 L.-P.; = Sapph. fr. 117 Bᵇ Voigt) and to Wilamowitz' remarks on Ἀδώνιοc inscribed on a vase (*Sappho und Simonides*, Berlin 1913, pp. 36 and 37 n. 1). For the possibility of τοῦ Ἀδωναίου θεοῦ, cf. e.g. Ἀδωναίου θεοῦ in **49**, 34 f.; **50**, 36; **51**, 3; PGM IV 1560 ὁ μέγας θεός, Ἀδωναῖε; XVI 9 τοῦ Ἀδωναίου Cαβαωθ.

9 δεῦρό μοι: see **65**, 31 comm.

Κύπρι[c] : Κύπρι[c̣]̣ ed.pr., but ε is not written above deleted c. Either c was simply deleted or it was altered to ε. We are probably dealing with the common epithet of Aphrodite (cf. LSJ *s.v.* Κύπρις; PGM VII 388). For a possible mention of Kypris in a *charitesion*, cf. P.Berol. inv. 11734, 67 with comm. (ed. W.Brashear, *APF* 36, 1990, 49-74). According to the first editors, Κύπριε may have been intended, and they suggested that the reference may have been to Adonis. Κύπριος, however, is not attested as an epithet of Adonis, although it is true that he had numerous connections with the island (see W.W.Baudissin, *Adonis and Esmun*, Leipzig 1911, pp. 81-85).

10 ονϩ. ε[ị] : ονϩε ed.pr. The Coptic word means 'life'.

10-12 ε[ị] | ἐχάρισεν τὸ κρυπτόν | cου ὄνομα: cf. e.g. PGM II 5-8 (= *hymn.* 9, 4-6) εἴ ποτε δὴ φιλόνικον ἔχων κλάδον ἐνθάδε δάφνης [cῆ]c ἱερῆc κορυφῆc ἐφθέγγεο πολλάκις ἐσθλά, καὶ νῦν μοι σπεύσειας; XXXV 22-24 δότε κἀμοὶ χάριτα κα⟨ὶ⟩ νίκην ἔ⟨μ⟩προσθεν πάντων, ὡς τἀγαθὰ δωρήματα ἐχαρίσου τῷ Αλβαναθαναλβα καὶ Αχραμαχαμαρι.

12 *fin.* -θα: last letter most uncertain.

13 *fin.* -ιθι: last two letters most uncertain.

Oxyrhynchos   II-III AD[1]

T.Köln inv. 8.
ED.PR.: D.Wortmann, "Neue magische Texte. Nr. 8: Amulett", *Bonner Jahrb.* 68 (1968)
106.
TRANSL.: ed.pr.
COMM.: ed.pr.
DESCR.: silver, not lead (ed.pr.), tablet; 5 × 5 cm. Inscribed on one side only. Broken away
on the right.
LOC.: Institut für Altertumskunde, Universität zu Köln.

On inscribed amuletic metal *lamellae* (usually gold or silver) such as **64**
(cf. **2** and **5** intr. with line 2) and their various contents, see R.Kotansky in:
Faraone-Obbink, *Magika Hiera*, pp. 107-137. Here we have a conventional
charitesion; see **63** intr., note 1.

1   αεηιουω ια[   ]
Αδωναιε Cαβ[αωθ,]
δὼc χάριν, φ[ιλίαν,]
4   εὐπραξίαν, ἐ[πα-]
φροδιcίαν τῶ [φο-]
ροῦντι τὸ φυ[λα-]
κττήριον.

3 δὼc   5 τῷ   6-7 φυλακτήριον

aeêiouô iaô - - - Adônaie Sabaôth, give favor, love, success, charm to the wearer of this
amulet.

---

[1] VI AD according to the first editor.

1 ια[: ια[ω ed.pr. The latter is the most likely possibility, but by no means the only one; cf. e.g. the words, names and vowel combinations beginning with ια- in Indexes VII, VIII and IX.

4-5 ἐ[πα]Ιφροδιcίαν : κ[αὶ ἀ]Ιφροδιcίαν ed.pr.

6-7 φυ[λα]Ικττήριον (r. φυλακτήριον) : φυ[λ]Ιαττήριον ed.pr.

APPLIED MAGIC:

DIVINATORY CHARMS

Antinoopolis[1]   Plate IV   III AD[2]

Museo del Vicino Oriente, inv. 181/665.

ED.PR.: I.Crisci in: *Antinoe (1965-1968). Missione Archeologica in Egitto dell'Università di Roma* (Istituto di Studi del Vicino Oriente. Serie Archeologica 21, Rome 1974), p. 121 f. "Testo magico."

COMM.: ed.pr.

DESCR.: terra-cotta sherd from a shallow bowl; 16 × 8 cm. The letters were incised on the concave side when the clay was still moist. The bowl's original height was 6 cm, its diameter 33 cm.

LOC.: Museo del Vicino Oriente, Rome.

A potsherd from a shallow terra-cotta bowl inscribed to serve as a vessel for divination; as such, a unique document of applied magic.[3]

The sherd preserves part of a Schwindeschema and seven lines of a Greek formula that summons the great god. The top of the Schwindeschema runs parallel to the bowl's rim, about 1.5 cm below it. The design will have bottomed out roughly at the center of the bowl. The top of the Schwinde-schema was originally 20-25 cm broad. The seven lines of Greek run parallel to the left edge of the Schwindeschema. The reconstructed text accounts for writing on about a quarter to a third of the bowl's interior surface; quite possibly more or all of this surface was inscribed as well.

The form of divination for which the bowl was used is *lekanomanteia*, a subcategory of *hydromanteia*: A vessel was filled with one or more liquids (usually water and oil). Various other substances and objects could be added, and mirrors were often employed. The vessel was exposed to the light of the

---

[1] Found to the northeast of the ancient city, close to the wall.

[2] IV-V AD according to the ed.pr.

[3] For other kinds of magical inscriptions incised or written in ink on bowls, vases and lamps, cf. e.g. **51**; PGM O 5; further material in D.Wortmann, *Bonner Jahrb.* 168 (1968) 81 note 12. See also Naveh-Shaked, *Amulets and Magic Bowls*, pp. 19-28, 124-214.

sun, the moon, a lamp or a torch, and a god was summoned to enter it. The soothsayer or his child medium could see or even hear the god; as the one or the other gazed into the filled vessel he could foretell the future by interpreting the reflections on the surface or the slicks of oil on the water. Literature: *RE* XII.2, *s.v.* Λεκανομαντεία, coll. 1879-89 (R.Ganszyniec); Th.Hopfner, *Offenbarungszauber* II, esp. §§ 228-272; idem, "Mittel- und neugriechische Lekano-, Lychno-, Katoptro- und Onychomanteia," in *Studies Presented to F.Ll.Griffith* (London 1932), pp. 218-232; F.Cunen, "Lampe et coupe magiques (PGM V, 1-52)," Symb. Osl. 36 (1960) 65-71. For a discussion of this and related practices not only throughout late antiquity, but also among various peoples through the nineteenth century, see E.Lefébure, "Le Vase divinatoire," *Sphinx* 6 (1903) 61-85.

For prescriptions that specify writing or drawing on vessels for *lekano-manteia*, cf. PGM IV 3209-17 Ἀφροδίτης φι⟨α⟩λομαντεῖον. ἀγνεύcαc ἡμέρας ζ′ καὶ λαβὼν φιάλην λευκὴν πλῆcον ὕδατος καὶ ἐλαίου, πρότερον γράψαc εἰς τὸν πυθμένα ζμυρνομέλανι· 'ηιοχ χιφα· ελαμ-ψηρ ζηλ αεηϊουω' (γράμματα κ̄ε̄), ὑπὸ τὸν πυθμένα δὲ ἔξωθεν· 'Ταχιηλ, χθονίη, δραξω' (γράμματα ῑη̄), καὶ κήρωcον λευκῷ κηρῷ. εἰc δὲ τὸν κύκλον ἔξωθεν τὸν ἄνω· 'ϊερμι, φιλω ς ερικωμα δερκ[ω] μαλωκ γαυλη Ἀφριηλ ἐρωτῶ'; and 3247-54; Delatte, *Anecdota Athenien-sia*, pp. 54, 1-6; 504, 5-12; 586, 5 f. Cf. also Griffith-Thompson, *Demotic Magical Papyrus*, XIV 17 ff. (cited here is the translation of J.H.Johnson in Betz, *Translation,* p. 219) "You bring a copper cup; you engrave a figure of Anubis in it; you fill it with settled water guarded which the sun cannot find; you fill the top (of the water) with true oil - - -." Pliny knew of a similar practice: *N.H.* XXXIII 46 *tinguit Aegyptus argentum, ut in vasis Anubim suum spectet.*

The present inscription differs from those cited above in that it was incised when the clay was still moist, and the bowl was baked subsequently. This suggests that the artifact was used repeatedly. The person who commissioned it to be made was probably a professional diviner.

1 [ιαεωβαφρενεμουνοθ]ιλαρικριφια[ευεαιφιρκιραλιθοννομενερφαβωεαι]

[αεωβαφρενεμουνοθιλα]ρικριφιαευε[αιφιρκιραλιθοννομενερφαβωεα]

[εωβαφρενεμουνοθιλα]ρικριφιαευεαιφι[ρκιραλιθοννομενερφαβωε]

4 [ωβαφρενεμουνοθιλα]ρικριφιαευεαιφι[ρκιραλιθοννομενερφαβω]

[βαφρενεμουνοθι]λαρικριφιαευεαιφι[ρκιραλιθοννομενερφαβ]

[αφρενεμουν]οθιλαρικριφιαευεαιφ[ιρκιραλιθοννυζομενερφα]

[φρενεμο]υνοθιλαρικριφιαευ[εαιφιρκιραλιθοννομενερφ]

8 ρενεμουνοθιλαρικριφιαευ[εαιφιρκιραλιθοννομενερ]

ενεμουνοθιλαρικριφιαε[υεαιφιρκιραλιθοννομενε]

νεμουνοθιλαρικριφιαε[υεαιφιρκιραλιθοννομεν]

εμουνοθιλαρικριφ[ιαευεαιφιρκιραλιθοννυομε]

12 μουνοθιλαρικρ[ιφιαευεαιφιρκιραλιθοννυομ]

ουνοθιλαρικρ[ιφιαευεαιφιρκιραλιθοννυο]

υνοθιλαρικ[ριφιαευεαιφιρκιραλιθοννυ]

νοθιλαρι[κριφιαευεαιφιρκιραλιθον]

16 οθιλαρ[ικριφιαευεαιφιρκιραλιθο]

θιλ[αρικριφιαευεαιφιρκιραλιθ]

ιλ[αρικριφιαευεαιφιρκιραλι]

[λαρικριφιαευεαιφιρκιραλ]

20 [αρικριφιαευεαιφιρκιρα]

[ρικριφιαευεαιφιρκιρ]

[ικριφιαευεαιφιρκι]

[κριφιαευεαιφιρκ]

24 [ριφιαευεαιφιρ]

[ιφιαευεαιφι]

[φιαευεαιφ]

[ιαευεαι]

28 [αευεα]

[ευε]

[υ]

δεῦρό μοι, ὁ αὐτο-

32 γεννήτωρ θεέ, ἀσπερ-

μοβόλητε, αὐτοπάτω[ρ, αὐ-]

τομήτωρ, ἀφανής, [2-4]

[. . ἀ]σώματε, δέσποτα,

36 [. . . . .]ς κρύφια [?

[. . . . .] αληθ[

iaeobaphrenemounothilarikriphiaeyeaiphirkiralithonuomenerphaboeai (etc.). (Lines 31-
37) Hither to me, self-begotten god, (created) without cast seed, father of yourself, mother
of yourself, invisible, incorporeal, ruler - - - hidden - - - true (?) - - -.

1-30 ιαεωβαφρενεμουνοθιλαρικριφιαευεαιφιρκιραλιθονυομενερ-
φαβωεαι etc.: a very common palindrome; cf. **48** A; **49**, 1+3; **74**, 11-16;
and see PGM, Vol. 3 (Index), p. 280. The formula often occurs in solar
contexts. According to K.Fr.W.Schmidt, it is based on the Hebrew divine
name ιαεω + Egyptian f3j.f-rn-ỉmn *'ḏ, mr (= rw?)-R^c (m-)k3r.f* 'Iao is the
bearer of the secret name, the lion of Re secure in his shrine' (*GGA* 196,
1934, 177 f.; also *GGA* 193, 1931, 443 f.; Th.Hopfner, *Archiv Orientální* 7,
1935, 119). But this is not convincing for linguistic reasons (H.J.Thissen)

31 δεῦρό μοι: cf e.g. PGM IV 236-238 (*lekanomanteia*) δεῦρό ⟨μοι⟩,
ὅ τις θεός, ὄφθητί μοι ἐν τῇ ἄρτι ὥρᾳ καὶ μή μου θαμβήσῃς τοὺς ὀφ-
θαλμούς· δεῦρό μοι κτλ.; PGM VII 559 f. (*lychnomanteia*) ἧκέ μοι, τὸ
πνεῦμα τὸ ἀεροπετές and 570 δεῦρό μοι, κύριε. The phrase δεῦρό μοι is
very common in prayers in the magical papyri. It begins e.g. the prayer
transmitted by PGM XII 238-257, XIII 761-800 and XXI (see the discussion
by Merkelbach-Totti, *Abrasax* I, pp. 127-222); cf. also PGM III 496; further
references in PGM, Vol. 3 (Index), p. 77, *s.v.* δεῦρό μοι. For the Egyptian
equivalent αμου νηι, cf. **6**, 3 comm.

31-32 αὐτο|γεννήτωρ: attested also in Irenaeus, *Haer.* I 8, 4 (I, p. 135
Harvey), and Epiph., *Panar.* 34, 5, 8 (GCS 2, p. 13, 9). Cf. αὐτογενέτωρ
(PGM IV 1561; XIII 269; P 13a, 1), αὐτογένεθλος (PGM I 342 *lychno-
manteia*; IV 943 *lychnomanteia*, 1989 necromancy), and αὐτογέννητος
(XIII 63, 572).

32-33 ἀσπερ|μοβόλητε : ασπερ| . . . ολητε ed.pr. *Addendum lexicis*;
cf. σπερμοβολέω, σπερμοβόλημα, σπερμοβολία and σπερμοβόλος.
The similar ἀσπερμολόγητος is used by Dioskoros of Aphrodito in P.Cairo
Masp. II 67188 (= PGM P 13a), line 1 π[αν]τοκράτωρ, πρωτογεν[έτω]ρ,
[α]ὐτογενέτωρ, ἀσπερμολόγητε. Preisendanz altered the last word to
ἀσπερμογόνητε ("ohne Samen Erzeugter"), but a compound based on
-γόνητος is unparalleled. The transmitted reading ἀσπερμολόγητε, however, can be defended, though not as was recently done by L.S.B. MacCoull
(*Tyche* 2, 1987, 95 f.), suggesting that Dioskoros based the word on
σπερμολόγος 'babbler' (used of Paul in Acts 17, 18), positing that he gave it

a new meaning under the influence of the Stoic concept of the λόγος σπερματικός, and translating it as "not bound by the ordinary laws of human nature." Dioskoros rather had in mind NT Ep. Hebr. 7, 3 ἀπάτωρ, ἀμήτωρ, ἀγενεαλόγητος (of Melchizedek), and he may have been familiar with the word as used of Christ's divinity – e.g. Orig., *in Lucam* 28 (GCS 9, p. 161, 9) and Ps.Justin Martyr, *Quaestt. et responss. ad orthodoxos* 67 (III, 2, p. 98 Otto). The meaning of ἀγενεαλόγητος is 'of unrecorded descent', 'without geneology'. In Dioskoros' ἀσπερμολόγητε, the element -σπερμο- is probably synonymous with γενεα-; the word, then, should be translated 'without known seed' or 'without known descent'.

33 αὐτοπάτω[ρ: also in Aristid., *Or.* 43, 9 Keil, of Zeus; *Orph. hymn.* 10, 10, of Physis; Iambl., *Myst.* VIII 2 (261, 13), of God; Porphyr., *Hist. Philos.*, fr. 17 (p. 15 Nauck), of the Platonic Good and Beautiful; Synes., *Hymn.* 1, 146, of God; Clem. Rom., *Recogn.* 3, 3, 8 (GCS 2, p. 9, 9) of God; Greg. Naz., *Carm.* 2.2, 7, 254 (Migne, PG 37, col. 1571A), of Christ.

33-34 αὐ]|τομήτωρ: the word is probably attested in Semonides 7, 12, but in a different sense. It is also transmitted in Epiph., *Panar.* 31, 6, 4 (GCS 1, p. 394, 1), where it has been emended to αὐτοπάτωρ.

34-35 ἀφανής, [2-4]|[. ἀ]σώματε : αφανης ι] . . . τε ed.pr. The restoration ἀ]σώματε (cf. **57**, 36 with comm.; PGM IV 1777 ἀϊδῆ, ἀσώματε) is considerably likelier than ὑπερα]σώματε (cf. Lampe, *s.v.*). One can probably rule out πυρι- and πυρο]σώματε (PGM IV 595 f. and VII 701), because the context seems to require the concept of incorporeality. Other compounds based on -σώματος are still less suitable. If ἀ]σώματε is correct, an entire word is missing before it.

37] . αληθ[:] . αλη[ed.pr. The god should reveal the 'truth' or make the revelation 'truthfully'. Cf. from divinatory charms PGM I 320 ἀληθείην καταλέξας; II 10 ἐπ' ἀλ[η]θείας, 115 τῇ ἀληθείᾳ; IV 913 πάντα ἀληθῆ διηγεῖται; XIV 6 f. χρημάτισον ἐπ' ἀληθείας, ἀληθῶς, ἀψευδῶς, ἀναμφιλόγως; also III 288 ἀψευδῶς; IV 1033 ἀψεύστως, 2504 ἀψευδῶς; V 421 ἀψευδῶς; VII 248 ἀψεύστως, 571 ἀψευδής. A stone scarab found on the Tusculan hill (ed. R.Wünsch, *Bullettino della Commissione Archeologica Comunale di Roma* 27, 1899, 294-299) contains the following Greek inscription accompanied by magical words and the seven vowels: χρημάτισόν μοι ἐν τῇ νυκτὶ ταύτῃ ἐπ' ἀληθείᾳ μετὰ μνήμης. Numerous requests for truthful revelation in demotic texts, e.g. Griffith-Thompson, *Demotic Magical Papyrus*, XXVII 23 f.; XXIX 8, 12, 20; etc.

66

Fayum ?   III/IV AD

T.Moen s.n.

ED.PR.: P.J.Sijpesteijn, "Ein Herbeirufungszauber," *ZPE* 4 (1969) 187-191.

COMM.: ed.pr.; (line 21) F.Maltomini, *ZPE* 87 (1991) 253.

TRANSL.: ed.pr.

PHOTO: ed.pr., plate 10.

DESCR.: lead tablet; 10.7 × 12.5 cm. There are two breaks where the tablet had been folded vertically (3 and 7 cm from the left margin). After these folds were made, the tablet was folded from the top towards the bottom so as to form a packet of about 4 × 3 cm. Inscribed on one side only.

LOC.: private collection of E.Moen, Baarn, Holland (previously in the private collection of A.M.Hakkert).

The nature of this text is clearly shown by lines 19-22: a daemon is commanded to come, to enter into Alexander, to appear and speak; he should be articulate, peaceful and not frightening. Requests of this sort characterize charms for divination in which a daemon is supposed to speak through a living medium.[1] In all likelihood Alexander was a child.[2] He wishes that the divination be successful and that he remain unharmed during the possession.[3] Since it is written on lead, the charm is likely to be directed towards a corpse-daemon, and so we are probably dealing with an example of necromancy.

---

[1] On such divinatory charms, see Hopfner, *Offenbarungszauber* II, §§ 75 II b, 273-295.

[2] Children, especially boys, were almost always the mediums in magical divination. See Th.Hopfner, "Die Kindermedien in den griechisch-ägyptischen Zauberpapyri," in: *Recueil d'études dédiées à la mémoire de N.P.Kondakov* (Prague 1926), pp. 65-74; idem, "Mittel- und neugriechische Lekano-, Lychno-, Katoptro- und Onychomantien," in: *Studies Presented to F.Ll.Griffith* (London 1932), p. 219.

[3] For the dangers to which child mediums were exposed, see Hopfner, *Offenbarungszauber* II, § 69; idem, *Studies Griffith* (cit. above, note 2), p. 225 f.

1 ⳤⲋⲋⲃⲓⲍⲍⲐⲉⳙⲉⲛⲏⲏⳝⲕⲛⲑ ⲭ ⲭ
  ⲟ ⲝ ⳾ ⲧⳤ ⲅ ⳦ ⳝ Ⳛ ⲁ ⲱ . ⲓ ⲱ ⲉ ⲓ ⲟ ⲋ

  ⳝ ⲋ ⲱ ⳤ τουραιαρ ̇ υητιρωχοχε
4 μαβαντεανα αγατα αμαψουουρου
   ανααπαντο ροδαμιτ Cατραπερκμηφ
   θυρcερψε ̇ αμαχθεν θουφ καρχρηθχρωινε
   κρομιορφι ζθο θονινευκτευ Θωουθιθωθ
8 Ιαω τεωαντιcιρονμυραε βωδρομωω
   αλεου παονενε παντιενε λυμβρεκλαρυζ
   κρογεακετοριψαραβαθαεο παχνευχανωρ
   φοβερόμματε πανεργέτ⟨α⟩ Cεcενγεν Βαρ-
12 φαραγγηc ομοιβαcκο / βερωουνηρ
   θωβαφ θαμβαμι οψνωοιμφυτι
   cθομψιμ φιηιοινδυcδωμηλελωθε
   αδυναιcα / ιοιναθαψαωcευ βιρααριν
16 δαλημ αζαθοαθαγενγη ψουανε
   πουραθα ̇ ουαμωθ ἀέἠἰόὑώ επεη
   ωιουθευα ̇ υυυ ιιι θεcμαοαθαα
   ἐλθέ, λάλησον, εἰcκρίθητι
20 ἐμοὶ Ἀλεξάνδρῳ, ὃν [ἔ]τεκε
   Διδύμη, πάνητί μοι εἰρηνικῶc,
   διὰ φωνῆc, ἀβόφωc.

4 αγότα Pap.   9-18 in ecthesi   17 ἀέἠἰόὑώ Pap.   19-22 in eisthesi
21 φάνηθί μοι   22 ἀφόβωc

(Mag. signs) *touraiar ̇ yêtirôchoche* |⁴ *mabanteana agata amapsouourou anaapanto roda-mit Satraperkmêph thyrserpse ̇ amachthen thouph karchrêthchrôine kromiorphi ztho thonineukteu Thôouthithôth* |⁸ *Iaô teôantisironmyrae bôdromôô aleou paonene pantiene lymbreklaryz krogeaketoripsarabathaeo pachneuchanôr*, you with terrible eyes, you the doer of all, *Sesengen Barpharaggês* |¹² *omoibasko berôounêr thôbaph thambami opsnôoimphyti sthompsim phiêioindysdômêlelôthe adynaisa ioinathapsaôseu biraarin* |¹⁶ *dalêm azathoathagengê psouane pouratha ̇ ouamôth aeêioyô epeê ôioutheua ̇ yyy iii thesmaoathaa.* Come, speak, enter |²⁰ me Alexandros, whom Didyme bore, appear to me peacefully, by (your) voice, without causing fear.

3 τουραιαρ-: cf. PGM I 133 f. -ρουρραιαλ.

4 αγο͞τα Pap.: interpret as αγατα or αγ`α΄οτα or αγο`α΄τα.

5 Cατραπερκμηφ: cf. PGM XII 185; XIII 917; Delatte-Derchain, *Intailles*, nos. 48, 408 (?), 510; line 2 of the silver amulet from Homs (Syria) published by P.J.Sijpesteijn, *OMRO* 59-60 (1978-1979) 189-192 (= SEG XXVIII 1334); Griffith-Thompson, *Demotic Magical Papyrus*, XVII 19; verso XXII 14 (cf. Betz, *Translation*, pp. 223 and 248). Cf. also PGM O 2, 24 f. Cατραπειν; IV 2485 f. Cατραπαμμων.

As for the final κμηφ, it occurs as a name of the Sun in PGM III 142, 471; IV 1705; as a name of Osiris in IV 2094 (Κμηφι); cf. also VII 583 (Κμηφιc) and col. 17, where Κνηφιc is written within an ouroboros (see Vol. 2, Taf. I, Abb. 4); Audollent, *DT*, 242, 7; and see PGM, Vol. 3 (Index), p. 225. The name is likely to indicate the primitive serpent-deity of Thebes *Km-3t.f* ('he who has completed his age'), on which see Griffiths, *Plutarch's de Iside et Osiride*, p. 374. The interpretation of K.Fr.W.Schmidt, *GGA* 193 (1931) 449 and Th.Hopfner, *Plutarch. Über Isis und Osiris* II (Prague 1941), pp. 100, 101 nn. 2-3, who equated Κμηφ with Egyptian *k3 mwt.f* 'bull of his mother', is probably to be dismissed. For the possible connection of the Theban serpent-god and Chnoubis, see the discussion by H.M.Jackson, *The Lion Becomes Man. The Gnostic Leontomorphic Creator and the Platonic Tradition* (Society of Biblical Literature, Diss. Series 81, Atlanta 1985), pp. 101-103 n. 78. R.K.Ritner (in Betz, *Translation*, p. 22 n. 35), however, interprets κμηφ as Egyptian *ẖm3.f* 'his shrine'.

6 -αμαχθεν: cf. PGM IV 862 αμαχθα; XIII 987 αμαρχθα.

-χρηθ-: cf. PGM XII 116 χρ[η]θ.

7 κρομιορφι: for the ending, cf. PGM XIXa 5 χοου[χ]ορφι.

Θωουθιθωθ: based on Θωθ; cf. **45**, 25, and see W.Brashear, *APF* 36 (1990) 59, comm. on 113-114.

8 Ιαω τεω-: after Ιαω a small oblique scratch in the lead, seemingly accidental. Also possible Ιαωτ εω-; cf. PGM V 141 Ιαωτ, 479 Ιαωθ.

10 -αραβα-: cf. PGM XIII 758 αραβα.

-αχνευ-: cf. PGM XII 169 μα]ρμαραχνευ.

-νωρ: for magical words ending in -ωρ, see PGM, Vol. 3 (Index), p. 277 f.

11 φοβερόμματε: the word occurs in PGM V 437, and on a magical gem (Bonner, *SMA*, p. 168 = Guarducci, *Epigrafia Greca* IV, p. 273): φοβερόμματε Βριμὼ Αρωριφρασι.

πανεργέτ⟨α⟩: elsewhere only in Aesch., *Ag.* 1486, of Zeus.

11-12 Cεcενγεν Βαρφαραγγηc: see **10**, 2 comm.

13 θαμβαμι: cf. PGM IV 1214 θαμβραμι; I 218 f. Αμβραμι.

14 cθομ-: cf. PGM II 15 cθομ and **96 A** 37 cθωμβαυλη.

15 αδυναιcα: possibly for Αδωναι or Αδωναιοc.

ιοινα-: instead of ι̣, perhaps an upright connected with the preceding oblique stroke.

βιρααριν: cf. PGM I 136 βιραθαυ; XIII 952 βιραιθαθι; and IV 2415 αριν.

16 αζαθο- : α' γαθο- ed.pr.   The reading, however, is difficult, since what was written between the two alphas is partially lost in a vertical break of the tablet.

19-22. This section is indented also compared with 1-8.

19 εἰcκρίθητι: the verb εἰcκρίνω (active 'cause to enter', passive 'enter into') is technical for the entry (εἴcκριcιc) of the soul as well as of a daemon into the body; for the latter, cf. Iambl., *Myst.* III 6 (112, 11); 13 (131, 12); Porph., *De philos. ex orac. haur.* II, *apud* Eus., *P.E.* IV 23, 5 (GCS 8.1, p. 214, 23); V 8, 6 (*ibid.*, p. 238, 3) = *Orac. Chald.*, fr. dub. 223, 5 des Places; Psell., *De oper. daem.* 13 (Migne PG 122, 849C = p. 21 Boissonade); and see Dodds, *The Greeks and the Irrational*, p. 295 f. Somewhat different is the sense of εἰcκρίνω in PGM IV 3025, 3083 f. and probably VII 432 ('cause to enter into his proper place'); see K.Preisendanz, *Wiener Studien* 42 (1921) 128; Eitrem, *Some Notes*, p. 16 f.

21 πάνητί μοι (r. φάνηθί μοι) Maltomini, *loc. cit.* : πανάτιμοc ("ganz ohne Ehre") ed.pr. Cf. PGM II 166; IV 999, 1002, 1007, 1015, 1019, 1024, 1041, 1045; VII 331, etc.

εἰρηνικῶc: cf. PGM IV 1041 f. εἴcελθε, φάνηθί μοι, κύριε, ἱλαρόc, εὐμενήc, πραΰc, ἐπίδοξοc, ἀμήνιτοc (also 1045 f.), 1972-74 πραΰc, μειλίχιοc μηδ' ἀντία μοι φρονέοιτο. μηδὲ cὺ μηνίcηc κτλ.; V 44 f. διατήρηcόν με καὶ τὸν παῖδα τοῦτον ἀπημάντουc, 420 ἵλεώc μοι γενοῦ.

22 διὰ φωνῆc: the daemon is supposed to speak articulately and intelligibly. Cf. PGM IV 1032 f. ἀποκρίθητί μοι διὰ τῆc ἱερᾶc cου φωνῆc, ἵνα ἀκούcω δηλαυγῶc; LXXVII 21 f. εὔδηλον χρηματιεῖ.

ἀβόφωc (r. ἀφόβωc): cf. **97** → 9; PGM LXXVII 21 ἀφόβωc, ἀτρόμωc; IV 237 f. μή μου θαμβήcηc τοὺc ὀφθαλμούc, 1062-64 cυντηρήcαc με - - - ἀνειδωλόπληκτον, ἄπληγον, ἀθάμβητον, 1079 f.; LXII 36 f.; Griffith-Thompson, *Demotic Magical Papyrus*, II 14 *aph-'o-b-'o-s* (= ἀφόβωc); XVII 19: "watch this boy, do not let him be frightened, terrified, or scared" (cf. Betz, *Translation*, pp. 197, 223); Kropp, *Koptische Zaubertexte* II, XXXII 44 f.: "Du mögest mir erscheinen in einem Gesichte, das mir nicht Furcht einflößt."

TEXTS OF UNCERTAIN NATURE

Narmouthis   I/II AD

O.Mil. Vogl. inv. 85.

ED.PR.: A.Vogliano, *Secondo rapporto degli scavi condotti dalla missione archeologica
d'Egitto della R. Università di Milano nella zona di Medinet Madi* (Milan 1937), pp.
49-51, nos. 15-16.

COMM.: ed.pr.

DESCR.: ostracon; 7 × 4 cm. Inscribed on both sides. Broken away at the right edge of the
concave side, respectively the bottom edge of the convex side.

LOC.: Istituto di Papirologia, Università degli Studi, Milan.

The writing on both sides is by the same hand, but one cannot be certain
that the two texts are related to each other. Side A is clearly magical. Side B
may be from a medical prescription.

A (concave side)

1   αβλαν[αθαναλβα
         βλαν[αθαναλβ
         λαν[αθαναλ
4   αν[αθανα
         να[θαν
         α[θα
         θ

B (convex side)

1   ⟦δρ⟧[
         νη βοτάνη καὶ ῾ϲ᾽μύρνα
         καὶ ἰϲχάδεϲ καὶ βῆτι ῾ἔκλευκα᾽

(A) *ablanathanalba* (etc.).

(B) - - - herb and myrrh and dried figs and white pennyroyal (?).

A (concave side)

1-7 αβλαν[αθαναλβα in a symmetrical Schwindeschema as e.g. in **9**, 1-7 (see comm.) and **21**, 3-13. The first editor suggested that it is also possible that the Schwindeschema had the following flush-right wing shape:

αβλαν[αθαναλβα
βλαν[αθαναλβα
λαν[αθαναλβα
etc.

This formation can be paralleled for αβλαναθαναλβα (cf. PGM XIXa 29-41; XLIII 1-13), but it can be ruled out here, because the bottom of Side A must be complete, as it corresponds with the left side of B.

B (convex side)

1 ⟦δρ⟧[: not transcribed in the ed.pr.

3 βητι: perhaps βήτι⟨α⟩ for βαίτια. The herb βαίτιον, a kind of pennyroyal, is discussed in Diosc. III 32, 1 (II 41, 14 - 43, 2 Wellmann). On the use of pennyroyal to promote childbirth and abortion, see J.Scarborough, "The Pharmacology of Sacred Plants, Herbs and Roots," in Faraone-Obbink (edd.), *Magika Hiera*, p. 144 f.

ἔκλευκα : ευλευκα (?) ed.pr. The first kappa is not certain, but it is preferable to upsilon. To our knowledge εὔλευκος is attested only as a variant of ἔκλευκος in Athenaeus 679d (III, p. 502, 14 Kaibel).

68

Karanis   III AD

O.Cairo inv. CP 25/8/37/1-2 (9883).
ED.PR.: H.C.Youtie, "Ostraca from Karanis," *ZPE* 16 (1975) 274 (= *Scriptiunculae Post.* I, p. 178).
COMM.: ed.pr.
DESCR.: ostracon; 8 × 5.8 cm. Inscribed on one side only.
LOC.: Egyptian Museum, Cairo (previously Ann Arbor, Michigan, inv. 9883).

Short instructions copied from a formulary for the preparation of an amulet. The instructions now written on the ostracon may have served as the amulet itself. The amulet was to contain magical figures (ζῴδια), vowels and drawings of a woman and a child. "If the latter were perchance intended to represent Isis and the young Horus (Harpocrates), we might think of an amulet for promoting conception, childbirth, or lactation, although the more general purposes of maintaining domestic harmony or preventing illness would not be excluded" (ed.pr.).

1   traces
           ]ως ζῴδια
           οοοοοο εεεεεε
4   γυνή· παιδίν

3 γυνη· Pap.   παιδίον

- - - figures, *οοοοοο εεεεεε*, woman, child.

Fayum   II-V AD[1]

P.Palau Rib. inv. 3.

ED.PR.: G.Michailides, "Papyrus contenant un dessin du dieu Seth à tête d'âne," *Aegyptus*
    32 (1952) 45-53.

REPUBL.: S.Bartina, "Set o el horrendo y gruñidor jabalí verrugoso," *Stud. Pap.* 6 (1967)
    109-121.

COMM.: ed.pr.; Bartina, *loc.cit.*

PHOTO: ed.pr.; Bartina, *loc.cit.*

DESCR.: papyrus; 9 × 13. Four horizontal folds. The writing runs against the fibers, and
    the back is blank. The height of the drawing is 7.5 cm and its maximum breadth is 4.7
    cm. To its left, some 3-4 cm of blank papyrus; below it, about 5.5 cm of blank
    papyrus. Unevenly broken away at the left and right; evenly cut away at the top and
    bottom.

LOC.: Seminario de Papirología de la Facultad Teológica (San Cugat del Vallés), Barcelona
    (previously in the private collection of G.Michailides, Cairo).

It is not certain that the present text is a piece of magic, but it is included
here because the drawing of donkey-headed Seth with bow in left hand and
arrow in right is similar to the drawing of Seth holding a spear in each hand in
col. IV of the demotic section of P.Leiden inv. J 384 (the Greek part of this
papyrus is PGM XII).[2] The demotic text that accompanies the drawing in the
Leiden papyrus consists of instructions for a disjunctive spell (lines 13-26):
among other things one draws the figure of Seth on a potsherd, says
"separate NN, born of NN, from NN, born of NN" repeatedly and deposits
the sherd in the house in which the couple lives. Text, translation and
photograph of this part of the demotic papyrus in J.Johnson, *OMRO* 56
(1975) 38 f. with plate X; translation and drawing also in Betz, *Translation*,

---

[1] A date was not assigned in the ed.pr. Late I BC to early II AD according to Bartina.

[2] For other drawings of Seth (both certain and uncertain ones) in magical texts, see
Moraux, "Une défixion judiciaire," pp. 19-21.

p. 169 f. (PDM xii 62-75); a photograph of the drawing also in PGM, Vol. 2, Tafel II, Abb. 11. Possibly the present text was also a disjunctive charm or part of one, and in light of the folds it might have been an applied one.

The three words that describe the god, cμερδαλέος ἠπύτης θεός, yield the acrostic Cηθ; see *RAC* I, *s.v.* Akrostichis, coll. 235-238 (J.H.Waszink). The poetisms cμερδαλέος 'terrible' and ἠπύτης 'loud-voiced' are appropriate for Seth, the god who 'raises the voice' (*šd ḫrw*) to cause confusion; see *Lexikon der Ägyptologie* V, *s.v.* Seth, coll. 908-911 (H.te Velde); further bibliography on Typhon-Seth in Brashear, *Magica varia*, p. 56 f.

The papyrus apparently contains the first ancient attestation of the nominative form ἠπύτης that has been presupposed on the basis of epic ἠπύτα (*Iliad* 7, 384).

cμερδαλέος
ἠπύτες
θεός

2 ἠπύτης

FORMULARIES

Oxyrhynchos   II-I BC[1]

P.Wash. Univ. II 74.

ED.PR.: Z.M.Packman, "Three Magical Texts from the Washington University Collection.
    2: Description of Magical Figures," *BASP* 13 (1976) 177-179.

REPUBL.: P.Wash. Univ. II 74 (Z.M.Packman).

COMM.: Packman, *locc.citt.*

TRANSL.: Packman, *locc.citt.*; R.Kotansky in Betz, *Translation*, no. CXI.

PHOTO: ed.pr., between pp. 176 and 177.

DESCR.: papyrus; 16 × 10.5 cm. To the left, blank space of 2.5 cm representing most of
    the width of an intercolumniation; to the left of line 9 survives ̣v from a preceding
    column. Part of the top margin is preserved to a height of 1.2 cm. Broken away on all
    other sides. The writing runs along the fibers on the recto; on the verso, written against
    the fibers, remnants of two columns of an account (in P.Wash. it is mistakenly stated
    that the verso is blank).

LOC.: Washington University Library, St. Louis, Missouri. Inv. 139.

An obscure text for which we know of no close parallel. Mention is made
of the Egyptian god Kneph, and he is equated with Greek the "great (?)
modeller" (lines 1-2). There follow instructions to mould (presumably out of
clay or wax) two bulls (3-4) and then to form other magical figures. Whether
these other figures were also to be moulded or whether they were to be drawn
or painted, perhaps on the bodies of the bulls, is not clear.

Restorations proposed in the commentary suggest that at least 10 to 15
letters are missing after the break; the column will therefore have run to at
least 30 letters or 12 cm.

Paragraphus between lines 2 and 3, 4 and 5. First line in ecthesis.

---

[1] So dated in P.Wash. Univ. II at the suggestion of E.G.Turner.

1 . .[. . . .]λοις Αἰγυπτιστὶ Κνη[φ

 Ἑλληνιστὶ δὲ πλάςτης μέγ[ας

 καὶ πλάςας βοῦς δύο ἴςους [

4 καὶ τὰς φύςεις ἄρρενας καὶ . [

 καὶ ἄλλον cχηματοποήςας [

 τὸ cῶμα ὄφεως μὴ ἔχοντο[ς

 ἀλλ' ἐξ ἑκατέρου τοῦ μέρους [

8 [. .] μὲν ἀνθρώπων κεφαλ[άς

 χηναλωπέκων κεφαλάς [πτε-]

 ῥύγων χρυςοειδῶν ἔχον[

 τοὺς ταῖς μορφαῖς κ[

12 ἔχοντα τὸ μὲν cῶμ[α

 μορφὴν ἱέρακος π[

 Αἰγυπτιστὶ εη[

 λεπτὰς ἑρμην[

— — —

2 Ἑλληνιςτὶ: τ ex corr.   5 cχηματοποιήςας

- - - in Egyptian, Knêph - - - in Greek, the great (?) modeller - - - and having modeled two bulls, equal - - - |4 and their natures masculine, and - - - and having formed another - - - the body of a snake which has not one (?) head (?) but at each end - - - |8 - - - heads of men - - - heads of geese - - - golden wings having (?) - - - the shapes - - - |12 having the body - - - the face of a sea (?) hawk - - - in Egyptian eê - - - subtle interpretations (?).

In the following commentary reference is usually made to Packman's republication, P.Wash. Univ. II 74, only. Readings that were correctly rejected there are not referred to here. Reference to the suggestions of other scholars are all *apud* P.Wash.

1 . .[. . . .]λοις or . .[. . . .] coις : [. . . .] . . . . P.Wash.
1-2 Αἰγυπτιστί - - - Ἑλληνιςτί: late ancient syncretism was polyglot. Greek and Egyptian predominated, Hebrew exerted great influence, and other languages (not only human ones) are referred to. Cf. e.g. PGM XII 263-265

ἐπικαλοῦμαί ce κατὰ Αἰγυπτίους· 'Φνω εαι Ιαβωκ', κατὰ δ' Ἰουδαίους· ''Αδωναῖε Cαβαωθ', κατὰ ''Ελληνας· 'ὁ πάντων μόναρχος βασιλεύς', κατὰ δὲ τοὺς ἀρχιερεῖς· 'κρυπτέ, ἀόρατε, πάντας ἐφορῶν', κατὰ δὲ Πάρθους· 'Ουερτω'; XIII 443 f. ἐπικαλοῦμαί ce πάcῃ φωνῇ - - - καὶ πάcῃ διαλέκτῳ and 455-463 ὁ δὲ πρῶτος ἄγγελός ce φωνεῖ ὀρνεογλυφιcτί· 'αραι', ὅ ἐcτιν· 'οὐαὶ τῷ ἐχθρῷ μου' - - - ὁ δὲ ''Ηλιος ὑμνεῖ ce οὕτως ἱερογλυφιcτί· 'Λαϊλαμ'· ἀβραϊcτὶ διὰ τοῦ αὐτοῦ ὀνόματος· 'αναγ Βιαθιαρβαρ κτλ' - - - τὸ δὲ φυcικόν cου ὄνομα αἰγυπτιcτί· 'Αλδαβαειμ' (λέγει τὴν βᾶριν, ἐφ' ἣν ἀναβαίνει ἀνατέλλων τῷ κόcμῳ). For further references, see PGM, Vol. 3 (Index), p. 210 f., *s.vv.* ᾿Αβραϊcτί, Αἰγύπτιος, Αἰγυπτιcτί etc. In Greek literary texts, Αἰγυπτιcτί occurs especially for the purpose of distinguishing between the Greek and Egyptian names of the gods: cf. e.g. Herod. II 46, 79, and 156; Plat., *Tim.* 21E; Plut., *De Iside* 375F. On the bilingual (Egyptian and Greek) magical papyri of which only the Greek sections are included in PGM, see the remarks of J.H.Johnson in Betz, *Translation*, pp. xv-xvii.

1 Κνη[φ : Κν[P.Wash. with reference to R.Merkelbach's suggestion Κν[ηφ. After a certain ν, the lower left of what could easily be η. The possibility that Κνουφι stood here, as was suggested by C.Rine, can now be excluded. On Kneph (= Kmeph), see **66**, 5 comm.

2 πλάcτης μέγ[ας: cf. Porph. *apud* Eus., *P.E.* III 11, 45 (GCS 8, 1, p. 143, 1) τὸν δημιουργόν, ὃν Κνὴφ οἱ Αἰγύπτιοι προσαγορεύουσιν. The term πλάcτης is also appropriate of Kneph as identified with Chnum, the creator god who shaped mankind on a potter's wheel; see *Lexikon der Ägyptologie* I, coll. 950-954 *s.v.* Chnum (E.Otto); L.Koenen, "Die Prophezeiungen des 'Topfers'," *ZPE* 2 (1968) 178 ff.

μέγ[ας or μετ[(Merkelbach).

3 ἴcους [τὸ μέγεθος H.C.Youtie.

4 καὶ τ[ὴν χροιὰν μέλανας M.Totti, if the reference is to the Apis bull, which is generally black; cf. Herod. III 28; Strab. XVII 1, 31; Bonnet, *Reallexikon*, p. 49 f.

5 cχηματοποήcας (r. -ποιήcας): the participle might refer (a) to further three dimensional modeling (cf. 3 πλάcας) or (b) either line-drawing or painting. In the latter case, it could be that the figures are to be drawn or painted on the bodies of the moulded bulls.

At the end of the line, perhaps ἐχέτω] *vel sim.* governing τὸ cῶμα in 6.

6 μὴ ἔχοντο[c κεφαλήν R.Merkelbach : μὴ ἔχοντο[c μόνον μίαν κεφαλήν M.Totti : μὴ ἔχοντο[c μηδένα κέρκον ed.pr.

7 τοῦ μέρους [κεφαλὰc δύο M.Totti : [τρικεφάλου ed.pr.

7-8. It seems likely that lost portions of these lines further defined the expression ἑκατέρου μέρους. The ed.pr. proposed ἐκ δε]ι[ξιᾶc, M.Totti ἐκ δε]ι[ξιῶν; if either suggestion is correct in substance, divide rather δεξι]ι[ᾶc or δεξι]ι[ῶν (see 8 comm.).

8 *init*. [.] : [. . .] P.Wash.
[- - - ἐξ ἀριcτερᾶc ed.pr. : [- - - ἐξ εὐωνύμων M.Totti.

11 μορφαῖc: perhaps 'faces' or 'heads' as was pointed out by M.Totti. Cf. Eus., *P.E.* I 10, 48 f. (GCS 8, 1, p. 53, 4-9) Φοίνικες δὲ αὐτὸ Ἀγαθὸν Δαίμονα καλοῦcιν· ὁμοίως καὶ Αἰγύπτιοι Κνὴφ ἐπονομά-ζουcι· προcτιθέαcι δὲ αὐτῷ ἱέρακος κεφαλὴν - - - καί φηcιν Ἐπήειc ἀλληγορῶν - - - "τὸ πρῶτον ὂν θειότατον ὄφιc ἐcτὶν ἱέρακος ἔχων μορφὴν κτλ."
κ[αὶ ἄλλον R.Merkelbach.

12 cῶμ[α, τὴν δὲ κεφαλὴν εἰc] R.Merkelbach : κροκοδείλου, τὴν δὲ M.Totti. The hawk-headed crocodile (κορκόδειλοc ἱερακοπρόcωποc) occurs in PGM XIII 41, 42 f., 46, 51, 412, 416 and 421; see also P.Perdrizet, "La tunique liturgique historiée de Saqqara," *Monuments Piot* 34 (1934) 105 f.

13 ἱέρακος π[ελαγίου ed. pr. : τι[, as read by V.Schuman, cannot be excluded. For the sea-hawk as one of a set of three heads, cf. PGM IV 3131-35 λαβὼν κηρὸν Τυρρηνικὸν πλάcον ἀνδριάντα παλαιcτῶν γ'. ἤτω δὲ τρικέφαλοc· ἡ μέcη κεφαλὴ ἤτω ἱέρακος πελαγίου, ἡ δὲ δεξιὰ κυνοκεφάλου, ἡ δὲ ἀριcτερὰ ἴβεωc. In Ps.Callisth. I 8, 1 (p. 8 Kroll), Nektanebo sends a dream to Philip by means of a sea-hawk. It is predicted to be a portent in PGM IV 211-213, and its blood is drunk in PGM IV 2597 f. and 2660.

14 *fin*. - - - Ἑλληνιcτί] R.Merkelbach.

15 ἑρμην[: ἑρμη[P.Wash. Perhaps ἑρμην[είαc. In PGM XII 401 ἑρμηνεύματα are Greek translations of the secret code names by which Egyptian temple scribes referred to herbs and other ingredients used in rites.

Provenance   I BC[1]
  unknown

P.Monac. II 28.

ED.PR.: P.Fabrini-F.Maltomini in: P.Lett. Carlini (Pisa 1978), pp. 237-266, no. 34.

REPUBL.: P.Monac. II 28 (P.Fabrini-F.Maltomini).

COMM.: ed.pr.; P.Monac. II 28.

TRANSL.: R.Kotansky in Betz, *Translation*, no. CXVII.

PHOTO: ed.pr., plates XIII a-b; P.Monac. II, fig. 10, pp. 124-126.

DESCR.: papyrus; twenty-three fragments from the bottom of a roll. All are broken away at
    left, top and right, and fr. 1 also at the bottom. All except fr. 1 preserve much of the
    lower margin (maximum height in fr. 20, col. i: 4.3 cm). Fr. 21 shows an inter-
    columnium of 2.5 cm. The writing runs with the fibers on the recto, and the verso is
    blank.

LOC.: Bayerische Staatsbibliothek, Handschriftenabteilung, Munich. Inv. Gr. 216.

The original order of all fragments other than 2 + 21 cannot be ascertained. Also uncertain is the number of preserved columns and original length
of line. Fr. 2 + fr. 21 col. i preserve beginnings and ends of some lines of the
same column; the precise width of the gap that separates the two fragments
cannot be established.

Most of the scraps are too fragmentary to allow one to identify the nature
of their charms. When this is possible, however, we are certainly or probably
dealing with erotic charms (frr. 2 + 21, 5, 9, 11, 14 and 22). Remnants of
poetry are preserved in frr. 18, 19, 22, and probably also 6 and 13.

Different sections are separated by extra space between lines (frr. 10, 11,
17), ecthesis (frr. 9, 17, probably 11), larger size of the first letter (frr. 9, 11,
17) and, at least in fr. 17, paragraphus.

---

[1] Probably the second half of the century. E.G.Turner (*apud* ed.pr., p. 238) suggested a
comparison with P.Oxy. XIV 1635 (44-37 BC) and P.Oxy. XII 1453 (30-29 BC).

Sometimes a blank space is left in the line to indicate a pause in sense (frr. 5, 3; 12, 3; cf. also 14, 2, 4). Elision is not marked (frr. 2, 4; 6, 4; 13, 2; 18, 2; 19, 2 (*bis*?); possibly 20 ii 1). Iota adscript occurs in frr. 12, 3 and 23, 2; it is omitted in frr. 14, 3 and 22, 4, probably in fr. 7, 3, possibly in fr. 7, 4.

Fr. 2 (7.6 × 6.2 cm) + Fr. 21 (6.1 × 5.3 cm)

— — —

```
1                        ] ͵ ͵ [          i                    ii
                     ] ϲιων ελ[            — — —
     οἰκίαν λιπο ͵ [ c. 5 ] ἄνδρα λ[   ]υτου           ͵ [        1
  4  ἥδιϲτα καθεύδιν ὑπ' ἐμοῦ ιξ[     ]αιηϲ καὶ       τοϲε[
     λ ͵ ͵ ͵ ͵ ͵ ͵ τεωϲ γῆ καὶ οὐρανό[ϲ   τελ]έαν ἐπα-   εχ ͵ [
     οιδήν.                                            ϲεμ[       4
```

Fr. 1 (2.1 × 2 cm)   Fr. 3 (2.4 × 5.3 cm)   Fr. 4 (2.4 × 4.6 cm)

```
— — —              — — —                    — — —

1    ] ͵ μυ[        1    ] ͵ ͵ [             1   ] ͵ [
    ]την[              ]ομαι ουδ[               ] ͵ ν βοῦϲ ε ͵ [
    ]ην πρεϲ[β-        ]ενακου ͵ [
                    4    ]φορηϲω ͵ [
    — — —
```

Fr. 5 (4.9 × 5.5 cm)   Fr. 6 (1.5 × 4.2 cm)

```
— — —                                 — — —

1      ] ͵ [   ] ͵ [              1      ] ͵ [
    ] μέλανι κολλήϲ[η                  ]εϲθαι ε[
  ]                  μα[                ]νεχα[
4  ]ειϲ τρύβλιον καινὸ[ν            4   ]κ' ἴθι μο[ι
```

Fr. 2, 4 καθεύδειν   Fr. 5, 3 ante μα[spatium vacuum in Pap.

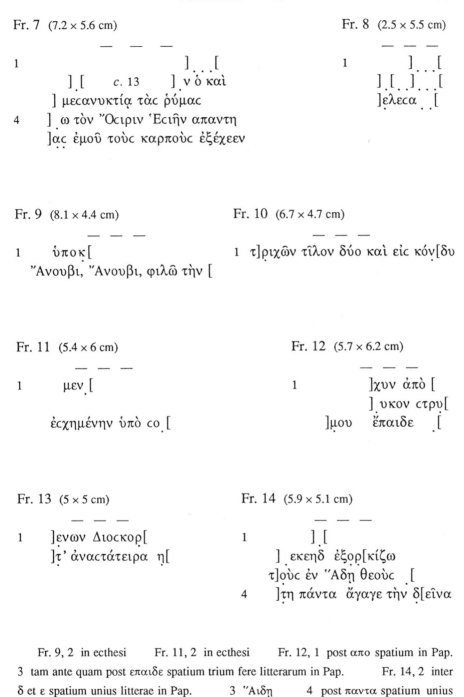

Fr. 7 (7.2 × 5.6 cm)

1   ]...[
    ].[c. 13   ].ν ὁ καὶ
    ] μεcανυκτίᾳ τὰc ῥύμαc
4   ] ω τὸν ῞Οcιριν ῾Εcιῆν απαντη
    ]ας ἐμοῦ τοὺc καρποὺc ἐξέχεεν

Fr. 8 (2.5 × 5.5 cm)

1   ]...[
    ].[.].[...[
    ]ελεcα..[

Fr. 9 (8.1 × 4.4 cm)

1   ὑποκ[
    ῎Ανουβι, ῎Ανουβι, φιλῶ τὴν [

Fr. 10 (6.7 × 4.7 cm)

1 τ]ριχῶν τῖλον δύο καὶ εἰc κόν[δυ

Fr. 11 (5.4 × 6 cm)

1   μεν.[

    ἐcχημένην ὑπὸ cο.[

Fr. 12 (5.7 × 6.2 cm)

1   ]χυν ἀπὸ [
    ] υκον cτρυ[
    ]μου   ἔπαιδε .[

Fr. 13 (5 × 5 cm)

1]ενων Διοcκορ[
    ]τ᾽ ἀναcτάτειρα η[

Fr. 14 (5.9 × 5.1 cm)

1   ].[
    ] .εκεηδ ἐξορ[κίζω
    τ]οὺc ἐν ῞Αδη θεοὺc .[
4]τη πάντα ἄγαγε τὴν δ[εῖνα

Fr. 9, 2 in ecthesi   Fr. 11, 2 in ecthesi   Fr. 12, 1 post απο spatium in Pap.
3 tam ante quam post επαιδε spatium trium fere litterarum in Pap.   Fr. 14, 2 inter
δ et ε spatium unius litterae in Pap.   3 ῞Αιδη   4 post παντα spatium unius
litterae in Pap.

Fr. 15 (1.1 × 4.3 cm)   Fr. 16 (0.9 × 3.9 cm)   Fr. 17 (3 × 6.9 cm)

— — —   — — —   — — —

1   ]μο . [1   ] . νδ[1   δ[
     ]δεςο[   ]λ̣ειτ[——

                                             ἐκγ[
                                             ω[
                                        4   α . [

Fr. 18 (4.9 × 5 cm)   Fr. 19 (6.7 × 5.5 cm)

— — — —   — — — —

1   ] πολυιδρ[.] . . . . . [1   ] . . . . . οι δεινὴν ἀέν[αον
     ] αἴτ' οὐρανὸν ἀςτε[ρόεντα   χαλε]ποῖςίν τ' ἄλγεςιν εντοδυν̣[
     π]ότνια ἀθανάτη τε τ[

Fr. 20 (6.8 × 6.9 cm)   Fr. 21

        i   ii   (see above Fr. 2 + Fr. 21)

                         — — —
                         ηδεκα[1
                         ουςιν[
         — — —
1   ]ρθεις δ[

Fr. 22 (6.8 × 5.9 cm)   Fr. 23 (6.3 × 5.2 cm)

— — — —   — — — —

1   ] . ακρα[1   ]νουκ . [
     ] . . ςο . ορ[. . .] . ς καὶ [   ] αὐτῶι ὡςεὶ πῶμα κ . [
     ]τε κελαινὴ τήν ςε τεκοῦ[ςαν   ]ηι λάβε αὐτό. ἔςτιν γὰρ [
4   ]αςιν ἀγρυπνίαν δότε τῆ δῖνα . [

     Fr. 17, 2 in ecthesi   Fr. 22, 4 δεῖνα

Fr. 1 - - - the elder (?) - - -. Frr. 2 + 21 i - - - house, abandoning her husband - - - to sleep with me (?) very sweetly, by me - - - and - - - so long as (?) earth and heaven - - - (fulfill) this charm completely. Fr. 4 - - - a cow - - -. Fr. 5 - - - (so that) she join (her black) to my black - - - into a new cup - - -. Fr. 6 - - - come to me - - -. Fr. 7 - - - also called (?) - - - in the middle of the night the streets - - - Osiris *Hesiês* - - - my fruits, he (?) poured out - - -. Fr. 8 - - - fulfill (?) - - -. Fr. 9 - - - what is prescribed below (?) - - - "Anubis, Anubis, I love her, NN (?) - - -. Fr. 10 - - - pluck two hairs and (put them) into a drinking-vessel - - -. Fr. 11 - - - her, possessed by you (?) - - -. Fr. 12 - - - from - - - speak the spell - - -. Fr. 13 - - - daughter of Zeus (?) - - - overthrower - - -. Fr. 14 - - - whom NN bore (?) I adjure - - - by the gods in Hades - - - all, drive her, NN - - - -. Fr. 18 - - - of much knowledge - - - who (live) in the starry heaven - - - mistress and immortal - - -. Fr. 19 - - - dreadful, everlasting - - - with grievous sufferings and with pains (?) - - -. Fr. 20 - - - and Hecate (?) - - -. Fr. 22 - - - black, her who bore you - - - give insomnia to her, NN - - -. Fr. 23 - - - on it as a cover - - - take it, for it is - - -.

Frr. 2 + 21.

Fr. 2 preserves the beginnings of lines whose ends appear in fr. 21 col. i. The size of the gap that separates the two fragments cannot be established; just possibly it should be filled by the damaged fr. 8 (see fr. 8, 3 comm.).

2-6. Logos of an erotic spell. Many details cannot be ascertained, but the general sense is clear: the woman must abandon her husband and come to the lover.

3 οἰκίαν: probably the house where the beloved is to join the lover (line 2 ἐλ[θεῖν ?); cf. e.g. PGM IV 2756 f. ἡ δ(εῖνα) ἥκοι ἐπ' ἐμαῖcι θύραιcι; 2909; Audollent, *DT*, 271, 7 f.; also Theocr. 2, 17, 22, etc. ἴυγξ, ἕλκε τὸ τῆνον ἐμὸν ποτὶ δῶμα τὸν ἄνδρα. Otherwise the reference might be to the house that the woman should leave; cf. PGM O 2, 27-31 πύρωcον τὴν ψυχὴν 'Αλλοῦτος - - - ἕωc ἀποcτῇ ἀπὸ τῆc οἰκίαc 'Απολλωνίου.

λιπο [: the traces are minimal. In all likelihood the feminine participle, possibly accusative λιποῦc[αν (see 4 comm.); after this, probably τὸν. Cf. **45**, 47 f.

]υτου: e.g. μετ' ἐμα]υτοῦ.

4 καθεύδιν (r. -ειν): the infinitive and the possible λιποῦc[αν in 3 could be governed by something like ποίηcον or ποιήcατε (cf. e.g. **45**, 46; PGM XVI 3, 11, 19, etc.; XXXVI 147). For the phrase ἥδιcτα καθεύδειν, cf. Plat., *Crit.* 43B and Soph., *Trach.* 175 (εὕδειν).

ιξ[: perhaps a form of ἰξύc.

5 λ . . . . τεωc: first the foot of an upright; then the base of an oval (as of ε, θ, o, c); then minimal traces. At the end of the sequence, perhaps τέωc (= ἕωc), in which case the reference might be to a love that is to endure eternally like heaven and earth (for these as symbols of eternity, cf. e.g. NT Matth. 5, 18; D.H., *Ant. Rom.* VI 95, 2; Aster. Amas., *Homil.* X 5 [p. 138, 11 f. Datema]; also Theogn. 252); we would then have a reinforcement of the usual request for life-long love (cf. e.g. **38**, 12 f.; **39**, 12 f.; **46**, 26; **48** J 14; **49**, 80, etc.). Another possible articulation is (-)τε ὡc, in which case there may be a comparison to the love which linked Sky and Earth.

5-6 τελ]έαν ἐπαλοιδήν: certainly preceded by an imperative of τελέω (see below, fr. 8, 3 comm.). For this common formula, see **45**, 53 comm.; cf. also **73** ii 18.

Fr. 3.

3]ενακου .[: a form of ἐνακούω (unattested elsewhere in the Greek magical papyri) or rather]εν ἀκου .[.

. [: o or c.

4 . [: at the break, a vertical.

Fr. 4.

2 βοῦc: the animal (always feminine) is usually mentioned in praxeis (cf. e.g. PGM I 5; III 383; IV 909; XIII 129, 361, etc.). It could, however, be that it is here mentioned in a series of divine 'symbols' (cημεῖα or cύμβο-λα), as in PGM VII 780, where βοῦc is a symbol of Mene.

. [: γ, η, π possible.

Fr. 5.

2] μέλανι κολλῆc[η: cf. the passages cited in **38**, 12 comm. On τὸ μέλαν as pubic hair, see Henderson, *The Maculate Muse*, p. 143, § 163a.

3. The blank space in the line may mark a transition from logos to praxis; or else the beginning of a new charm.

4]ειc: probably] ειc, but also a second pers. sing. ending is possible. καινό[ν: see **97** ↓ 25 comm.

Fr. 6 (logos).

1] . . [: a vertical followed by a round letter.

3]νεχα[: e.g. τύραν]νε, κοίρα]νε or παρθέ]νε χα[ῖρε.

4]κ' ἴθι μο[ι: certainly addressed to a divinity; cf. PGM IV 2543, 2548 δεῦρ' ἴθι μοι; III 249 δεῦρ' ἴθι. As for]κ', one might think of Homeric βάσκ' ἴθι.

Fr. 7 (logos).

1] ͟ ͟ [: the base of a round letter; an upright; a short oblique that descends from left to right.

3-4. Possibly in reference to Isis wandering the roads by night in search of Osiris after his death.

3 μεσανυκτίᾳ: the spelling μεσαν- (in place of μεσον-) occurs in PGM XIII 123 (cf. app.cr.); P.Oxy. XIV 1768, 6; *v.l.* in NT Marc. 13, 35 and Luc. 11, 5. Cf. modern Greek τὰ μεσάνυχτα, and see Blass-Debrunner-Funk, *Grammar*, § 35.2. The dative singular of the adjective (probably agreeing with ὥρᾳ lost in the lacuna) seems likelier than the plural of τὸ μεσονύκτιον (on the tendency of compound adjectives to form a special feminine in later Greek, see Blass-Debrunner-Funk, *Grammar*, § 59; Gignac, *Grammar* II, pp. 105-111). Midnight was, of course, an appropriate time for many magical operations: cf. PGM VII 435; XIa 4; also IV 447, 1968 f., 2091 f.; and see W.Speyer, *Mittag und Mitternacht als heilige Zeiten in Antike und Christentum*, in: *Vivarium. Festschrift Th.Klauser* (JbAC Ergänzungsband 11, Münster 1984), pp. 314-326 (with literature).

4] ͟ : probably τ, but γ, ν possible.

Ἐςιῆν: from Egyptian ḥsy, literally 'praised'. The word is frequently an epithet of Osiris (cf. e.g. PGM XII 80 f.; also IV 875; V 270, 273). It can also indicate a person or animal made divine by drowning (cf. PGM III 1 f.) or merely by immersion; see esp. J.Quaegebeur, *ZPE* 24 (1977) 246-250; idem, *Orient. Lovan. Period.* 8 (1977) 138-142.

απαντη(-): a form of ἀπαντάω or cognates; or else ἀπάντη.

5 ἐμοῦ τοὺς καρποὺς ἐξέχεεν: the context is hard to discern, but one should probably assume that τοὺς καρπούς is the object of a verb in lacuna and that the object of ἐξέχεεν followed. ἐμοῦ indicates that the line is part of a logos.

Fr. 8.

3]ελεϲα ͟ ͟ [: perhaps τ]ελέϲατε (but the last two letters are illegible). If so, it would be tempting to place fr. 8 between fr. 2 and fr. 21 in such a way

as to have τ]fr.8,3ελέςατε [μοι τελ]fr.21i3έαν έπαlfr.2,6οιδήν. Examination of the physical condition of the fragments provides no lead.

Fr. 9.

Ecthesis of line 2 and larger size of the first letter of Άνουβι indicate the beginning of a new section, namely a logos.

1 ὑποκ[: since we are near the end of the praxis, one might consider a supplement such as ὑποκ[άτω (cf. e.g. PGM VII 359 γράφε εἰς αὐτὸ τὸ ὑποκάτω ὄνομα) or ὑποκ[είμενον *vel sim.* (cf. e.g. PGM VII 364 λέγε ζ' τὸν ὑποκείμενον λόγον; also XXXVI 2, 72, 102, 362; **94**, 19, 24, 28, 31).

2 Άνουβι: for Anubis in love spells (see the following note), cf. PGM XVIIa 3; also IV 340 and the parallel texts **46**, 3; **47**, 3; **48** J 3; **49**, 10.

φιλῶ τὴν [: erotic charm. In all likelihood [δεῖνα. The only passages in which the lover mentions his love are PGM IV 1540-43 ὡς ἐγώ ςε κατακάω καὶ δυνατὴ εἶ, ὅυτω ἧς φιλῶ, τῆς δεῖνα, κατάκαυςον τὸν ἐγκέφαλον, and, apparently, **72** fr. 1. See also **72** ii 1-25 comm.

Fr. 10 (praxis).

Wider interlinear space above 1 marks the beginning of a new section.

1. Hairs of animals and persons were frequently used as *ousia* in magical praxeis; cf. **48**, 7, 21 and the parallel texts **49**, 20 f., 26 f.; **50**, 2 f., 21 f.; **51**, 1 f.; PGM I 4; V 386-388; Griffith-Thompson, *Demotic Magical Papyrus*, verso XVII 6 (cf. Betz, *Translation*, p. 246); Luc., *Dial. mer.* 4, 4; Apul., *Metam.* III 16; Psell., *De oper. daem.* 21 (Migne PG 122, 869A = p. 32 Boissonade). Hair was found attached to **40**, PGM XVI, XIXa, and the Athenian lead tablet published by D.R.Jordan, *Hesperia* 54 (1985) 251-255 = "Survey" no. 38 (at p. 251 he refers to an unpublished defixio from Egypt in the Ashmolean Museum). See *RAC* XIII, *s.v.* Haar, col. 179 f. (B.Kötting).

κόν[δυ or κον[δύλιον.

Fr. 11.

1 μεν [: probably μενυ[.

2. Ecthesis, larger size of the first letter, and extra interlinear space indicate the beginning of a new section.

έςχημένην: probably of a woman 'possessed' by a man; cf. PGM XIII 320 f. ἐὰν θέλῃς γυναῖκά ςου μὴ ςχεθῆναι ὑπὸ ἄλλου ἀνδρός (cf. Betz, *Translation*, p. 181 n. 73 for the articulation γυναῖκά ςου).

co [: a high point at the edge, suggestive of υ. If cου, it refers either to the user of the spell (praxis) or to a god (logos).

Fr. 12 (praxis).

2] : ε or c, not λ.

λ]ευκὸν cτρύ[χνον? Theophrastus (*H.P.* IX 11, 6) mentions a kind of cτρύχνον (called μανικόν) whose *white* root causes madness; see also Diosc. IV 73 (II 231 f. Wellmann). Note that in Diosc. IV 70 [RV] (II 228, 7 Wellmann) another kind of cτρύχνον, a black one normally called cτρύχνον κηπαῖον, is labeled cτρύχνοc μέλαc κηπαῖοc. But other supplements are possible, e.g. οἶνον λ]ευκὸν cτρυ[φνόν or] cῦκον cτρυ[φνόν.

3 ἔπαιδε: the blank spaces before and after the word indicate pauses in sense; probably the praxis ended before the imperative and the logos (the same epode that ends in frr. 2 + 21 col. i?) began after it. For the imperative λέγε between praxis and logos, cf. PGM I 94 λέγε δέ; also VII 333.

[: a piece of writing that resembles a sort of tau with a horizontal stroke joining the left of its foot. It is like no other letter in the text; a magical sign?

Fr. 13 (logos).

1 Διοcκορ[: either Διόcκορ[οι or Διὸc κόρ[η. On the popularity of the Dioscuri in Graeco-Roman Egypt, see H.C.Youtie, *ZPE* 16 (1975) 272 f. (= *Scriptiunculae Post.* I, p. 176 f.). On the latter possibility, see the following note.

2 ἀναcτάτειρα: an otherwise unattested feminine of the rare ἀναcτατήρ 'overthrower' (Aesch., *Sept.* 1015, *Ch.* 303; cf. also ἀναcτάτηc in *Ag.* 1227). In the present text the adjective possibly refers to Hecate (for Hecate as causing turmoil in nature, cf. Verg., *Aen.* VI 256 f.; Luc., *Philops.* 22, *Nec.* 9 f.; also Ap. Rh. III 1218 and Sen., *Oed.* 570 f.; for magical texts, cf. esp. PGM IV 2244 ἀναcτατοῦcα πάντα, on which see K.Preisendanz, *Byz. Jahrb.* 4, 1923, 406; cf. also Hecate's epithet ῥηξίχθων). If Hecate is meant here (cf. also below, frr. 19, 1 comm. and 20 ii 1 comm.), Διὸc κόρ[η is preferable in line 1. Hecate was commonly identified with Artemis; and already in the classical and Hellenistic periods there were traditions about her being a daughter of Zeus and the following consorts: Demeter (Call., fr. 466 Pfeiffer); Hera (Sophr., p. 161 Kaibel); Pheraia (Σ Theocr. 2, 35/36a, p. 278, 11-12 Wendel; Σ Lycophr. 1180, p. 341, 7-8 Scheer). See J. Heckenbach, *RE* VII.2, *s.v.* Hekate, col. 2772.

The *nomina agentis* in -τήρ (-τώρ), fem. -τειρα, proliferate in the poets of the Hellenistic and Roman periods, who freely use the endings to coin new nouns; an impressive contribution is made by the Orphic hymns, with their long series of epithets (see Ernst Fraenkel, *Geschichte der griechischen Nomina agentis auf* -τήρ, -τωρ, -της (-τ-) I, Strasbourg 1910, p. 124 f.). Possibly, then, ἀναcτάτειρα belonged to a poetic section, in iambics (the same rhythm could be recognized in 1).

Fr. 14 (logos from an erotic spell).

2] ̣ : the horizontal of γ or τ.

] εκενδ: possibly ὅν or ἥν ἔ]τεκε ἡ δ(εῖνα), which presupposes that the usual abbreviation ⌰ was here executed incompletely; cf. PGM IV 2756 f., where MAINOMENHHΔHKAI was convincingly interpreted by Preisendanz as μαινομένη ἡ δ(εῖνα) ἥκοι. In fr. 22, 4 we have the full form δῖνα, but the scribe need not have been consistent (cf. e.g. **72** and **79**). We might have here the earliest attestation of the formula ὅν (ἥν) ἔτεκε NN in magical texts (see **73** ii 11 comm.). On the formula, see D.R.Jordan, *Philologus* 120 (1976) 127-132.

3 τ]οὺς ἐν ῞Αδη (ῑ. ῞Αιδη) θεούς: possibly the authorities by whom a daemon (cf. singular ἄγαγε in 4) is adjured. If so, ἐξορκίζω was here constructed with a double accusative. For the expression οἱ ἐν ῞Αιδη θεοί, cf. Audollent, *DT*, 22, 44 f.; 23, 4 f.; 29, 30; 30, 36; 31, 29; also **52**, 11 f.

4]τη or]γη.

πάντα: possibly used of 'everything' that the above mentioned gods in Hades can do or over which they are in charge. On this hyperbolic style in Greek prayer, see Keyßner, *Gottesvorstellung*, pp. 30-34.

Fr. 18 (logos in dactylic hexameters).

1-3. To whom this refers cannot be determined: Aphrodite? Hecate (-Selene)? Isis?

2 αἴτ' οὐρανὸν ἀcτε[ρόεντα: a common Homeric formula.

3 π]ότνια ἀθανάτη τε: either the part up to the feminine caesura, or the final three feet. The sequence does not seem to be attested elsewhere.

Fr. 19 (logos in dactylic hexameters).

1] ̣ ̣ ̣ ̣οι: minimal traces of the bottoms of three letters; οι could be ωι.

δεινὴν ἀέν[αον: if the adjectives refer to a divinity (as seems probable), it is most likely Hecate. There are five occurrences of feminine δεινή of a goddess in PGM; four of them refer to Hecate: IV 1404, 2530 (but see app.cr.), 2542, 2611; and cf. also IV 2729 and 2800. Hecate's name is perhaps to be read in fr. 20 ii 1; see also above, fr. 13, 2 comm.

2 χαλε]ποῖcίν τ' ἄλγεcιν εντοδυν[: the nexus χαλεπὸν ἄλγοc is Homeric, cf. *Il.* 5, 384; *Od.* 2, 193; 11, 582; 22, 177; also Theogn. 555 and 1178a. The interpretation of the final sequence is problematic. An articulation ἔντο seems to lead nowhere. Better ἔν τ' ὀδύν[ηcι (κακῆcι?; cf. Hom., *Od.* 9, 440 f. ὀδύνηcι κακῆcι / τειρόμενοc), which, however, implies a hexameter without caesura (unless χαλεποῖcίν τ' ‖ ἄλγεcιν; cf. Call., *Epigr.* 41, 1-2 Pfeiffer [= 4 Gow-Page; see note *ad loc.*]).

Fr. 20.
The last line of col. i is lower than the last line of col. ii. Possibly in col. ii the writer reached the end of a section and left a line blank (as in frr. 10, 11, 17).

Col. ii 1 ηδεκα[: perhaps ἠδ' Ἑκά[τη among other possibilities. See above, frr. 13, 2 comm.; 19, 1 comm.

Fr. 22 (logos from an erotic spell).
3. Here the text presents dactylic rhythm, and κελαινή is a poetic word. Line 4 is prose, which means either that 3 ended a poetic section or that it is a metrical fossil (cf. e.g. PGM III 552 f., 557 f.; IV 385 f.; 3102 f.; and see PGM, Vol. 2, p. XIII f.). To whom (or to what) ce refers cannot be established.

4 ἀγρυπνίαν δότε τῇ δῖνα (r. δεῖνα): that 'a certain woman' is to suffer from sleeplessness makes it certain that we are dealing with an erotic spell. For the motif of sleeplessness in other contexts, cf. **53**, 18; also PGM LXX 24 f.

Fr. 23 (praxis).
1 [: a vertical at the edge.
2 ὡcεὶ πῶμα: 'as a cover' rather than 'as a drink'. Cf. e.g. Paul. Aegin. V 24 (CMG IX.2, p. 22, 20) ἐπιθείc τε πώματοc δίκην τῷ ἀγγείῳ κόcκινον; also VI 86 (CMG IX.2, p. 128, 4) οἷον πῶμά τι; Gal., *De instr. odor.* 5, 4 (CMG Suppl. V, p. 48, 28) ὥcπερ πῶμά τι; Ps.Gal., *Rem.* 2, 24 (XIV 468, 3 K.) ὡc πῶμα. Perhaps something like ἐπίθεc] αὐτῷ ὡcεὶ πῶμα κτλ.

Abusir el Melek   Plate V   Augustan Age

P.Berol. inv. 21243.

ED.PR.: W.Brashear, "Ein Berliner Zauberpapyrus," *ZPE* 33 (1979) 261-278, with corrigenda in *ZPE* 35 (1979) 152.

COMM.: ed.pr.; (col. i 1-14) C.A.Faraone, *Phoenix* 44 (1990) 230-238; (i 6-8) R.Janko, *ZPE* 72 (1988) 293; (i 8-9, ii 1) F.Maltomini, *ZPE* 74 (1988) 247 f.; (i 24, 25-26, ii 15, 16, 19) idem, *Civ. Class. Crist.* 1 (1980) 375 f.

TRANSL.: ed.pr.; H.D.Betz, *Translation*, no. CXXII; (i 1-14) C.A.Faraone, *art. cit.*, 234.

PHOTO: S.Schoske *et al.*, *Schönheit – Abglanz der Göttlichkeit. Kosmetik im Alten Ägypten* (Schriften aus der Ägyptischen Sammlung 5, Munich 1990), p. 148.

DESCR.: papyrus, from mummy cartonnage. A large sheet (33.9 × 29.7 cm) and five small unplaced fragments. The writing runs with the fibers on the recto, and the verso is blank. Two columns of different width are preserved (col. i ± 8.5 cm; col. ii ± 17 cm). Upper margin 3.4 cm; left 2-3 cm; lower col. i 3 cm, col. ii 1.5 cm; right 2.5-3 cm; intercolumnium 0.6-2.2 cm. A kollesis 16.2 cm from the left margin.

LOC.: Ägyptisches Museum, Berlin.

The text falls into five sections: col. i 1-5 remarks explaining the source of the charms; 5-14 love charm; 15-27 love charm; col. ii 1-25 love charm in three parts; 26-30 charm against headache. The sections are separated by a wavy line. The whole preface (i 1-5) is in ecthesis, and so are the opening lines of each section and subsection (i 15, ii 1, 4, 9), with the exception of ii 26. The initial letter of i 1 and that of ii 1 are larger than normal.

The first love charm consists of an incantation in hexameters (i 6-14). This is dealt with between the translation and the commentary.

Diaeresis on ι in i 7. Elision unmarked (i 9, 10, 23, ii 6). In the hexameters i 6-14, scriptio plena in 10 μαίνοιτο ἐπ', 11 ἦτε ἐν, 12 ἦ ἐν; in the iambic trimeter ii 2, scriptio plena καὶ ἀγρυπνία. Iota adscript is inconsistently written, but never in error. ⳤ for δεῖνα in i 19 (*bis*), 20, 23, ii 22; the full form in i 16, 17, ii 7 (*bis*), 11, 21, 30. καί is abbreviated in ii 13, 16, fr. 3, 1.

col. i

1 ἐξαγωγὴ ἐπῳδῶν ἐκ τῆc εὑρεθείcηc
  ἐν Ἡλίου{c} πόλει ἐν τῆ ἱερᾳ βύβλωι τῆι καλου-
  μένη Ἑρμοῦ ἐν τῶι ἀδύτωι Αἰγυπτίοιc
4 γράμμαcιν καὶ διερμηνευθέντων Ἑλληνι-
  κοῖc. ἐπὶ μήλο[υ] ἐπῳδή· τρίc·
  βα[λ]ῶ μή[λ]οιc [c. 4]δώcω τόδε φάρμα-
  κ[ον] καίριον αἰεὶ βρωτὸν θνητοῖc ἀν-
8 θρώποιc καὶ ἀθανάτοιcι θεοῖcιν. ᾗ ἂν
  δῶ μήλῳ τ' ἔβαλον μήλῳ τε πατάξω,
  πάντα ὑπερθεμένη μαίνοιτο ἐπ' ἐμῆι
  φιλότητι, ἤτε ἐν χειρὶ λαβο[ῦ]cα φάγοι
12 . . . . ἢ ἐν κόλπωι καθῆται μὴ
  παύcαιτο φιλῶν με. Κυπρογένεια τέλει
  τελέαν ἐπαοιδήν.
  φ . . . cται [c. 9] θελεηλε τα
16 ε . [ ]ται[ ] δ. ἔλαβόν cου [τὸ ὄ]μμα. ὁ δε⟨ῖ⟩να·
  ἔλαβόν cου [τὴ]ν ψυχήν. ὁ δεῖ[να· c. 5]μην cου
  τοῦ αἵματοc. [ὁ δ(εῖνα)·] ἐχρηcάμη[ν cου c. 7]
  ὁ δ(εῖνα)· κατέφα[γόν] cου τὸ ἧπαρ. ὁ δ(εῖνα)· [c. 5]cά-
20 μην cου τ[ὸ δέ]ρμα. ὁ δ(εῖνα)· ἐποίηcα. ἡ θεὰ ἡ
  ἐν τῶι οὐρ[αν]ῶι αὐτὸν προκ[α]τῖδε καὶ ἐ[γ]έ-
  νετο αὐτῶ[ι π]άντα κατὰ ψυχὴν [.] . . . .
  ὁ δ(εῖνα)· ἀφ' ἧc ἡ[μ]έραc ⟨καὶ⟩ ὥραc cοι [. . .]
24 ναν . [ ]θεῖcα ἡ cταθειc[?]' ἔμπεc[.] εἰc ἔρωτα,
  εἰc φιλ[ί]αν [κ]αὶ εἰc ⟨c⟩τοργὴν [. . .] . [. .]
  ἀποθάνω. [ὦ] πότνια θεὰ ι[c. 8]εραιωι
  τέλεcόν μ[οι] τελέαν ἐπαοιδήν.

col. ii

1 ἄραc τὰc χεῖραc π[ρὸc] τὰ ἄcτρα κατάcειε λέγω[ν c. 8] . . εινα
  καὶ [3-5]

Col. i 1-5 in ecthesi   1-3 vid. comm.   5 post κοιc spatium trium fere litterarum
in Pap.   7 αϊ ειβρωτον Pap.   9 τε βάλω   τεπαταξᾶⁱ⁾] Pap.   11 εἴτε   15
in ecthesi   19 (bis), 20 д̄ Pap.   21 προκατειδε   23 д̄ Pap.
    Col. ii 1 in ecthesi

καὶ νὺξ μέλαινα καὶ cτάcιc καὶ ἀγρυπνία καὶ εμη[c. 9   ]δο-
    κρεμωι ὑπ[3-5]

χρηc ἴδη πρὶν ἥλιον.

4   λαβὼν μύρον ἔπαcον καὶ χρεῖcον τὸ πρόcωπον· cὺ εἶ τὸ μ[ύ-]
    ρ[ο]ν ᾧ ἡ Εἶcιc χρε[ι]cαμένη

ἐπορεύθη εἰc τὸν τοῦ Ὀcείριοc κόλπον τοῦ αὐτῆ[c ἀνδρὸc καὶ
    ἀδ]ελφοῦ καὶ ἔδωκαc αὐτῇ{c}

τὴν χάριν ἐπ' ἐκείνη τῆι ἡμέρᾳ· δόc μοι ταcε[c. 10   ] ταc
    [c. 10   ]

η[.] . [c. 25   ]ειρε τὸν δεῖνα ἢ τὴν δεῖνα. δέc[ποι-]

8   να ᵓΙcι τέλει τελέαν ἐπαοιδήν.

χαῖρε Ἥλιε, χαῖρε ἀνατέλλων, χαιρέτωcαν δὲ οἱ cὺν coὶ ἀναθέλ-
    λοντεc θεοί,

χαιρέτω δὲ κ . . . . . . · οὐ περὶ θ . [.] οὐ περ[ὶ   c. 20   o]ὐδὲ

περὶ ἀργυρίου ἀλλὰ περὶ τοῦ δεῖνα τ[c. 30   ]

12   μένει· κατατρ[έ]χω, αὐτὸc δέ με φεύγει [c. 25   ]

θέντα coι τὴν δ[.] . . . κ(αὶ) ποιήcαντά cε βαc . . [c. 5]ε . νοc . .
    [c. 10   ]

ἀνατολῶν μήτε δύcεων μήτε . . . . ν . [c. 10   ]φ[.]τι μὴ πίοι
    μ[ήτε]

καθίcαι μήτε [.] ωcαι ἀλλὰ ἔχοι με ἐν . [c. 25   ]

16   κ(αὶ) ἄδημοc ἤτω ἕωc ἂν πρὸc ἐμὲ ἕωc [c. 25   ]

αἰώνιον θεῖον [c. 5] . τον[. . .] μὴ ε . . [c. 8] . . . . [c. 6]

ἐντολ . [.] . . [.] . . ἐὰν μὴ [c. 18   ]εμη ημω[c. 6]

ἐὰν διαλίποιc [.]ε . . βαcαν[ι]ῶ cε ἕωc ἂν πρὸc ἐμὲ ἔλθ[η]c καὶ
    πορεύ[η   c. 5   ]

20   traces   traces   αν . [.]δεκ . ε   traces   [c. 5]

. . . . τὸν δε[ῖ]να ἀγάγηc ['Η]λιε . ι . [.]ωcα   traces   [c. 5]

τὴν αἰεὶ εμ[.] . . . . ηι . ον ἡμέρᾳ τὸν δ(εῖνα) . . . . ονε . υμαι αμφ .

εζωμαι χα . [.] . . . traces   [.] . μαι .   traces   μαιτον . νειδη .

24   επαν . . . πα   traces   [.] . εαν καὶ . [c. 8   ] . . πότνια

Κυπρογένεια τέλει τελέαν ἐπαοιδήν.

⌒

3 χρήcη πρὶν ἴδηc ἥλιον?   4 in ecthesi   χρῖcον   ειcιc: alterum c ex

corr., l. ᵓΙcιc   χριcαμένη   5 Ὀcίριοc   8 ἐπαοιδήν: ο ex corr. (ex γ?)

9 in ecthesi   ἀνατέλλοντεc   13 κ̄ Pap.   16 κ̄ Pap.   22 Δ̄ Pap.

πρὸς κεφαλαλγίαν· Ὄcειρις πονεῖ τὴν κεφαλήν, ὁ Ἄμ[μων
πο]νεῖ τοὺς κροτάφους τῆς
κεφαλῆς, Ἡ[c]ενεφθυς πο[ν]εῖ τὸ περίμετρον τῆς κεφαλ[ῆ]ς.
οὐ μὴ παύcηται [Ὄc]ειρι[c]
28   πονῶν τὴν κεφαλήν, οὐ μὴ παύcηται ὁ Ἄμμων πονῶν τοὺς
κροτάφους τῆς κεφαλῆς,
οὐ μὴ παύcητ[αι Ἡc]ενεφθυ[c πονοῦcα] τὸ περίμετρον τῆς
κεφαλῆc, ἕωc παύcηται
πρῶτον ὁ δεῖνα πάντ [c. 9]

26 Ὄcιρις   27 Ὄcιρις   30 post lacunam spatium vacuum in Pap.

Fr. 1 (5.2 × 0.8 cm)   ] δειν`ε′ ου ἐγὼ φιλῶ αυ [

Fr. 2 (1.5 × 1 cm)   ] ιο ἐὰν [

Fr. 3 (4.4 × 1 cm)   ] ειλωι κ(αὶ) λάβοι ο [
                           ] θαι Ἥλιε ε [

Fr. 4 (1 × 1.5 cm)   ] cα [

Fr. 5 (1.2 × 0.5 cm)   ]νημε[

Fr. 6 (1.6 × 0.3 cm)   ] cε τον[

Fr. 3, 1 ϙ Pap.

(Col. i) Publication of charms from the 〈 〉 (?) found in Heliopolis, in the holy book called 'of Hermes', in the innermost shrine, (written) in Egyptian |4 letters and translated into Greek.

Charm by means of an apple. Three times. "I shall throw apples - - - I shall give (?) this always timely love spell to eat both for mortal people |8 and immortal gods. The woman to whom I give it and at whom I throw the apple and whom I hit with the apple, setting everything else aside, may she fall madly in love with me, whether she, taking it in her hand, eats it |12 - - - or places it in her bosom, and may she not stop loving me. O goddess born in Cyprus, fulfill this charm completely."

- - - |16 - - - NN (?) (says): "I have taken your eye." NN (says): "I have taken your soul." NN (says): "I have tasted (?) your blood." NN (says): "I have used - - -." NN (says): "I have devoured your liver." NN (says): "I have - - - |20 your skin." NN (says): "I have done it." The goddess in heaven looked down upon him, and everything happened according to the wish of his soul - - -. NN (says): "From the day and from the hour - - - |24 - - - or standing (?), falling (?) in love, friendship and affection - - - until (?) I die." O lady goddess Isis (?) - - - fulfill this charm completely.

(Col. ii) Having raised the hands toward the stars, move them saying: - - - and black night and trouble and sleeplessness and - - - you shall use before you see the sun. |4 Having taken perfume, chant and anoint your face: "You are the perfume with which Isis anointed herself when she went to the bosom of Osiris, her husband and brother, and you gave charm to her on that day. Give me - - - him, NN, or her, NN. Mistress |8 Isis, fulfill this charm completely.   Hail Helios, hail you who rise, hail to the gods who rise with you, and hail also to - - -. (I pray you ?) not for appearance (?), not for - - -, nor for money, but about him, NN, - - - he does not (?) |12 remain, I am running and he flees from me - - - who assigned (?) to you the - - - and made you - - - neither of rising nor of setting nor - - - may he not drink nor sit down nor eat (?), but may he have me in his mind (?) - - - |16 and let him be abroad until he comes to me - - - everlasting divine - - - if you (?) do not - - - if you wait - - - I shall torture you until you come to me and go - - - |20 - - - that you bring him, NN, o Helios - - - the always - - - today (?) him, NN, - - - bronze - - - |24 - - -. O lady goddess born in Cyprus, fulfill this charm completely."

Against headache. "Osiris has a headache, Ammon has a pain in the temples of his head, Esenephthys has a pain all over her head. Osiris will not stop |28 having a headache, Ammon will not stop having a pain in the temples of his head, Esenephthys will not stop having a pain all over her head, until first he, NN, stops completely (?) - - -."

Fr. 1 - - - I do not (?) love him (?) - - -. Fr. 2 - - - if - - -. Fr. 3 - - - and may he (?) take - - - o Helios - - -. Fr. 4 - - - day - - -.

Metrical Section

Lines 6-14, dactylic hexameters

1-2 βα[λ]ῶ μή[λ]οις ़ [c. 4]δώςω τόδε φάρμα|7κ[ον] καίριον αἰεὶ βρωτὸν θνητοῖς ἀν|8θρώποις καὶ ἀθανάτοισι θεοῖσιν.

ᾗ ἄν |9 δῶ μήλῳ τε βάλω μήλῳ τε πατάξω, |10
4   πάντα ὑπερθεμένη μαίνοιτ' ἐπ' ἐμῆι |11 φιλότητι,
εἴτ' ἐν χειρὶ λαβο[ῦ]ςα φάγοι |12 ◡ ◡ _ ◡ ◡ _ ≍
ἢ ἐν κόλπωι καθίσαι ⟨καὶ⟩ μὴ |13 παύςαιτο φιλῶν με.
⟨πότνια⟩ Κυπρογένεια τέλει |14 τελέαν ἐπαοιδήν.

1-2 papyri textum dedi ([: ε vel θ vel c, vix κ; αϊ ειβρωτον). Genuinos versus vix restituas. Varia temptaverunt viri docti: βά[λ]⟨λ⟩ω μή[λ]οις [καὶ] δώςω τόδε {φάρμακ[ον]}, καίριον αἰεί, / βρωτὸν θνητοῖς⟨ίν τε) {ἀνθρώποις} καὶ ἀθανάτοιςι θεοῖςιν R.Merkelbach (apud ed.pr.); βά[λ]⟨λ⟩ω μή[λ]οις [καὶ] δώςω τόδε {φάρμακ[ον]}, καίριον αἰεί, / βρωτὸν ⟨δ'⟩ {θνητοῖς} ἀνθρώποις⟨ι) καὶ ἀθανάτοιςι θεοῖςιν R.Janko (ZPE 72, 1988, 293); βά[λ]⟨λ⟩ω μή[λ]οις [καὶ] δώςω τόδε φάρμα-κ[ον] {καίριον} αἰεί / βρωτὸν θνητοῖς⟨ίν τε) {ἀνθρώποις} καὶ ἀθανάτοιςι θεοῖςιν L.Koenen (apud Janko, loc.cit., adn. 1). Sed prius hemistichium v. 1 displicet: metrum claudicat, [καὶ] nec spatio nec vestigiis congruit   2 θνητοῖς dispexi (θνητὸν ed.pr.)   3 ἦ ἂν δῶ dispexi (νδω ed.pr.) | τεβαλον Pap., correxi | τεπαταξᾶ̣ Pap.   4 hiatus vix tolerabilis, ⟨δ'⟩ add. ed.pr. (etiam ⟨θ'⟩ possis); an πάντα⟨ς⟩? (P.J.Parsons per litt.) | μαινοιτο Pap.   5 ητε Pap., correxi | λαβο[ῦ]ςα proposui (λάβο[ι] ed.pr.); vid. comm. | post φαγοι vestigia dubia octo litt.   6 καθίςαι Parsons : καθηται Pap. : καταθῇ Henrichs | ⟨καὶ⟩ Henrichs, Parsons | φιλῶν dispexi (φιλεῖν ed.pr.)   7 versus lacunosus, ⟨πότνια⟩ addidi (cf. ii 24) : Κυπρογένεια ⟨θεά, cὺ⟩ ed.pr. (cf. PGM IV 2938 f. = hymn. 22, 19; ad Κυπρογένεια θεά cf. Panyas. fr. 13, 3 Davies)

Col. i

1-5. This preamble, claiming the content of the papyrus to be a translation of ancient Egyptian spells found in a sacred book of Hermes kept in the innermost shrine of the temple at Heliopolis, aims to create an aura of mystery, antiquity and authority. An Egyptian source is quite possible for some of the spells; however, the first charm (lines 5-14), as well as some other sections (as e.g. ii 12), appear to belong completely to a western tradition. In fact, such claims are a well-known topos; cf. PGM XXIVa 2-4 ἀντίγραφον ἱερᾶς βίβλου τῆς εὑρεθείςης ἐν τοῖς τοῦ Ἑρμοῦ ταμίοις; IV 884-887 ἐπεί cου λέγω τὰ ὀνόματα, ἂ ἔγραψεν ἐν Ἡλιουπόλει ὁ τρισμέγιστος Ἑρμῆς ἱερογλυφικοῖς γράμμαςι; VII 863-865 ἡ βίβλος ἥδ' αὐτή, ⟨δ⟩ώδεκα ἰδία θεῶν, ηὑρέθη ἐν Ἀφροδιτοπόλει ⟨παρὰ⟩ τῇ θεᾷ μεγίςτῃ Ἀφροδίτῃ Οὐρανίᾳ; VIII 41 f. τὸ δὲ ἀληθινὸν ὄνομά cου ⟨ἐπ⟩εγραμμένον ⟨ἐςτὶ⟩ τῇ ἱερᾷ ςτήλῃ ἐν τῷ ἀδύτῳ ἐν Ἑρμουπόλει; P.Oxy. XI 1382, 19 f. (= Totti, Texte, no. 13) καταχωρίζεται ἡ ἀρετὴ ἐν ταῖς Μερκουρίου βιβλιοθήκαις; Cat. Cod. Astr. Gr. VII, p. 62 (fol. 177v) βίβλος εὑρεθεῖςα ἐν Ἡλιουπόλει τῆς Αἰγύπτου ἐν τῷ ἱερῷ ἐν ἀδύτοις ἐγγεγραμμένη ἐν ἱεροῖς γράμμαςι κτλ.; VIII.4, p. 105, 4 f. τὸ δὲ ἕτερον βιβλίον εὑρέθη ἐν Ἡλιουπόλει τῆς Αἰγύπτου ἐν τῷ ἱερῷ ἐν ἀδύτοις γεγραμμένον ἱεροῖς γράμμασιν ἐπὶ βασιλέως Ψαμμητίχου; Reitzenstein, *Poimandres*, p. 121 n. 6 ἀντίδοτος ἐκ τῶν Ἡφαίστου ἀδύτων τοῦ ἐν Μεμφίτιδι μεταληφθεῖσα κρίσει καὶ φιλανθρωπίᾳ, φασί, τοῦ Τρισμεγίστου Ἑρμοῦ; cf. also Gal., *Comp. medic. per gen.* V 2, XIII 776, 17-19 K. (= Hopfner, *Fontes*, p. 363, 10-12) ἐν ἑτέροις δ' ἂν εὕροις γεγραμμένην ἐκ τῶν ἀδύτων εἶναι καὶ τήνδε κατὰ τὸ Ἡφαίστειον ἐν Αἰγύπτῳ; 778, 6-8 K. (= Hopfner, *Fontes*, p. 363, 15-17). See A.J. Festugière, *La révélation d'Hermès trismégiste* I (Paris 1950[2]), pp. 319-323, and especially W.Speyer, *Bücherfunde in der Glaubenswerbung der Antike* (Hypomnemata 24, 1970), p. 125 for Egypt (with secondary literature); idem, *Die literarische Fälschung im heidnischen und christlichen Altertum* (Handbuch der Altertumswissenschaft I.2, Munich 1971), esp. pp. 67, 70 f. For the Greek magical papyri in particular, see H.D.Betz, "The Formation of Authoritative Tradition," pp. 161-170. Further literature in the ed.pr. of the present text.

1 ἐξαγωγή: problematic, but probably genuine (at any rate, no satisfactory emendation has been proposed: neither ἐξ ἀγωγῶν καὶ ἐπῳδῶν nor ἐξ ἀγωγῶν καὶ ἐπῳδῶν, mentioned in the ed.pr., are attractive). Brashear, as well as Betz and Faraone, take it as "excerpt" ("Auszug"), a meaning apparently unparalleled elsewhere, but which seems a not impossible extension of the normal range of application of the word. However, we incline to think that the basic sense of 'bring out of' refers rather to the whole 'publishing' operation claimed by the magician, i.e. the recovery of the charms *out of* the recesses of the temple, their translation and introduction *into* the Greek world; then, a sort of "exportation", or "diffusion" or "disclosure" of them. Some support for this interpretation might come from Themist., *Orat.* 23, 299A (p. 95, 8-9 Downey-Norman) - - - ὥστε κύριοι γενέσθαι τῆς ἐξαγωγῆς τῶν Πλάτωνος μαθημάτων. It has passed unnoticed that ἐξαγωγή is glossed *divulgatio* in *Gloss.* II 54, 4 (*divulgatio*: ἐξαγωγή, δημοθηνία [?]).

ἐπῳδῶν: on the *epode*, see F.Pfister, *RE Suppl.* IV, coll. 323-344.

1-3 ἐκ τῆς εὑρεθείσης - - - Ἑρμοῦ: emendation is required. The first editor changed the text into ἐκ τῆς εὑρεθείσης ἐν Ἡλίου πόλει ἐν τῶι ἀδύτωι ἱερᾶς βύβλου τῆς καλουμένης Ἑρμοῦ, which implies a serious corruption. A satisfactory sense can perhaps be made out by assuming the omission of a noun with which εὑρεθείσης agreed, e.g. ἐκ τῆς ⟨πραγματείας τῆς〉 (or 〈cυγγραφῆς τῆς〉) εὑρεθείσης κτλ. (saut du même au même?).

2 ἐν Ἡλίου{c} πόλει: the town that had been the most important religious center of Ancient Egypt continued to enjoy a great reputation in later magic. See P.Oslo I 1, 106 comm.; more in general *Lexikon der Ägyptologie* II, *s.v.* Heliopolis, col. 1113 (L.Kákosy); S.Sauneron, *Le papyrus magique illustré de Brooklyn* (Wilbour Monographs 3, New York 1970), p. ix.

ἐν τῆ ἱερᾷ βύβλωι: cf. PGM III 424 ἀντίγραφον ἀπὸ ἱερᾶς βίβ[λο]υ; XIII 3 βίβλος ἱερὰ ἐπικαλουμένη Μονὰς ἢ 'Ογδόη Μοϋcέως, 15 f. 'Ερμῆς - - - 〈ἐν〉 ἑαυτοῦ ἱερᾷ βύβλῳ ἐπικαλουμένη 'Πτέρυγι', 231, 232 f., 341 f.; XXIVa 2 f., quoted above, 1-5 comm. J.Quaegebeur pointed out that ἱερὰ βύβλος was the usual Greek rendering of Egyptian *dm'-ntr* (transcribed in Greek as Cεμ(ε)νουθι) 'book of the gods', 'divine book', i.e. a sacred book written by a hierogrammateus (*Anc. Soc.* 11-12, 1980-1981, 230-234; 233 for the present text).

3 'Ερμοῦ: Hermes-Thoth, lord of wisdom and magic, divine scribe and inventor of writing, to whom many sacred books were attributed; see A.Rusch, *RE* VI A.1, *s.v.* Thoth, col. 359; Griffiths, *Plutarch's de Iside et Osiride*, pp. 519-521; Hopfner, *Fontes*, p. 863 f., *s.v.* liber.

ἐν τῶι ἀδύτωι: the innermost recess of the temple. For sacred writings said to be kept in the *adyta*, in addition to several passages quoted above (1-5 comm.), cf. Philo Bybl., *FGrHist* 790 F 1 (p. 805, 9); Luc., *Sacr.* 14 (= Hopfner, *Fontes*, p. 310, 12 f.); Dio Cass. LXXV 13, 2 (= Hopfner, *Fontes*, p. 377, 2); Ach. Tat. 3, 25, 6 (= Hopfner, *Fontes*, p. 461, 20); Syncell., *Chron.* 72 f. (p. 72, 7 Mosshammer = Hopfner, *Fontes*, p. 74, 21); Apul., *Metam.* XI 22 (with Griffiths' note); for texts of Ancient Egypt, see *Lexikon der Ägyptologie* III, *s.v.* Krypta, col. 827 (Cl.Traunecker). In fact, in the Egyptian temples sacred books were normally kept in the 'House of Life' and in the 'House of papyrus rolls'; see *Lexikon der Ägyptologie* III, *s.v.* Lebenshaus, coll. 954-957 (M.Weber); *ibid.* I, *s.v.* Bibliothek, col. 784 (V.Wessetzky); G.Burkard, "Bibliotheken im alten Ägypten," *Bibliothek. Forschung und Praxis* 4.2 (1980) 79-115.

3-4. 〈γεγραμμένων〉 Αἰγυπτίοις | γράμμασι would be easier.

4 διερμηνευθέντων: this refers to ἐπῳδῶν in 1. Apparently, unless it is a mere mistake (the writer may have been influenced by the preceding γράμμασι), another instance of the masculine participle used for the feminine (cf. 13 φιλῶν with comm.). That ἐπῳδῶν in 1 is from ἐπῳδός rather than

ἐπῳδή seems quite improbable; the usages of ἐπῳδός as substantive elsewhere do not support such an interpretation (and cf. 5 ἐπῳδή!).

3-5 Αἰγυπτίοις | γράμμασιν καὶ διερμηνευθέντων Ἑλληνι‌κοῖς: see esp. W.Speyer, "Angebliche Übersetzungen des heidnischen und christlichen Altertums," *JbAC* 11/12 (1968/1969) 26-41; idem, *Die literarische Fälschung* (cit. above, 1-5 comm.), p. 70 f.

5-14. 'Charm by means of an apple'. The motif of the apple as a love token has a long tradition in Greek and Latin literature (cf. Theocr. 5, 88 with Gow's note; many passages are gathered by A.R.Littlewood, "The Symbolism of the Apple in Greek and Roman Literature," *HSCP* 72, 1967, 147-181). Our charm shares terms and features of the topos (see below). Its peculiarity, however, lies in making the apple, over which the epode is recited, a powerful, irresistible φάρμακον: the woman who bites it or places it in her bosom will become mad with love. This charm has no parallel in the Greek magical papyri, but it can be compared with Kropp, *Koptische Zaubertexte* II, X (= W.Beltz, *APF* 29, 1983, 74 f.; 9th cent.): "Ich beschwöre [euch nebst] euren Namen und euren Kräften und euren Amuletten und euren herrlichen Orten, an denen ihr euch befindet, daß ihr herabkommet auf diese (Früchte?), die in meiner rechten Hand sind, ich (NN), damit [zur Stunde, da ich der NN davon geben werde], daß sie davon esse, ihr dieser ein Liebesverlangen nach mir gebet, daß sie mir anhange mit unaufhörlicher Begier, etc." Ancient Mesopotamian apple incantations are quoted by C.A. Faraone, *Phoenix* 44 (1990) 235 f. For medieval folklore, see *Handwörterbuch des deutschen Aberglaubens* I, *s.v.* Apfel(baum), col. 512 f.; IX *Nachträge*, col. 362.

5 ἐπὶ μήλο̣[υ] : ἐπὶ μήλο̣[ις] ed.pr. The expression ἐπὶ μήλο̣[υ] ἐπῳδή seems to be comparable with ἀγωγὴ ἐπὶ ζμύρνης (PGM IV 1496; XXXVI 333); ἀγωγὴ - - - ἐπὶ παντὸς σκύφου (IV 1928 f.); ἀγωγή, ἔμπυρον ἐπὶ θείου ἀπύρου (XXXVI 295); ἀγωγὴ ἐπὶ ἡρώων ἢ μονομάχων ἢ βιαίων (IV 1390 f.); μαντεῖον Cαραπιακὸν [ἐπὶ] παιδός, ἐπὶ λύχνου καὶ φιάλης [κ]αὶ β[ά]θρου (V 1-3). Or else the meaning is 'charm (to be recited) over an apple'. If so, also ἐπὶ μῆλο̣[ν] would be possible (cf. PGM IV 931 f. ἐπὶ τοῦ λύχνου ὁ αὐτὸς λόγος λεγόμενος and VII 232 f. λόγος ὁ λεγόμενος ἐπὶ τὸν λύχνον). In the light of these passages, the dative μήλο̣[ις] (ed.pr.) does not seem likely.

τρίς: the spell is to be recited three times. Betz connects τρίς with βα̣[λ]ῶ, which seems quite improbable. For the number three in magic, cf. PGM, Vol. 3 (Index), p. 190, *s.v.* τρίς, and see the literature indicated by Brashear, *Magica varia*, p. 41.

6-14. Hexameters.

6-8. The original hexametric form seems to be almost hopelessly lost here. The attempts to reconstruct it (see above, app.cr.) are based on the assumption that some glosses entered the text. On the other hand, as L. Koenen pointed out (*apud* Janko, note 1), one cannot exclude that the text of the papyrus originates from more than two hexameters. However that may be, in those reconstructions v. 1 is exceptionable: (i) its inner meter is poor; (ii) the supplement [καὶ] does not account for the trace before the lacuna (see below, 7 comm.); furthermore, it is rather too short for the space.

6 βα[λ]ῶ μή[λ]οιc: a stereotyped phrase (cf. also 9); cf. Hesych. *s.v.* μήλῳ βαλεῖν (II, p. 661 Latte); Suid. *s.v.* βάλλειν μήλοις (I, p. 451, 22 Adler; cf. also III, p. 386, 14, 24); Aristoph., *Nub.* 997; Plat., *Anth. Pal.* V 79, 1 (= Page, *Further Greek Epigrams*, 590); Theocr. 5, 88; 6, 6 f. See Littlewood, cit. (above, 5-14 comm.), 154 f.

[*c.* 4]δώcω: before the lacuna the base of a round letter: ε, θ, ω possible (the oval is too large to be reconciled with a cursive κ, as in ii 5 ἔδωκαc and 16 κ(αὶ)). After the lacuna a horizontal on line: δ possible but not altogether certain. The putative sigma is much larger than normal, but an alternative seems to be excluded. This is a crucial point for the reconstruction of v. 1, and a satisfactory solution has not yet been found.

7 θνητοῖc : θνητὸν (r. θνητοῖc) ed.pr.   ι links at the top with c, which has no parallel in this text, but ν cannot be read.

8-9 ἦ ἄν | δῶ Maltomini, *loc.cit.* :   ν|δω ed.pr. For the relative pronoun used only once, although governed by different verbs in different constructions, see Kühner-Gerth, *Grammatik* II, p. 432. The text of the papyrus needs no emendation. Hiatus between a longum and a monosyllabic biceps in the first foot occurs in Ap. Rh. I 271, 334, 827, 1189; II 279, 1224; III 846, 1113; Theocr. 4, 22; 10, 30; 17, 38, 114; [Mosch.], *Megara* 54; Nic., *Ther.* 540, 566, 623, 854, 933, *Alex.* 516 (always after ἤ); also Call., *Hymn.* 4, 30 and fr. 260, 55 (though after ἤ, and in 'quotations' from Homer).

9 τεπαταξᾶ] Pap. ω is written above α and the two letters are flanked by a vertical stroke, curved to the left at the foot. Brashear inclined to regard it as an indication of two alternative forms: τ' ἐπάταξα and τε πατάξω (future); consequently, he suggested that three different moments were possibly being considered: "Ich ... (Gegenwart), ich bewarf mit einem Apfel

(Vergangenheit) und ich werde mit einem Apfel schlagen (Zukunft)."
However, in view of the new reading at the beginning of v. 3 (ἦ ἂν δῶ), it
seems more likely that the writer intended to correct to τε πατάξω (aor.
subj.); accordingly, τεβαλον of the papyrus should be emended to τε βάλω.

10 πάντα ὑπερθεμένη: a common phrase in papyrus letters since the
third century BC, introducing urgent requests (cf. P.Hal. 13, 10 f.; P.Eleph.
11, 5; also Preisigke, *Wörterbuch*, 649.45-49; add P.Oxy. I 120 verso 4
[misplaced in Preisigke, *Wörterbuch*, 649.42]; XVII 2154, 3; LV 3817, 15 f.;
P.Herm. 11, 16; P.Mich. VIII 494, 4 f.; P.Oslo II 59, 2; P.Wisc. II 74, 3).
The hiatus is very harsh and probably results from corruption. Parsons'
πάντα⟨ς⟩ is attractive, especially in the light of **45**, 49 f. εἰ δὲ καὶ ἕτερο[ν]
ἔχει ἐν κόλποις, ἐκεῖνον μὲν ὑπερθέσθω. The familiar epistolary formula
might have replaced the less common ὑπερτίθεσθαι + acc. of person.

μαίνοιτο: cf. **41**, 12 ἔρωτι μανικῷ; **45**, 7, 31, 43, 49; PGM IV 2756 f.
μαινομένη ἡ δ(εῖνα) ἥκοι ἐπ' ἐμαῖσι θύραισι; Audollent, *DT*, 271, 6 f.
ἐρῶντα μαινόμενον, ἀγρυπνοῦντα ἐπὶ τῇ φιλίᾳ αὐτῆς, 40 f.; also e.g.
Plat., *Resp.* 9, 578A, *Phaedr.* 253C; Men., *Mis.* A 11 f.; Theocr. 2, 49-51;
Luc., *Philops.* 14 (ἐμμανέστατα ἐρῶσα).

ἐπ': for μαίνομαι constructed with ἐπί and the (causal) dative, cf. Eur.,
Phoen. 535; Theocr. 10, 31; 20, 34 (see Gow's note on 13, 49).

10-11 ἐπ' ἐμῆι ǀ φιλότητι: cf. PGM IV 2743 f. (= *hymn.* 21, 21) δαμνομένη ψυχῇ ἐπ' ἐμῇ φιλότητι καὶ εὐνῇ.

11-12. To pick up the apple, to take a bite of it, to place it in the bosom:
all of these gestures are literary topoi (see below).

11 λαβο[ῦ]ϲα : λάβο[ι] . . . ed.pr. Since the traces after the lacuna
are so scanty, the reading proposed must be regarded as conjectural. λαβο[ῦ]ϲα does not fill the entire space available between the gap and φάγοι,
but the scribe often leaves blank spaces between words. However, with the
first editor's restoration (which implies a disjunctive before φάγοι), it is difficult to imagine a syntactically and metrically plausible text. Cf. Plat., *Anth.
Pal.* V 79, 3 (= Page, *Further Greek Epigrams*, 592) τοῦτ' αὐτὸ λαβοῦσα.

φάγοι: cf. Luc., *Dial. mer.* 12, 1 τοῦ μήλου ἀποδακών, *Tox.* 13
μῆλά τινα ἀποδεδηγμένα; Alciphr., *Epist. paras.* 26 [III 62], 2 (p. 91
Schepers); Aristaen. I 25, 21 Mazal.

12. If, as is probable, a new hexameter begins with ἢ ἐν κόλπῳ and if
the meter at the beginning of the line was not disturbed, then eight letters
would have filled two and a half feet.

ἤ: Brashear is probably correct in regarding this as answering ἤτε in 11. But ἤ will then stand at the beginning of v. 6, with aphaeresis, rather than at the end of v. 5 (ed.pr., p. 267). ἤτε - ἤ is, as far as we can see, unparalleled (Homer has ἤτε - ἤτε); therefore, probably, r. εἴτε (for εἴτε - ἤ, cf. LSJ, *s.v.* εἴτε *sub fin.*).

ἐν κόλπωι: cf. Catull. 65, 19-22; Luc., *Dial. mer.* 12, 1; Long. III 34, 3 ἐντίθηϲι τοῖϲ κόλποιϲ; Aristaen. I 10, 29 f.; 25, 21-23 Mazal; Nicetas Choniates, *Hist.* p. 148, 88 f. van Dieten (Corpus Fontium Historiae Byzantinae XI.1) ἡ δὲ παρθένοϲ καταθεμένη τοῦτο (i.e. τὸ μῆλον) τῷ κόλπῳ ἐκμαίνεται.

καθῆται: unmetrical. P.J.Parsons (*apud* ed.pr.) suggested καθίϲαι ⟨καὶ⟩, A.Henrichs (*apud* ed.pr.) καταθῇ ⟨καὶ⟩. The verb κατατίθημι would be appropriate (cf. the previous note), but the optative seems required (cf. 11 φάγοι).

13 φιλῶν : φιλεῖν ed.pr. The ω is faded but certain. For the use of the masculine participle in place of the feminine as early as in poetry of the 5th cent. BC, see the notes of E.Fraenkel on Aesch., *Ag.* 562 τιθέντεϲ (II, pp. 283-285) and of W.S.Barrett on Eur., *Hipp.* 1102-50 (pp. 366-368). It is well-attested in later Greek; see **31**, 3 comm. See also above, 4 comm.

Κυπρογένεια: cf. PGM IV 2928, 2938 (= *hymn.* 22, 12, 19).

13-14 τέλει | τελέαν ἐπαοιδήν: see **45**, 53 comm.; also **73** ii 18.

15-27. Love charm. Because the papyrus is badly damaged here and because of a total lack of parallels, this is an extremely difficult section. The one thing certain is that we are dealing with a mythological exemplum that contains both utterances (16-20 ἐποίηϲα; 23-26 ἀποθάνω) and narrative (20 ἡ θεὰ-22).

A preliminary difficulty lies in deciding whether throughout this section ὁ δεῖνα is to be taken (i) as the subject who utters each phrase (e.g. 16: NN (says): "I have taken your eye"; text and translation given above are arranged according to this interpretation); (ii) as the subject of the action contained in each utterance (e.g. 16: "I, NN, have taken your eye"; so Betz); or (iii) as the person addressed in each utterance (nominative for vocative; e.g. 16: "you, NN, I have taken your eye"). The first editor was probably correct in preferring (i), as (ii) would imply an ambiguous use of ὁ δεῖνα, where one would expect rather ἐγὼ ὁ δεῖνα, and (iii) would leave the intervention of the goddess (20-22) unexplained. As for the whole section, Brashear inclines to interpret it as follows: the practitioner (probably while handling some *ousia* regarded as the body of the goddess) refers to a mythical episode in which a personage (ὁ δεῖνα) claims to have eaten several parts of the body of a goddess (evidently on the occasion of a sacrificial meal; 16-20); this resulted in a mystic union and so the goddess granted his wishes (narrative section 20-22). Then, a new utterance by the personage follows, this time addressed to the beloved: (in outline) "From now on you have to love me until death" (23-26). Finally, the practitioner himself (who, it is implied, now enjoys the same divine favor as the mythical character) utters the concluding request: "O Lady goddess etc." (26-27).

The above is probably correct as regards the general frame, but it can be questioned on two points: (a) it is unlikely that ὁ δεῖνα refers to a mythical personage ("die Figur der mythischen Geschichte"); such a personage would be indicated by his proper name, whereas ὁ δεῖνα implies, as usual, its replacement with the name of a real person when the charm would be applied; (b) the 'eucharistic' interpretation is not convincing: some of the bodily parts mentioned seem incompatible with it: ὄμμα, ψυχή, δέρμα. On the contrary, ὄμμα and especially δέρμα suggest an aggressive attitude towards the deity.

It is much more difficult to pass from criticism to positive proposals. Perhaps the practitioner refers to a magical action which he himself carried out in the past and by which he constrained the goddess to comply with his wishes; the utterances in 16-20, then, would function as threats and ὁ δεῖνα would be the practitioner himself.

[Only as a working hypothesis: lines 16-20 are a 'slander' (διαβολή), the magical procedure consisting of slandering a person before a god, by ascribing to him some impious acts and, more often, impious words; see S. Eitrem, "Die rituelle διαβολή," *Symb. Osl.* 2 (1924) 43-61, and cf. PGM VII 604 ff. αὕτη γὰρ εἴρηκεν, ὅτι ὁ Ιαω πλευρὰς οὐκ ἔχει, ⟨ἡ δεῖνα εἴρηκεν,⟩ ὅτι Αδωναι ἐπὶ χόλῳ βίᾳ ἐβλήθη, ⟨ἡ δεῖνα εἴρηκεν,⟩ ὅτι - - -, ⟨ἡ δεῖνα εἴρηκεν,⟩ ὅτι - - - ἡ δεῖνα εἴρηκεν, ὅτι κτλ.; IV 2654 ff. ἡ δεῖνά σε δεδρακέναι τὸ πρᾶγμα τοῦτ' ἔλεξεν· κτανεῖν γὰρ ἄνθρωπόν σε ἔφη, πιεῖν δὲ αἷμα τούτου, σάρκας φαγεῖν, μίτρην δὲ σὴν λέγει τὰ ἔντερα αὐτοῦ καὶ δέρμα ἑλεῖν δορῆς ἅπαν κτλ.; 2478 ff. ἡ δεῖνά ἐστιν ἡ εἰποῦσα ὅτι — ⟨οὐκ⟩ ἐγώ εἰμι εἰποῦσα ὅτι· ἐγὼ εἶδον τὴν μεγίστην θεὸν καταλιποῦσαν τὸν πόλον τὸν οὐράνιον - - -. ἡ δεῖνά ἐστιν ἡ εἰποῦσα· κτλ. As can be seen from these passages, such an interpretation would explain the dramaturgic structure perfectly: NN (says): "I etc." Let us suppose that the charm is a *diakopos*: ὁ δεῖνα is the rival in love; he is accused of having uttered some sacrilegious phrases against the goddess; she listens to this calumny and grants the wishes of the practitioner. Against this, (a) αὐτόν 21 and αὐτῷ 22 would refer to the practitioner, which seems rather unnatural; (b) it would be difficult to account for 23-26 (ὁ δεῖνα - - - ἀποθάνω)].

16] δ̣ : ὁ δ(εῖνα) is what one expects, but there is no ink where the vertical stroke ought to be, and there is some ink after the putative delta.

17 ὁ δεῖ[να· c. 5]μην: possibly ἐγευcά]μην (H.Maehler *apud* ed.pr.); the poetic ἐπαcά]μην (W.G.Arnott *apud* ed.pr.) seems improbable; ἐκο-ρεcά]μην would be too long.

18 ἐχρηcάμη[ν cου c. 7]: perhaps ἐχρηcάμη[ν cου τῷ cώματι]? For χράομαι of sexual intercourse, cf. LSJ, *s.v.*, IV 2; *TGL*, *s.v.*, 1612B. Brashear thought of ἐχρηcάμη[ν cου τῇ καρδίᾳ], and entertained the possibility of a misspelling of ἐχριcάμην.

19 *fin.*]cα: after α, a squiggle that we cannot explain.

19-20. [ἐνεδυ]cά]μην cου τ[ὸ δέ]ρμα A.Henrichs (*apud* ed.pr.). Cf. e.g. Dio Cass. LXVIII 32, 1 τὰ ἀπολέμματα ἐνεδύοντο.

20 τ[ὸ δέ]ρμα: the space is rather short for τ[ὸ cπέ]ρμα.

22 κατὰ ψυχήν: here, it seems, 'according to his mind' (like κατὰ νοῦν), though the expression usually means 'in the soul'.

23 ἀφ' ἧc ἡ[μ]έραc ⟨καὶ⟩ ὥραc: cf. PGM VII 649 f. ἐφ' ἧc ὥραc ἐὰν καταβῇc κτλ.; XII 62 ἀφ' ἧc ἂν παραι[τ]ῶ ὥραc.

24 ναν . [ ]θεῖcα : ναν [.] [.]θεῖcα ed.pr.

'η cταθειc[?]' : possibly ἢ (or ἡ?) cταθεῖc[α], but we are unable to establish a context.

ἐμπεc[. .] : a form of ἐμπίπτω seems likely (F.Maltomini, *loc.cit*). ἐμπεc[οῦc]α would suit space and trace, but the syntax of the passage is not clear. For the nexus ἐμπίπτειν εἰc ἔρωτα, cf. Plat., *Resp.* 608A; Antiphan. fr. 235, 3 (II, p. 114 Kock); Diod. Sic. XXXVI 2, 2 (cf. also 2a, 1); Strab. XIV 1, 41; Plut., *Quaest. conv.* 622D (IV, p. 25, 16 Hubert); Ps.Luc., *Asin.* 50; Athen., *Deipnos.* XII 552F, 554C (III, pp. 219, 16; 223, 11 f. Kaibel).

24-25 εἰc ἔρωτα, | εἰc φιλ[ί]αν [κ]αὶ εἰc ⟨c⟩τοργήν: for such detailed enumerations, cf. **45**, 7, 30 f.; also **42**, 13, 36 f., 45, etc.; **50**, 60, etc.

25-26 [. .] . [.] . | ἀποθάνω: the ink is badly faded and the traces are indecipherable. Possibly [μου] ἄχ[ρι] ἂν ἀποθάνω (F.Maltomini, *loc.cit*); cf. e.g. **46**, 24 f.; **48** J-K 25, 39; PGM XVI 8 (also 17, 24 f., 33, etc.).

26. θεὰ ꞌῙ[cι? (R.Merkelbach *apud* ed.pr.).

]εραιωι: H.Maehler (*apud* ed.pr.) suggested ἐν χρόνῳ ἡμ]εραίωι, which, however, seems too long for the space.

Col. ii

1-25. Love charm in three parts (1-3, 4-8, 9-25). An interesting feature of this charm is the fact that, at least in 9-25, the beloved appears to be a man (cf. 12 αὐτός). Then, either the charm is conceived from the point of view of a woman (i.e. it is a woman who performs the magical action) or it is homosexual in intent (line 4 λαβών is not decisive, since the situation in 1-8 may have been different, or it might be a generic masculine). Either case is unparalleled in formularies, which regularly assume the client to be a man desiring a woman (PGM IV 2089-91 seems to envisage a double possibility); the applied charms, of course, reflect the actual situation (for homosexual love charms, see **42**, intr.). Also unusual is that the performer refers to his own feeling and experience as he does in 12 κατατρ[έ]χω, αὐτὸς δέ με φεύγει and, it seems, in fr. 1 φιλῶ. Somewhat comparable are **71** fr. 9, 2 φιλῶ τὴν [δεῖνα (see comm. *ad loc.*); **49**, 77-79 ἀγρύπνησον Ματρῶναν - - - ἣν ἔχει ἐν νόῳ Θεόδωρος; and PGM IV 1405-11 ὁ δεῖνα ἐκ τῆς τροφῆς ἑαυτοῦ καταλείψανα δάκρυcιν ἔμιξεν καὶ cτενάγμαcιν πικροῖc, ὅπωc αὐτὸν καρπίcηcθε βαcάνοιc ἐχόμενον, ἥρωεc ἀτυχεῖc, - - - · τὸν δεῖνα καρπίcαcθε τὸν πονοῦντα καρδίαν, ἕνεκεν τῆc δεῖνα κτλ.

1 ἄραc τὰc χεῖραc: for τὰc χεῖραc αἴρειν as gesture of prayer, see the instances collected in Bauer, *Wörterbuch, s.v.* αἴρω 1a. Cf. also PGM III 621 f. προcκύ]νει ἀνατείναc τὰc χεῖραc καὶ λέ[γε]; IV 904-906 καὶ τὰc χεῖραc ἀνατείναc εἰc οὐρανὸν πρὸc τὰc τοῦ ἡλίου ἀκτῖναc λέγε τὸν λόγον ζʹ; XIII 827-829 ἀμφοτέραc χεῖραc προτείναc, λέγε; and see C.Sittl, *Die Gebärden der Griechen und Römer* (Leipzig 1890), p. 174 f.; A. Hermann, *JbAC* 6 (1963) 112-128; *RAC* VIII, *s.v.* Gebet I, coll. 1141, 1158, 1167 (E.von Severns).

κατάcειε λέγω[ν Maltomini, *loc.cit.* : καταcτελέτω [ed.pr.   For τὰc χεῖραc (τὴν χεῖρα) καταcείειν, cf. *Vita Aes.* 87 (p. 98, 14 f. Perry); Philo, *Jos.* 211, *Legat.* 181; NT Act. Ap. 19, 33; Heliod. 10, 16, 3 τὴν χεῖρα προτείναc καὶ καταcείων (for τῇ χειρὶ καταcείειν, cf. Pol. 1, 78, 3; Jos., *A.J.* 4, 323; 8, 275; NT Act. Ap. 12, 17; 13, 16; 21, 40; Heliod. 10, 7, 2; for καταcείω used absolutely, cf. Xen., *Cyr.* 5, 4, 4; Jos., *A.J.* 17, 257;

B.J. 2, 46; App., *Illyr.* 25, § 73; *Bell. civ.*, 2, 60, § 247). For ἄρας τὰς χεῖρας - - - λέγων, cf. the passages quoted in the previous note.

] ̣ ̣ εινα :] ̣ δεῖνα ed.pr., but the remains of the second letter suggest a curved base, as of ε, θ, c, whereas δ shows consistently a flat or nearly flat base in this text. If by chance δ, then probably δεινὰ rather than δεῖνα (see the following note).

2. καὶ νὺξ μέλαινα καὶ cτάcιc καὶ ἀγρυπνία is an iambic trimeter (iambic rhythm might be recognized in what remains as far as line 3). Brashear is probably right in comparing the verse with the apostrophes and laments of the shut-out lover in the paraclausithyra, e.g. Men., *Mis.* A 1; *Anth. Pal.* V 164 (Asclep.); 191 (Mel.); *Fragm. Grenf.* 11 Cunningham. It cannot be ruled out, however, that 'night, trouble and sleeplessness' are the torments invoked against the beloved.

καὶ νὺξ μέλαινα: cf. Aesch., *Eum.* 745 ὦ νὺξ μέλαινα μῆτερ; Eur., *El.* 54 ὦ νὺξ μέλαινα.

καὶ εμη[: likely καὶ ἐμὴ [.

]δοκρεμωι: the articulation is problematic. At the end, ἐμῷ? But what went before? Or perhaps κρεμῶ (with iota adscript written in error)? Brashear tentatively suggested κρε⟨γ⟩μῷ 'with the sound of stringed instruments'.

3 χρηc ἴδη πρὶν ἥλιον: we see no way of recovering something plausible without spoiling the iambic rhythm (see 2 comm.); a text such as χρή c' ἰδεῖν πρὶν ἥλιον (for πρίν as preposition with the accusative, cf. Bauer, *Wörterbuch*, *s.v.* 2) does not seem attractive. Brashear was therefore probably right in emending to χρήcῃ πρὶν ἴδῃc ἥλιον. Cf. PGM IV 286 χρῶ πρὸ ἡλίου, 33 πρὶν ἀνατείλη ὁ ἥλιος, 3173 πρὸ ἡλίου ἀνατολῆc; I 20 πρὶν ἀνατολῆc ἡλίου; VII 418, 420 f. On dawn as an appropriate time for magical operations, see W.Brashear, *APF* 36 (1990) 67 with n. 21. For χρήcῃ in directions, cf. PGM II 64; XIII 748, 752; for the future in directions, see **86** fr. A ii 1 comm. on λήμψε[ι].

4 χρεῖcον (r. χρῖcον) τὸ πρόcωπον: for the use of facial ointments in love charms and in *charitesia*, cf. Griffith-Thompson, *Demotic Magical Papyrus*, XII 14, 30 (cf. Betz, *Translation*, pp. 215, 216) and PGM XXXVI 211-214. See C.A.Faraone, *Phoenix* 44 (1990) 224 and n. 10 for parallels in neo-Assyrian magic.

4-6. For the love of Isis for Osiris as mythical paradigm, see **38**, 9 comm.

4 μ[ύ]ρ[ο]ν ᾧ: restored by M.Smith (*apud* ed.pr.).

5 ἐπορεύθη εἰς τὸν τοῦ 'Οϲείριοϲ (r. 'Οϲίριοϲ) κόλπον: this refers to the sexual union of Isis with the dead Osiris: Isis lay on the corpse of Osiris, took in his seed and conceived Horus. The story, reported also by Plut., *De Iside* 358D, is already attested in the Pyramid Texts (632a-d): "Your sister Isis *comes to you* rejoicing for love of you. You have placed her on your phallus and your seed issues into her" (R.O.Faulkner, *The Ancient Egyptian Pyramid Texts*, Oxford 1969, p. 121, § 632); cf. also P.Louvre I 3079, col. 110, 10, where Isis is made to say: "I have played the part of a man though I am a woman..." (transl. by Griffiths, *Plutarch's de Iside et Osiride*, p. 353; text in J.C.Goyon, *BIFAO* 65, 1967, 95; see 111 n. 22). (An active role is assigned to Isis also in the Aretalogy from Maroneia, line 17 ϲύνοικον δ' ἔλαβεϲ Ϲέραπιν; cf. SEG XXVI 821 = Totti, *Texte*, no. 19.)

τοῦ αὐτῆ[ϲ ἀνδρὸϲ καὶ ἀδ]ελφοῦ: cf. PGM XXIVa 7-10 ἡ Ἴϲιϲ ζητοῦϲα ἑαυτῆϲ τὸν ἀδελφὸν καὶ ἄνδρα "Οϲιριν; IV 1471-73 ἡ Ἴϲιϲ ἔβη ϲυνόμευνον ἀδελφὸν ἔχουϲα ἐν ὤμοιϲ; Diod. Sic. I 21, 3 (= Hopfner, *Fontes*, p. 100, 39) τὴν δὲ Ἴϲιν ἀδελφὴν οὖϲαν 'Οϲίριδοϲ καὶ γυναῖκα; 27, 4 (= Hopfner, *Fontes*, p. 106, 26) ἐγώ εἰμι γυνὴ καὶ ἀδελφὴ 'Οϲίριδοϲ (cf. the Isis-Aretalogy from Cyme, line 6 and that from Ios, line 5; see Totti, *Texte*, no. 1, § 6).

αὐτῆ{ϲ}: probably a case of erroneous addition of final -ϲ (see Mayser, *Grammatik* I.1, p. 183; Gignac, *Grammar* I, p. 125 f.), but one cannot exclude an early example of genitive with verbs of 'giving' (on which see Kapsomenakis, *Voruntersuchungen*, p. 114).

6 χάριν: here 'attractiveness' 'charm', not "du gabst ihr deine Gunst" (ed.pr.). See **63**, 8-9 comm.

δόϲ μοι ταϲε[*c.* 10] ̣ : possibly τὰϲ ἐ[παφροδιϲία]ϲ. In similar contexts, however, the word occurs only in the singular: cf. **64**, 4 f.; PGM VIII 4 f. δόϲ μοι χάριν, τροφήν, - - - ἐπαφροδιϲίαν; IV 1674; VII 392; VIII 62; XII 69; XIII 803 f.; XXXVI 224 f.; P.Louvre E 3229, 5 (ed. Brashear, *Magica varia*, p. 73); possibly P.Berol. inv. 11734, 31 (ed. W.Brashear, *APF* 36, 1990, 49-74); see also Preisigke, *Wörterbuch*, *s.v.* The first editor suggested τὰ ϲε[αυτῆϲ.

7]ειρε: Brashear prints -έγ]ειρε (see also comm. *ad loc.*).

8 ἐπαοιδήν : ἐπαγοιδήν ed.pr., but it seems rather that an omicron was superimposed over another letter, probably γ (or γο?). The opposite (i.e. γ ex ο) seems unlikely (the word is correctly written in i 14, 27, ii 25).

9-10 χαῖρε - - - χαῖρε - - -χαιρέτωσαν - - - χαιρέτω: for a similar transition from the second to the third person, cf. PGM IV 1048-51 χαῖρε, θεὲ θεῶν - - - χαιρέτωσάν cου αἱ Ὧραι - - - χαιρέτωσάν cου αἱ Δόξαι. Also Sapph. 117 Voigt †χαίροιc ἀ νύμφα†, χαιρέτω δ' ὁ γάμβροc; Liban., Decl. XXII 35.

9 ἀναθέλλοντεc (r. -τέλ-) : ἀνατέλλοντεc ed.pr.

οἱ cὺν coὶ ἀνατέλλοντεc θεοί: as Brashear pointed out, the gods who compose the retinue of Ra in his ship. See J.Assmann, Ägyptische Hymnen und Gebete (Zurich-Munich 1975), no. 11, p. 110 "Gegrüßet seiest du, Re! Gegrüßet seiet ihr, jene Götter, die die Vorhut des Re bilden und die einherziehen im Gefolge der Großen Barke, die ihn geleiten in Frieden zu seiner Stunde, etc.;" W.H.Worrell, "Coptic Magical and Medical Texts," Orientalia 4 (1935) 33, lines 116-117 "Hail Sun, Hail to them that are with thee." Cf. also PGM XIII 395-397 διὸ τῶν ἐννέα θεῶν τῶν ἀνατελλόντων cὺν τῷ ἡλίῳ ἔλαβε τὰc μορφὰc καὶ τὴν δύναμιν; XXXVI 215 ὃν (the Sun) δορυφοροῦcιν οἱ θεοὶ πάντεc (see Markelbach-Totti, Abrasax II, p. 59, ad loc.). It could also be, however, that "the gods who rise together with you" are, more directly, the stars and planets which rise at dawn.

cὺν coί: not cὺν ἐοῖ (ed.pr.; cf. also Corrigenda, ZPE 35, 1979, 152).

10 δὲ κ . . . . . . · οὐ περὶ θ . [ ] οὐ περ[ὶ : δεκ . . . . περιθ . [.] ουπερ[ed.pr. Between κ and π, indecipherable traces; the reading οὐ is conjectural, but see below, 10-11 comm.

δὲ κ . . . . . . : one might consider, e.g., δὲ καὶ Ἰcιc (Isis-Sothis; or Isis-Venus, see G.Roeder, RE IX.2, s.v. Isis, col. 2120, 21-23). A reading δὲ Κύπριc (for Κύπριc said of the planet Venus, cf. Nonn., Dion. 6, 238; 38, 384) seems rather short for the space.

10-11 οὐ περὶ θ . [.] - - - ἀλλὰ περὶ τοῦ δεῖνα: the general context is lost, but what remains suggests a formula such as that discussed by A.D.Nock in: Bell-Nock-Thompson, Magical Texts from a Bilingual Papyrus, p. 262 f.: "I am not asking you to do x or y (generally difficult or impossible tasks), but z (something much simpler)." Cf. PGM IV 1505-08 οὐ πέμπω cε μακρὰν εἰc τὴν Ἀραβίαν, οὐ πέμπω cε εἰc Βαβυλῶνα, ἀλλὰ πέμπω cε πρὸc τὴν δεῖνα; LXI 13 f. οὐκέτι ἐπὶ ταῦτά cε πέμψω, οὐδὲ χρεία ἐcτὶν τούτων, ἀλλὰ ἐπὶ τὴν δεῖνα; and especially Kropp, Koptische Zaubertexte II, VI 8-10 (cf. W.Beltz, APF 29, 1983, 72 f.) "ich verlange (αἰτεῖν) weder [dieses] noch (οὔτε) etwas anderes derart von dir, sondern (ἀλλά) ich verlange (αἰτεῖν) [deine] ganze [Kraft] herab auf meine Kraft etc." (cf. also lines 20-21).

οὐ περὶ θ [ ]: after θ, ε seems the best reading; then, only a high speck of ink and a low one, possibly from the apex and left foot of alpha. Probably θέα[c]. Cf. PGM III 576-579 διδοὺς ἐμοὶ - - - μορφήν, κάλλος; VIII 4 f. δός μοι - - - προcώ⟨π⟩ου εἶδος; 26 f. δός μοι τὴ⟨ν⟩ χάριν, μορφήν, κάλλος; 30 f. δός μοι - - - μορφήν; XXIIa 23 ποίη[cóν] με καλὸν παρ' αὐτῇ γενέcθαι.

οὐ περ[ὶ c. 20 ο]ὐδὲ ǀ περὶ ἀργυρίου ἀλλὰ κτλ.: purely e.g. οὐ περ[ὶ χρυcοῦ προcεύχομαι ὑμῖν ο]ὐδὲ ǀ περὶ ἀργυρίου ἀλλὰ κτλ. (cf. PGM IV 2439 f. φέρε μοι ἀργύρια, χρυcόν, ἱμ[ατ]ι[c]μόν, πλοῦτον πολύολβον ἐπ' ἀγαθῷ, and VIII 31 f. δότωcάν μοι χρυcὸν καὶ ἄργυρον καὶ τροφὴν πᾶcαν ἀδιάλειπτον).

11-12. E.g. ἀλλὰ περὶ τοῦ δεῖνα τ[οῦ ἀcεβοῦc καὶ ἀνοcίου. διώκω, αὐτὸc δ' οὐ] ǀ μένει (for τ[οῦ ἀcεβοῦc καὶ ἀνοcίου, cf. PGM IV 1411 f.; also XXXVI 144; Audollent, *DT*, 155 B, 9; 188, 9 [cf. PGM LVIII 11 f.]).

12 κατατρ[έ]χω, αὐτὸc δέ με φεύγει: a well-known motif in erotic Greek literature since Sapph. 1, 21 Voigt καὶ γὰρ αἰ φεύγει, ταχέωc διώξει (see the instances collected by Gow on Theocr. 11, 75 and 6, 17), but unparalleled in the Greek magical papyri.

13 ποιήcαντά cε βαc [c. 5]: first, upright: γ, ι, τ possible; second, speck at mid-height. In view of the preceding θέντα cοι, the proposed articulation seems preferable to cεβαcτ [(ed.pr.). Seemingly, the Sun is prayed to or commanded in the name of some more powerful authority who assigned (? θέντα) something (τὴν δ[ύ]cιν?) to him and caused him to do something (a form of βαcτάζω? or 'made him king', βαcιλέα, βαcιλεύειν? cf. e.g. Orph., Fr. 96 Kern, quoted in **87**, 4 comm.). In line 14 the Sun is possibly threatened with cosmic disorder of the rhythm of his rising and setting.

14 μήτε δύcεων : ed.pr.

μήτε v [: probably another word connected with the course of the Sun.

]φ[ ]τι μὴ :] ἐφ' [ὅ]τι μὴ ed.pr., without comment ('on condition that'?), but we have not been able to parallel such a nexus ([ᾧ]τε cannot be read). Perhaps [ὅ]τι μὴ 'save that' (cf. LSJ, *s.v.* ὅ τι II), preceded by an elided word? But all is most uncertain.

μὴ πίοι: cf., e.g., **43**, 9; **45**, 45; **73** ii 6; PGM IV 354 (and the parallels **46**, 11; **47**, 10; **48** J 9, 23), etc.

15 καθίcαι : κάθηται ed.pr., but one would expect to see the second vertical of η. Moreover, the optative seems required. Cf. PGM IV 1510 f.

[ ] ωϲαι: scattered ink; [β]ρώϲαι? Brashear suggested [ἀ]πώϲαι.

ἔχοι με ἐν [: probably ἐν φ[ρεϲί or ἐν ν[όῳ (the minimal trace before the lacuna does not help); cf. **49**, 63, 78; PGM IV 1519 f. ἀλλ' ἐμὲ μόνον, τὸν δεῖνα, κατὰ νοῦν ἐχέτω, 2741 f. ἐμὲ δ' ἐν φρεϲὶν ἐγκαταθέϲθω, 2960 f. κατὰ νοῦν μηδένα ἔχουϲα, εἰ μὴ ἐμὲ τὸν δεῖνα μόνον; Audollent, *DT*, 266, 19 *solum me in mente habeat*; 231, 29 f.

16 ἄδημος ἤτω: to our knowledge, the adjective occurs only in Soph., Fr. 639 Radt. For the sense, cf. lines 10-13 of the Coptic love charm published by P.C.Smither, *JEA* 25 (1939) 173 f.: "But let him seek after me from village to village, from city to city, from field to field, from country to country, until he comes to me etc." It is probably not necessary to think of a mistake for ἀδήμων (another *hapax*, attested for Hipp., *Epid.* I 18 in Gal., *In Hipp. Epid. I*, II 76 [CMG V 10.1, p. 89, 23]) ἤτω or ἀδημονείτω.

ἤτω Maltomini, *loc.cit.* : η . . ed.pr. The ink is badly faded, but the reading seems inescapable. On this form of imperative, frequent in the magical papyri, see Gignac, *Grammar* II, p. 407.

ἕωϲ ἂν πρὸϲ ἐμὲ ἕωϲ [: one expects ἔλθῃ in place of the second ἕωϲ (cf. 19).

17 θεῖον [: θε[όν ed.pr. The new reading is by Brashear (letter of 5 July 1991).

] . . τον[ ] :]ϲον ed.pr.

18 ἐντολ [ ] : εντο[ ] ed.pr. The new reading is by Brashear (see 17 comm.), who suggests for 17-18 something like [μή μου παρακούϲῃϲ τῶν] | ἐντολῶ[ν] (cf. PGM IV 367 f. and the parallel **48** J-K 19 f., 30).

Above the first two illegible letters after the first gap (tops of two uprights) is a horizontal for which we have no explanation; Ⲇ̄ seems improbable.

] . . ἐάν :] ἐάν ed.pr.

19 ἐὰν διαλίποιϲ: ἐάν with optative is unusual at this time, and one might suspect a misspelling of διαλίπῃϲ. However, οι for η does not occur elsewhere in this text. For ἐάν with optative in later Greek, see Radermacher, *Grammatik*, p. 200; LSJ, *s.v.* εἰ B III; *TGL*, *s.v.* ἐάν, p. 4B-C; also G. Anlauf, *Standard Late Greek oder Attizismus? Eine Studie zum Optativgebrauch im nachklassischen Griechisch*, Diss. Cologne 1960, pp. 87, 111, 118, 119, 124, 141, 146-147, 156. Cf. PGM IV 1903 ἐὰν ϲυρίϲειεν; VII 980 ἐὰν ἄψαιμι.

βαϲαν[ι]ῶ ϲε: apparently it is the beloved, not Helios, that is addressed here (cf. ἔλθ[η]ϲ at this line).

βαcαν[ι]ῶ Maltomini, *loc.cit.* : βαcανῶ (for βαc⟨κ⟩ανῶ) ed.pr., but after ν there is a gap wide enough for 1 or 2 letters; and βαcκαίνω would be out of place here. For βαcανίζω in similar contexts, cf. **42**, 16, 37, 60; PGM IV 1412 f.; XIXa 50 f.; XXXVI 201; Audollent, *DT* 271, 14, 41; L.Robert, *Journal des Savants* 1981, p. 35 n. 1 (= Jordan, "Survey," p. 186 f.; an unpublished *defixio* from Carthage or Hadrumetum) πυρούμενοι τὰc ψυχάc, τὰc καρδίαc, τὰc cπλάνχναc (*sic*) αὐτῶν, βαcανιζόμενοι κτλ.

20-24. In most places nothing can be read.

22 εμ[.] . . . ηι ον ἡμέρᾳ: a reading ἐν [τῇ] cήμερον ἡμέρᾳ does not seem allowed.

ἀμφ . : after the trace, some ink, probably accidental. Perhaps 22-23 ἀμφιέζωμαι.

χα . [.] . . : χαλ[κ]ὸν ed.pr.

24] . . πότνια :] . . οcυνν . [ed.pr.   Cf. PGM IV 2927 f. (= *hymn.* 22, 12).

26-30. Against headache. Other such charms: **14**, 5; **22**, 4; **32**, 7; **94**, 39; PGM VII 199-201, 201 f.; XVIIIa 2 f.; XX col. II 1 f., 15 ff.; LXV 4 f. The present spell is based on threat (see **45**, 9-11 comm.; cf. also **94**, 52-58). Its scheme (*x* is in such and such condition and it will remain so until...) is rather unusual. Brashear quotes a parallel from a demotic magical papyrus, P.Louvre E3229, coll. 5, 23 - 6, 1: "The copper is bent down. The neshmet-bark will not stop sinking. The great river draws blood. Isis is ill, [Neph]thys... The copper will not stop bending. The neshmet-bark will not stop sinking. The great river will not stop drawing blood. Isis will not stop being sick. Nephthys will not stop - - - until they [make] him do the thing which so and so desires from him" (transl. by J.H.Johnson, *Enchoria* 7, 1977, 72). Cf. also A.Klasens, *A Magical Statue Base* (Leiden 1952), p. 57 (f 21 ff.): "The boat of Re stands still and does not sail. Aton is in his place of yesterday, until Horus will be healthy for his mother Isis, until the patient will be healthy for his mother likewise. - - - The foods are stopped up, the temples blocked, until Horus will be healthy etc. - - - The misery which is yonder will turn the disturbance to its place of yesterday, until Horus etc. - - - The demon of the dark goes about, the seasons are not separated, the figures of the shadow are not seen, until Horus etc. - - - The sources are blocked, the crops are withering, the food is taken from mankind, until Horus etc."

27 Ἠ[c]ενεφθυc (also 29): cf. PGM XII 235 Ἠcενεφ⟨θ⟩υc; PGM LXII 5 Cενεφθυc; on a bone tessera from Alexandria Cενεφθυc (cf. E.Alföldi-

Rosenbaum, *Chiron* 6, 1976, 237, no. 92 with plate 29); Epiph., *De fide* III 2, 11 (GCS 3, p. 512, 12 = Hopfner, *Fontes*, p. 609, 6) Cενεφθυ (dative); and, probably, PGM IV 101 ϲενεβθω (*v.l.* ϲενεφθω). The name is in all likelihood a combination of Ἰϲιϲ and Νεφθυϲ; see the discussion by J.Quaegebeur, "Le théonyme Senephthys," *Orient. Lovan. Period.* 22 (1991) 111-122.

30 πάντ ̣ [: πάντα ̣ [ed.pr. The letter before the lacuna is illegible. Possibly πάντα ̣ [or πάντω ̣[ϲ.

Fr. 1 φιλῶ: see above, ii 1-25 comm.
    αυ ̣ [: αὐτ[όν? ed.pr.

Fr. 3, 1] ̣ ̣ειλωι :] ̣ ̣ ̣ ̣ ̣ ed.pr.

Fr. 5]νημε[: possibly]ν ἡμε[ρ- as suggested in the ed.pr.

Fr. 6: not transcribed in the ed.pr.

Provenance   I AD[1]
   unknown

P.S.A.Athen. 70.

ED.PR.: G.A.Petropoulos, P.S.A.Athen. (Athens 1939), p. 430 f., no. 70.

REPUBL.: F.Maltomini in: *Miscellanea Papyrologica* (Papyrologica Florentina VII, 1980),
   pp. 169-172.

COMM.: ed.pr.; Maltomini, *loc.cit.*

TRANSL.: R.Kotansky in Betz, *Translation*, no. CIII.

PHOTO: *Miscellanea Papyrologica*, plate XI.

REF.: Preisendanz, "Überlieferung," no. LXXXVII.

DESCR.: papyrus; 7×12 cm. Broken away on all sides except the bottom, where there is a
   blank space of 2 cm. The writing runs with the fibers, and the back is blank. Parts of
   two columns are preserved; the intercolumnium is between 2 and at least 3 cm.

LOC.: Archaeological Society of Athens.

Col. ii 1-18: love charm. The general flow is relatively clear. Lines 2-12
consist of a logos. A daemon is commanded to drive the beloved from whatever place she happens to be in (3); he must go everywhere (3-4) and cause
her to suffer torments (5-6) until she comes to the lover (6-7); the lover is to
be dear to her (? 9); the command is to be carried out rapidly (10); the gist of
the command is repeated in 11-12. Lines 13-14 contain directions to be carried
out after the recitation of the logos. 15-16 appear to contain magical words,
which suggests that we are again within a logos. It ends with a well-known
concluding formula (17-18).

   To judge from the probable supplements in ii 5-6, the lines of this column
lack ca. 20 letters to the right.

---

[1] II AD according to the ed.pr. G.Cavallo (letter of 30.8.1991) does not exclude the
late first century BC, and compares the hand to Roberts, *Greek Literary Hands*, pll. 8b
(30-29 BC), 9a (between 7 and 4 BC) and 11a (assigned to the second half of the first
century AD).

An illustrative textual restoration of ii 2-14 is offered in *Miscellanea Papyrologica*, p. 172.

Iota adscript incorrectly written in ii 6 φαγέτωι, omitted in ii 5 καθεύδη, possibly written in 8 (see 8 comm. and 7-8 comm.). ⳠΔ for δεῖνα (ii 7).

col. ii

```
[ . . . ]ταρ ουτω[                                           1
π . ωθοι και ο [
ἐκ παντὸς τόπ[ου            ὕπαγε εἰς πάντα]
τόπον καὶ πᾶϲα[ν οἰκίαν καὶ ἄξον μοι τὴν δ(εῖνα).] 4
ἐὰν καθεύδη μὴ [καθευδέτω, ἐὰν φάγῃ μὴ]
φαγέτωι, ἐὰν πίν[ῃ μὴ πινέτω, ἕωϲ ἔλθῃ πρὸϲ]
ἐμέ, τὸν δ(εῖνα), καὶ μ[
   . [ . ] . . καὶ τὸ μ[                                     8
   [ . . . ] φίλτατον [
   [ . . ἤ]δη ἤδη    [
[δ(εῖνα)   . . ] ἔτεκεν ἡ [δ(εῖνα)
εἰς πάντα τόπον [                                            12
θῦε δέ, μὴ ε[
πῦρ καὶ βαλὼν [
ε . ρ ιαλφηϲ θι[
   . [ . ] . . χιωχ[                                         16
ου[ . . . ] ἐπὶ τ[
[τελεί]αν ἐπα[οιδήν.
```

col. i
```
- - -
1  ]η
   ] . ν
   ]μ
4  ] .
   ] . πα
   ] . αν
```

Col. ii 6 φαγέτω   7 ⳠΔ Pap.   10 post alterum ηδη spatium vacuum in Pap.

(Col. ii, lines 3 ff.) - - - from every place - - - go into every |⁴ place and into every house and drive her, NN, to me. If she is sleeping, let her not keep sleeping; if she is eating, let her not keep eating; if she is drinking, let her not keep drinking, until she comes to me, NN, and - - - |⁸ - - - and the - - - very dear - - - now now. - - - NN, whom NN bore - - - |¹² into every place - - - sacrifice, not - - - fire and throwing - - - *e r ialphês thi*- - - |¹⁶ - - - *chiôch* - - - (fulfill this) charm completely.

Col. i: not transcribed in the ed.pr.

Col. ii

3 ἐκ παντὸς τόπ[ου: cf. e.g. **42**, 17, 38; **45**, 46 f.; **48** J 11, etc.

3-6. Supplements by Maltomini, *loc.cit.* In 4 slight variations are possible (cf. the parallels indicated in the next note).

3-4. Cf. PGM IV 348-350, 371 f. (and the parallels **46**, 7 f., 19 f.; **47**, 7, 18 f.; **48** J-K 6 f., 20 f., 32 f.; **49**, 17-19; **50**, 17-20); XXXVI 354.

5-6. Cf. PGM IV 1510-19 εἰ κάθηται, μὴ καθήϲθω, εἰ λαλεῖ πρός τινα, μὴ λαλείτω, εἰ ἐμβλέπει τινί, μὴ ἐμβλεπέτω, εἰ προϲέρχεταί τινι, μὴ προϲερχέϲθω, εἰ περιπατεῖ, μὴ περιπατείτω, εἰ πίνει, μὴ πινέτω, εἰ ἐϲθίει, μὴ ἐϲθιέτω, εἰ καταφιλεῖ τινα, μὴ καταφιλείτω, εἰ τέρπεταί τινι ἡδονῇ, μὴ τερπέϲθω, εἰ κοιμᾶται, μὴ κοιμάϲθω. In the present text the list of torments was certainly much less elaborate. If one supplies only what the surviving text requires, the result is continuous sense and two lines (5 and 6) with nearly equal length. Probably, then, nothing more is lost in the lacuna. The beloved is simply not to eat, drink and sleep, as in **43**, 8 f.

6 φαγέτωι (r. φαγέτω): for iota adscript incorrectly added to the third person imperative, see Mayser, *Grammatik* I.1, p. 113 f.; Gignac, *Grammar* I, p. 185.

6-7 ἕως ἔλθη πρὸς] | ἐμέ: cf. e.g. **39**, 15 f.; **40**, 17-20; **43**, 10, etc.

7 ἐμέ, τὸν Maltomini, *loc. cit.* : β̣ ̣ϲον ed.pr.

καὶ μ[: possibly καί μ[ε φιλῇ or καὶ μ[είνη. For the former, cf. e.g. PGM LXI 17 f. καὶ μὴ δυνηθῇ μήτε πιεῖν μήτε φαγεῖν, ἄχρι οὗ ἔλθη πρὸς ἐμέ, ἵνα με φιλῇ; for the latter, cf. e.g. PGM IV 378-380 μέχρι οὗ ἔλθη πρὸς ἐμέ, τὸν δεῖνα, καὶ ἀχώριϲτός μου μείνη; XVI 6-8, 15 f., 22-24, etc. ἕως ἔλθη - - - καὶ διαμείνη. Perhaps better is καὶ μ[ηρὸν μηρῷ πελάϲη (or κολλήϲη), for this would suit the possibility of καὶ τὸ μ[έλαν τῷ μέλανι in 8; cf. PGM IV 400-404 and the other passages gathered in **38**, 12 comm.; also **71** fr. 5, 2.

8 ̣[̣ ̣] ̣ : before the lacuna an upright; after the lacuna possibly ηι or πι in ligature.

7-8. The two lines may have run as follows:

ἐμέ, τὸν δ(εῖνα), καὶ μ[ηρὸν μηρῷ πελάϲη καὶ κεφαλὴν κε-]
φ[αλ]ῇ̣ι̣ καὶ τὸ μ[έλαν τῷ μέλανι

(line 7, however, would be rather long compared with the restorations suggested for 5-6).

10 ἤ]δη ἤδη [: because of the blank space after the second ἤδη, one should probably refrain from supplementing with the usual ἤ]δη ἤδη [ταχὺ ταχύ. Possibly ἤδη ἤδη was written alone (cf. PGM XII 86), but either ταχὺ τα]ι[χύ (cf. PGM VII 472 f.) or ἄρτι ἄρ]ι[τι (cf. PGM IV 1245) might have preceded.

11 [δ(εῖνα)   ] ἔτεκεν: it is not possible to tell whether the lacuna contained ὃν or ἣν. This is the earliest certain attestation of the formula ὃν (ἣν) ἔτεκε NN in magical texts. See, however, 71 fr. 14, 2 comm.

ἡ [δ(εῖνα) Maltomini, loc. cit. : [ed.pr.

13 θῦε δέ : [   ]δε ed.pr. Cf. 75, 8 with comm.

15 ιαλφης: cf. ιαρφε in PGM XXXVI 287 and ιαϲφη in PGM II 123. The first editor read this line [   ]ρι ἀλφῆϲ θι[and interpreted ἀλφῆϲ as a misspelling of ἀλοιφῆϲ or ἀλυφῆϲ.

16 χιωχ: cf. χιω χιωχα in 42, 52.

17 ου[: ο [ed.pr.

] ἐπὶ τ[: the writer tends to divide words; the spaces before ε and after ι suggest the articulation proposed.

18 [τελεί]αν ἐπα[οιδήν : [   ]λ[   ]επε[ed.pr. At the end of 17 will have stood an imperative of τελεῖν, with the possible additions of μοι and τήν. Also [τελέ]αν is possible. Parallels for this concluding formula are collected in 45, 53 comm.

74

Provenance
unknown

II AD

P.Genav. inv. 186.

ED.PR.: F.Maltomini, "Due papiri magici della Bibliothèque Publique et Universitaire di
Ginevra," *SCO* 36 (1986) 293-298.

COMM.: ed.pr.

TRANSL.: ed.pr.

PHOTO: ed.pr., plate XIII.

DESCR.: papyrus; 8 × 12.8 cm. Remains of a column preserved to its full height, but
damaged at the right and at the mid- and lower left. Blank spaces above and below the
text of 0.7 and 0.5 respectively; to the left, blank space of 2.2 cm. The writing runs
with the fibers on the recto, and the verso is blank.

LOC.: Bibliothèque Publique et Universitaire, Geneva.

Two spells, separated by a long horizontal stroke with coronis and a
wider line-space. The first spell (1-7) is against insomnia, the second (8-21)
probably against sciatica.

Diaeresis on upsilon in 1. ō-for ὄνομα (1, 4, 7); ⳁ for δεῖνα (17, *bis*).
καί is consistently abbreviated.

1   τοῦτο τὸ (ὄνομα) ὕπνον πο[ιεῖ. ἐὰν]
       γάρ τις ἀcθενῶν ἀγρ[υπνῇ, λα-]
       βὼν φύλλ[ο]ν̣ δάφνη[c ἐπίγρα-]
4   ψον τὸ (ὄνομα) τ[ο]ῦτο κ(αὶ) ὑπ[όθεc ὑπὸ]
       τὴν κεφαλὴν ἢ εἰc τὸ[
       λέγε δὲ κ(αὶ) τοῦ ἀcθενοῦ[ντοc τὸ]
       (ὄνομα) κ(αὶ) ὑπνώcει ἐκπλήκτω̣[c.

1 in ecthesi   ō- Pap.   ϋπνον Pap.   4 ō- Pap.   κ̢ Pap.   6 κ̢ Pap.
7 ō- Pap.   κ̢ Pap.

8   [*c.* 9]δα   [
     [...κασς]ιτέρινον λ...[
     [*c.* 7] ἐπίγραφε·
        [ια]εωβαφρε-

12   [νε]μουνοθι-
       [λα]ρικριφιαευε-
       αιφιρκιραλιθο-
       νυομενερφα-

16   βωεαι.
     ἀπάλλαξον τὸν δ(εῖνα) τῆς δ(εῖνα) [παντὸς]
     δεινοῦ πόνου κ(αὶ) πάςης ν[όςου
     νω...νεύρων κ(αὶ) ὀστέω[ν

20   [....]ςτος[...]ρυπεριτ[
     [*c.* 10   ]ενειλη[

8 post]δα spatium vacuum in Pap.   17 ∠ (bis) Pap.   18 κ̄ Pap.   19 κ̄ Pap.

This name causes sleep. If a patient suffers from insomnia, take a leaf of laurel, write on it |[4] this name and put it under his head or in the mattress (?). Utter also the name of the patient and he will sleep amazingly. |[8] Against sciatica (?). On white tin (?) - - - write: *iaeôbaphre*|[12]*nemounothilarikriphiaeyeaiphirkiralithonuomenerpha*|[16]*bôeai*. Deliver him, NN, son of her, NN, from every terrible suffering and every illness of tendons (?), sinews and bones - - - |[20] - - - roll up (?) - - -.

1-7. Cf. Ps.Gal., *Rem.* 2, 27, 3 (XIV 489, 4-6 K.) = Heim, *Incantamenta*, no. 202 εἰς φύλλον δάφνης ἐπίγραφε καὶ ὑποτίθει ἐπὶ τὴν κεφαλὴν λεληθότως ὀνομάζων· κόνκοφον βραχερέον; *ibid.* 3 (XIV 526, 18-527, 2 K.); Delatte, *Anecdota Atheniensia*, pp. 90, 1-3 εἰς ὕπνον· γράψον εἰς φύλλα δάφνης τὰ ςτοιχεῖα ταῦτα καὶ θές τα εἰς τὸ προσκέφαλόν του μὴ νοοῦντος· ξς χυ φθ; 551, 11-13 γράφε εἰς φύλλον δάφνης τὰ ςτοιχεῖα ταῦτα· ξ.ξ.χ.ς.υ.φ.θ. καὶ θὲς αὐτὸ ὑποκάτω τοῦ ςτρώματος, ἀγνοοῦντος αὐτοῦ· καὶ κοιμᾶται; also 142, 9-11; 550, 5-7, 8-12, 16-19; Legrand, *Bibliothèque grecque vulgaire* II, p. 11, 314-316. Similar, though more concise, is **96 A** 51 f.

1 τοῦτο τὸ (ὄνομα): if the ecthesis marks the beginning of the recipe, one might wonder where 'this name' is; perhaps it is lost in the lacuna at the end of 7 (for instances of the delayed mention of 'this name', cf. PGM IV 3143 and 3156-64). If we are dealing with a roll, however, the ecthesis could mark a new section of a recipe that began earlier, and the 'name' could have stood in the previous column.

(ὄνομα): for the sign ⊡ (also ◻ ⊡ ⬓) = ὄνομα, cf. PGM, Vol. 2, p. 269 f. As was pointed out by R.Ganszyniec (*ARW* 21, 1922, 229), the sign may have had its origin in the Egyptian cartouche ◯| that encircled the names of kings and deities. This cartouche had an apotropaic function and as a hieroglyph was read *rn* 'name'.

ὕπνον πο[ιεῖ: for the nexus, cf. e.g. Hipp., *Affect.* 36 (VI 246, 15 L.); *Aphor.* IV 15 (IV 506, 8 L.); Diosc. IV 75, 4 (II 235, 15 Wellmann); *Eupor.* I 12, 13 (III 156, 9, 18 Wellmann), etc.

5 εἰς τὸ[: perhaps εἰς τὸ [στρῶμα as in Delatte, *Anecdota Atheniensia*, p. 551, 12 (quoted above, 1-7 comm.). Both εἰς τὸ [προσκεφάλαιον and [προσκέφαλον (as in Delatte, *Anecdota Atheniensia*, p. 90, 3, quoted above, 1-7 comm.; Legrand, *loc.cit.* above, 1-7 comm.; *v.l.* in *Cyranides* I 10, p. 63, 24 Kaimakis) would be rather long compared with the restorations in 1-4, 6.

6-7 λέγε δὲ κ(αὶ) τοῦ ἀσθενοῦ[ντος τὸ] | (ὄνομα): cf. Delatte, *Anecdota Atheniensia*, p. 550, 10 f. καὶ γράψον καὶ τὸ ὄνομαν τοῦ ἀρρώστου εἰς χαρτὶν κτλ.

7 ἐκπλήκτῳ[ς: stressing the astonishing efficacy of recipes is a common feature both in magical and in medical texts. θαυμάζω and its derivatives are the words usually employed (cf. e.g. PGM IV 161, 233, 775, 3126, 3170 f., etc.), but ἐκπλήσσομαι occurs in PGM VII 921 καὶ ἐκπλαγήσει. For the adverb in an active sense, cf. Epiph., *Panar.* 76, 28, 7 (GCS 3, p. 377, 20).

8. The short line at the beginning of a new section probably contained the title of the second charm; the ending]δα suggests the usual heading πρὸς (or εἰς) + accusative; the space requires 8/9 letters; line 19 shows that this charm was concerned with sinews and bones; so, very probably: [πρὸς ἰσχιά]δα. There is no other prescription against sciatica in the Greek magical papyri, but cf. W.H.Worrell, *Orientalia* 4 (1935) 27, line 221 for one in a Graeco-Coptic magical text; cf. also the magical gems discussed by Bonner, *SMA*, pp. 71-77, and by Delatte-Derchain, *Intailles*, pp. 196-200.

9 κασσ]ιτέρινον: on tin in magic, see **94**, 37 comm.

λ ‸ ‸ [: first, probably ε; second, perhaps υ; third, κ or β.

10] : probably the right curve of ω.

9-10. The general sense is that the ιαεω logos in lines 11-16 is to be written on a tin object, probably a tablet. Restoration, however, is problematic. One would expect λαμν[ίον at the end of 9, but this reading seems impossible (see 9 comm.). Perhaps [εἰc καcc]ίτερ{ιν}ον λευκ[ὸν χαλ|κῷ γραφί]ῳ ἐπίγραφε, which, however, implies a mistake in an otherwise correct text (for white tin, cf. e.g. P.Leid. X 255, p. 95 Halleux; for the illustrative χαλκῷ γραφ(ε)ίῳ, cf. the numerous occurrences in PGM, Vol. 3 [Index], p. 74, *s.v.* γραφεῖον). Alternatively: (i) [εἰc καcc]ιτέρινον λευκ[ὸν λαμ|νίον ἤλ]ῳ ἐπίγραφε (λαμ|νίον or πέται|λον or πτύ|χιον; for ἤλῳ, cf. PGM VII 466; LXXVIII 4). (ii) 8-10 πρὸc ἰcχιά]δα· [λ(αβὼν) πέται|λον καcc]ιτέρινον λευκ[ῆ γραφίδι ἐν αὐτ]ῷ ἐπίγραφε (for λευκῆ γραφίδι, cf. PGM III 303).

11-16. On this palindrome, see **65**, 1-30 comm.

18 δεινοῦ πόνου: cf. PGM P 3, 3-6 διαφύλαξον τὸν οἶκον τοῦτον μετὰ τῶν ἐνοικούντων ἀπὸ παντὸc κακοῦ - - - καὶ πόνου δεινοῦ κτλ.

ν[όcου: of ν only the left corner is preserved.

19 νω : scattered ink. Probably the genitive plural of a noun, e.g. τό]|νων. If so, 18-19 πάcηc ν[όcου τό]|νων.

20] : the top of an upright.

]ρυπεριτ[: instead of]ρ also]ο is possible; ιτ seems preferable to η[. Perhaps]ρ ὑπὲρ ιτ[or]ρυ περὶ τ[.

21] : α or λ.

] ενειλη[: probably] ἐνειλη[c- (ἐνειλήcαc? ἐνείληcον?) or] εν εἰλη[c- (cf. PGM II 51, 63 f. and IV 2702 f. respectively). This line belonged to a praxis.

Provenance   II AD
  unknown

P.Genav. inv. 293.

ED.PR.: F.Maltomini, "Due papiri magici della Bibliothèque Publique et Universitaire di
    Ginevra," *SCO* 36 (1986) 298-305.

COMM.: ed.pr.

PHOTO: ed.pr., plate XIV.

DESCR.: papyrus; 5.8 × 11.7 cm. Remains of a column damaged at the right, the lower
    left and the bottom. The upper margin measures 1.1 cm; to the left a blank space of
    1.2 cm. The writing runs with the fibers on the recto, and the verso is blank.

LOC.: Bibliothèque Publique et Universitaire, Geneva.

Praxis and logos of a prescription. Its beginning is lost, and its precise
nature cannot be determined. The praxis (1-11) prescribes a sacrifice (8): the
operator, facing south (2), has to lick a magical inscription written with
myrrh-ink (3-4) and to anoint something with honey (5) on the occasion of an
astral conjunction (7). The victim is a young white pig (9); its innards are to
be eaten (10) and the rest burnt (11). The logos follows: divine entities are
commanded (12) to come to the practitioner (14, 19), to hear him (19) and to
complete the operation (19-20). The text breaks off in the middle of a well-
known magical litany.

The supplements proposed for 19-21 suggest an original column width of
7-8 cm with about 30 letters to the line.

1 μόρια ȳ κ[
   πρὸς νότο[ν
   τος καὶ ἔγλειξο[ν
4 ζμυρνομέλανι [
   χρίσας μέλιτι [
   ἔχουσιν τὸν κα [
   συνοδεύοντος [
8 θῦε δὲ καὶ ἀπογε[υ-
   [ ]ε χοῖρος λευκὸς [
   αν καὶ τὰ σπλάνχνα [
   λοιπὰ ὁλοκαύτου.   [
12 [ἐ]πικαλοῦμαι ὑμᾶς κ[
   [ ] ματος οὗ ἐστήρισεν [
   [ ] ουθ· ἔλθατέ μοι, α[
   [ ] ὁρέων καὶ κορυφῶν [
16 [ ] τῶν ὁρέων ο [ ] [
   [το]ῦ [οὐρα]νοῦ καὶ τῆς γῆς [
   [τὰ] πάντα διατάξαντα ς[
   [ἐπα]κούσατε, ἔλθατε κα[
20 [τήν]δε τὴν πρᾶξιν ἣν β[ούλομαι
   [Βαρ]βαραθαμ χελουβρυ β[αρουχ αβραμ Σε-]
   [σε]γγεν Βαρφαρανγης [

———   ———   ———

3 ἔκλειξον   10 σπλάγχνα   11 post ολοκαυτου spatium vacuum in Pap.
14 post ουθ spatium unius litterae in Pap.   22 inter βαρ et φαρανγης spatium unius
litterae in Pap.

- - - three portions - - - towards south - - - and lick - - - |⁴ with myrrh ink - - -
anointing with honey - - - they have the - - - being in conjunction - - -. |⁸ Sacrifice and
taste - - - a white piglet - - - and the innards - - - burn the rest entirely - - -. |¹² "I invoke
you - - - which (?) he fixed - - - come to me - - - of the mountains and summits - - - |¹⁶ - -
- of the mountains - - - of the heaven and the earth - - - who ordered all things - - - hear,
come and complete for me (?) |²⁰ this operation, which I want, by (?) *Barbaratham
cheloubry barouch abram Seseggen Barpharangês* - - -.

2 πρὸς νότο[ν: cf. PGM II 79 f. κοιμῶ τὴν κεφαλὴν ἔχων πρὸς νότον; XIII 829 f. ⟨ε⟩ἰ⟨ς⟩ τὸ⟨ν⟩ νότον - - - λέγε; 858 πρὸς τὸν νό-το⟨ν⟩ βλέπων λέγε, etc.; see PGM, Vol. 3 (Index), *s.vv.* ἀπηλιώτης (ἀνατολή), βορέας, λίψ, νότος. On geographical orientation in magical procedures, see Th.Hopfner, *RE* XIV.1, *s.v.* Mageia, col. 358 f.; idem, *Offenbarungszauber* I, § 837; P.Oslo I 1, 240 comm.

3 ἔγλειξο[ν (r. ἔκλειξον): cf. PGM IV 782-785 γράψον ἐπὶ φύλλου περσέας τὸ ὀκταγράμματον ὄνομα, ὡς ὑπόκειται, καὶ - - - ἀπόλειχε τὸ φύλλον, 788 f. τὸ δὲ ὄνομά ἐστιν τοῦτο· ϊ εε οο ϊαϊ. τοῦτο ἔκλειχε, ἵνα φυλακτηριασθῇς; VII 521-523 τὸ ὄνομα γράφε ζμυρνομέλανι εἰς ᾠὰ δύο ἀρρενικά· καὶ τῷ μὲν ἑνὶ περικαθαίρεις σεαυτὸν καὶ ἐκλείξας τὸ ὄνομα ἔκβαλε κατάξας; XIII 131-133 (quoted in **97** ↓ 3-4 comm.; also 434-436; 688-692), 889 f., 1042-51. To lick a magical inscription is to ingest it and to acquire its force; see Fr. Preisigke, *Die Gotteskraft der frühchristlichen Zeit* (Pap. Inst. Heidelberg 6, 1922), p. 32 f. This technique is well attested also for Ancient Egypt; cf. J.F.Borghouts, *Ancient Egyptian Magical Texts* (Leiden 1978), p. 55, no. 84; *Coffin Texts* II, 44 (spell 81; see R.O.Faulkner, *The Ancient Egyptian Coffin Texts* I, Warminster 1973, p. 87); and see M.Heerma van Voss, *Phœnix* 30 (1984) 32. A comparable procedure was to drink a liquid in which a magical inscription had been dissolved (cf. PGM I 232-236; XIII 131-136) or which was poured over a statue or stela (as was the case for Egyptian healing statues and Horos cippi; see R.K.Ritner, "Horus on the Crocodiles," esp. pp. 106-108). See Dornseiff, *Das Alphabet*, pp. 20, 50; A.A.Barb, *Mitteil. d. anthropol. Gesellsch. in Wien* 82 (1953) 17 f.; also *Handwörterbuch des deutschen Aberglaubens* VIII, *s.v.* Trinken, col. 1156 f.; IX, *Nachträge, s.v.* schreiben, Schrift, Geschriebenes, col. 354.

4 ˍ[: upright; γ, ι, κ, ν possible. Probably a form of γράφω.

3-4. Purely e.g.: καὶ ἔκλειξο[ν τοὺς χαρακτῆρας τῷ] | ζμυρνομέ-λανι γ[ράψας εἰς χάρτην.

5 ˍ[: probably a round letter.

6 ˍ[: foot of a descender hooked to right, perhaps ρ.

7 cυνοδεύοντος: very probably 'to be in conjunction' in an astronomical sense (cf. LSJ, *s.v.*, II). The verb does not occur elsewhere in the Greek magical papyri, but cf. cύνοδος in PGM III 482, IV 780, XIII 5, 116, 672, referring to conjunctions of the moon and sun (new moon). In the present passage, however, the gender of the participle implies a different heavenly

body (see *TGL*, *s.v.*, 1422B; also, e.g., *Cat. Cod. Astr. Gr.* II, p. 123, 12; VIII.3, p. 105, 15, etc.). For temporal directions of astronomical character in magic, see Th.Hopfner, *RE* XIV.1, *s.v.* Mageia, col. 354 f.; idem, *Offenbarungszauber* I, §§ 825-835.

8-11. The victim is a white piglet; a part of it (the σπλάγχνα) is to be roasted and eaten, the rest burnt. This seems the most probable reconstruction (see 10-11 comm.). If this is correct, the background appears to be Greek, not Egyptian, since in Egypt the pig, sacred to Seth and regarded as unclean, normally was neither sacrificed nor eaten; see A.B.Lloyd, *Herodotus. Book II. Commentary 1-98* (EPRO 43, Leiden 1976), pp. 216-218; *Lexikon der Ägyptologie* V, *s.v.* Schwein, coll. 762-764 (W.Helck). This repugnance is evidenced also by PGM I 105 f. and IV 3079 f. (the latter within a λόγος Ἑβραϊκός: cf. 3084 f.). There is probably no relationship with Isis, for she was connected with a white *sow*; see J.Bergman, "Isis auf der Sau," *Boreas* 6 (1974) 81-109.

8 θῦε δὲ (or ἐπίθυε δὲ): cf. **73** ii 13 (also **100**, 1); PGM XIII 369; IV 2641, 3096.

ἀπογε[υ-: imperative or participle. In the Greek magical papyri, γεύομαι and ἀπογεύομαι occur always in connection with sacrificial operations; cf. PGM III 320, 428, 430, 434, 470; XIII 377 (and cf. ἀπόγευσις 360 f. and 376).

10 ̣αν: a little hook on the line, suggesting the lower right of η, κ, λ, π, υ.

σπλάνχνα (r. σπλάγχνα): roasting and eating innards was an essential moment in Greek sacrifice.

10-11 ̣αν καὶ τὰ σπλάνχνα̣ [⏐ λοιπὰ ὁλοκαύτου: this sequence suggests a distinction of use between the σπλάγχνα (and perhaps that of which ̣αν is the rest) and λοιπά; and also 8 ἀπογε[υ- points in the same direction. For something similar cf. PGM IV 2395-98 θῦε αὐτῷ λευκομέτωπον ⟨ὀν⟩άγριον καὶ ὁλοκαυστήσας ἰδὲ τὰ σπλάγχνα ἀποπυρίσας ἐπὶ ξύλοις ἰτεΐνοις οὕτω κατάφαγε. When the whole victim is to be consumed by fire, no such distinctions are made (cf. PGM IV 3148 f.; XII 36, 214). E.g. καὶ τὰ σπλάγχνα [κατάφαγε, τὰ δὲ] ⏐ λοιπὰ ὁλοκαύτου.

11 ὁλοκαύτου: in view of the middle ὁλοκαυστοῦ in PGM IV 3148 (though see S.Eitrem, *Les papyrus magiques grecs de Paris*, Oslo 1923, p. 19), one cannot exclude that it is from ὁλοκαυτέω, in which case r. ὁλοκαυτοῦ. The following blank space marks the end of the praxis. In the lost part of the line, probably, λόγος *vel simm.* (λόγος λεγόμενος, etc.).

12 κ[: κ[ύριοι? κ[ραταιοὶ (θεοί PGM VII 422; δαίμονες II 9)?

13] . : probably γ, possibly ϲ.

12-13. E.g. κ[ύριοι, οἱ ἐπὶ τοῦ ϲτηρ]|[ί]γματοϲ οὗ (i.e. ὅ) ἐϲτήριϲεν (for ϲτήριγμα as 'firmament', cf. PGM VII 509); or οἱ ἐπὶ τοῦ ἑδρ]|[ά-] ϲματοϲ (cf. PGM IV 1149, 1153); or also κ[ύριοι θεοὶ τοῦ κτλ. However this may be, ϲτηρίζω suggests a cosmic image; the verb is frequently used of the creator god: cf. PGM IV 1153 f. τὴν δὲ γῆν ἑδράϲμαϲιν αἰωνίοιϲ ϲτηρί-ϲαϲ (also ϲτηριγμοθέταϲ in 1356); Alex. Trall. II 585 Puschmann (= Heim, *Incantamenta*, no. 167) ὁ θεὸϲ ὁ ϲτηρίξαϲ τὴν γῆν; lines 1-4 of the magical bracelet published by A.A.Barb, "Magica varia," *Syria* 49 (1972) 364 τὸν βροντήϲαντα καὶ ἀϲτράψαντα καὶ ϲτηρίϲαντα γῆν καὶ οὐρανόν; also *1 Clem.* 33, 3 οὐρανοὺϲ ἐϲτήριϲεν; *Corp. Herm.* IV, fr. 31 (p. 137, 11 Nock-Festugière); Arat., *Phaen.* 10; Orph., Fr. 299, 3 Kern; Eus., *Comm. in Ps. 23*, Migne PG 23, 220D, etc. For the aorist in -ϲα, see Blass-Debrunner-Funk, *Grammar*, § 71; Gignac, *Grammar* II, p. 268 and n. 1.

14] . ουθ (]ῳουθ,]λουθ,]μουθ) rather than]ωυθ. Either the name of a god, subject of 13 ἐϲτήριϲεν, or a magical word. Perhaps [Θ]ῳουθ; for Hermes-Thoth as almighty world-ruler, see A.Dieterich, *Abraxas* (Leipzig 1891), pp. 64, 66 f.; M.P.Nilsson, "Die Religion in den griechischen Zauber-papyri," *Bull. de la Soc. de Lettres, Lund*, 1947-1948, II, 10 f. (= *Opuscula selecta* III, p. 140); G.Fowden, *The Egyptian Hermes* (Cambridge 1986), p. 25. Other magical names with the same ending: Αβεραμενθωουθ, Αρμιωουθ, Φωουθ (see PGM, Vol. 3, Index VI, *s.vv.*), Cουαρμιμωουθ (Audollent, *DT*, 242, 16). 13-14 e.g. [ὁ μέγιϲτοϲ Ἑρμῆϲ] | [Θ]ῳουθ.

ἔλθατε (cf. also 19): for the form ἦλθα, see Gignac, *Grammar* II, p. 340 f. Above ατ is a horizontal for which we have no explanation.

ἀ[κούϲατέ μου? ἄ[γγελοι? ἄ[γιοι ἄγγελοι?

15-17. The genitives can be governed again by a phrase such as οἱ ἐπὶ τῶν (on which see **2**, 2-3 comm.) or by a noun such as κύριοι (cf. e.g. PGM IV 640 f.), οἰκήτορεϲ (VII 351), ἄρχοντεϲ (VII 687), δεϲπόται (XII 48), etc.

15] . : the top of an upright.

ὀρέων: for the uncontracted gen. pl. of ὄροϲ (also in 16), see Gignac, *Grammar* II, p. 67.

18. διατάξαντα ϲ[rather than διατάξανταϲ [, because the extended tail of the last α suggests word end; cf. the final ε of 19 ἐπα]κούϲατε. The participle will refer to a god as orderer of the universe. Because the invoca-tion is addressed to *several* entities (12, 14, 19), the accusative is probably an

accusative of swearing. So, 17-18 e.g. [ὅτι ὁρκίζω ὑμᾶς τὸν] | [τὰ] πάντα διατάξαντα. For διατάccω and cognates in similar contexts, cf. PGM XIII 270 f. cὲ μόνον ἐπικαλοῦμαι, τὸν μόνον ἐν κόcμῳ διατάξαντα θεοῖc καὶ ἀνθρώποιc; also, e.g., Men. Rh. 438, 24, p. 208 Russell-Wilson; *Corp. Herm.* IV, fr. XXIII, 20 (p. 7, 2 Nock-Festugière); fr. 35 (p. 142, 3 Nock-Festugière), etc.

19-20. Certainly the text ran here (cυν-, δια-) τελέcατέ μοι] | [τήν]δε τὴν πρᾶξιν; cf. PGM XII 258 ἐπάκουcόν μου καὶ τέλεcόν μοι τήνδε τὴν πρᾶξιν; also IV 2098 διατέλεcόν μοι τὸ δεῖνα πρᾶγμα; III 85 cυντέλεcόν μοι τὸ δεῖνα πρᾶγμα, etc. In 19 a reconstruction ἔλθατε κα[ὶ τελέcατε is probable; cf. Audollent, *DT*, 38, 14 f. ἔλθετε καὶ τελειώcατέ μοι τὴν πραγματείαν ταύτην.

20 ἢν β[ούλομαι: cf. PGM XXXVI 229 ποίηcον ὃ βούλομαι πρᾶγμα.

21-22. On the Βαρβαριθα logos, see **2**, 5-7 comm. Because this logos has a great variety of forms, the parallels cannot serve to determine original length of line. Some of its occurrences (PGM III 109 f.; Delatte-Derchain, *Intailles*, nos. 516, 520, 521), however, correspond with the length of line that has been posited above (see intr. and 19-20 comm.).

The following partial reconstruction of 12-22 is purely illustrative, but it may give some concreteness to the observations made in the commentary.

```
12   [ἐ]πικαλοῦμαι ὑμᾶc, κ[ύριοι οἱ ἐπὶ τοῦ cτηρ-]
     [ί]γματοc οὗ ἐcτήριcεν [ὁ μέγιcτοc Ἑρμῆc]
     [Θ]ωουθ· ἔλθατέ μοι, ἀ[κούcατέ μου, οἱ ἐπὶ]
     [τῶ]ν ὀρέων καὶ κορυφῶν [
16   [ . . ] τῶν ὀρέων ο . . [ . ] [
     [το]ῦ [οὐρα]νοῦ καὶ τῆc γῆc, [ὅτι ὁρκίζω ὑμᾶc τὸν]
     [τὰ] πάντα διατάξαντα· c[υνεργήcατέ μοι,]
     [ἐπα]κούcατε, ἔλθατε κα[ὶ τελέcατέ μοι]
20   [τήν]δε τὴν πρᾶξιν ἢν β[ούλομαι, κατὰ τοῦ]
     [Βαρ]βαραθαμ χελουβρυ β[αρουχ αβραμ Cε-]
     [cε]γγεν Βαρφαρανγηc [
```

Tebtunis   II/III AD[1]

P.Yale II 134.

ED.PR.: G.M.Parássoglou, "Greek Papyri from Roman Egypt. No. 9: Magico-Medical
Prescriptions," *Hellenika* 27 (1974) 251-253.

REPUBL.: SB XIV 11909; P.Yale II 134 (S.A.Stephens).

COMM.: ed.pr.; P.Yale II 134; (line 7) F.Maltomini, *Civ. Class. Crist.* 1 (1980) 374;
M.Marcovich, *ZPE* 65 (1986) 58; F.Maltomini, *ZPE* 68 (1987) 105 f.

TRANSL.: ed.pr.; R.Kotansky in Betz, *Translation*, no. CXXVII; P.Yale II 134.

PHOTO: ed.pr., plate 11.

DESCR.: papyrus; the last column of an otherwise fragmentary roll measuring 75 × 16.5
cm. The writing runs with the fibers on the recto, and the verso is blank.

LOC.: The Beinecke Rare Book and Manuscript Library, Yale University, New Haven,
Connecticut. Inv. 1206, col. vi.

The earlier, as yet unpublished portion of the roll (remains of five
columns) contains a very fragmentary series of magical charms. Col. vi
preserves six prescriptions which are similar in style and content to the
Jocular Recipes of Democritus (Δημοκρίτου παίγνια, PGM VII 167-185[2]):
lines 1-2 to relax an erect penis, 3-4 to pick someone up at the baths, 5-6 for
amorous dalliance with a woman, 7-8 to cause a fight at a banquet, 9-10 to
turn wine sour, 11-12 for frequent sexual intercourses.

The prescriptions are separated by paragraphus and extra interlinear
space. The scribe correctly gave iota adscript in 5 and 10, but omitted it in 2,
3 and 7. Unmarked elision (10, possibly 8).

---

[1] Early fourth century according to Stephens (III-IV Parássoglou), but cf. Schubart,
Griechische Palaeographie, Abb. 47, 47a, 47b, 47c.

[2] On which see F.Maltomini in: *Corpus dei papiri filosofici greci e latini* I.1** 43a 1T
(Florence 1992).

1 κατακύψαι καὶ μὴ ἀνακύψαι· νάρκης
θαλασσίας ἐνκεφάλῳ [χ]ρῖε τὴν ἐcφῦν.

ἐν βαλανείῳ τινὰ ἔρεcθαι· κυνὸc νε-
4 κροῦ κροτῶνα θλᾷcον ἰc τὴν ἐcφῦν.

γυναικὶ ἐμπαῖξαι· θαψίαc χ[[ει]]υλῶι
χρεῖε τὸ αἰδοῖον.

ἐν cυ[μ]ποcίῳ μάχην γενέcθαι· κυνό-
8 δηκτον λίθον βάλε ἰc τὸ μέcον.

ὄξοc δριμὺ ποιῆcαι· ψήφουc πυρώ-
cac βάλ' ἐν [αὐ]τῶι.

πρὸc πολλὰ βεινῖν· cελείνου
12 καὶ εὐζώμου cπ[έρ]μα πρόπιε.

2 ἐγκεφάλῳ   ὀcφῦν   3 αἴρεcθαι?   4 εἰc   ὀcφῦν   6 χρῖε
8 εἰc (an βάλ' εἰc ?)   11 βινεῖν· cελίνου

So it will droop and not stand up: anoint the loins with the brain of an electric ray. To pick up (?) someone at the baths: squeeze a tick from a dead dog |4 against the loins. To 'play' with a woman: anoint your genitals with juice of deadly carrot. To cause a fight at a banquet: throw a dog-bitten |8 stone into the midst. To turn cheap wine sour: throw red-hot pebbles into it. To fuck a lot: drink in advance celery |12 and rocket seed.

1-2. A prescription for relaxing an erect penis. The recipe could be against priapism, if it is not a joke that can be explained by the salacious and mischievous nature of these *paignia*. For ἀνακύπτω said of the penis, cf. Aristoph., *Thesm.* 1187b (cod. R, excised by Bentley as *parepigraphe*) ἀνακύπτῃ (-ει) καὶ παρακύπτι (-ει) ἀπεψωλημένοc. The electric ray was generally believed to have antaphrodisiac power; cf. Plin., *N.H.* XXXII 139 *venerem inhibet - - - fel torpedinis vivae genitalibus inlitum*; Ps.Gal., *Rem.* 2, 27, 1 (XIV 487, 7 f. K.); *Cyranides* IV 44 (p. 277, 9-11 Kaimakis) ἐὰν δὲ καὶ γυνὴ ἐπιχρίcῃ τὸ μόριον αὐτῆc ἐκ τοῦ cτέατοc, οὐ cυγγενήcεται ἀνὴρ μετ' αὐτῆc οὐδὲ cυνουcιάcει ὅλωc. (Quite different is PGM XXXVI 284: the gall of an electric river-eel is used in a φυcικλείδιον, a charm to open the female genitals.) A prescription for relaxing a penis occurs in Bell-Nock-Thompson, "Magical Texts from a Bilingual Papyrus," p. 254 (recto B, 4-5). For recipes to prevent an erection, see e.g. Ps.Gal., *Rem.* 2, 27, 1 (XIV 486 f. K.).

1 ἀνακύψαι : ἀν[α]κύψαι ed.pr., Stephens.

2 ἐcφῦν (r. ὀcφῦν): cf. also 4. For o > ε, see Gignac, *Grammar* I, p. 289 f. The loins were believed to be the seat of sexual desire. Adams' statement that ὀcφῦc is used of the penis in Ps.Luc., *Asin.* 9 and 51 is unconvincing (Adams, *The Latin Sexual Vocabulary*, pp. 48, 92; see also Macleod's translation in the Loeb Lucian, Vol. VIII, pp. 65, 135).

3 ἐν βαλανείῳ: the baths were haunted by voyeurs and exhibitionists and were regarded as a good place for picking up both girls and boys. Cf. e.g. Petron. 92, 7 f.; Mart., *Epigr.* I 23 (with Howell's and Citroni's comm.) and XI 63 (with Kay's comm.).

ἔρεcθαι (r. αἴρεcθαι?) : according to Stephens, the verb may be ἐρέcθαι "to solicit someone," but that ἔρομαι could have this meaning seems quite improbable; moreover, given its high literary level and its rarity in post-classical prose, it would not be at home in the present text. Parássoglou suggested that one read αἴρεcθαι "to win someone" ("to get a certain [lover]" Kotansky in Betz, *Translation*), and we incline to agree with this interpretation, although we have not been able to find parallels.

4 κροτῶνα: on the tick in folklore and magic, see *RE Suppl.* XIV, *s.v.* Zecken, col. 983 f. (W.Richter); cf. also **78** ii 12-13 comm.

θλάcον : θλ[ῖ]ψον Parássoglou, Stephens, but (i) there are some traces after λ consistent with part of the loop and oblique of α (certainly not with ι), (ii) one would expect to see the bottom of the vertical of ψ, (iii) the verb required is θλάω: cf. Philum., *Ther.* 7, 2 (CMG X.1, 1, p. 11, 9) κροτῶνος τεθλαcμένου; Aesop., *fab.* 231, 2 Perry οἷός τε ἦν cυνθλάcαι τὴν ψύλλαν; Soran., *Gyn.* III 29 (CMG IV, p. 112, 9) κόρεcι τεθλαcμέναιc; *Geopon.* XIII 17 (p. 403, 16 Beckh) κόρειc θλάcαc.

5 γυναικὶ ἐμπαῖξαι: for the meaning of ἐμπαίζω here, cf. LXX *Judic.* 19, 25 ἐνέπαιξαν αὐτῇ ὅλην τὴν νύκτα ἕωc τὸ πρωί. For παίζω and cυμπαίζω of amorous dalliance, see Henderson, *The Maculate Muse*, p. 157, § 240; Adams, *The Latin Sexual Vocabulary*, p. 162.

θαψίαc: on the properties of deadly carrot, see Diosc. IV 153, 3 f. (II 299, 6 ff. Wellmann). Its juice, applied to the glans, makes it swell (II 300, 4-7 Wellmann).

7-8. Cf. Aelian., *N.A.* I 38 ἔριν δὲ εἴ τις καὶ ϲτάϲιν ἐθέλοι ἐν τῷ ϲυν-δείπνῳ ἐργάϲαϲθαι, δηχθέντα ὑπὸ κυνὸϲ λίθον ἐμβαλὼν τῷ οἴνῳ λυπεῖ τοὺϲ ϲυμπόταϲ ἐκμαίνων; Manuel Philes, *De animalium proprietate* 54, 5 f. οἴνῳ δὲ κυνόδηκτον ὁ κρύψαϲ λίθον, / ϲτάϲιν πονηρὰν ἐξεγεί-ρει τοῖϲ φίλοιϲ; also Plin., *N.H.* XXIX 102 *minus hoc miretur qui cogitet lapidem a cane morsum usque in proverbium discordiae venisse* (on which see F.Maltomini, *Materiali e discussioni per l'analisi dei testi classici* 16, 1986, 153 f.). A Coptic parallel is preserved in a codex of the 11th century, BKU I 26, p. 29 line 15 f.; see O.von Lemm, *Bull. Acad. Impér. des Scien-ces de St. Pétersbourg*, VI-me Série, 1 (1907) 497 f., no. XVII (= *Koptische Miscellen* [Subsidia Byzantina XI, 1972], p. [15 f.]): "Nimm den Stein, in den der Hund gebissen hat, wirf ihn in den Wein trinkender Leute, so prügeln sie sich einander" (Lemm also cites an Arabic parallel). For medieval examples, see *Handwörterbuch des deutschen Aberglaubens* IV, *s.v.* Hund, col. 481; VIII, *s.v.* Streit, Zank, coll. 527, 530 n. 75. For sympotic quarrels, see E.Pellizzer in: M.Vetta (ed.), *Poesia e simposio nella Grecia antica* (Roma-Bari 1983), pp. 29-41.

7 μάχην Maltomini (*Civ. Class. Crist.* 1, 1980, 374), Stephens (μά[χ]ην) : μά[ν]ην Parássoglou.

8 βάλε ἰϲ (r. εἰϲ) τὸ μέϲον: "The variant offered by the papyrus, to throw a stone into the midst of the symposium rather than into the wine, brings to mind the apple of discord at the Wedding of Peleus and Thetis or the tale of the Spartoi the number of whom Cadmus reduced by casting a stone into their midst, causing them to fight with each other. The intent must be mischievous, in the nature of a practical joke in this case" (S.A.Stephens). But it could also be that βάλε means here 'put', not 'throw'; see the charm quoted by C.Bartsch, *Zeitschr. f. deutsche Mythologie u. Sittenkunde* 3 (1855) 321 (from a manuscript of the late 16th or early 17th cent.) "vneynig-keit zu machen. Eynen stein genommen, der nach eynem hunde geworffen würdt, vnd der hundt dorein gebiessen hatt, diesen stein alsdan gelegett vnder eynen tysch, oder sonsten an ein ortt, da leutte beysamen sein."

τὸ μέϲον: the text is irreproachable. Marcovich's conjecture τὸ μέθυ (*ZPE* 65, 1986, 58) is to be rejected; see F.Maltomini, *ZPE* 68 (1987) 105 f.

11 πρὸϲ πολλὰ βεινῖν (r. βινεῖν): cf. PGM VII 182 f. πολλὰ βι[ν]εῖν δύναϲθαι; **83**, 5. For the anarthrous infinitive with πρόϲ, cf. P.Lips. 37, 15; on the prepositional infinitive without article in general, see Ljungvik, *Beiträge zur Syntax*, pp. 3-6; Mandilaras, *Verb*, §§ 839-864.

cελείνου (r. cελίνου): on the aphrodisiac properties of celery, cf. *Geopon.* XII 23, 3 (p. 372, 4-6 Beckh) βρωθὲν δὲ τὸ cέλινον κατωφερεcτέραc εἰc τὰ ἀφροδίcια ποιεῖ τὰc γυναῖκαc; see *Handwörterbuch des deutschen Aberglaubens* VI, *s.v.* Petersilie, col. 1529; VII, *s.v.* Sellerie, col. 1635.

12 εὐζώμου: on the rocket plant as an aphrodisiac, cf. Diosc. II 140 (I 210, 5 f. Wellmann) εὔζωμον πλεῖον βρωθὲν cυνουcίαν παρορμᾷ, καὶ τὸ cπέρμα δ'αὐτοῦ τὸ αὐτὸ ποιεῖ; Gal., *Alim. fac.* 2, 53 (VI 639, 11 f. K.); Ps.Gal., *Rem.* 2, 27, 2 (XIV 487 f. K.); *Cyranides* I 5, 15-20; V 5, 3 f. (pp. 44 f.; 301 Kaimakis); Plin., *N.H.* XIX 154; Marcell. Emp., *De medicam.* 33, 46; **83**, 5-9. See also *RE* I A.1, *s.v.* Rauke, col. 287, 36-39 (F.Orth); P.T. Eden, *Hermes* 91 (1963) 458. In *Cyranides* I 5, 12-14 (p. 44 Kaimakis), however, it is said that rocket, eaten green, prevents erection and ejaculation during sleep and hence is eaten regularly by temple attendants (similar is Ps.Gal., *Rem.* 3 [XIV 543, 15-18 K.]).

Provenance   II-III AD[1]
unknown

P.Bon. 3.

ED.PR: O.Montevecchi in: O.Montevecchi-G.B.Pighi, "Prima ricognizione dei papiri dell'
    Università di Bologna," *Aegyptus* 27 (1947) 182, 183 f.

REPUBL.: A.Vogliano, *Acme* 1 (1948) 226-228; idem, *Acme* 5 (1952) 405-407; P.Bon. 3
    (O.Montevecchi).

COMM.: Montevecchi, *locc.citt.*; Vogliano, *locc.citt.*; F.Maltomini in: *Miscellanea
    Papyrologica* (Papyrologica Florentina VII, 1980), p. 172 f.; (fol. 6r, 6) J.Schwartz,
    Rev. Phil. 28 (1954) 292. On codicological matters, see F.Maltomini, *ZPE* 85 (1991)
    239-243, with reference to previous discussions.

PHOTO: *ZPE* 85 (1991), plates III, IV, V.

REF.: Pack[2] 645+1034; Preisendanz, "Überlieferung," no. LXXXV.

DESCR.: the last three pages (foll. 5v-6) of an incomplete papyrus codex of mixed content
    (foll. 1-5r contain a hexameter katabasis, P.Bon. 4 = Pack[2] 1801). Estimated page
    height ca. 22 cm. Estimated page breadth ca. 18 cm. Column height of the Homer
    oracle ca. 18 cm with 25 lines per column.

LOC.: Biblioteca Universitaria, Bologna. Inv. 24 f recto + 24 b[2].

A Homer oracle, like P.Lond. I 121 (= PGM VII 1*-66*, 1-148a) and
P.Oxy. LVI 3831. These oracles consisted of a list of 216 disconnected
Homeric verses, each of which was preceded by three figures, from ααα
(1.1.1) to ϛϛϛ (6.6.6). The inquirer cast a single die three times, and the result
indicated the verse to be consulted (cf. P.Oxy. 3831, 4-6).

All of the verses on fol. 5v can now be identified on the basis of P.Oxy.
3831, which gives the same verses in the same order. P.Lond. 121, as
reconstructed in PGM VII, appears quite different, but this reconstruction is

---

[1] II-III AD with Vogliano, Montevecchi and Turner, *Typology*, pp. 81, 90, 107 no.
107, 116; II AD according to C.H.Roberts, "The Codex," *Proc. Brit. Acad.* 40 (1954) 184 f.
(see also C.H.Roberts-T.C.Skeat, *The Birth of the Codex*, London 1983, p. 71 f.).

defective.[2] In fact, fol. 6r, 6-9 correspond exactly to PGM VII 24*-27*; the figures given by Preisendanz to the section 24*-34*, αδϛ-αϛδ, are wrong, the correct ones being 31-41, αϛα-βαε.[3] Fol. 6r, 5 corresponds to PGM VII 66*: the verse was misplaced by Preisendanz, its true number being 30, αεϛ.[4] Fol. 6v, 1-11 correspond with PGM VII 51*-61*, and hence it follows that fol. 6r contained 25 lines just like fol. 5v.

Diaeresis on iota (fol. 6v, 5, 9). Elision is marked in foll. 6r, 5 and 6v, 8, 10, but not in 6v, 7. καί is abbreviated (fol. 6v, 6).

The figures in parentheses indicate the position of the verses in the Homer oracle.

Fol. 5v (→)

1	[ααα	ἄνδρ' ἀπαμύνασθαι, ὅτε τις πρότερος χαλε]πήνῃ	Ω 369 etc.
	[ααβ	θαρϛῶν νῦν Διόμηδες ἐπὶ Τρώεσσι μάχεσθα]ι	Ε 124
	[ααγ	ἦ ῥά νύ τοι μεγάλων δώρων ἐπεμαίετο θυ]μός	Κ 401
4	[ααδ	νίκην καὶ μέγα κῦδος, ἀτὰρ Δαναοῖϛί γε πῆ]μα	Θ 176
	[ααε	ἀλλ' οὐ πείϛονται Τρῶες καὶ Δαρδανίωνε]ϛ	Θ 154
	[ααϛ	εἰ δ' ἄγε τοι κεφαλῇ κατανεύϛομαι ὄφρα π]εποίθῃϛ	Α 524
	[αβα	οὐκ ἐᾷ Κρονίδης ἐπαμυνέμεν Ἀργεί]οιϛιν	Θ 414
8	[αββ	ϛοὶ δ' ἐγὼ οὐχ ἅλιος ϛκοπὸϛ ἔϛϛομαι οὐδ'] ἀπὸ δόξης	Κ 324
	[αβγ	ἔγρεο Τυδέος υἱέ· τί πάννυχον ὕπνον ἀ]ωτεῖς;	Κ 159
	[αβδ	παύϛειε κλαυθμοῖο γόοιό τε δακρυόεντ]οϛ	δ 801
	[αβε	οὐκ οἶδ'. οὐ γάρ πώ τις ἑὸν γόνον αὐτὸϛ] ἀνέγνω	α 216
12	[αβϛ	εἶμι μέν, οὐδ' ἅλιον ἔποϛ ἔϛϛεται ὅττι κ]εν εἴπω	Ω 92
	[αγα	ἔϛϛεται ἢ ἠὼϛ ἢ δείλη ἢ μέϛον ἦμαρ]	Φ 111
	[αγβ	ἴϛχεο, μηδ' ἔθελ' οἷος ἐριζέμεναι βαϛιλ]εῦϛιν	Β 247
	[αγγ	ἀντίον εἶμ' αὐτῶν· τρεῖν μ' οὐκ ἐᾷ Π]αλλὰϛ Ἀ[θήνη	Ε 256

— — —

___

[2] P.J.Parsons already expressed doubt about it in P.Oxy. 3831 intr. This is not the appropriate place for a detailed discussion of Preisendanz' reconstruction of the London Homer oracle. Only a few points relevant to 77 are dealt with here.

[3] This was established by Wessely, *Neue griechische Zauberpapyri*, p. 16 f., and accepted by Preisendanz in *Philologus* 72 (1913) 553. Subsequently, Preisendanz referred the unplaced fr. XXV (IX Wessely) to vv. 32-34 (PGM VII 25*-27*), whereas we now know that the fragment bears the beginnings of vv. 25-27 (see 77, fol. 6r, 1-2). This was the origin of the setbacks that PGM VII shows in comparison with the earlier reconstructions by Wessely and Preisendanz himself.

4 See Wessely, *op. cit.* (note 3), p. 16, and Preisendanz, *loc.cit.* (note 3).

Fol. 6r (↓)

1 (26) αεβ τοῦ μὲν φθίν[οντος μηνός, τοῦ δ᾽ ἱσταμένοιο]   ξ 162 =τ 307
      αεγ οὐκ ἄν τοι χρα[ίσμ-   { Γ54
                                    Λ387
      αεδ μήτε τι τὸν ξε[ῖνον στυφελίζετε μήτε τιν᾽ ἄλλον]   c 416 = υ 324
4 (29) αεε αἰσχρόν τοι δη[ρόν τε μένειν κενεόν τε νέεσθαι]   B 298
      αες μὴ παῖδ᾽ ὀρφα[νικὸν θῆῃς χήρην τε γυναῖκα]   Z 432
      ασα ἔσται ταῦτα Σκ[άμανδρε διοτρεφές, ὡς σὺ κελεύεις]   Φ 223
      ασβ δυσμενέσιν [μὲν χάρμα, κατηφείην δὲ σοὶ αὐτῷ]   Γ 51
8 (33) ασγ τ[ο]ῦ[δ᾽] αὐτοῦ λ[υκάβαντος ἐλεύσεται ἐνθάδ᾽ Ὀδυσσεύς]   ξ 161 =τ 306
      [ασδ] [οὐδὲν] σοί [γ᾽ ὄφελος, ἐπεὶ οὐκ ἐγκείσεαι αὐτοῖς]   X 513

—   —   —

Fol. 6v (→)

1 (51) [βγγ ἔρχεο· πάρ τοι ὁδός, ν]ῆες δέ το[ι] ἄγχι θαλάσσης   I 43
      [βγδ ψευστήσεις, οὐδ᾽ αὖτε τ]έλος [μ]ύθῳ ἐπιθήσεις   Τ 107
      [βγε μήτηρ δ᾽ αὖθ᾽ ἑτέρωθε]ν ὀδύρετο δάκρυ χέουσα   X 79
4 (54) [βγς οὐδ᾽ εἰ πεντάετές γε κα]ὶ ἑξάετες παραμίμνων   γ 115
      [βδα ὣς φάτο, καὶ Παιήον᾽ ἀ]νώγει ἰήσασθαι   E 899
      [βδβ ταῦτά τοι, ὦ δύστηνε, τ]ελευτήσω τε κ(αὶ) ἔρξω   λ 80
      [βδγ πῶς ἐθέλεις ἅλιον θε]ῖναι πόνον ἠδ᾽ ἀτέλεστον   Δ 26
8 (58) [βδδ ὄψιμον, ὀψιτέλεστον ὅ]ου κλέ[ο]ς [ο]ὔ ποτ᾽ ὀλ[εῖ]ται   B 325
      [βδε   π]ατρίδα [γαῖα]ν ἵκητα[ι]   γ 117?
      [βδς ἐλθεῖν. ὄφρ᾽ ἔνθεν θυμοφθόρα φάρμ]ακ᾽ [ἐνείκῃ]   β 329
      [βεα   ] [Ω 725?

—   —   —

Fol. 6r, 5 παιδ᾽ορφα[Pap.   5/6 paragraphus finem sectionis αεα-αες indicat
Fol. 6v, 5 ἰησασθαι Pap.   6 κ, Pap.   8 ποτ᾽ολ[Pap.   9 ἵκητα[Pap.
10]ακ᾽ Pap.

Fol. 5v.

1. This line (Ω 369, π 72, φ 133) appears in PGM VII 84 as εββ.

6. P.Oxy. 3831 appears to have ἐπινεύσομαι instead of κατανεύσομαι of all MSS (see *ad loc.*).

10. P.Oxy. 3831 has παυεσθ( ) at the beginning of this verse (see *ad loc.*).

12. εἴπω also in P.Oxy. 3831; εἴπῃ in Homer, as the context requires.

Fol. 6r.

2 οὐκ ἄν τοι χρα[ίσμ- Maltomini, *loc. cit.* : ουκαις χρο[Vogliano : ουκαιμ ςχρ[Montevecchi. Either Γ 54 οὐκ ἄν τοι χραίςμη κίθαρίς τά τε δῶρ' Ἀφροδίτης or Λ 387 οὐκ ἄν τοι χραίςμηςι βιὸς καὶ ταρφέες ἰοί.

6. Identified as Φ 223 by J.Schwartz, *Rev. Phil.* 28 (1954) 292.

Fol. 6v.

9 π]ατρίδα [γαῖα]ν ἵκητα[ι Maltomini, *loc. cit.* :]ιλα[   ]ϊμυ[Montevecchi :]ιδα[   ]ϊκητ[αι Vogliano (1952). P.Lond. has γ 117 here (PGM VII 59*) πρίν κεν ἀνιηθεὶς [ςὴν πατρίδ]α γαῖαν [ἵκοιο], and in all likelihood **77** bore the same verse (rather than ε 26 = ε 144 ὥς κε μάλ' ἀςκηθὴς ἦν πατρίδα γαῖαν ἵκηται or η 193 πομπῇ ὑφ' ἡμετέρῃ ἦν πατρίδα γαῖαν ἵκηται). In this case, the oracle has replaced the original Homeric ἵκοιο by ἵκηται: compare εἴπω for Homer's εἴπῃ in fol. 5v, 12 (in both places, is this a matter of carelessness, or of deliberate adaptation?).

11] [: not recorded by Montevecchi and Vogliano. Ω 725 in PGM VII 61*. The trace is too scanty to allow a reading. However, of the letters which form the end of this verse, it suits μ best. If so, [ἆνερ ἀπ' αἰῶνος νέος ὤλεο, κὰδ δέ] μ[ε χήρην].

Oxyrhynchos   II/III AD[1]

P.Köln inv. 1886.

ED.PR.: D.Wortmann, "Neue magische Texte. Nr. 13: Fragment eines Zauberbuches (?),"
   Bonner Jahrb. 168 (1968) 109-111.

COMM.: ed.pr.; (lines 12-13) F.Maltomini in: *Miscellanea Papyrologica* (Papyrologica
   Florentina VII, 1980), p. 176.

TRANSL.: ed.pr.; H.D.Betz, *Translation*, no. XCVII.

PHOTO: ed.pr., plate 14.

DESCR.: papyrus; 9.5 × 15 cm. Remains of two columns with intercolumnium (2.5 cm)
   and upper margin (3 cm). The writing runs with the fibers on the recto, and the verso is
   blank.

LOC.: Institut für Altertumskunde, Universität zu Köln.

Col. ii has remnants of six iatromagical prescriptions. The first five of
them (lines 1-14) are likely to have dealt with various remedies for the same
ailment; in this portion of the text, it seems that every recipe is introduced by
ἄλλο and marked by a short paragraphus; as one can see from ii 2-3 and 12-
13 (cf. also i 7), the new recipe did not have to start after the paragraphus,
but could already begin in the preceding line. Since 3-6 probably concern eye
disease, this may well be the subject of the whole section. A new section
begins in line 15: the transition is marked by a full heading, longer paragraphus, indentation of the opening line and the first letter of this line placed
between two short horizontal strokes (one above and one below).

---

[1] III/IV according to the ed.pr. The hand can be compared e.g. to P.Oxy. XXI 2300
(pl. IX; II-III AD, assigned) and P.Oxy. XXVIII 2487 (pl. VI; III AD, assigned).

col. i   col. ii

	col. i	col. ii
1	] ˌ ντος	φεθέντος β[αλὼν εἰς φοινι-]
	]ιφαλα	κοῦν ῥάκος [*c.* 6 ἄλλο·]
	] ˌˌ ρας κακ-	c̅α̅ύρας δεξι[ὸν ὀφθαλμὸν]
4	] ˌˌˌ ωδι	ἐκκόψας κ[αὶ αὐτὸν βα-]
	] ˌˌˌˌ ης	λὼν ἐν αἰ[γείῳ δέρματι]
	] ˌˌˌ ας	ἅπτε ἀριστ[ερ- *c.* 9]
	] ἄλλο·	ἄ̅λ̅λο· νυκ[τιβαοῦτος τὴν]
8	]κιν ˌˌˌ ς	καρδία[ν *c.* 13]
	]ε[ˌ] ˌ ον	τ̅ω̅ τρ[ίψας *c.* 12]
	]δα	ἄλλο· κρ[*c.* 14]
	]ν πε	[ˌ] ˌ ης καὶ τω[*c.* 11]
12	— — —	ος ὁμοῦ περία[πτε. ἄλλο· κρο-]
		τ̅ῶνος βοὸς μ[*c.* 10 αἰ-]
		γ̅είῳ δέρματι π[*c.* 10]
		π̅ρ[ὸς] πᾶσαν [νόcον· *c.* 4]
16		κάνθαρον το[
		κ[ˌ] ιο[ˌˌ]θεν[
		[ˌˌˌ] ˌˌˌ [
		— — —

Col. ii 15 in eisthesi

(Col. ii) - - - having put (it) in a red rag - - -. Another: gouge out the right eye of a lizard, |⁴ put (?) it in goat skin and fasten it to the left - - -. Another: the |⁸ heart of an owl (?) - - - after pounding it - - -. Another: - - - |¹² all together, fasten it. Another: - - - of a tick from a black (?) cow - - - in goat (?) skin - - -. Against every illness: (take) |¹⁶ a beetle - - -.

Col. i

7 ἄλλο: also in ii [2], 7, 10, [12]. It introduces analogous recipes also e.g. in **89**, 5; PGM IV 1323; VII 201, 206, 255, 376. The same in medical and alchemical writings; see Martinez, *P.Mich 757*, p. 7 n. 31.

Below 11. According to the first editor, the present column contained a twelfth line bearing]ε[, but this cannot be verified either on the original or on the plate in the ed.pr.

Col. ii

1. ἀ]ιφεθέντος?

1-2 εἰς φοινι]ικοῦν ῥάκος: cf. PGM II 71 φοινικῷ ἐρίῳ; IV 2703 φοινικίνῳ δέρματι; V 388 ἅμματι φοινικίνῳ. Greeks regarded the color red as having apotropaic and protective power. For the Egyptians, red as the color of Seth and the desert often had negative value, especially in the Late Period, but the color is also known to have positive associations. See Hopfner, *Offenbarungszauber* I, § 615; *Lexikon der Ägyptologie* II, *s.v.* Farben, col. 124 (E.Brunner-Traut); *RAC* VII, *s.v.* Farbe, coll. 362-371 and 405-408 (A.Hermann). For Egyptian red amulets, see esp. J.Gw.Griffiths, "The Symbolism of Red in Egyptian Religion," in: *Ex orbe religionum. Studia G.Widengren oblata* I (Leiden 1972), pp. 85-87 (= Griffiths, *Atlantis and Egypt, with Other Selected Essays* [Cardiff 1991], p. 212 f.).

3-4 cαύρας δεξι[ὸν ὀφθαλμὸν] | ἐκκόψας: the restoration proposed by the first editor seems highly probable. The verb ἐκκόπτω is frequently used of the gouging out of an eye (e.g. Aristoph., *Ach.* 92, *Av.* 583, 1613; Arist., *M.M.* I 33, 14; Demosth. XXIV 140 f.; Luc., *Tox.* 40, *Pseudol.* 27, etc.), and the lizard was the animal employed *par excellence* in remedies against eye disease (see W.Drexler, *Philologus* 58, 1899, 610-616; Bonner, *SMA*, pp. 69-71). For the supplements proposed, cf. *Cyranides* II 14 (p. 139, 8 f. Kaimakis) οἱ δὲ ὀφθαλμοὶ αὐτῆς (i.e. τῆς cαύρας) ἀφαιρεθέντες ζώσης εἰς ὄνομα τοῦ πάσχοντος πᾶσαν ὀφθαλμίαν ἰῶνται; Marcell. Emp., *De medicam.* VIII 50 *lacerti viridis - - - oculos erues acu cuprea et intra bullam vel lupinum aureum claudes colloque suspendes: quod remedium quamdiu tecum habueris, oculos non dolebis*; also Plin., *N.H.* XXIX 131- - - *aiunt - - - serpentis oculum dextrum adalligatum contra epiphoras prodesse, si serpens viva dimittatur*. As an alternative restoration, one might consider cαύρας δεξι[ὰν χεῖρα] | ἐκκόψας κ[αὶ αὐτὴν κτλ.; cf. *Cyranides* II 14 (p. 139, 4-7 Kaimakis) ταύτης τὴν δεξιὰν χεῖρα ἐὰν φορῇ τις κτλ. (against every serious illness); cf. also PGM VII 187-189 (a charm for favor and victory) ἄρας αὐτοῦ (i.e. τοῦ καλαβώτου) τὴν δεξιὰν χεῖρα ἐν καλάμῳ κόψας κτλ.

In general, for the lizard in ancient folklore, see A.D.Nock in: Bell-Nock-Thompson, "Magical Texts from a Bilingual Papyrus," 274-279 (= Nock, *Essays on Religion and the Ancient World* I, pp. 271-276); also G.Wolff, *Porphyrii de philosophia ex oraculis haurienda librorum reliquiae* (Berlin 1856), pp. 198-202.

4-5. βα]ιλῶν, or else εἰ]ιλῶν or its compounds, though these normally take the simple dative (cf. PGM II 51 ἐνειλήϲαϲ τῷ αὐτῷ ῥάκει τὸ ζῴδιον, 48, 63 f.; IV 2702 f.; LXII 23). Certainly not ἐγκυκ]ιλῶν (ed.pr.).

6 ἀριϲτ[ερ-: possibly ἀριϲτ[ερῷ βραχίονι or ἀριϲτ[ερᾷ χειρί. The first editor supplemented ἀριϲτ[ερῷ ὄμματί ϲου.

7. νυκ[τιβαοῦτοϲ with the ed.pr. (cf. PGM I 223; XXXVI 265), but νυκ[τερίδοϲ and νυκ[τικόρακοϲ are equally possible. For the owl in magic, see P.Oslo I 1, 265 comm.; for the bat, see *RE* VI.2, *s.v.* Fledermaus, col. 2742 (M.Wellmann); *RAC* VII, *s.v.* Fledermaus, col. 1099 (I.Mundle).

8-9 καρδία[ν - - - τρ[ίψαϲ: cf. PGM III 427.

9. After τρ[ίψαϲ, the first editor supplemented χρῖϲόν ϲε, which is unwarranted.

12. The paragraphus under this line was not recorded in the ed.pr.

12-13. Possibly κρο]ιτῶνοϲ βοὸϲ μ[ελαίνηϲ (F.Maltomini, *loc.cit.*); for the black cow, cf. PGM I 5; III 383; IV 909, 1440, 3149; VII 652 f.; XIII 129; XXXVI 239. Probably ἄλλο preceded this; αἷμα and a verb might have followed. This, however, would make a considerably longer line than those proposed in 3-5; yet cf. Griffith-Thompson, *Demotic Magical Papyrus*, XXV 25, 28 (cf. Betz, *Translation*, pp. 235, 236) "the blood of the tick of a black cow;" Plin., *N.H.* XXVIII 256 *e bove silvestri nigro si sanguine ricini* etc.

13-14 αἰ]ιγείῳ (cf. 5) or else τρα]ιγείῳ (ed.pr.) or λα]ιγείῳ.

14-15. To the lower left of the paragraphus at the break is a vertical that curves to the left at the bottom. It does not and did not join the paragraphus, but it also does not seem to have been part of a letter (e.g. from a remark in the margin, or from a long line in the preceding column). Possibly it is from a decorative squiggle at the beginning of this new section.

79

Oxyrhynchos　　　　　　　　　　Plate VI　　　　　　　　　　　III AD

P.Oxy. LVI 3834.

ED.PR.: R.W.Daniel in: P.Oxy. LVI (London 1989), pp. 54-57, no. 3834.

COMM.: ed.pr.

TRANSL.: ed.pr.

DESCR.: papyrus; 21 × 21 cm. Two columns of unequal height written along the fibers. The back is blank. The first column is a short one with space of c. 4 cm at the head, and at least 7.5 cm at the foot. The intercolumnium ranges in size from almost nothing to 2 cm, whereas 2.5-3.5 cm of unwritten papyrus survives to the left of col. i, and as much as 4.5 cm to the right of col. ii. This suggests that we have almost the whole of an independent piece of papyrus, not just a fragment from a longer roll. The edge of a kollesis can be seen 4-4.5 cm in from the left, with an overlap of c. 2 cm; it is a three layer join, since the upper sheet has had its lower (vertical) layer of fibers removed before joining (see P.Harris II, p. 115). The overlap, as the reader of the text sees it, is from right to left: it seems that the piece, after being cut from the roll, was turned 180 deg. before writing.

LOC.: Ashmolean Museum, Oxford.

　　Six short charms. The first two (lines 1-5 and 6-11) promote conception; the third (12-18) induces a prophetic dream; the fourth (19-25) restrains wrath; the fifth (26-32) is for victory against legal adversaries; the mutilated sixth (33 f.) is against fever.

　　Ϟ (5?, 9, 21, 25 *bis*, 31) and Ϟνα (8) for δεῖνα. ᾱ for ἄλλο (6). Raised horizontal for final ν (7). Diaeresis above ι (12) and υ (18). Paragraphus after lines 25 and 32. Lines 19-20 and 26 in ecthesis, 33 in esthesis.

col. i

1   ἐπὶ ἐκκρίματος, καλόν.
        cυνγενόμενος λέγε·
        ἐκκέχυκα τὸ ἔμα
4   τοῦ Αβραθιαου εἰς τὴν
        φύcιν τῆς δ(εῖνα).
        ἄλ(λο).
        [δ]ὸς coῦ τὴν ἡδονὴν
8   τῷ δ(εῖ)να· μετέδωκά coι
        τὴν ἐμὴν ἡδονήν, ἡ δ(εῖνα).
        ἐν δὲ τῇ κοιλίᾳ cου ἔχευcα
        τὸ αἷμα τοῦ Βαβραωθ

col. ii

12   ὄνειρον ἰδεῖν ἀληθει-
        νόν. κοιμώμενος
        λέγε ἁγνὰ φαγών·
        ν ἡ Νειθ, ἵ Νειεθ
16   εἰ ἐπιτυγχάνω τοῦ
        δεῖνα πράγματος, δεῖξόν
        μοι ὕδωρ, εἰ δὲ μή, πῦρ.

        θυμοκάτοχον.

20   προσερχόμενος πρὸς αὐτὸν
        λέγε· μή μοι ὀργίζου, ὁ δ(εῖνα),
        ἀλλὰ μεταστράφητι· ἐγώ εἰμι
        ὁ θεὸς ὁ ἐν οὐρανῷ, Αφφου
24   αχ [. .] Αβραc[α]ξ · λῆξον
        ὀργήν, ὁ δ(εῖνα), εἰς ἐμέ, τὸν δ(εῖνα).
        ἐπὶ ἀ[ν]΄τι΄δίκο[υ] νεικητικ[όν].
        ἀποβλέπων τὴν ἀκτ[ῖνα τοῦ]

2 cυγγενόμενος   3 αἷμα   5 ⳽ Pap.?   6 ἇ Pap.   7 ηδονῇ Pap.
8 ⳽να Pap.   9 ⳽ Pap.   12 ϊδειν Pap.   12-13 ἀληθινόν   18 ϋδωρ
Pap.   21 ⳽ Pap.   25 ⳽ (bis) Pap.   26 νικητικόν

28   θεοῦ λέγε· c̄ιc̄ιc̄ρω̣ [
        θιανοηρ Αβρααξ, ἐ[ναντι-]
        ώθητε ἐν τῆ cήμ[ερον ἡμέ-]
        ρᾳ τῷ δ(εῖνα), ἐπὶ ἀντίδικ[όc ἐcτι]
32   _τοῦ [θ]εοῦ._
                ἐπὶ πυρετοῦ.
        [c. 12   ]νθηc . . .

                — — —

31 ⏓ Pap.   ἐπεὶ

Over (seminal) secretion; a good charm. Having made love say: "I have poured out the blood I[4] of Abrathiaou into the *natura* of woman NN."

Another. "Give your pleasure I[8] to NN; I gave you my pleasure, woman NN. In your womb I poured the blood of *Babraoth*."

I[12] To see a true dream. Upon going to sleep say after you have eaten ritually pure food: "Verily by *Neith*, verily by *Neieth*, I[16] if I shall succeed in a certain activity, show me water, if not, fire."

A restrainer of wrath. I[20] Go to him and say: "Be not angry with me, NN, but have a change of heart. I am the god in heaven, *Aphphou* I[24] *ach- - - Abrasax*. Put an end to anger, NN, against me NN."

Victory charm over a legal adversary. Looking at the ray of the I[28] god say: "*Sisisrô - - - thianoêr Abrasax*, oppose on the present day NN, because he is an adversary I[32] of the god."

In case of fever - - -.

1-11. Two formulas to be recited by a man after copulation so that a woman conceives. Cf. PGM XXXVI 283-294 φυcικλείδιον. - - - cοι λέγω, μήτρα τῆc δῖνα, χάνε καὶ δέξαι τὸ cπέρμα τοῦ δεῖνα καὶ cπ[έ]ρ[μ]α τὸ ἀκρατὲc τοῦ ιαρφε αρφε κτλ. Greater similarity is displayed by a charm for conception inscribed on a gold lamella from Ballana, Nubia (IV or V AD) edited by L.P.Kirwan (based on notes and transcription of S.Eitrem) in: W.B.Emery, *The Royal Tombs of Ballana and Qustul* I

(Cairo 1938), pp. 405-407, no. III (printed here with hitherto unpublished, improved readings proposed by R.Kotansky and R.Merkelbach):

ἐλθαὶ πρὸς αἰμαί, ᾿Ιϲιϲ Ι² ὅτι αἰγώ ἰμι{ν} ῎Οϲιριϲ, Ι³ ὁ ἄρ⟨ρ⟩ην
ἀδαιρφόϲ ⟨ϲ⟩ου. Ι⁴ ταῦτα τὰ ὕδατα ἃ Ι⁵ ϲοι προϲφέρω{ϲ} ὕΙ⁶δρω
αἰϲτη ⟨ἱ⟩αίρακοϲ Ι⁷ ϲτηθινιον ἴβαιοϲ Ι⁸ ὕδρω τοῦ ᾿Ανούβαιωϲ Ι⁹
ἀδελφόν φνηθΙ¹⁰βεν κατὰ νότον Ι¹¹ ενναι, ἄνυξόν Ι¹² ϲου τὴν
μήτραν Ι¹³ ἐν ταύτη τῇ ὥρᾳ καὶ Ι¹⁴ ἐν ⟨ταύ⟩τη τῇ ῥοπῇ καὶ
ἄΙ¹⁵ρπαξον τὸ ϲπαραιΙ¹⁶ν ἔν ϲου ὕδρω ἐν τῷ Ι¹⁷ ϲου ὀνόματι,
᾿Ιϲι, ἄνα⟨ϲ⟩Ι¹⁸ϲα, βαϲίλιϲ⟨ϲ⟩α Ταιντύρων, Ι¹⁹ ἤδη, ταχὺ ταχύ,
διὰ Ι²⁰ τὴν δύναμιν ὑΙ²¹μῶν, ταχύ.

1 ἐλθὲ	ἐμέ	2 ἐγώ εἰμι	3 ἀδελφόϲ	4 ὕδατα Tab.
5-6 ὕδρω Tab., l. ὕδωρ	6 ἐϲτι ἱέρακοϲ	7 ἴβαιοϲ Tab., l. ἴβεωϲ
8 ὕδωρ	᾿Ανούβεωϲ	9 αδελφον: φνηθ: Tab.	11 ἄνοιξόν	15-16
ϲπαρὲν	16 ϲοι	ὕδρω Tab., l. ὕδωρ	18 Τεντύρων	20-21 ὑμων
Tab.

Whereas in the Ballana charm the male semen is referred to as water of various gods, in the present two charms it is the blood of a great god. The general notion can be explained in light of the fact that blood and semen (also saliva, milk, urine, wine, water, honey, etc.) were though to emanate from or to share something with an eternal flow of divine light, which was also viewed as a liquid. See especially E.R. Goodenough, *Jewish Symbols in the Greco-Roman Period* V (New York, 1956), pp. 112-197. On the interrelationship of the bodily fluids and on their divine origin in Greek thought, see R.Muth, *Träger der Lebenskraft. Ausscheidungen des Organismus im Volksglauben der Antike* (Vienna 1954), and F.Rüsche, *Blut, Leben und Seele. Ihr Verhältnis nach Auffassung der griechischen und hellenistischen Antike, der Bibel und der alten Alexandrinischen Theologen* (Paderborn 1930). On the blood of the Egyptian gods and creation from it, see *Lexikon der Ägyptologie* I, *s.v.* Blut, col. 841 (W.Westendorf); Goodenough, *op.cit.,* V, p. 159.

1 ἔκκριμα = ἔκκριϲιϲ 'secretion', here specifically of semen; cf. Arist., *HA* 544B 14 τὸ ϲπέρμα ἐκκρίνεϲθαι and similarly *GA* 765B 10-11.

καλόν: for similar recommendations in the titles, see **82** fr. B 5 comm.

4 Αβραθιαου: a variant of Αρβαθιαω and Αβραθιαω, 'tetrad of Iao'; cf. the similar Αρβατιθοθ in **50**, 43. Parallels and discussion in W.Fauth, "Arbath Jao," *Oriens Christianus* 67 (1983) 64-103, esp. 64-75.

8 τῷ δῖνα: palaeographically it is difficult to decide between this and τῇ δῖνα, but the former seems as preferable in light of 8-9 μετέδωκά coι τὴν ἐμὴν ἡδονήν, ἡ δῖ(να). Conception was thought to result from the union not only of male and female seed, but also of heat and pleasure; cf. Hipp., *Genit.* 4 (VII 474, 19 - 476, 5 L.), and see the commentary on this passage in I.M.Lonie, *The Hippocratic Treatises "On Generation", "On the Nature of the Child," "Diseases IV"* (Berlin-New York 1981), pp. 119-122. If τῇ δῖνα is the correct reading, the situation is more complicated: the man addresses first his ejaculated semen (cf. Ps.Callisthenes I 7, 1 Kroll cπέρματα ἀνίκητα καὶ ἀνυπότακτα, διαμείνατε) and then the woman.

11 Βαβραωθ: PGM, Vol. 3 (Index), p. 236 lists the similar Βαρβ[α]-ωθ for PGM XII 72 αραας c Cηβαρβ[α]ωθ.

12-18. Of the many charms to induce prophetic dreams, the closest to the present one are PGM VII 249-254, 255-259 and XXIIb 27-30. The first of these runs as follows: ὀνειραιτητόν, ὃ ἀεὶ κέχρηται. λόγος ὁ λεγόμενος πρὸς τὸν καθημερινὸν λύχνον· ναιενχρη, ναιεν[χρ]η, μήτηρ πυρὸς καὶ ὕδατος· cὺ εἶ ὁ προανατέλλων Ἀρχ[εντε]χθα· χρημάτιcόν μοι περὶ τοῦ δεῖνα πράγματος. ἐὰν ναί, δεῖ[ξόν μ]οι φυτὸν καὶ ὕδωρ, εἰ δὲ μήγε, πῦρ καὶ cίδηρον, ἤδη [ἤδη, ταχὺ] ταχύ. On this passage, see Hopfner, *Offenbarungszauber* II.1, § 209. Artemidorus criticized such prognostic dream-charms: IV 2 (p. 246, 14 ff. Pack) ἔτι δὲ καὶ τῶν νομοθετούντων τοῖc θεοῖc καταγέλα, λέγω δὲ τῶν εὐχομένων οὕτως "εἴ μοι πρακτέον τόδε" καὶ "εἴ μοι ἔcται τόδε" και "εἰ νῦν ἴδοιμι Δήμητρος καρπόν· εἰ δὲ μή, Διονύcου" κτλ. Artemidorus discusses the significance of fire and water in dreams in II 9-10 and II 27 respectively.

14 ἀγνὰ φαγών: PGM IV 52-57 prescribes a seven-day abstention from bloody and uncooked food and from wine; cf. also 73 f. ὅταν δὲ μέλλῃc καθ' ἡμέραν ἐν τῇ ἀγνείᾳ ἐcθίειν καὶ κοιμᾶcθαι, εἰπὲ λόγον. Other passages in divinatory charms that prescribe ritual purity are PGM II 148, 151; IV 784, 3209; VII 334, 846; XIII 151; XXIIb 27.

15 νὴ Νειθ, ι Νειεθ: according to H.J.Thissen, one may recognize the name of the goddess Neith twice, the first time preceded by the Greek particle νή, the second time preceded by the synonymous Egyptian particle *j3* (cf. Crum, *s.v.* ειε (c), p. 74 b). On the goddess, see *Lexikon der Ägyptologie* IV, *s.v.* Neith, coll. 392-394 (R.Schlichting). Cf. PGM VII 341 νηιθι with app.cr. and XIXa 1 Νηίθ, Νηίθ with app.cr.

19-25. On θυμοκάτοχα, see **57** intr.

23 Αφφου: cf. PGM LVII 10 'Αφο]υθ, χεννονευ, 'Αφουθ. Both Αφφου and Αφουθ might derive from the name of the 18th Egyptian decan, for whom W.Gundel (*Dekane*, p. 77 ff.) gives the following forms: Aposot, ἀφοсο, Afut (var. Asut), Aphut, ἀφοδω ἀμφαταμ (see K.Preisendanz, *GGA* 201, 1939, 143).

27-28 τὴν ἀκτ[ῖνα τοῦ] Ι θεοῦ: Helios. Cf. e.g. PGM IV 905 f. πρὸς τὰς τοῦ ἡλίου ἀκτῖνας.

28 сιсιсρω: see **42**, 49-50 comm.; cf. also **57**, 14.

29 θιανоηρ: possibly based on the solar θηνωρ; see **42**, 52 comm.

29-30 ἐ[ναντι]Ιώθητε: this verb occurs commonly in Cypriot curse tablets against legal adversaries; the formula runs κατακοιμίсατε τὴν γλῶссαν τὸν θυμὸν τὴν ὀργὴν τὴν εἰс ἐμὲ ἔχει τὸν NN ὁ NN ἵνα μὴ δύνηταί μοι μηδενὶ πράγματι ἐναντιωθῆναι (cf. e.g. Audollent, *DT*, 22, 27-30; 24, 14-16; 25, 14 f. [= Mitford, Inscr. Kourion, nos. 127, 129, 130]). Cf. also PGM P 15c 1-4 Κ(ύρι)ε, ὁ δεсπ(ότηс) τῆс οἰκουμένηс, ἐκδίκηсόν με μετὰ τοῦ ἐναντιοῦντόс με; XII 261 f. μηδεὶс δαιμ(όν)ων ἢ πνευμάτων ἐναντιωθήсεταί μοι. See also **54**, 24 comm. on ἀντίοс ἐλθεῖν.

31-32 ἐπὶ (r. ἐπεὶ) ἀντίδικ[όс ἐсτι] Ι τοῦ [θ]ε̣οῦ: for such justifications, cf. **89**, 3-4 comm.

33. This line may have consisted of nothing more than the lemma indented a space of about six letters.

Provenance   Plate VII   III AD[1]
unknown

P.Reinach II 89.

ED.PR.: P.Collart, P.Reinach II (Cairo 1940), p. 32 f., no. 89.

COMM.: ed.pr.

TRANSL.: R.Kotansky in Betz, *Translation*, no. LXXXVI.

DESCR.: papyrus; 4.5 × 10 cm. Remains of a column damaged at the left, right and
bottom. Upper margin 2.5 cm. The writing runs with the fibers on the recto, and the
verso is blank.

LOC.: Institut de Papyrologie, Université de Paris-Sorbonne. Inv. 2176.

Two recipes separated by a long horizontal stroke and extra interlinear
space (2.5 cm). The first is concerned with the making of an amulet; the
purpose of the second cannot be determined.

Ϟ for δεῖνα (1). Iota adscript correctly written in 3 (the only word which
requires it).

1   φ]ύλαξον τὸν δ(εῖνα) ὃν ἔτ[εκεν ἡ δ(εῖνα)
           π]ερίαψον περὶ τὸν τρά[χηλον

           _____

           ἀνα]τολῆι Διδύμων [
4   ]ριον ὥρας θ̄ γραφ[
           ] ω αἰγὸς θηλίας ει [
           ] ξεοντα [. . . .]δονο[
                          ] ξου [
8   ] [

           _   _   _

1 Ϟ Pap.   5 θηλείας

[1] IV AD according to the ed.pr. The writing can be compared to literary hands of the
early and middle third century; cf. Roberts, *Greek Literary Hands*, pl. 20 a-c.

Protect him, NN, whom NN bore - - - attach (it) around the neck.   At the rising of the
Twins - - - at (?) the 9th hour, write - - - of a female goat - - -.

2 περὶ : π[ε]ρὶ ed.pr., but epsilon is clearly visible.

περὶ τὸν τρά[χηλον: parallels in Brashear, *Magica varia*, p. 55.

3 ἀνα]τολῆι Διδύμων : ἀνα]τολῆ ῑ Διδύμων ed.pr.   Probably ἐν τῆι
ἀνα]τολῆι as in PGM III 122, 128, XIII 402 f. Also possible is the synonymous ἐπι]τολῆι (cf. PGM XIII 390).

4]ριον: the first editor restored αὔ]ριον.

5. On female goats and their properties, cf. *Cyranides* II 4 (p. 120 f.
Kaimakis).

ει ̣[: a form of εἰλέω?

7] ̣ξου ̣[:] ̣ζου[ed.pr.

8] ̣[: not recorded in the ed.pr.

81

Fayum ? III AD

P.Berol. inv. 21260.

ED.PR.: F.Maltomini, "Due papiri magici inediti," *SCO* 31 (1981) 115-117.

COMM.: ed.pr.

TRANSL.: R.Kotansky in Betz, *Translation*, no. CXXIX.

PHOTO: ed.pr., plate IX.2.

DESCR.: papyrus; 5 × 8.2 cm. Broken away on all sides except the bottom, where there is a margin of 4.3 cm. The writing runs against the fibers on the verso. On the recto, along the fibers, a documentary text from the second half of the second century AD.

LOC.: Ägyptisches Museum, Berlin.

```
1        ] . [ . ] . [ . . . . ] . . . [ . ] . [
         ]ι τινος πράγματος κα[
         ] πέταλον ἀπό τινος μ . [
4        ] καὶ δήcαc αὐτὸ λίνῳ  [
         ]α λύκου μέλανος ἀποτ[
         ] καὶ ἐν [κ]ανιcκίῳ αὐτὸ α[
         ]τακιc διακονήcι cοι —[
```

7 διακονήcει

- - - about such and such matter - - - a lamella from a certain - - - and having tied it with linen - - - of a black wolf - - - and (put) it in a little case - - - it will serve you very often.

2]ι: probably περ]ί (cf. PGM IV 718, 872 f., 896, 1033, 1329 f., 2502 f., 3107, 3207; V 445; VII 248, 253, 332 f., 358, 479, 1015; LXXVII 22 f.). In our text τινος seems to mean τοῦ δεῖνα, though, when τις has this value, it is normally preceded by the article; see LSJ, *s.v.* τις A II 10 b *in fine*; PGM, Vol. 3 (Index), p. 188, *s.v.* τις *in fine*; especially PGM VII 479 περὶ τοῦ τινος πράγματος. The expression περὶ τοῦ δεῖνα πράγματος *vel simm.* occurs always in divination charms and, with the exception of PGM LXXVII 22 f., in logoi. Whether the prescriptional section in 3-7 belonged to the same recipe cannot be determined.

κα[: perhaps κα[ὶ or κα[ccιτέρινον. In the latter case, the reference might be to πέταλον in the following line, but see below.

3 πέταλον: in all likelihood a metal tablet. For their use in magic, see Martinez, *P.Mich. 757*, pp. 2-6; and cf. PGM, Vol. 3 (Index), *s.vv.* λᾶμνα, λεπίς, πέταλον, πλάξ, πλάτυμμα, πτύχιον (most of these occurrences can be found also in R.Kotansky, "Incantations and Prayers for Salvation on Inscribed Greek Amulets," in: Faraone-Obbink, *Magika Hiera*, p. 129 f. n. 46).

ἀπό τινος μ [: before the break, the left side of ε, ο or ω. The damaged word probably indicates the place from which the lamella is to be taken, e.g. μο[λιβοῦ cωλῆνος or μο[ύλων ζυγοῦ (cf. PGM IV 2130 f. λαβὼν cίδηρον ἀπὸ ἀναγκοπέδηc; VII 397 λαβὼν μόλιβον ἀπὸ ψυχροφόρου cωλῆνος, 432 f. πλάκαν ἐc μολιβῆν ἀπὸ ψυχροφόρου τόπου ἐγχάραξον, 925 f. λαβὼν λεπίδα μολιβῆν ἀπὸ ζυγοῦ μούλων; X 37 ἀπὸ ἡμιόνων).

4 αὐτό: probably the πέταλον, and so in 6.

λίνῳ: for the use of linen in magic and religion, see **44** footnote 1. For the tying of amulets with linen thread, cf. PGM IV 81, 1082 f.; Plin., *N.H.* XXVIII 29; Marcell. Emp., *De medicam.* VIII 27; XIV 68.

[: oblique rising from left as of μ.

5. E.g. τρίχ]α λύκου μέλανος ἀποτ[εμών.

λύκου μέλανος: the wolf plays a great role in magical beliefs; for the Graeco-Roman world, see *RE Suppl.* XV, col. 970 f. (W.Richter). There is no other mention of a black wolf in the Greek magical papyri (for a white wolf, see **34** C 1-4). The Greeks identified the Egyptian warrior god Upuaut with a black wolf; see *Lexikon der Ägyptologie* VI, *s.v.* Upuaut, col. 863 (E.Graefe).

6 α[: ἀ[πόθου?

7]τακις: πλεις]τάκις seems a very likely supplement.

διακονήςει: διακονέω is a technical term in magical literature to indicate "the willing obedience of the spirits to the incantation" (S.Eitrem, P.Oslo I 1, 279 comm.); cf. **39**, 2; PGM IV 1508 f., 2045, 2065, 2076; VII 884 f.; XII 40, 47, 49; XIXa 49 f.; XXXVI 304; LXI 11; LXII 4, 8; Audollent, *DT*, 15, 35.

The horizontal stroke after coι might indicate the end of a section, or it might be merely a line-filler.

Provenance   III AD
  unknown

P.Laur. III 57.

ED.PR.: R.Pintaudi, P.Laur. III (Florence 1979), pp. 34-36, no. 57.

COMM.: ed.pr.

TRANSL.: R.Kotansky in Betz, *Translation*, no. CXIX.

PHOTO: ed.pr., plate LII.

DESCR.: papyrus; two fragments whose position in relationship to each other cannot be
determined. Fr. A (8.5 × 8.3 cm; not 7.5 × 8.4 as stated in the ed.pr.), broken away at
right, top and bottom, preserves the left side of a column; to the left a blank space of 2
cm. Fr. B (9.3 × 2.7 cm; not 8.4 × 2.7 as stated in the ed.pr.) is broken away on all
sides. The writing runs along the fibers on the verso. On the recto of fr. A, remnants of
seven lines in a different hand run along the fibers at right angles to the text on the
verso; the right side of the recto corresponds with the top of the verso. The recto of fr.
B is blank.

LOC.: Biblioteca Medicea Laurenziana, Florence. Inv. PL II/52.

Remains of five short prescriptions on fr. A and of three on fr. B: A 1
probably a love charm, 2-3 touch-charm, 4-6 charm to drive (the beloved), 7-
9 subjugation charm, 10-11 probably a charm to win favor; B 1-3 medical
(wounds), 4 undetermined, 5 against fever.

As far as can be ascertained, the first line of every prescription was in
ecthesis. There is extra interlinear space between lines 1 and 2 on fr. A. The
restored text of fr. B shows that the column of writing was broader than 11
cm.

αγω^γ for ἀγώγιμον or ἀγωγή (4). ✳ for χρηςτόν or χρήςιμον (9, in
marg.). καί is abbreviated (fr. B 3, 5).

Fr. A

1 ὕπνου τυχ[εῖ]ν· ἐξορκίζω [

παράψιμον. λαβὼν γα[
θ̄εχθει ῑβ̄εαλη[
4 ἀγώγ(ιμον). ἐπὶ ὀςτρακι[
βολcακ' cαρ[
τὰς φρένας [
ὑποτακτικόν. [
8 ὑπόταξον [
χρ(ηςτόν) γράψον [
τ [c. 5] [
ἐπαφροδι[cίαν

Fr. B

1]α [c. 4] [
]εδηc τραύματα [ ] [
] κυνὸc λόγοc. μίcγε δὲ κ(αὶ) [
4]ν. λαβὼν φύλλον ἐλέαc ἐπίγρ[αψον
πρὸc καθημερι]νὸν κ(αὶ) νυκτερινόν, κέλλιcτον. λαβὼν [

Fr. A 2 in ecthesi   4 in ecthesi   ἀγώγ(ιμον) vel ἀγωγ(ή), αγωγ̄ Pap.   5
βολcακ' Pap.   7 in ecthesi   9 χρ(ηςτόν) vel χρ(ήcιμον), ✳ Pap.   10 in ecthesi
Fr. B 3 κοινὸc   κ̄ Pap.   4 ἐλαίαc   5 κ̄ Pap.   κάλλιcτον

(Fr. A) - - - (not) get sleep. I adjure - - -.   Contact-charm. Take milk (?) - - - *thechthei ibealê*- - -. |⁴ Charm to drive (the beloved). On a sherd (?) - - - *bolsak sar*- - - the wits - - -. Charm to subject. - - - |⁸ subject - - - (on the left margin: useful) write - - - loveliness - - -.

(Fr. B) - - - wounds - - - any formula at all. Mix and - - -. |⁴ Against fever with shivering (?). Take an olive-leaf and write on it - - -.   Against diurnal and nocturnal fever, excellent. Take - - -.

Fr. A

1 ὕπνου τυχ[εῖ]ν : τ̣ου τύχ[η]ν ed.pr. The phrase, certainly negated, suggests a love charm. See **71** fr. 22, 4 comm.

2 παράψιμον: a love charm that acts by contact; cf. PGM VII 973-980 ἀγώγιμον παράψιμον· - - - ἐπαναγκάσατε τὴν δεῖνα τῆ[c] δεῖνα, ἐὰν ἄψαιμι, ἐπακολουθῆcαι; PGM XII 62, where the reading of the papyrus ἐν τούτῳ τῷ παραψίμῳ must be retained (see K.Fr.W.Schmidt, *Philol. Wochenschrift* 55, 1935, 1174; and PGM, Vol. 3 [Index], p. 158); also IV 2173 f. ἧc δ' ἂν παράψῃ γυναικὸc ἢ ἀνδρόc, φιληθήcει.

γα̣[: the first editor suggested γά̣[λα.

3 θ̅ε̅χθει ι̅β̅εαλη[: perhaps only magical words with bars above the first two letters. One might also consider numeral letters and magical words: θε′ χθει (or rather θ′ εχθει) ιβ′ εαλη[(cf. PGM IV 2615 f. εαλανινδω).

4 ὀcτρακι[: a form of ὀcτράκιον or ὀcτράκινοc. Neither ὄcτρακο̣[ν nor ὀcτράκῳ̣ can be read.

5 βολcακ: cf. PGM II 32 βολcοχ and IV 2027 βολ cαχυ.

6 τὰc φρέναc: the wits of the beloved that are to be tormented, as e.g. in PGM IV 2489; also **48**, 10.

7 ὑποτακτικόν: cf. PGM VII 396, 925, 940; X 36. Subjugation charms were dealt with by Th.Hopfner, *Archiv Orientální* 10 (1938) 128-148, to whose references may be added Bonner, *SMA*, D. 395 (reverse) and the Syrian coin amulet published by C.Bonner, *HThR* 43 (1950) 165-168.

9 marg. χρ(ηcτόν) or χρ(ήcιμον): see Turner-Parsons, *Greek Manuscripts*, p. 15; McNamee, *Abbreviations*, p. 109; cf. especially P.Oxy. VIII 1088 (medical prescriptions); also app.cr. to PGM LXII 44 (but see P.Warren 21, 44).

10. The ecthesis marks the beginning of a new section, and a heading is expected. The first editor suggested τε[λετή]. To judge by the word ἐπα- φροδι[cίαν in 11, the text is probably a *charitesion*, possibly a love charm (see **72** ii 6 comm.).

Fr. B

1]α̣ . . [̣: foot of an upright below the line; then minimal traces on the line.

2] ̣[̣: short diagonal ascending to right followed by a minimal rest of a diagonal from right: λ? Then the foot of an upright.

3] κυνὸc (r. κοινὸc) λόγοc :] κενολόγοc ed.pr. See **95** → 7 comm. μίcγε: on the form μίcγω in papyri, see Gignac, *Grammar* II, p. 281.

.[: left part of a round letter, probably α.

4]ν: possibly πρὸϲ ῥιγοπυρέτιο]ν as suggested by the first editor, who compares the present line with PGM VII 211 and line 5 with VII 213.

5 κέλλιϲτον (r. κάλλιϲτον) : κελλιοτον ed.pr., who however suggests κάλλιϲτον in the commentary. Cf. **79**, 1; PGM VII 385, 459, 462. For α > ε, cf. Gignac, *Grammar* I, pp. 278-282. Recommendation of the efficacy of the recipes is a feature that magical formularies share with many other sorts of technical literature of later antiquity (medicine, alchemy etc.); see P.Oslo I 1, comm. on 1 εἰϲ ταῦτα ποιῶν; also **74**, 7 comm.

Provenance   Plate VII   III AD
unknown

P.Lit. Lond. 171.

ED.PR.: H.J.M.Milne, P.Lit. Lond. (London 1927), p. 137, no. 171.

COMM.: ed.pr.

REF.: Pack[2] 2405; Gazza, "Prescrizioni mediche" (I), p. 95; Marganne, *Inventaire*, no. 107.

DESCR.: papyrus; 9.6 × 14.5 cm. A short column complete in height and breadth, but damaged at the upper left. Upper margin 2.3 cm; lower margin 5.4 cm. The writing runs against the fibers on the verso; on the recto, an account or list of property.

LOC.: British Library, London. Inv. 2558 verso.

Two recipes reminiscent of the Jocular Recipes of Democritus (Δημοκρίτου παίγνια, PGM VII 167-185) and **76**. The second is concerned with sexual intercourse, and probably also the first. After each recipe a paragraphus.

```
1        .λ[.].ικ... ἥδεςθαι·
         [ . . . . . . ] μετὰ κόπρ[ο]υ
         χ[ε]λιδό[ν]ος cὺν μέλειτι
4        π[ερίχ]ρειcαι.
         ‾‾‾‾‾‾‾‾‾‾‾‾‾‾‾
         πολλὰ cυνουcιάζειν·
         εὐζώμου cπέρμα
         μετὰ cτροβιλίων cὺν
8        οἴνῳ τρείψας νῆςτης
         πίε.
         ‾‾‾
```

3 μέλιτι   4 περίχριcαι   8 τρίψας

To have fun with a concubine (?): rub on yourself - - - and the excrement of a swallow together with honey. To copulate a lot: bruise seed of rocket and small pine-cones together with wine and drink it on an empty stomach.

1 λ̣[ ]ικ̣ : λε λικὸν ed.pr. Variously assignable traces, letter-count uncertain. First, top of an upright with a high horizontal to the right (π? ιτ?); second, diagonal descending to right (α? λ?); after the gap αικ or λικ; then possibly ι (certainly not ο); the traces that follow suggest *prima facie* ν, but the first vertical cannot be verified, and there seems to be some ink to the left of where the vertical ought to be: so, λι or δι might be considered, even though no horizontal on the lower level is visible. This may point to a dative singular ending in -κιδι. If from παλλακίς, it would seem to have been spelled παλ[λ]αικίδι. Cf. **76**, 5 γυναικὶ ἐμπαῖξαι.

3 χ[ε]λιδό[ν]ος: Crönert's reading (*apud* ed.pr.) is definitely preferable to ἀ[λέ]κδο[ρ]ος (r. ἀλέκτορος), suggested as a possible alternative in the ed.pr. For the pharmacological use of the excrement of the swallow, cf. Diosc., *Eupor.* II 48 (III 263, 14 Wellmann); Gal., *Comp. medic. sec. loc.* VI 6 (XII 939, 5 K.); Ps.Gal., *Rem.* II 1, 1; 2, 2 (XIV 391, 17 f.; 399, 12 f. K.); Aëtius VII 96; 97 (CMG VIII.2, pp. 341, 25 f.; 342, 8 f.); Alex. Trall. II 135, 20 f. Puschmann; see also *RE* II A.1, *s.v.* Schwalben u. Segler, col. 774, 46-49 (H.Gossen).

4 π[ερίχ]ρεισαι (r. περίχρισαι) as suggested in the app.cr. of the first edition, not τρεί[ψας]̣ ̣ ̣ cαι as given in the transcription (Crönert's]ρεισαι looks the likeliest reading, and π[is possible). *Pace* Milne, τρίψας is not demanded by sense, for the missing substance in 2 need not have been a solid.

5-9. Cf. PGM VII 182-184 πολλὰ βι[ν]εῖν δύνασθαι· στροβίλια πεντήκοντα μετὰ δύο κυά[θ]ων γλυκέος καὶ κόκκους πεπέρεως τρίψας πίε; also **76**, 11 f.

6 εὐζώμου: for rocket as an aphrodisiac, see **76**, 12 comm.

8 νῆστης: see Moeris, p. 204, 10 Bekker νῆστις Ἀττικοί, νήστης Ἕλ-ληνες; Phryn., *Ecl.*, no. 298 Fischer νήστης βάρβαρον, τὸ δὲ ἀρχαῖον νῆστις διὰ τοῦ ι; also [Hdn.], ζητ. 248, 20 Cramer. The form νήστης is the usual one in papyri: cf. PGM I 235; III 334, 412, 427; P.Oxy. VIII 1088, 44; P.Berol. inv. 9765, ii 2 (BKT III, p. 31). PSI X 1180, 69-70 νῆστι (dative) is ambiguous. Cf. also Dittenberger, *Syll.*³ 1171, 9 = I.Cret. I, XVII 17, 9 (1st cent. BC).

Aboutig?[1]   III-IV AD[2]

P.Yale II 130.

ED.PR.: P.Proulx-J.O'Callaghan, "Papiro mágico cristiano (PYale inv. 989)," *Stud. Pap.*
    13 (1974) 83-88.

REPUBL.: R.W.Daniel, *ZPE* 25 (1977) 145-149; SB XIV 12113; P.Yale II 130 (S.A.
    Stephens).

COMM.: ed.pr.; Daniel, *loc.cit.*; C.H.Roberts, *Manuscript, Society and Belief in Early
    Christian Egypt* (London 1979), p. 82; F.Maltomini in: *Miscellanea Papyrologica*
    (Papyrologica Florentina VII, 1980), pp. 173-175; P.Yale II 130.

TRANSL.: Daniel, *loc.cit.*; R.Kotansky in Betz, *Translation*, no. CXIV; P.Yale II 130.

PHOTO: ed.pr.

DESCR.: papyrus; 7.0 × 12.8 cm. Above the text, as much as 2 cm of an upper margin.
    Broken away unevenly on the other sides. The writing runs along the fibers, and the
    back is blank.

LOC.: The Beinecke Rare Book and Manuscript Library, Yale University, New Haven,
    Connecticut. Inv. 989.

A fragment from a protective charm to be used by a woman (cf. 1 τὴ[ν
δ]εῖνα and see 4-5 comm.).

According to Roberts the abbreviation κ̄ε̄ in line 1 characterizes this text as
Christian. This may well be the case, even if κύριος and θεός abbreviated as
nomina sacra are occasionally found in pagan syncretistic magical texts; cf.
93, 3 κ(υρί)ῳ θεῷ 'Οcί[ριδι (κω without bar Pap.), and see PGM, Vol. 2,
p. 270. Another possible indication of Christianity is 7 κωφῶν δεμόν[ων,
which is reminiscent especially of Christian exorcisms (see 6-7 comm.).

The restorations proposed for 1, 2 and 8 suggest a length of line of between 22 and 26 letters. All restorations provided should be regarded as

---

[1] "- - - acquired from Maurice Nahman in 1931; it is said to be from Aboutig" (P.Yale
II 130).
[2] So dated according to the ed.pr., III AD according to P.Yale II 130.

illustrative, for one cannot exclude the possibility that more letters should be restored to the left of the fragment and fewer to the right.

1   [φύλα]ξον τὴ[ν δ]εῖνα, κ(ύρι)ε, [ἀπὸ πάντων]
        [πον]ηρῶν πραγμάτῳ[ν καὶ ἀπὸ παν-]
        [τὸ]ς cυναντήματος κ[αὶ   c. 5-8   ]
4   [ˌ]cεκτηсιου καὶ ἀπ[ὸ   c. 7-10   ]
        [ˌˌˌ]μου πτώcε[ωс] π[c. 9-12   ]
        [ˌˌˌˌ]ωcεωс ὑπνο [c. 9-12   ]
        [ˌˌˌˌ] κωφῶν δεμόν[ων καὶ ἀπὸ πά-]
8   [cης] ἐπιλήμψεωс [καὶ ἀπὸ παν-]
        [τὸс с]εληνιαсμοῦ κ[αὶ   c. 7-11   ]
        [ˌˌˌˌˌ]ματος καὶ ἀ[πὸ   c. 7-11   ]
        [ˌˌˌˌˌ ἐ]πιπ[ο]μπῆс [c. 8-11   ]
12   [c. 8-11   ]κατ [c. 10-14   ]
        [c. 8-11   ] ˌcε[c. 10-14   ]
        [c. 8-11   ]δυν[c. 10-14   ]

—   —   —

1 κε̄ Pap.   7 δαιμόνων   8 ἐπιλήψεως

The proposals made by Daniel and Maltomini (*locc. citt.*) are included here without explicit attribution. Readings and restorations proposed in the ed.pr. and subsequently rejected are likewise not referred to.

1 [φύλα]ξον: also possible διαφύλα]ξον or ἀπάλλα]ξον, either if there was a different distribution of letters to the right and left of each line, or if the charm continued from a preceding column.

τὴ[ν δ]εῖνα on the basis of a photograph superior to the plate in the ed. pr. : τὴ[ν δε]ῖνα Daniel, SB XIV 12113, P.Yale II 130. Before the break, the bottom of a vertical; therefore τὴν rather than τὸν δεῖνα. See also 4-5 comm.

κ(ύρι)ε: see intr.

1-2 [ἀπὸ πάντων] | [πον]ηρῶν πραγμάτῳ[ν: cf. PGM LXXI 6 f. φύλακξόν μοι (r. φύλαξόν με) ἀπὸ παντὸс κακοῦ πράγματος.

3 cυναντήματοc: cf. PGM XIII 798 f. οὐκ ἀντιτάξεταί μοι πᾶν πνεῦμα – οὐ δαιμόνιον, οὐ cυνά⟨ν⟩τημα οὐδὲ ἄλλο τι τῶν καθ' Ἅιδου πονηρῶν.

3-4 κ[αὶ   c. 5-8   ]|[. .]cεκτηcιου: the adjective κτηcίου, read in the ed.pr., does not seem appropriate here and leaves]cε a complete mystery, nor is εκτηcιοc attested as a word or the ending of a word. Given these difficulties, one might consider Ἐκ⟨α⟩τηcίου, even if it entails a correction *juxta lacunam*. The following lines 5-7 are concerned with warding off daemons, and so here perhaps there was a reference to the Ἐκατικὰ φάcματα (see E.Rohde, *Psyche* II [Freiburg i.B. 1898²], pp. 407-411, and cf. PGM IV 2728 f. Ἐκάτη, τριοδῖτι, πυρίπνοα φάcματ' ἔχουcα). Since Ἐκατικόc and Ἐκατήcιοc are synonymous, the present passage may have run κ[αὶ παντὸc φάcμα]|[το]c Ἐκ⟨α⟩τηcίου or, less likely, κ[αὶ φαντάcμα]|[το]c Ἐκ⟨α⟩τηcίου. Another possibility is suggested by Manetho, *Apotel.* 5, 302 f., where the adjective Ἐκατήcιοc occurs in a specifically magical context: δόξαν ἔχει τέχνηc Ἐκατηcίου εἵνεκα κέρδουc, / καὶ μαγικῇ cυνέcει πέπιθεν τὰ πνεύματα φεύγειν. For the text of the papyrus, then, perhaps κ[αὶ πάcηc τέχ]|[νη]c Ἐκ⟨α⟩τηcίου 'and all the witchcraft of Hekate'.

4-5 ἀπ[ὸ   c. 7-10   ]|[. . .]μου πτώcε[ωc]: cf. the phylactery PGM P 13, 15 f. πτῶcιc δαίμονεc (r. -νοc) μεcεμβρ[ιναῖ]c ὥραιc, where πτῶcιc denotes the attack of a daemon. Hence, for the present passage perhaps ἀπ[ὸ πάcηc φαν]|[ταc]μοῦ πτώcε[ω]c. There is some support from the immediately surrounding context, which in general is concerned with the onslaught of daemons. It cannot be excluded, however, that here the papyrus contained something which would explain τὴ[ν δ]εῖνα in line 1. Hence R.Merkelbach (*apud* Daniel, *loc.cit.*) suggested ἀπ[ὸ πάcηc τῆc μή]|[τραc] (or ὑcτέ]|[ραc]) μου πτώcε[ωc] (cf. PGM VII 260-271, a spell labeled πρὸc μήτραc ἀναδρομήν, and XXIIa, 9 ⟨πρὸc⟩ μαζῶν καὶ μήτραc πόνον). In this case πτῶcιc μήτραc would be a more general term for πρόπτωcιc μήτραc 'prolapse of the womb'. This possibility is supported by the ms. reading of the title Περὶ πτώcεωc (rather than προπτώcεωc) μήτραc of Soranus, *Gyn.* IV 35 (CMG IV, p. 147, 8). On the widespread belief in and fear of the dislocation, or wandering, of the womb and on the many magical amulets intended to check it, see A.Delatte, *Musée Belge* 18 (1914) 75-88; Bonner, *SMA*, pp. 79-94; A.A.Barb, "Diva Matrix," *Jour. Warb. Court. Institutes* 16 (1956) 193-238; J.-J.Aubert, "Threatened

Wombs: Aspects of Ancient Uterine Magic," *GRBS* 30 (1989), esp. pp. 423-425.

5 πτώϲε[ωϲ] π[*c.* 9-12] : πτώϲε[ω]ϲ κ̣[αὶ ἀπὸ πάϲηϲ *c.* 0-2] Daniel, SB XIV 12113, P.Yale II 130.

6]ωϲεωϲ: perhaps [ἐμπτ]ώϲεωϲ or κα]ι̣[ταπτ]ώϲεωϲ. Cf. Delatte, *Anecdota Atheniensia*, p. 243, 7 ἐμπιπτικόν (*sc.* δαιμόνιον) and 246, 4 f. καταπίπτοντεϲ (*sc.* δαίμονεϲ).

ὑπνο̣ [: perhaps ὑπνοφ[ανῶν, less likely ὑπνοφ[όβων. In favor of the former: it is commonplace that daemons act on people during their sleep; cf. e.g. PGM P 10, 36-40 πνεύματα - - - ποιοῦντα τὸν ἄνθρωπον δυϲόνει[ρον] ἢ ἔκθαμβ[ον] ἢ ἀμαυρίαν ποιοῦντα ἢ ἀλλοιωϲύνην φρενῶν ἢ ὑπ[ο]κλοπὴν καὶ ἐν ὕπνῳ καὶ δίχ[α] ὕπνου; Delatte, *Anecdota Atheniensia*, pp. 100, 13-19 ὁρκίζω ὑμᾶϲ - - - ἀπὸ τὴν ϲτρωμήν του καὶ ἀπὸ τὸν ὕπνον του (also 243, 22-26); the word ὑπνοφανήϲ, however, is rare – apparently attested only in Manetho, *Apotel.* 4, 363 f., though in a suitable context: βλαβερὸν δ' ἐπὶ πᾶϲιν ὁρίζει, / ϲκυλμοὺϲ ὑπνοφανεῖϲ, φαντάϲματά τ' ἠδ' ἐπαγωγάϲ. Also ὑπνοφόβηϲ is rare; to our knowledge it occurs only in *Anth. Pal.* IX 524, 21, where it is an epithet of Dionysos

6-7 ὑπνο̣ [*c.* 9-12]ι̣[. . .] κωφῶν δεμόν[ων: probably ὑπνοφ[α-νῶν ἢ ἀλά]ι̣[λων ἢ κω]φῶν δεμόν[ων. Cf. especially Delatte, *Un office byzantin d'exorcisme*, p. 35, 19 f. ἢ νυκτόλαλον ἢ κωφὸν ἢ ἄλαλον (so also p. 49, 25). For the frequent combination of ἄλαλοϲ and κωφόϲ elsewhere, cf. NT Marc. 9, 25 τὸ ἄλαλον καὶ κωφὸν πνεῦμα; PGM P 17, 16 ἢ ὅϲα τυφλὰ δαιμόνια ἢ κω[φὰ ἢ ἄλ]αλα ἢ νωδά; Orig., *Comm. in Matth.* XIII 6 (GCS X, p. 193, 5) πῶϲ ϲεληνιάζεϲθαι λέγεται ὁ ὑπό τινοϲ πνεύματοϲ ἀκαθάρτου καὶ κωφοῦ καὶ ἀλάλου ϲκοτούμενοϲ καὶ καταβαλλόμενοϲ; Delatte, *Anecdota Atheniensia*, p. 122, 24 f. ϲυναπαντήματοϲ ἢ ἐπιβουλητικὸν ἢ ἐγκαταχθόνιον ἢ πλάγιον ἢ μαγευμένον ἢ κουφὸν (*sic*) ἢ ἄλαλον κτλ. (similar: p. 127, 4-6); Pradel, *Gebete*, p. 9, 1 f. τῷ κωφῷ καὶ ἀλάλῳ πνεύματι; p. 11, 2 τὰ πνεύματα τὰ οὐρανοειδῆ, τὰ ἀϲτεροειδῆ, κωφά, ἄλαλα; Psell., *De operat. dem.* (p. 21 f. Boissonade) ἄλαλον καὶ κωφόν; Goar, *ΕΥΧΟΛΟΓΙΟΝ sive rituale Graecorum* (Venice 1730²), p. 580, 15 f. ἢ κωφὸν ἢ ἄλαλον (similarly p. 584 *ad fin.*). The possibility of e.g. ὑπνοφ[ανῶν φανταϲ]ι̣[μῶν ἢ κω]φῶν δεμόν[ων, originally proposed by Daniel (*loc.cit.*), seems less likely.

8 ἐπιλήμψεως: on the Hellenistic spellings λήμψομαι, εἴλημπται, ἐλήμφθη, λημπτός and its compounds and λῆμψις, ἐπίλημψις, ἀπόλημψις etc., common in papyri and medical writers, cf. **86** fr. A ii 1, and see Gignac, *Grammar* II, p. 269 with note 4, and esp. Crönert, *Memoria Graeca Herculanensis*, pp. 65-68. On the Latin pronunciation with -*mps*-, see *TLL* V.2, 667, *s.v. epilepsia*. On the demonic nature of the illness, see *RAC* V, *s.v.* Epilepsie, coll. 819-831 (E.Lesky-H.J.Waszink).

9-10 κ[αὶ *c.* 7-11]ἰ[. . . .]ματος: perhaps κ[αὶ ἀπὸ παντὸς] Ι [φαντάς]ματος or [πνεύ]ματος or [cυμπτώ]ματος or κ[αὶ ἀπὸ πάcης νό]ἰ[cου cώ]ματος.

11 ἐ]πιπ[ο]μπῆc: for the meaning 'demonic visitation' (LSJ), cf. PGM IV 2698-2702 φύλαξόν με ἀπὸ παντὸc δαίμονοc ἀερίου καὶ ἐπιγείου καὶ παντὸc ἀγγέλου καὶ φαντάcματος καὶ cκιαcμοῦ καὶ ἐπιπομπῆc; V 166-170 πᾶc δαίμων οὐράνιος καὶ αἰθέριος καὶ ἐπίγειος καὶ ὑπόγειος καὶ χερcαῖο[c] καὶ ἔνυδρος καὶ πᾶcα ἐπιπομπὴ καὶ μάcτιξ ἡ θεοῦ. On the term, see Fr.Pfister, "Zur antiken Daemonologie und Zauberei. Ἐπιπομπή, immissio, incursus und Verwandtes," *Woch. kl. Philol.* 29 (1912) 753-758.

Oxyrhynchos   Plate VIII   Later III AD[1]

P.Oxy. XLVI 3298 verso, 41-44.
ED.PR.: J.R.Rea, P.Oxy. XLVI (London 1978), pp. 59-63, no. 3298.
COMM.: ed.pr.
TRANSL.: ed.pr.
DESCR.: papyrus; 19 × 7 cm. On the recto, the upper part of three columns containing
  horoscopes (photo: P.Oxy. XLVI, plate VIII). On the verso, against the fibers, remains
  of another column of horoscopes, then a second column with one horoscope and,
  separated by a long horizontal stroke, the present charm.
LOC.: Ashmolean Museum, Oxford.

41   ὀνειρετηϲία.
      γρ(άψον) τὸ ὄνο(μα) [το]ῦτ[ο εἰ]ϲ χαρτάριον
      ἢ εἰϲ φύλλ[ο]ν ..... ϲ καὶ ἐπι [ ]αϲ
44   δι ανα .[.]... [.].. τη[.]....[

41 ὀνειραιτηϲία   42 γ Pap.   ονο Pap.

Request for a dream. Write this name on a piece of papyrus or on a leaf of - - -.

42 τὸ ὄνο(μα) [το]ῦτ[ο εἰ]ϲ (more a guess than a reading) : τὸ
ὄνο(μα) ..... ed.pr. For τὸ ὄνομα τοῦτο, cf. 74, 4; PGM I 146, 259;
IV 1321, 2695 f., 3116; also XII 179. For instances of delayed mention of
'this name', see 74, 1 comm.

---

[1] The *terminus post quem* is AD 249/50; see ed.pr., line 22 comm.

43 φύλλ[ο]ν . . . . . .c (ed.pr.), in which case the letter following the ν is the bottom of a vertical. Also possible φύλλ[ο(ν)], in which case the next two letters might be πι or νι. Mention of the laurel leaf (δάφνη) is normally expected in a dream request (cf. PGM V 370-399; VI; VII 795-828); according to J.R.Rea, however, delta cannot be read where it would be required.

Oxyrhynchos   Plate IX   III or early IV AD

P.Oxy. LVI 3835.
ED.PR.: F.Maltomini in: P.Oxy. LVI (London 1989), pp. 57-61, no. 3835.
COMM.: ed.pr.
DESCR.: papyrus; two fragments from a roll. Fr. A (17.2 × 14.8 cm), broken away to left
and right and at the bottom, contains remains of two columns written against the fibers
on the verso. Upper margin 1.8 cm; intercolumnium 1.3-1.9 cm. On the recto, written
with the fibers, remains of three columns from a philosophical text. The position of
the small Fr. B (1.3 × 1.3 cm), whose recto is blank, is not now determinable, but the
physical condition of the papyrus makes it more likely that it belonged to the first
column.
LOC.: Ashmolean Museum, Oxford.

The surviving portion of the text is homogeneous; all of the spells are
concerned with the identifying of a thief. At least five spells can be
distinguished, separated by extra interlinear space (i 8-9, ii 8-9, 11-12, 16-
17) and — in the one case where it can be determined — by dividing paragraphus and ecthesis of the new line (ii 8-9).

Spells to catch a thief are PGM V 70-95, 172-212; also III 479-494.
Demotic: Griffith-Thompson, *Demotic Magical Papyrus*, III 29 (cf. Betz,
Translation, p. 200); Bell-Nock-Thompson, "Magical Texts from a Bilingual
Papyrus," 244, col. vi (cf. Betz, *Translation*, p. 288 f.).

There is no certain evidence to establish the original line-length. The
supplements suggested for ii 1-8 seem to be the most economical way of
producing continuous sense.

Diaeresis on upsilon (fr. A i 9, 10; ii 13); dicolon to close a section in fr.
A ii 8.

Fr. A

col. i

— — —

1　　　　　　　　　　　　　　　]οιο
　　　　　　　　　　　　　　　]αν
　　　　　　　　　　　　　　　].
4　　　　　　　　　　　　　　]
　　　　]...[　　　　　　].[.]ν
　　]. [.....]δ.ριοβαλ[..]το.[.] κύριε
　　].[.]...ιρ...αχ[.]υς.ι βάλε
8　　].αρφ.[.]θ παράδος τὸν κλέπ[την

　　　　].φυρα.ν ὕδατι....τ[
　　　　].[.].[.].υποκ.....γ[

— — —

col. ii

1　εἰς τόπον καὶ λήμψε[ι] τ[ὴ]ν [σφῦραν]
　　καὶ κατακρούσεις εἰς τὸν [ὀφθαλμόν,]
　　κρούων καὶ λέγων· ἐκβαλ[
4　ὀφθαλμὸν ὁ κλέψας κα[
　　εἰπάτω ὁ κλέψας πρὶν ε.[
　　τὸν ὀφθαλμόν. ὅταν ο[
　　γη λύσις ἐλαίῳ ἢ οἴν[ῳ
8　κλύσον.　　　　　　[
　──────────
　κητε· κρόμβυα βαλεῖς εἰς [
　εἰπὼν ὅτι· ὁ κλέψας δακνετ[
　ἐὰν μὴ χαλάσῃ, δῆλος.　[

12　[....] σφυρίδα βαλε[ῖς.] αμμον εἰς α[
　　[....]..η ἄγγος ὕδατο[ς] καὶ ἐρεῖς βρε[

Col. i 9 ὕδατι Pap.　　10 ὑπο Pap.

Col. ii 8 κλυσον: Pap., deinde spatium vacuum　9 in ecthesi　κ΄ ἦτε?　κρόμμυα　11 post δηλος spatium vacuum　13 ἄγγος　ὕδατο[Pap.

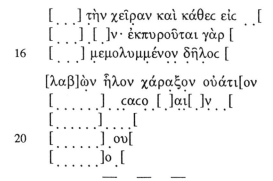

[. .] τὴν χεῖραν καὶ κάθες εἰς . . [
[. . .] . [.]ν· ἐκπυροῦται γὰρ [
16 [. . .] μεμολυμμένον δῆλος [

[λαβ]ὼν ἦλον χάραξον οὐάτι[ον
[. . . . .] . caco . [.]αι[.]ν . . [
[. . . . .] . . . [
20 [. . . . .] . ου[
[. . . . .]ο . [

14 χεῖρα   16 δῆλος: δ ex corr.? (ex ζ?)

Fr. B

1   ] . [.] . [
]δος φ . [
] . . [

(Fr. A col. i) - - - Lord - - - throw - - - hand over the thief - - - hammer in water (?) - - -.

(Col. ii) - - - to a place and you will take the hammer and strike on the eye and, while striking, say: "Thief, I will extrude (?) your |4 eye." And add (?): "Let the thief speak before I extrude his eye." If the thief speaks, freeing: |8 wash him (?) with oil and wine. 20 (?). Or (?): you will place onions on the eye (?), saying: "Thief, let the onion bite you (?)." If (the irritation) does not subside, it is clearly him. |12 - - - basket you will put - - - vessel of water and you will say: "I wet (?) your hand" and dip his hand into the vessel (?). For the water (?) boils - - - whomever you find |16 scalded (?), it is clearly him. Take a nail and engrave an Udjat-eye - - -.

(Fr. B) - - - hand over the thief (?) - - -.

Fr. A , col. i

6 κύριε: this spell contains a logos addressed to a deity: perhaps Hermes (PGM V 173, 188) κλεπτῶν εὑρετής or the Sun (PGM V 189) who sees all. It is to the κύριος that the imperative in 8 is directed.

8 παράδος τὸν κλέπ[την: cf. PGM V 77 f. παράδος τὸν κλέπτην τὸν ἄραντά τι; also 91 f.

9. cφῦρα ἐν ὕδατι?

Col. ii

1-8. There are clear similarities to PGM V 70-95 (4th cent. AD): λαβὼν βοτάνην χελκβει καὶ βούγλωccον ὕλιcον καὶ τὰ ἐκπιάcματα καῦcον καὶ μεῖξον τῷ χυλῷ χρηcτῶc καὶ γράψον εἰc τοῖχον χοω ἐν αὐτοῖc καὶ λαβὼν πανουργικὸν ξύλον γλύψον cφῦραν καὶ ἐν ταύτῃ κροῦε εἰc τὸ οὐ⟨άτιον⟩ λέγων [τ]ὸν λόγον· "ἐξορκίζω cε κατὰ τῶν ἁγίων ὀνομά- των· παράδος τὸν κλέπτην τὸν ἄραντά τι (here follow magic words) καὶ κατὰ τῶν φρικτῶν ὀνομάτων (here follow vowels and the drawing of an eye), παράδος τὸν κλέπτην τὸν κλέψαντά τι. ὅcον κρούω τὸ οὐάτιον cφύρῃ ταύτῃ, ὁ τοῦ κλέπτου ὀφθαλμὸς κρουέcθω καὶ φλεγμαινέcθω, ἄχρι οὗ αὐτὸν μηνύcῃ." λέγων ταῦτα κροῦε τῇ cφύρῃ. This spell, and the one in the present papyrus, represent the earliest evidence for a type of thief-detection spell (*Diebeszauber*) of which we have many late examples which show its success and wide diffusion, probably from Egypt to Byzantium, to Italy and then to a large part of western Europe even as far as distant Iceland (see the literature noted in the app.cr. to PGM V 70-95; *Hand- wörterbuch des deutschen Aberglaubens* II, *s.v.* Dieb, Diebstahl, coll. 222 f., 248; III, *s.v.* Hammer, col. 1376; Byzantine examples in Delatte, *Anecdota Atheniensia*, pp. 67, 11-17; 611, 1-7; 625, 17-22). It is not possible to deter- mine whether col. i 9-10 preserves the beginning of this spell or of an earlier one. In the section now lost the writer must at least have given instructions for drawing the eye. This spell, unlike PGM V 70-95, envisages the loss (not just a disorder) of the eye, as commonly in the later survivals of this practice.

1 εἰc τόπον: probably the place where the eye was to be drawn, or else the place where the suspects were to be assembled.

λήμψε[ι]: future, like κατακρούcειc (2), βαλεῖc (9, 12), ἐρεῖc (13); contrast κάθες (14), χάραξον (17). For the future in directions, cf. e.g. PGM II 76, 176; IV 1897, 1899, 1924, 1926 f.; XIII 135 (= 695); LXII 39, 40, 43; also **72** ii 3 with comm. For the form λημψ-, see **84**, 8 comm.

2. Cf. PGM V 75 κροῦε εἰς τὸ οὐ⟨άτιον⟩.

3-4. A restoration "ἐκβαλ[έτω τὸν] | ὀφθαλμὸν ὁ κλέψας" seems suggested by εἰπάτω ὁ κλέψας in 5. That ὀφθαλμὸν ἐκβάλλειν could mean 'extrude', 'get rid of', i.e. 'lose an eye', seems possible on the basis of the idiomatic ὀδόντα ἐκβάλλειν; cf. Aristot., *H.A.* 576A, 13; *Geopon.* XVI 1, 14 (p. 454, 12 Beckh); also Solon 27 W. (= 23 G.-P.), 1-2; Eur., *Cycl.* 644; cf. also the metaphorical ἐκβαλεῦcι τὰς κούρας of Herod. IV 64. But perhaps it would be better to supplement "ἐκβαλ[ῶ (or ἐκβάλ[λω) cou τὸν] | ὀφθαλμόν, ὁ κλέψας", with ὁ κλέψας nominative for vocative, as probably in ii 10 (for ὀφθαλμὸν ἐκβάλλειν in the sense of 'put out an eye', cf. e.g. NT Marc. 9, 47 καὶ ἐὰν ὁ ὀφθαλμός cou cκανδαλίζη cε, ἔκβαλε αὐτόν; *Acta Andreae et Matthiae* 1 [p. 66 Bonnet] καὶ ὀρύccοντες ἐξέβαλλον αὐτοῦ τοὺς ὀφθαλμούς; Epiph., *Panar.* 33, 11, 6 [GCS 1, p. 462, 25 f.]). See also next note.

4. E.g. κα[ὶ ἐπερεῖς]. Alternatively, 3-5 "ἐκβαλ[ῶ cou τὸν] | ὀφθαλ-μόν." ὁ κλέψας κα[υθήcεται. καί·] | "εἰπάτω κτλ." 'the thief will experi-ence a burning sensation. And (add): "Let him speak etc." Cf. φλεγμαινέ-cθω in PGM V 94.

5. The trace on the broken right-hand edge suggests the left side of a cursive kappa as in 10 δακνετ[and 15 ἐκπυροῦται. So: ἐκ[βαλεῖν or ἐκ[βάλη (for πρίν with the subjunctive after a positive proposition, cf. e.g. PGM III 264; IV 28, 2249, 2298 f.; VII 621); or else ἐκ[βάλω or ἐκ[βαλεῖν με, if ἐκβαλ[ῶ (or ἐκβάλ[λω) were right in 3.

6-7. E.g. ὅταν ὁ [κλέψας λέ]|γη (cf. 5 εἰπάτω).

7. With the reconstruction so far proposed it would come naturally to take λύcιc as a verb, λύcειc; but it seems a pity to destroy the exact correspond-ence with PGM VII 178 λύcιc· ἐλαίῳ (though cf. M.Wellmann, *Die Georgika des Demokritos* [APAW 1921.4], p. 29: "wohl λύcειc"). λύcιc here is the 'untying', the 'freeing' of the thief from the spell. Many examples of λύcιc by means of anointing are noted by Wellmann, *op.cit.*, p. 29 f. Some late thief-detection spells also contemplate the freeing of the thief: see *Handwörterbuch des deutschen Aberglaubens* II, *s.v.* Dieb, Diebstahl, coll. 204 and 247.

E.g. οἴν[ῳ αὐτὸν] or οἴν[ῳ τὸ ὄμμα].

8. It seems preferable to interpret this as κλύcον (cf. e.g. Arist., *H.A.* 603B, 11 κλύζοντες τοὺς μυκτῆρας οἴνῳ) rather than ἔ]|κλυcον (e.g. λύcιc· ἐλαίῳ ἢ οἴν[ῳ αὐτὸν ἔ]|κλυcον).

The following reconstruction of 1-8, combining suggestions made thus far, is offered *exempli gratia*:

1   εἰς τόπον καὶ λήμψε[ι] τ[ὴ]ν [cφῦραν]
      καὶ κατακρούcειc εἰc τὸν [ὀφθαλμόν,]
      κρούων καὶ λέγων· "ἐκβαλ[ῶ cου τὸν]
4   ὀφθαλμόν, ὁ κλέψαc." κα[ὶ ἐπερεῖc·]
      "εἰπάτω ὁ κλέψαc πρὶν ἐκ[βαλεῖν με]
      τὸν ὀφθαλμόν." ὅταν ὁ [κλέψαc λέ-]
      γῃ, λύcιc· ἐλαίῳ ἢ οἴν[ῳ αὐτὸν]
8   κλύcον.   [

9-11. We know of no other evidence for the use of onions in charms to catch a thief. Nonetheless, combining the facts of normal experience with what remains of this prescription, one can perhaps guess that onions were placed on a 'magic' eye (drawn or incised) and that this produced irritation in the eye of the thief.

9 κητε: the sequence is problematic. Just possibly κ is a numeral-letter (= 20), i.e. the serial number of the spell within the collection (for an instance of numeration in magical prescriptions, cf. **100**, 7), with ἤτε 'or' introducing a spell similar to the one before (even though ἄλλο is the usual way of introducing analogous spells or recipes; cf. **78** i 7 comm.). A reading κητα (= κη′ τὰ) seems decidedly improbable.

κρόμβυα (r. κρόμμυα): the same spelling in PGM IV 3260a and SB VI 9017, no. 12, 10; and cf. κρομβυοπώληc in UPZ II 180a xx 8, on which see Mayser, *Grammatik* I.1, 157.11-13.

εἰc [τὸν ὀφθαλμόν? εἰc [τὸ ὄμμα?

10 δακνετ[: "ὁ κλέψαc, δακνέτ[ω cε τὸ κρόμβυον"? (But it would be rather long compared with the restorations proposed for 1-8.) For the onion as δηκτικόν, cf. Diosc. II 151 (I 216, 5 Wellmann). For δάκνω used of things which irritate the eye, cf. LSJ, *s.v.* II, and see J.Taillardat, *Les images d'Aristophane* (Paris 1965²), § 296.

11 ἐὰν μὴ χαλάcῃ: 'if (the irritation) does not subside'? The same syntactic structure in PGM V 211 f. ἐὰν δέ τιc αὐτῶν μὴ καταπίῃ - - -, αὐτόc ἐcτιν ὁ κλέψαc.

δῆλοc: as at the end of the next spell (16), the word seems to be used absolutely with the meaning 'there he is revealed', 'it is clearly him', equivalent to αὐτός ἐcτιν ὁ κλέψας in PGM V 212 (see previous note). Here the style is more concise.

12-16. What remains of this spell seems to be closely related to the type of trial by ordeal which was widely current in the medieval West and known by the name of *iudicium (examinatio) aquae ferventis (calidae), aenei, caldariae,* etc. (German *Kesselfang*): the accused had to put his hand into a vessel of boiling water (normally to recover a stone or a ring which had been thrown into it); if his hand came out uninjured, he was judged innocent, if it was scalded, guilty. Up to now the earliest known evidence for this sort of *iudicium* was represented by the *Pactus Legis Salicae* ch. 53, 56, from the beginning of the sixth century; cf. *Monumenta Germaniae Historica. Legum sectio I*, vol. IV.1, pp. 200-203, 210-214. See H.Brunner, *Deutsche Rechtsgeschichte* II (2. Aufl. neu bearb. von C.von Schwerin, Munich-Leipzig 1928), pp. 545-550, and Register, p. 909, *s.v.* Kesselfang; *Handwörterbuch des deutschen Aberglaubens* III, *s.v.* Gottesurteil (Ordal), col. 1021 f.; many examples of *Kesselfang* are collected in *Monumenta Germaniae Historica. Legum sectio V*, p. 604 ff.

In the papyrus, many details remain uncertain, partly because of doubtful readings.

12 cφυρίδα: a reading cφυρίδ[ι]ν for cφυρίδιον seems unlikely; the space is too small, and the trace after the gap suggests the tail of alpha rather than the diagonal of nu. For the form cφ-, already prevalent in the papyri of the Ptolemaic period, see Gignac, *Grammar* I, p. 87 f.

] ͅ : the traces (the ends of two parallel horizontals, the lower one projecting further towards the right) seem hardly suitable to any letter in this hand.] ψάμμον,] ͅ ἄμμον, -]γραμμον, (-)]κάλαμον, (-)]θάλαμον, -]πάλαμον all are palaeographically unsatisfactory and, in any case, of no direct relevance in the context. Whatever the answer, the content of 12 will be difficult to relate to the known forms of *Kesselfang*.

13-14. "βρέ[χω] | [cου] τὴν χεῖραν" or "βρέ[χε] κτλ."? Or indeed, if the trial involves more than one suspect, "βρε[χέτω] | [πᾶc] τὴν χεῖραν" or "βρέ[χετε ὑ]|[μῶν] κτλ."

14 χεῖραν (r. χεῖρα): see Gignac, *Grammar* II, p. 46.

ͅ ͅ [: two high points of ink.

14-15. E.g. κάθεc εἰc τὸ [ἄγγοc (or ὕδωρ) τὴν] | [χεῖ]ρ[α]ν. It is difficult to decide whether the clause still belongs to the direct speech introduced by ἐρεῖc (13) or is part of the instructions.

15 ἐκπυροῦται γὰρ [τὸ ἄγγος? τὸ ὕδωρ? Such a combination seems tolerable, cf. e.g. LXX 2 Mac. 7, 3 προσέταξεν τήγανα καὶ λέβητας ἐκπυροῦν; Philostr., *Vit. Apoll.* I 16 ἐκπυροῦν τὰ βαλανεῖα. (Probably one cannot say, of a scalded hand, ἐκπυροῦται - - - [ἡ χείρ.) And yet the passive form, the present tense and the γάρ are ill-suited to describing the operation of heating the water. Perhaps the water comes to the boil spontaneously, when the thief's hand touches it? In Hrotsvitha, *Gongolfus* 399-418 (ed. K.Strecker, *Hrotsvithae opera*, Leipzig 1930[2], p. 48 f.), the unfaithful wife burns her hand when she puts it in the cold water of the spring; see J.Grimm, *Deutsche Rechtsalterthümer* II (Leipzig 1899[4]), p. 580 f.

16 μεμολυμμένον: μεμόλυμμαι is the perfect of μολύνω 'dirty', 'stain'. Was the intention μεμωλυσμένον? (For oscillations and confusions between forms of μολύνω and μωλύω, cf. LSJ, *s.v.* μωλύω.) Perhaps 15-16 'Whomever you find scalded, there is the culprit revealed'.

17-21. Like ii 1-8, this spell presupposes the use of a picture (here incised with a nail) of an eye.

17 [λαβ]ών: of ω only the link-stroke is preserved.

οὐάτι[ον: a loan-word based on Egyptian *wḏꜣt* 'Udjat-eye'. Cf. PGM V 75, 92 (on XII 230, see H.J.Thissen, *ZPE*, forthcoming), and see Griffith-Thompson, *Demotic Magical Papyrus*, p. 64 note on line 8; A.Jacoby, *ARW* 16 (1913) 124; LSJ, *s.v.*

18]αι[:]ει[would also be possible.

Fr. B

2. παρά]δος φῶ[ρα? Cf. PGM V 178, 210 παράδος φῶρ', ὃν ζητῶ. See also fr. A i 8 comm.

Provenance   III-IV AD
  unknown

P.Berol. inv. 21227

ED.PR.: W.Brashear, "Vier Berliner Zaubertexte. Nr. 1: Anrufung an Sarapis," *ZPE* 17
    (1975) 25-27.

COMM.: ed.pr.; (line 5) F.Maltomini, *Civ. Class. Crist.* 1 (1980) 375.

TRANSL.: R.Kotansky in Betz, *Translation*, no. CV.

PHOTO: ed.pr., plate I b.

DESCR.: papyrus; 13.5 × 17 cm. Broken away at right and bottom. There is free space of
    1.5 cm above the text and of 3-3.5 cm to its left. Two vertical folds. The writing runs
    with the fibers on the recto, and the verso is blank.

LOC.: Ägyptisches Museum, Berlin.

The upper part of a column containing a prose hymn to the great god.
Probably between 10 and 15 letters are lost to the right of each line (see
comm. on lines 5-6, 10-11 and 14-15). ϟ for δεῖνα.

<pre>
1   ὁ π [ ]ω ὅλων ἀναφανεὶς κ[
       αἰώ[ν]ι[ο]ν φύcιν, ὁ ἀκάματ[οc] ο [
       ὁ τῆc μεcημβρίαc δ   ν με [
4   φύλ[α]ξ, ἐπικαλοῦμαί cε, κύριε πα[
       ἄγνωcτε, ὃν καθαρᾷ ψυχῇ ἐγὼ ο[
       νοc cε ἁγιαcτί· εἵλεώc μοι γεν[οῦ
       Ζ[ε]ῦ Ιαω Ζὴν Ἥλιε ιουc[
8   cανβαλχανβαλ θανωαμα[
       χωχ ἵνα εἰπ[   ] [   ] θεῶν [
</pre>

5 ἄγνωcτε: ε ex corr.   6 ἵλεώc   7-15 in eisthesi   9 χωχ: prius χ ex c

Αωτ Αβαωτ· βαϲυμ Ιϲα[κ Cαβαωθ Ιαω　　?　　]
Ιαβωκ· ἰϲάκουϲόν μου, τοῦ δ(εῖνα) [
12　　ωρου ωρου ωρου· αε ιαια[
　　[̣ ̣]ϲουω ιναοη ιαωα⟦ει⟧ [
　　θεόϲ, ὁ προπάτωρ θεόϲ, ὁ ̣[
　　τὴν οἰκουμέν[ην ̣] [̣ ̣ ̣ ̣] ̣[

————　　　　————　　　　————

10 αβαωτ· Pap.　　11 Ιακωβ　　εἰϲάκουϲον　　Ϩ Pap.　　12 ωρου· Pap.
13 ϲοϋῶ

You who appeared before all things (?) in accordance with your (?) eternal nature, the untiring one - - - you who - - - of the noon - - - |⁴ guardian, I summon you, lord almighty, unknown, whom with pure soul I, NN (?), praise (?) calling upon (?) you devoutly; be gracious to me - - - Zeus Iao Zeus Helios *ious*- - -|⁸ *sanbalchanbal thanôama*- - - *chôch* so that you (?) speak - - - of the gods - - - *Aôt Abaôt basym Isak Sabaôth Iaô Jakôb*. Hear me, NN, - - -|¹² *ôrou ôrou ôrou ae iaia*- - -*souô iyaoê iaôa* - - - god, primal father god, you who illumine (?) the entire (?) inhabited world - - -.

1-3 ὁ - - - ὁ - - - ὁ - - -: for the anaphora, see Norden, *Agnostos Theos*, pp. 141-239, esp. 201 ff.

1 ὁ π ̣[̣ ̣]ῳ ὅλων: perhaps ὁ πρ[ὸ τ]ῶ⟨ν⟩ ὅλων as suggested by A. Henrichs (*apud* ed.pr.). Cf. e.g. Philo, *Somn.* 1, 70 ὁ πρὸ τῶν ὅλων θεόϲ; Theophil. Ant., *Autol.* 1, 4 κύριος δέ ἐϲτιν διὰ τὸ κυριεύειν αὐτὸν τῶν ὅλων, πατὴρ δὲ διὰ τὸ εἶναι αὐτὸν πρὸ τῶν ὅλων.

1-2 κ[ ] | αἰώ[ν]ι[ο]ν φύϲιν: perhaps κ[ατὰ τὴν ϲὴν] | αἰώ[ν]ι[ο]ν φύϲιν as suggested by A.Henrichs (*apud* ed.pr.) or κ[αὶ κτίϲαϲ τὴν] | αἰώ[ν]ι[ο]ν φύϲιν. For the nexus αἰώνιοϲ φύϲιϲ, cf. Albin., *Intr. in Plat.* 9 ὁρίζονται δὲ τὴν ἰδέαν παράδειγμα τῶν κατὰ φύϲιν αἰώνιον; Eus., *Orat. coet. sanct.* 11, 9 (GCS 1, p. 168, 25) αἰωνίου φύϲεωϲ ἀρχὴ χρόνιος, of the immaculate conception.

2 ἀκάματ[οϲ]: cf. e.g. PGM VII 531 ἀκάματε, of Helios. If the article ὁ follows, then ἀκάματ[οϲ,] ὁ κτλ.

̣[or ̣ ̣[: the bottoms of two verticals. Among the possibilities are π (so ed.pr.), η, ν, γι, τι, etc..

3 δ....... v. με.[: τ. ε. ναθμεν[ed.pr. Between δ̣ and ṿ, perhaps 3 rather than 4 letters; the palaeographical possibilities are too manifold to be enumerated. The ṿ might possibly be λ with some stray ink to the upper right. After this letter, a blotch (any round letter or a deletion). The next letter was made *ex corr.*; it is probably γ, ε, ο or c. Before the break, the bottom of a vertical.

4 φύλ[α]ξ: probably the simplex rather than a compound beginning in the previous line. Cf. the phylactery inscribed on a gold lamella from Amphipolis, *Brit. Mus. Cat. Jewellery* (ed. F.H.Marshall), no. 3153, line 9 f. ἄγιε θεέ, ἀγίων μόνος αἰώνων φύλαξ κτλ. (the comma perhaps should be placed rather after ἀγίων); also *Orph. hymn.* 4, 5 οὐράνιος χθόνιός τε φύλαξ πάντων περιβληθείς (Ouranos); Orph., Fr. 113 Kern καὶ ὁ τοῦ Ὀρφέως Οὐρανὸς "οὖρος πάντων καὶ φύλαξ" εἶναι βούλεται· καὶ Φοίνικες δὲ καὶ Αἰγύπτιοι τῇδε τῇ τάξει τὸ φρουρητικὸν ἐγκατοικίζουσιν (similarly Cornut., *Theol. Gr.* 1 [p. 1, 1-4 Lang], and Achill. Tat., *Intr. Arat.* 36, 13-16 Maass). Cf. also Orph., Fr. 96 Kern τοῦτον (sc. Ἥλιον) γὰρ ἐπέστησε τοῖς ὅλοις ὁ δημιουργός (sc. Φάνης)· καὶ φύλακ' αὐτὸν ἔτευξε κέλευσέ τε πᾶσιν ἀνάσσειν, ὥς φησιν Ὀρφεύς.

κύριε πα[: probably κύριε πα[ντοκράτωρ] as suggested by the first editor. Cf. PGM XII 250; LXXI 3; P 13a, 1. The nexus occurs some 120 times in the Septuagint (cf. 2 Reg. 5, 11; 7, 8, 25, 27; etc.), where it translates *Jahweh Sabaoth*; see C.Capizzi, ΠΑΝΤΟΚΡΑΤΩΡ (Rome 1964), pp. 13-24. On παντοκράτωρ Cαβαωθ, see **29**, 5-6 comm.

5 ἄγνωστε ὃν καθαρᾷ ψυχῇ Maltomini, *loc.cit.* : ἄγωστε̣ [ας], ἡ καθαρὰ ψυχή ed.pr.

ἐγὼ ο̣[: probably ἐγώ, ὁ̣ [δ(εῖνα); cf. 10 μου, τοῦ δ(εῖνα).

5-6. An illustrative reconstruction: ὃν καθαρᾷ ψυχῇ ἐγὼ, ὁ̣ [δ(εῖνα), ὑμνῶ ἐπικαλούμε]ινός cε ἁγιαστί.

6 cε ἁγιαστί : δε ἁγιαστί[c] (r. ἁγιασθείς) ed.pr. There is space for one letter after αγιαστι, but the papyrus is not abraded here. Furthermore, ἁγιαστί[c] for ἁγιασθείς can no longer be accommodated to the present sentence, and the articulation ἁγιασθείς ἵλεώς μοι γεν[οῦ does not seem suitable. The adverb ἁγιαστί, assumed here, is elsewhere unattested. For adverbs based on -cτί, -ιcτί and -ιαcτί, see A.Debrunner, *Griechische Wortbildungslehre* (Heidelberg 1917), §§ 272, 353. Many of them refer to languages (Ἑλληνιcτί, Αἰγυπτιcτί, Ἑβραιcτί, Cυριcτί, etc.; several such instances in PGM XIII 455-463, cited in **70**, 1-2 comm.), but by no means

all; cf. e.g. ἀλογιcτί, ἀνδριcτί, ἀνθρωπιcτί, ἀφροντιcτί, γυναικιcτί, κυνιcτί, ὀνομαcτί, παιδιcτί, χιαcτί.

εἵλεώc (r. ἵλεώc) μοι γεν[οῦ as in PGM V 420; for such requests, see Keyßner, *Gottesvorstellung*, pp. 91-98.

7 ιουc[(with the ed.pr.) or ιουε[: on ιου, see **96**, 47 comm.

10-11 Αωτ Αβαωτ βαcυμ Ιcα[κ Cαβαωθ Ιαω?] Ι Ιαβωκ (r. Ιακωβ?): perhaps identical with PGM IV 1376 f. Αωτ· Αβαωτ· βαcυμ· Ιcακ· Cαβαωθ· Ιαω· Ιακωπ (*sic*), though there may have been an extra element in the lacuna in 10 (cf. the length of line suggested by the illustrative reconstruction of 5-6). The same logos in PGM V 134 f., though omitting the final Ιακωβ. Since the elements of the logos appear to be of Hebrew origin, the reading Ιαβωκ in **87** is probably not to be defended on the basis of PGM XII 263 ἐπικαλοῦμαί cε κατὰ μὲν Αἰγυπτίουc· Φνω εαι Ιαβωκ (cf. app.cr.).

βαcυμ: see **57**, 23 right comm.

11 δ(εῖνα) [: [ed.pr. At the top of what we take to be δ is a loop and what may be the beginning of a descender. Cf. e.g. PGM VII 528 f. εἰcάκουcόν μου, τοῦ δεῖνα.

12 ωρου ωρου ωρου: perhaps of Horos.

ιαια : over the last α appears to be a letter (θ?).

13 ιαωα⟦ει⟧ [: Ιαω α⟦ει⟧ ed.pr. After the deletion and before the break is blank space.

14 θεόc, ὁ προπάτωρ : [ὁ] θεὸc ὁ προ[c]τατῶν ed.pr. In προπάτωρ, the upper right of π is preserved after a lacuna (the letter will have been made larger than usual); then the upper part of α comparable to the third α in 2 ἀκάματ[οc] and to the first α in 5 ἁγιαcτί. For Helios as προπάτωρ, cf. PGM IV 457, 948, 1988. See also Bauer, *Wörterbuch*, *s.v.*, and Lampe, *s.v.*

14-15. At the right edge of 14, the bottom of a vertical. Possibly ὁ κ[αταλάμπων ὅλην or πᾶcαν] Ι τὴν οἰκουμέν[ην (cf. PGM VII 704 f.) or perhaps ὁ κ[υριεύων ὅλην (or πᾶcαν)] Ι τὴν οἰκουμέν[ην (cf. PGM VII 838).

Oxyrhynchos   Plate X   IV AD

P.Oxy. inv. 72/65 (a).

ED.PR.: P.Maas, "The Philinna Papyrus," *JHS* 62 (1942) 36 f. (Maas published the first 12 lines of this text with the readings and supplements of E.Lobel; lines 13-19 are published below for the first time).

COMM.: ed.pr.; R.Merkelbach, *APF* 16 (1958) 86.

REF.: Pack[2], no. 1872; Marganne, *Inventaire*, no. 130.

DESCR.: papyrus; 5.5 × 15 cm. Remains of a column complete in height but damaged at the right and the lower left. The writing runs with the fibers on the recto. Above the text a blank space of 1.3 cm and below it one of 2 cm. On the verso, against the fibers, the ends of 13 lines in a different hand.

LOC.: Ashmolean Museum, Oxford.

Two iatromagical recipes: lines 1-5 against erysipelas, 6 ff. against red eruption. It is not possible to say whether or not one or more charms began in lines 14-19.

The chief interest of this fragment is that the charm in lines 6-8 appears to be a close parallel to the second hexametrical charm in the so-called Philinna Papyrus, *Suppl. Hell.* 900 (see also PGM XX 6-14 = *hymn.* 28):

[*c.* 8]ας Cύρας Γαδαρηνῆc |⁷ [ἐπαοιδὴ] πρὸς πᾶν κατάκαυμ[α·]
⟨   ⟩ |⁸ . . . . . . μ]υcτοδόκοc κατεκα[ύθη] |⁹
[ὑψ]οτάτῳ δ' ἐν ὄρει κατεκαύθ[η] ⟨   ⟩ |¹⁰
ἑπτὰ λύ[κ]ων κρήνας, ἔπτ' ἄρ[κτων,] |¹¹ ἑπτὰ λεόντων·
ἑπτὰ δὲ παρθεⁱ|¹²νικαὶ κυ[α]νώπιδες ἤρυcαν [ὕ]|ⁱ³δωρ
κάλπ[ι]cι κυανέαιc καὶ ἔcⁱ|¹⁴βεcαν ἀκ[άμ]ατον πῦρ.

The first charm in the present text (lines 1-5) will have been similar, but not enough survives to warrant an attempt to reconstruct it. Apparently it was not hexametrical. Cf. also Apsyrtus in Oder-Hoppe, *Corp. Hippiatr. Graec.* II, p. 31, 5 f. (= Heim, *Incantamenta*, no. 65) τρὶς ἑπτὰ θαλάccια ζῷα, ἑπτὰ ἄρκοι, ἑπτὰ λέοντεc, ἑπτὰ δελφῖνοι ἐδίωκον τὴν ἀγρίαν μᾶλιν.

Paragraphus is used to divide the two charms and to separate the sections of the second one. The opening line of each charm is in ecthesis. Diaeresis on iota in 18. ⲓ̈ for πρός (1, 6).

1   πρ(ὸς) [ἐρ]υϲίπελα[ϲ λόγοϲ·
        ἑπτὰ λύκων, ἑ[πτὰ   παρ-]
        θένων ἄγριον [
4   μεγάλων ὀϲτῶν [
        ὦ Γῆ, ϲὺ δὲ ταῦτα πάντ[α
        πρ(ὸς) ἐρυθρὸν λόγοϲ· ἑπτὰ [λύκων   ἑπτ' ἄρκτων]
        ἑπτὰ λεόντων, ἑπτὰ [δὲ παρθενικαὶ κατε-]
8   κο`ΐμιϲαν αἰθέριον πῦρ. [
        λέγε·   [
        [.] . . ν ἐπικαλοῦμα[ι
        ω τοῦ Αβρααμ [ἐπικα-]
12   [λ]οῦμαι δὲ καὶ τὸ ὄν[ομα
        [. .]θ̣ρο̣ῦ κόλληϲον τὸ φ[
        [. . . . .] . . ον προϲ ον[
        [. . . . . δυ]νάμει καὶ ὑπα̣ [
16   [c. 6] καθαρὸϲ προϲθ[
        [c. 6] ν̣ . . . . ὀνοματ[
        [c. 7]μην ϊϲον ϊϲῳ [
        [c. 7]μ̣ων θέρμανο[ν

1 in ecthesi   ⲓ̈ Pap.   6 in ecthesi   ⲓ̈ Pap.   9 post λεγε spatium
vacuum in Pap.   18 ϊϲον ϊϲω Pap.

Formula against erysipelas. - - - of seven wolves, of seven - - - maidens (?) fierce fire (?) - - - |⁴ of big bones - - -. You, o Gê, all these things - - -.   Formula against red eruption. Of seven wolves - - - of seven bears, of seven lions, and seven maidens quenched |⁸ the ethereal fire. - - - say: - - - I call upon - - - of Abraham - - - and I call upon |¹² also the name - - - of red eruption (?) paste the - - - power and - - - |¹⁶ - - - pure - - - name(s) - - - in equal quantity - - - heat - - -.

1 πρ(òc) [ἐρ]υcίπελα[c (or-cιπέλα[τα) λόγοc : πρ(òc) [ἐρυ]cίπελα
λ[όγοc ed.pr.   A spell against erysipelas in PGM XIII 244-246 ἐὰν εἴπῃc
(sc. τὸ ὄνομα) ἐπὶ ἐρυcιπέλατοc, χρίcαc αὐτὸ κορκοδείλου ἀφοδεύ-
ματι, εὐθέωc ἀπαλλαγήcεται. In papyri, the ailment is mentioned in the
pharmacological recipes PSI X 1180, 56; SB XVI 13080, 8; P.Mich. inv. 21
A verso, 9 (ed. L.C.Youtie, ZPE 65, 1986, 132).

3 ἄγριον: quite possibly ἄγριον [πῦρ; cf. 8 αἰθέριον πῦρ and PGM
XX 14 (quoted in the intr.) ἀκ[άμ]ατον πῦρ; also Apsyrtus (quoted in the
intr.) ἀγρίαν μᾶλιν. Note that Hipp., *Epid.* VII 20 (V 392, 8 L.) has
ἄγριον πῦρ, of erysipelas (cf. Gal., *Ling. exolet. Hipp. explic.* XIX 134, 2
K.).

6 ἐρυθρὸν : ἐρυθρὰν ed.pr.   Cf. Hipp., *Liqu.* 6 (VI 130, 3 L.) τὰ
ἐρυθρά.

6-8. Restored *exempli gratia* by R.Merkelbach, *loc.cit.*, with PGM XX.

7-8 κατε]ⅼκο`ί'μιcαν Merkelbach, *loc.cit.* : καὶ ἐ]ⅼκο`ί'μιcαν *Suppl.
Hell.* 900, 13-14 app.cr.

9. The paragraphus under this line was not recorded in the ed.pr.

11 Αβρααμ[: Αβρααμ *vac.* [ed.pr.

12-13 ἐ]ⅼ[ρυ]θροῦ?

18 ἴcον ἴcῳ: cf. LSJ, *s.v.* ἴcοc I.2; for the expression in medical prescriptions, cf. e.g. Gal., *Comp. medic. sec. loc.* VI 8 (XII 964, 14 K.);
Paul. Aegin. IV 4, 3 (CMG IX.1, p. 326, 2), and the numerous occurrences
in J.-H.Kühn-U.Fleischer (edd.), *Index Hippocraticus* (Göttingen 1986-1989),
p. 399. Cf. PGM VII 485 ἴcα ἴcων.

Provenance   IV AD
unknown

O.Ashm. Shelton 194.

ED.PR.: J.C.Shelton, O.Ashm. Shelton (Papyrologica Florentina XVII, 1988), p. 140 f.,
   no. 194.

COMM.: ed.pr.

TRANSL.: ed.pr.

PHOTO: ed.pr., plate XLIV.

DESCR.: ostracon; 10 × 9 cm. Broken away at top, right and lower left; complete at the
   upper left and possibly at the bottom. Inscribed on the convex side.

LOC.: Ashmolean Museum, Oxford. Inv. G.O. 217.

Two charms, separated by a long horizontal stroke, against the sting of the
scorpion; cf. **16** intr., also **94**, 48-55 with comm. ⟄ for δεῖνα.

1   [
      καὶ μὴ μίνῃς α[
      τοῦ cώματοc τοῦ δ(εῖνα) [
4   ἐcτιν τοῦ ἁγίου θεοῦ [
      _____
           ἄλλο   [?
      [ὁ]ρκίcο ⟨cε⟩, πᾶν cκορπίε, ἐπι [
          ]υντα. ἐξοργίcω c[ε
8   ] καταβῆναι ἀπὸ τ[
             ] μὴ ψῦξο⟨ν⟩ μη[
             ] οτιθεc ημε[

              breaks off?

2 μείνῃς   3 ⟄ Ostr.   6 ὁρκίζω   πᾶc   7 ἐξορκίζω

- - - and do not remain - - - of the body of NN; for he is a man (?) of the holy god - - -. Another: I adjure you, every scorpion, - - - I adjure you - - - to come down from - - - do not cause ague, do (?) not - - -.

1-4. An illustrative reconstruction:

$$- - - μὴ πλῆξον]$$
$$καὶ μὴ μείνῃς, ἀ[λλὰ κατάβαινε ἀπὸ]$$
$$τοῦ cώματοc τοῦ δ(εῖνα)· [ὅτι ἄνθρωπόc]$$
$$ἐcτιν τοῦ ἁγίου θεοῦ [τοῦ ἐν οὐρανῷ]$$

2-4. Regarded as complete on the right by the first editor.

2 μὴ μίνῃς α[: μὴ λύπηcο[v] ed.pr. Before the break, what can hardly be anything else than the lower left loop of an alpha.

3-4. For the pattern of expression [ὅτι ἄνθρωπόc] Ι ἐcτιν τοῦ ἁγίου θεοῦ, cf. PGM IV 1177-80 ὅτι ἐγώ εἰμι ἄνθρωπος θεοῦ τοῦ ἐν οὐρανῷ, πλάcμα κάλλιcτον γενόμενον ἐκ πνεύματος καὶ δρόcου καὶ γῆc (PGM punctuates ἄνθρωπος, θεοῦ τοῦ ἐν οὐρανῷ πλάcμα κτλ.); PGM P 5a, 10 f. ὅτι δούλη ἐcτιν τοῦ θ(εο)ῦ τοῦ ζῶντος. The phrase ἄνθρωπος (± τοῦ) θεοῦ occurs several dozens of times in the Septuagint, especially as a designation of Moses (e.g. Deut. 33, 1; Josh. 14, 6) and of Elias (e.g. 3 Reg. 17, 18); other references in Bauer, *loc.cit.*

5 ἄλλο: see **78** i 7 comm.

6 πᾶν for πᾶc: on indeclinable πᾶν, see **47**, 7 comm.

ἐπι [: at the break, the left side of a round letter, probably c, possibly o.

6-7 τὸν] Ι [φορο]ῦντα ?

8 καταβῆναι : καταταβῆναι ed.pr. (printing error; correctly indexed). Quite possibly καταβῆναι ἀπὸ τ[οῦ cώματος τοῦ δ(εῖνα).

9 μὴ ψῦξο⟨ν⟩ : μὴ ψύξο (r. ψύξω) "lest I dry up (or, freeze)" ed.pr., adducing the coldness with which individuals are cursed in the Athenian curse tablets edited by D.R.Jordan, *Hesperia* 54 (1985) 205-255. The comparison, however, seems inappropriate. Probably here the verb is causative and refers to the ague resulting from the scorpion's sting (ψυγμόc); cf. Diosc. V 11, 2 (III 14, 7-8 Wellmann) τὰ τῶν θηρίων δήγματα, ὅcα τρόμους καὶ ψυγμοὺς ἐπιφέρει, μάλιcτα δὲ cκορπίων καὶ φαλαγγίων καὶ ἀcπίδων.

Oxyrhynchos   Plate XI   IV AD

P.Oxy. XXXVI 2753.

ED.PR.: A.H.S.el-Mosallamy, P.Oxy. XXXVI 2753 (London 1970), pp. 27-28, no. 2753.

COMM.: ed.pr.

TRANSL.: Betz, *Translation*, no. CII.

DESCR.: papyrus; Fr. E 2.5 × 3 cm; Fr. D 15 × 15.5 cm; Fr. B 3 × 3 cm; Fr. C 4 × 2.5
   cm. The text is written on the verso of P.Oxy. XXXVI 2751, a II/III AD text of Plato,
   Republic III (photo: Plate IV). Top edges of recto and verso are identical. The verso of
   Fr. A is blank. The writing of the magical text runs against the fibers. At the left edge
   of Fr. D, traces of a preceding column (intercolumniation between 0.5 and 2.5 cm). The
   last line of the text preserved on Fr. D was the last line of that column of writing;
   below it, some 1 cm of blank space. The recto shows that Fr. E has to be placed about
   5 cm above Fr. D; about 5 lines of writing are missing between the two fragments.

LOC.: Ashmolean Museum, Oxford.

The logos in Fr. D 4-16 is addressed to the headless god (ἀκέφαλος
θεός). With near certainty it is part of a 'Dream Request from Bes', for the
same logos occurs in two exemplars of a charm so entitled: PGM VII 221-
249 and VIII 64-110. In these parallels, the logoi are preceded by instructions
prescribe that one prepares a special ink, that one recites the logos to a lamp,
and that a piece of black cloth is wrapped around the throat. Similar, though
not identical instructions can be recognized in Fr. E and in lines 3-4 of Fr. D.

Literature on requests for prophetic dreams from Bes can be found in the
app.cr. to the passages in PGM cited above and in the notes on these sections
in Betz, *Translation*. For further commentary, see Preisendanz, *Akephalos*,
pp. 42-52. On the headless god as incorporating elements of Jahweh,
Sarapis, Aion, Seth-Typhon and, above all, Osiris, see also Merkelbach-
Totti, *Abrasax* 2, pp. 153-170 on PGM V 96-172.

Fr. E

1   ] ἐπὶ τ[
    το]ῦ ἐλλυ[χνίου
         ]ου[
4   ]οθ[
      ] ν[

Fr. D (col. ii)

1   μ[
    τ[c. 10   ] [ ] [
    ἀ[ναλά]μβανε ὕδατι ὀμ[βρίμῳ. ὁ λόγος ἐπὶ τοῦ]
4   λύχνου λεγόμενος οὗτ[ος· ἐπικαλοῦμαί σε,]
    τὸν ἀκέφαλον θεόν, τὸν [ἐπὶ τοῖς ποσὶν ἔχοντα]
    τὴν [ὅ]ρασιν, ⟨τὸν⟩ ἀστράπτοντ[α καὶ βροντάζοντα·]
    cὐ εἶ οὗ τὸ cτόμα πῦρ [δι]ὰ παντ[ὸς προσχεῖται· cὐ εἶ ὁ ἐπὶ]
8   τῆς Ἀνάγκης· ἐπι[καλο]ῦμαί cε [τὸν   c. 10   ]
    θεὸν [ιαεα] [c. 8   Ιαεω Cαβαωθ Αδωναι]
    χαρβα[θιαω· cὐ εἶ ὁ ἐπὶ τῇ ζμυρνίνῃ cορῷ κατα-]
    κείμενος καὶ πρὸς κεφαλῆ[c] ἔχ[ων ῥητίνης]
12 ὑπαγκώνιον καὶ ἀσφάλτου μ[c. 13   ]
    [ὅ]ν λ[έγο]υσιν A̅ν̅ο̅υ̅θ̅ A̅ν̅ο̅υ̅θ̅ ἄνακτα [c. 8   ]
    . . . . [οὐ]κ εἶ δαίμων, ἀλλὰ τὸ αἷμα τῶν [c. 8   ]
    καὶ τῶν λ̅ καὶ τῶν ρ̅δ̅ ἱεράκων. τῷ[ν πρὸς κε-]
16 φαλῆc τ[ο]ῦ Ὀcί[ρε]ωc λαλούντω[ν] καὶ ἀ[γρυ]‖[πνούντων]

Fr. B   Fr. C

1   ]π ο   1   ] καὶ ἀπ' ἀκαθαρτ[
    ]με   ] ἐπὶ τοῦ λύχν[ου
    ] ν   ἀκ]ρομέλαc π [

(Fr. D) - - - dissolve (the above-mentioned ingredients for the ink) in rain water. The formula to be recited over the lamp is this: "I call upon you, the headless god, the one with his sight by his feat, the one who lightens and thunders; you are the one whose mouth pours forth fire continually; you are the one over Necessity; I call upon you the - - - god - - - *Iaeô Sabaôth Adônai charbathiaô*; you are the one who lies on the coffin of myrrh and who has by his head an elbow-cushion of terebinth-resin (?) and a - - - of asphalt, you whom they call *Anouth, Anouth,* lord, demon (?) - - -; you are not a demon, but the blood of the x and the x (?) and the 30 and the 104 falcons and the - - - that chirp and keep watch by the head of Osiris - - -."

Fr. E

This fragment appears to have contained part of the instructions that preceded the logos. They must have varied considerably from the two parallels. They cannot be restored on the basis of PGM VII 226-230 as was stated by the first editor (n.b. one cannot read θεό[ς in line 4).

1 ἐπὶ τ[: ἐπὶ τ[οῦ λύχνου ed.pr., perhaps correctly.

2 το]ῦ ἐλλυ[χνίου : τ]οῦ ἐλλυ[χνίου ed.pr. (cf. comm.).

3]ου[: χεῖράν c]ου [καὶ σχεδόν coυ ἐγρηγοροῦντος ed.pr.

4]οθ[: ἥξει] ὁ θεὸ[ς καὶ λέξει coι καὶ ed.pr.

5] ν[: not indicated in the ed.pr.

Fr. D

1-3. The instructions are phrased differently than in the parallels.

1-2. The ed.pr. gave ἐμ?]ἰμ[άξῃς τὴν ζωγραφίαν τῷ Ἰσιακῷ μέλανι] τ[ὸ δὲ ῥάκος] . . ξ [ ] [, but a list of ingredients is expected here; see following note.

3 ἀ[ναλά]μβανε ὕδατι ὀμ[βρίμῳ: cf. PGM VII 222-225 λαβὼν μίλτον ⟨καὶ αἷμα⟩ περιστερᾶς λευκῆς, ὅμοιον καὶ κορώνης καὶ γάλα cυκαμίνου καὶ χυλὸν ἀρτεμιcίας μονοκλώνου καὶ κιννάβαρι καὶ ὕδωρ ὄμβριμον καὶ πάντα λειώcας ἀπόθου; VIII 68-73 ἔτι δὲ τὸ μέλα[ν], ἐν ᾧ γράφεις· αἷμα κορώνης, αἷμα περιστερᾶς λευκῆς, λίβανος ἄτμητος καὶ ζμύρνα καὶ μέλαν γραφικ[ὸ]ν καὶ κιννάβαρις καὶ ὀπὸς cυκαμίνου καὶ ὕδωρ ὄμβριον καὶ χυλὸς ἀρτεμι⟨cί⟩ας μονοκλώνου καὶ κατανάγκης. The two parallel passages lack the verb ἀναλαμβάνειν, for which cf. PGM IV 1832-37 μάννης δραχμαὶ δ', cτύρακος δραχμαὶ

δ' - - - (more ingredients)· μίξας ἀναλάμβανε οἴνῳ εὐώδει; cf. also IV 1317, 2681 and 2690.

3-4 ὁ λόγος ἐπὶ τοῦ] | λύχνου λεγόμενος οὗτ[ος : ἐπὶ τοῦ] | λύχ-[ν]ου λεγόμενος οὗτ[ος ὁ λόγος (?) ed.pr. The text appears to be close to PGM VII 232 f. λόγος ὁ λεγόμενος ἐπὶ τὸν λύχνον. What comes before the logos in PGM VIII 89-91 is quite different: λέγων τὸν λόγον, καὶ ἐλεύσεται πρὸς σέ. ἔχε ἔγγιστά σου πινακίδα, ἵνα ὅσα λέγει γράψῃς ἵνα μὴ κοιμη[θ]εὶς ληθαργήσῃς. For the text reconstructed here and for PGM VII 232-233, cf. e.g. **94**, 44; PGM IV 3098 ὁ δὲ λόγος ὁ λεγόμενος ἀλήθοντός σου ἐστιν οὗτος; XXXVI 137 ἔστι δὲ ὁ λεγόμενος λόγος οὗτος.

4-5 ἐπικαλοῦμαί σε,] | τὸν ἀκέφαλον θεόν: restored with PGM VII 233 f. and VIII 91; cf. V 98 σὲ καλῶ τὸν ἀκέφαλον. On the headless god, see intr.

5-6 τὸν [ἐπὶ τοῖς ποσὶν ἔχοντα] | τὴν [ὅ]ρασιν : τὸν [ἐν τοῖς ποσὶν ἔχοντα κεφαλὴν καὶ] | τὴν [ὅ]ρασιν ed.pr., following PGM VII 244; but this is not the corresponding part of the text, and the restoration is too long for the space available. In 5 one could restore [ἐν (as in the ed.pr.) or [παρά. Cf. PGM VII 234 τ[ὸ]ν ἐπὶ τοῖς ποσὶν ἔχοντα τὴν ὅρασιν and VIII 91 f. τοῖς παρὰ τοῖ⟨ς⟩ ποσὶν ἔχοντα τὴν ὅρασιν; also V 145 f. ἐγώ εἰμι ὁ ἀκέφαλος δαίμων ἐν τοῖς ποσὶν ἔχων τὴν ὅρασιν. The phrase here probably refers in the first place to the beheaded Osiris. It can be paralleled by the appellation 'He Whose Face Is in His Knee' used in the Egyptian *Book of the Dead*, Spell 130, 4 (p. 106 Allen), of Apophis, the beheaded enemy of the sun god.

6 ⟨τὸν⟩ ἀστράπτοντ[α : ἀστράπτοντ[α ed.pr. Cf. PGM VIII 92 f. τὸν ἀστράπτοντα καὶ βροντάζοντα; VII 234 f. ὁ ἀστράπ⟨τ⟩ων, ὁ βροντάζων; V 150 f. ὁ ἀστράπτων καὶ βροντῶν.

7 [δι]ὰ : [διὰ] ed.pr.

σὺ εἶ οὗ τὸ στόμα πῦρ [δι]ὰ παντ[ὸς προσχεῖται: so restored by the first editor following PGM VII 235 σὺ εἶ ⟨οὗ⟩ τὸ στόμα διὰ παντὸς προσχέεται. Cf. PGM VII 245 f. σὺ εἶ οὗ τὸ στόμα [δ]ι[ὰ] π[αν]τὸς καίεται; VIII 93 f. σὺ εἶ οὗ τὸ στόμα διὰ παντὸς πυρὸς γέμει; V 153 f. ἐγώ εἰμι οὗ τὸ στόμα καίεται δι' ὅλου; IV 3069-71 ᾧ τὸ ἄσβεστον πῦρ διὰ παντὸς αἰῶνος προσπαρακάεται.

7-8 σὺ εἶ ὁ ἐπὶ] τῆς 'Ανάγκης: cf. PGM VII 235 σὺ εἶ ὁ ἐπὶ τῆς 'Ανάγκης, Αρβαθιαω; PGM VIII 94 ὁ ἐπὶ τῆς 'Ανάγκης τεταγμένος.

8-10 ἐπι[καλο]ῦμαί cε [τὸν　c. 10　] Ι θεὸν [ιαεα̣] [　c. 8　Ιαεω
Cαβαωθ Αδωναι] Ι χαρβα̣[θιαω : ἐπι[καλ]οῦμαί cε [τὸν ἀκέφαλον]
Ι θεὸν [[　.　.　.　]], [τὸν ἐν τοῖc ποcὶν ἔχοντα κεφαλὴν καὶ ὅραcιν, Ἰc]Ιχυ-
ρ(ὸν) Β[ηcᾶν ἀμβλυωπόν ed.pr., freely adapting PGM VII 243-245,
although this is not the corresponding part of the parallel. The present passage
is restored, as far as possible, with PGM VIII 94-96 ἐπικαλοῦμαί cε τὸν
ἐπὶ τῆc Ἀνάγκηc τεταγμένον θεὸν Ιαεω· Cαβαωθ: Αδωναι: Ζαβαρβαθιαω. PGM VII omits the part of the logos that the present papyrus and PGM
VIII have here. As in PGM VIII 96, magical words must have been part if not
all of what was written in the lacunae in lines 9-10. After θεὸν in 9, ιαεα̣ is
canceled (cf. PGM VIII 95 f. θεὸν Ιαεω).

10-11 cὺ εἶ ὁ ἐπὶ τῆ ζμυρνίνῃ cορῷ κατα]Ικείμενοc: restored with
PGM VIII 96 f. by reason of space. The first editor restored the shorter cὺ εἶ
ὁ ἐπὶ cορῷ κατα]Ικείμενοc with PGM VII 236 f.

11-12 καὶ πρὸc κεφαλῆ[c] ἔχ[ων ῥητίνηc] Ι ὑπαγκώνιον καὶ ἀcφάλτου : καὶ πρὸ[c] κεφαλῆ[c]　.̣　[　ἔχων] Ι ὑπαγκώνιον καὶ ἀcφάλτου ed.pr. However, cf. PGM VII 237 f. καὶ πρὸc κεφαλῆc ἔχων ὑπαγκώνιον ῥητίνηc καὶ ἀcφάλτου and PGM VIII 97 f. ἔχων ὑπαγ⟨κ⟩ώνιον
ῥητίνην καὶ ἀcφαλτον.

14　.̣　.̣　.̣ [οὐ]κ : [　.̣　.̣　.̣ οὐκ] ed.pr.

13-14 [ὄ]ν λ[έγο]υcιν Ανουθ Ανουθ ἄνακτα　.̣ [　c. 8　]Ι　.̣　.̣　.̣ [οὐ]κ:
overlining not indicated in ed.pr. Cf. PGM VII 238 f. ὃν λέγουcιν Ανουθ.
ἀ[ν]άcτα, δαίμων; VIII 98 f. ὃν λέγουcιν Ανουθ: Ανουθ: ἀνάcτα,
δαίμων. The Oxyrhynchus papyrus had a longer text and gives ἄνακτα
where the parallels have ἀνάcτα. The two readings might have come from a
text which once ran ὃν λέγουcιν - - - ἄνακτα. ἀνάcτα, δαίμων, κτλ.
P.Oxy. might have had ὃν λέγουcιν - - - ἄνακτα [　c. 5　δαί]Ιμονα·
[οὐ]κ εἶ δαίμων, ἀλλὰ κτλ. or ὃν λέγουcιν - - - ἄνακτα, δ[αίμονα
c. 2]Ι　.̣　.̣　.̣ [οὐ]κ εἶ δαίμων, ἀλλὰ κτλ. For other passages in which the
magician displays his special knowledge similarly, cf. **95** → 16-19 comm.

14-16 ἀλλὰ τὸ αἷμα τῶν [　c. 8　] Ι καὶ τῶν λ̄ καὶ τῶν ρ̄δ̄ ἱεράκων
τῶ[ν πρὸc κε]Ιφαλῆc: cf. PGM VII 239 f. ἀλλὰ τὸ αἷμα τῶν β′ (ρ̄δ̄ Pap.)
ἱεράκων τῶν πρὸc κεφαλῆc; VIII 99 f. ἀλλὰ τὸ ⟨αἷμα⟩ τῶ⟨ν⟩ δύο
ἱεράκων τῶν πρὸc κεφαλῆc. Once again, the text of the Oxyrhynchus
papyrus is longer than its parallels. At the end of 14 one can imagine possibly
τῶν [x̄ καὶ τῶν x̄]. If by chance the readings of PGM VII 239 ῑβ̄ and VIII 99
δύο are both correct the lacuna might have had τῶν [β̄ καὶ τῶν ῑβ̄]. Above

line 15 is what appears to be an interlinear καὶ [. One might consider ʽκαὶ [τῶν substantive]ʼ τῷ[ν πρὸc κε]ǀϕαλῆc. The Oxyrhynchus papyrus shows to what a great extent the number of the birds varied in the tradition, and so the reading of PGM VII 239 ιβ̄ should not necessarily be changed so as to agree with PGM VIII 99 δύο. One or the other or both might be correct. When mention is made of *two* birds over the decapitated head of the headless god, the reference is almost certainly to Isis and Nephthys in the form of birds lamenting the corpse of Osiris; see *Lexikon der Ägyptologie* III, *s.v.* Klagefrau, coll. 444-447 (Ch.Seeber).

16 τ[ο]ῦ ʼOcί[ρε]ωc : τ[οῦ] Oὐcί[ρε]ωc ed.pr. Cf. PGM VIII 100 τοῦ ʼOcίρεωc; VII 240 τοῦ Oὐρανοῦ. As the first editor points out, ʼOcίρεωc rather than Oὐρανοῦ must be correct.

Fr. B

1]πο :]το ed.pr.
2]με :] υc ed.pr.
3] ν :]ν ed.pr.

Fr. C

This fragment may also belong to the instructions that preceded the logos.

1] καὶ ἀπ᾽ ἀκαθαρτ[: κ]αὶ ἀπ᾽ ἀκαθαρc[ίαc.

3 ἀκ]ρομέλαc : ὀλ]ομέλαc ed.pr. The traces after the break suit ρ rather than λ. For the compound restored, cf. PGM IV 802 f.

Provenance   III AD[1]
unknown

P.Laur. IV 149.

ED.PR.: R.Pintaudi, P.Laur. IV (Florence 1983), p. 54, no. 149.

COMM.: ed.pr.

PHOTO: ed.pr., plate CVI.

DESCR.: papyrus; 5.9 × 7 (not 6 as stated in the ed.pr.) cm. Broken away at left, right and
bottom; the blank space at the top (1 cm) may be a margin or extra interlinear space (as
at 4/5). The writing runs with the fibers on the recto, and the verso is blank.

LOC.: Biblioteca Medicea Laurenziana, Florence. Inv. PL III/508.

Remains of two recipes separated by extra interlinear space. Their purpose
is hard to discern. In the second one, ἐν ϲυμποϲίῳ (line 5) might suggest a
sympotic *paignion*.

Diaeresis on upsilon in 3.

```
1              ]κελαιθ[
         ] . . . . . βαλω τα[
         ] Ιαω καὶ ὑφαψα[
4        ]ᾱω Αδωναιο [

         ] ἐν ϲυμποϲίῳ γυ  [
         ]εϲϲχεθη λέγε ἐπὶ τ[
         ]ιε  θ[ ]ε[ c. 5 ] αθ  ε[
8        ] κ[    c. 7    ] ϲιο[
          —   —   —
```

3 ϋφαψα Pap.   7 post ιε spatium in Pap.   post αθ spatium in Pap.

---

[1] The hand can be compared e.g. to P.Oxy. XI 1364 (pl. V; early III AD, assigned);
Roberts, *Greek Literary Hands*, pl. 21a (early III AD, assigned); cf. also P.Heid. II 191
(Taf. VIb; III AD, assigned), though it differs somewhat in that it slopes to the right. The
first editor dated **91** to the 4th century, comparing the writing to Turner-Parsons, *Greek
Manuscripts*, pl. 70 (ca. 325 AD).

- - - I shall throw (?) - - - *Iaô* and having lit (?) - - - *Iaô (?) Adônaio* - - - at a banquet - - -
say over - - -.

2]_ _ _ _ _ : third, foot of an upright; ε or c; foot of an upright.

3 ὑφαψα[: 'to light' or 'to bind'?

4]αω: I]αω is the most likely, but not the only possibility.

Αδωναιο : Αδωναιε ed.pr. Αδωναιε is what one expects, but apparently it cannot be read. If ε, then oddly written.

5 ἐν cυμποcίῳ: see intr., and cf. **76**, 7; PGM XIb 1 f. [ἀνθρ]ώπους πίνοντα[c] ἐν cυμποcίῳ πρός[ωθεν] τοῖς ἔξωθεν ὀνορύγχους φαίνεcθαι.

γυ_[: foot of an upright at the edge. Perhaps a form of γυνή? See line 6, and cf. PGM XIII 320 f. (quoted in **71** fr. 11, 2 comm).

6]εccχεθη:] ἐc{c}χέθη?]εc cχεθῇ?

7 θ[_]ε[: θ[_ _ _]ε[ed.pr.

Provenance   Plate X   IV/V AD
unknown

P.Med. I 20.

ED.PR.: A.Traversa, "Dai papiri inediti della raccolta milanese. 25: Frammento di papiro magico," *Aegyptus* 33 (1953) 57-62.

REPUBL.: P.Med. I 20 (S.Daris).

COMM.: ed.pr.; P.Med. I 20.

TRANSL.: ed.pr.; H.D.Betz, *Translation*, no. XC.

PHOTO: ed.pr., between p. 60 and p. 61; P.Med. I, plate VII.

REF.: Preisendanz, *Überlieferung*, no. LXXXIV; van Haelst, *Catalogue*, no. 948.

DESCR.: papyrus; 9.5 × 12 cm. There are blank spaces above, below, to the left and to the right of the text. Six vertical and seven (?) horizontal folds. The writing runs with the fibers, and the back is blank. The ink is brick-red.

LOC.: Scuola di Papirologia dell'Università Cattolica del Sacro Cuore, Milan. Inv. 23.

The folds indicate that the sheet was used as an amulet. This is in seeming contradiction with the fact that from line 12 onwards the text appears to be that of a formulary. Therefore, either a section of a formulary was merely cut out of a roll or, more probably, a person who knew little Greek mechanically copied the directions of a handbook without understanding much of what he wrote (for other such cases, see **32**, 1 comm. and **58**, 1-2 comm.).

This text is filled with difficulties. The purpose of the first charm (1-13) is obscure (see, however, 11 comm.). The second charm (14-18) is against shivering and fever, but we are unable to say whether parts of lines 15-17 are Greek, Coptic, Hebrew or magical gibberish. Some Coptic letters occur in lines 5, 15 and 17 (and possibly in 6).

It cannot be ruled out that the charm issued from a Christian milieu ("chrétien (?)" van Haelst), though typically Christian features are lacking.

Portions of the papyrus have recently been unfolded (compare the photo published here with the earlier ones). As a result, the lacuna which previous editions show in lines 1-2 can now be partly filled, a few letters can be recovered to the left of lines 14 and 15, and a few letters or traces can be added to the right of lines 14-17.

κο╪ for κοι(νόν) or κοι(νά) (12, 13, 15); γρ/ for γράψον (14); φυλ/ for φυλακτήριον (14).

```
 1    τὸν κύριον  οσκαιμετας
      αυ τὸν κύριον μαγιὸν καὶ
      π  νν ἀνόματι Μιχαηλ
 4    Μιχαηλ Μιχαηλ Γαβριηλ
      ℈Ραφαηλ Ουριηλ Ηληλυ-
      θ αδεφαπαβα Ιαβαωθ
       θιηλ Φαβριηλ Εβριηλ
 8    θεὸς ςύ, Coβοως, οεοςτυου
       ωνα  μιν βηχε Νουρηλ Α-
      βηλ Αριηλ Αναηλ Κεμουηλ
      Αβααλ, λῖςον τὸμ ἵπ⟨π⟩ον, Ιαω
12    C[α]βαωθ βββ) κοι(νόν). ⊗ ⊗ ⊗
         ) ⊗ ⊗ ⊗ ⊗ ✝ κοι(νόν).
      φυλ(ακτήριον) ῥῖ⟨γ⟩ον πυρετόν. γρ(άψον) ῡῡυυυ
      ε[ ]βρεκον ℈η: κοι(νόν) τιταλομω  λ
16    [ ]  [ ]ι χαρ  τηρ [ ] ουας
      [ ]εκιρε οςπα  μαρ λο℈η  ϙ
      [ ]  ἤτη β, ταχὺ [β].
```

2 μαγειῶν (an μαγι⟨κ⟩όν?)   3 ὀνόματι   11 λῦcον τὸν   12 κο╪ Pap.
13 κο╪ Pap.   14 φυλ/ Pap.   γρ/ Pap.   15 dicolon in Pap.   κο╪ Pap.   18 ἤδη

The lord - - - and with you (?) the lord of magic and - - - in the name of *Michaêl*, |4 *Michaêl, Michaêl, Gabriêl, Rhaphaêl, Ouriêl, Êlêlyth, adephapaba, Iabaôth,* - - -*thiêl, Phabriêl, Ebriêl,* |8 you god *Soboôs,* you god (?) *ou ôna min bêche, Nourêl, Abêl, Ariêl, Anaêl, Kemouêl, Abaal,* deliver the horse (from evils) (?), *Iaô,* |12 *Sabaôth, bbb* (magical sign) what you wish (magical signs), what you wish. Protective charm against shivering, fever. Write *yyyyy,* Hebrew (?) or (?) something (?) as you wish. Solomon (?) - - - |16 - - - magical sign(s) - - - now now, quickly quickly.

When P.Med. I 20 agrees with the first edition, readings are contrasted only with the latter.

1-2. A portion of text has recently been recovered at the middle of these lines (see introduction).

τὸν κύριον - - - τὸν κύριον: a verb is needed to govern these accusatives, unless they are accusatives of adjuration (on which see **29**, 5-6 comm.).

.οсκαιμεταсιαυ τὸν : [καλοῦν]τας | αὐτὸν ed.pr.   Perhaps .ος (magical name) καὶ μετὰ сιαῦ (r. сοῦ) τὸν.

2 κύριον μαγιῶν (r. μαγειῶν or μαγι⟨κ⟩ὸν) : ν ὑγ[ιεινὸ]ν ed.pr.

3 π .νν ἀνόματι (r. ὀνόματι) : Π[ὰ]ν ν αν ομ ἔτι ed.pr.   The putative π could be τ; then an elusive trace. We have toyed with but rejected Πᾶν{ν}α ⟨ὀ⟩νόματι. Possibly the sequence π .νν arose from a misunderstood abbreviation of πνευμάτων.

ἀνόματι: on the confusion of α and ο, especially in the Coptic pronunciation of Greek, see Gignac, *Grammar* I, pp. 286-289, and cf. PGM XXVII 5 ἀνόματος; LXXXI 10 ἀνομασία. For ὀνόματι in place of ἐν (or ἐπὶ) ὀνόματι, see **20**, 5 comm.

5-6 Ουριηλ Ηληλυιθ αδεφαπαβα : Ουριη[λ, Ε]μανουιηλ, с[α-] χαφαπαβα ed.pr. : Ουριη[λ, Ε]μανουιηλ, с[.] αφαπαβα P.Med. I 20. For Eleleth, see J.Michl, *RAC* V, col. 211, no. 72; Davidson, *Dictionary of Angels*, pp. 104 (Eleleth), 140 (Heleleth); cf. also line 30 of the gold amulet published by R.Kotansky, *The J. Paul Getty Museum Journal* 8 (1980) 181-184 (= SEG XXX 1794). The δ in 6 might be Coptic Ϫ.

6 Ιαβαωθ : [С]αβαωθ ed.pr.   For Ιαβαωθ, cf. PGM IV 3263; VII 315; XII 473.

7 .θιηλ Φαβριηλ Εβριηλ : [βαω]θ ιη φα Βριηλ ε Βριηλ ed.pr.   At the beginning, the well-known Сαλαθιηλ cannot be read.

Φαβριηλ: see Davidson, *Dictionary of Angels*, p. 111.

Εβριηλ: see Davidson, *Dictionary of Angels*, p. 101.

8 θεὸς сύ, Соβοωс, οεοстυου : θεὸς [θε]ὸς Ιαω соεοс-τ-υου ed. pr. : εοс [θε]ὸς ιαω соεοстυου P.Med. I 20.   At the end of the line one should probably interpret the sequence οεοстυου as θεὸς сύ, ου- (the beginning of a magical word or name). For the acclamation сὺ εἶ (± ὁ) θεός, see A.J.Festugière, *La révélation d'Hermès trismégiste* IV (Paris 1954²), p. 165 with note 2. In our papyrus the noun (θεός) comes in the first position, which is rather unusual in acclamations and doxologies; one might compare

the phrase θεός μου εἶ cύ, which in the Psalms alternates with cὺ εἶ ὁ θεός μου (cf. also PGM IV 2860 ὀλέτιc cύ, Δίκη cύ). For the omission of the copula, cf. the acclamations in "Du-Stil" indicated by Peterson, ΕΙΣ ΘΕΟΣ, p. 181 n. 1; cf. also PGM IV 2858 f., 3264; VII 830 f.

Cοβοωc: probably a misspelling of Cαβαωθ.

9-10 ͅωνα ͅμιν βηχε Νουρηλ Α|βηλ Αριηλ : [ͅ]ωναααμινβιηχενο ͅ μαc | Ημραηλ ed.pr.

ͅωνα ͅμιν: at the beginning only scattered ink on damaged surface; after α, a round letter, possibly α or ο. Perhaps ἐῶνα ἀμίν (r. αἰῶνα ἀμήν)? But governed by what? Alternatively, one might take μιν as an independent word and recognize the Egyptian god Min. The following βηχε might be Egyptian *bjk*, Copt. ʙʜϩ (Boh. ʙɛxɪ), 'falcon'. The falcon was the sacred bird of Horos, and Min was identified with Horos; see Bonnet, *Reallexikon*, pp. 178-180 and 465 f. But all of this is most uncertain.

Νουρηλ probably stands for Νουριηλ, for whom cf. PGM P 21, 16, 35, and see J.Michl, *RAC* V, col. 224, no. 152; Davidson, *Dictionary of Angels*, p. 209.

Α|βηλ: cf. PGM XIa 8; W.Beltz, *APF* 29 (1983) 77 (P. 8330, 2) and 30 (1984) 98 (P. 9074, 1) ʌʙʜʌ. See Davidson, *Dictionary of Angels*, p. 4.

10 Αριηλ: cf. PGM P 14, 2; Delatte-Derchain, *Intailles*, no. 519; and see J.Michl, *RAC* V, col. 204, no. 21; Davidson, *Dictionary of Angels*, p. 54.

Αναηλ: cf. PGM P 14, 9; 21, 16, 35; and see J.Michl, *RAC* V, col. 203, no. 15; Davidson, *Dictionary of Angels*, p. 17.

Κεμουηλ: see Davidson, *Dictionary of Angels*, p. 166.

11 Αβααλ : βιαμ ed.pr. Cf. Abbael in J.Michl, *RAC* V, col. 201, no. 1 (add Kropp, *Koptische Zaubertexte* I, E 12 ʌʙʌʜʌ; Delatte, *Anecdota Atheniensia*, pp. 603, 12; 633, 29 ᾽Αβαήλ).

λῖcον (r. λῦcον) τὸμ (r. τὸν) ἵπ⟨π⟩ον : λιcοντομιπαν ed.pr. Our interpretation is tentative and based on the assumption that we have here meaningful Greek and not magical gibberish. A charm to deliver a horse from evils, however, comes as no surprise in itself; cf. the therapeutic and protective charms in Oder-Hoppe, *Corp. Hippiatr. Gr.* (these passages can all be located by means of Vol. II, Index VII, *s.v.* ἐπαοιδαί); see also G.Björck, *Apsyrtus, Iulius Africanus et l'hippiatrique grecque* (Uppsala 1944), pp. 57-70 and *Handwörterbuch des deutschen Aberglaubens* VI, *s.v.* Pferdesegen, coll. 1676-79. If λῦcον τὸν ἵππον sounds elliptical without a following ἀπό τινοc, this could be explained by the possibility that here, at the end of the charm, only its gist is being repeated (cf. e.g. **44**, 17-18 with 10-17). On the other hand, charms to protect or heal horses or other animals are unattested elsewhere in the Greek magical papyri. Another possibility might be to interpret λῦcον τὸν πόνον, which sounds much more familiar (cf. **32**, 12 with comm.) but implies a radical alteration of the text.

12 C[α]βαωθ : βαωβ ed.pr.
After the three betas, a piece of writing which resembles a round bracket.
κοι(νόν) (also 13, 15): see **95** → 7 comm.
At the end of the line we see three, not four (ed.pr.) magical signs.

13. Six (not five) magical signs. Of the first one, only the left side is preserved.

14-15. A few letters have recently been recovered to the left of these lines (see introduction).

14 φυλ(ακτήριον) ῥῖ⟨γ⟩ον πυρετόν : [κολ]λίριον. πυρετόν ed.pr. The heading is breviloquent; one should understand φυλακτήριον ⟨πρὸς⟩ ῥῖγος ⟨καὶ⟩ πυρετόν (cf. **96 A** 51 comm.). ῥῖ⟨γ⟩ον is for ῥῖγος by confusion of declensions; cf. **18**, 7; also **14**, 3, 4, 8; PGM XVIIIb 4. For the omission of γ, see Gignac, *Grammar* I, pp. 71-75 (before a back vowel, p. 73 f.).

ῡῡυυυ : four magical signs according to the ed.pr. Bars are visible above the first two upsilons only. Cf. the upsilons in the fever amulet **3**, 10 and 12.

15 ε[ ]βρεκον ϩη κοι(νόν) τιταλομω λ . : ['Α]βρα[ά]μ ηϩη κοι(νόν)· τιτ αα μ ωω ed.pr. A purely tentative reconstruction: Ε[ἰ]βρε-κὸν ϩῆ κοι(νόν) τι Ταλομῶν κτλ. = Ἑβραϊκὸν ἢ κοι(νόν) τι. Cαλο-μῶν κτλ. If Ἑβραϊκόν is correct, one must assume ει (?) for ε, ε for αι and a final ν that was made with the oblique stroke rising from the bottom of the left leg to the top of the right leg. ϩη for ἢ could be explained by false aspiration (Coptic influence? See Gignac, *Grammar* I, pp. 135-138). If Ταλωμων is for Cαλομῶν, one should probably assume a mistake in copying. The sequence κοι(νόν) τι, however, does not occur elsewhere.

16 χαρ . τηρ [ ] . ουαc : χαυ[ ]τηρ[ ]χουαc ed.pr. : χα . [ ] etc. P.Med. I 20. At the beginning, in all likelihood, a form of χαρακτήρ.

17 [ ]εκιρε . οcπα . . μαρ . λοϩη . ϥ : [.]εκιρα[ ]οcτα[.]μαρ[.]λο-ϩη ed.pr. We are unable to make any sense of this line.

18 [ ] . ήτη (r. ἤδη) β, ταχὺ [β] : [. .]cητη[.]τας ed.pr. Cf. the app.cr. to PGM VII 254; VIII 52; XII 143, 396; also VII 330; X 50; XII 86.

Provenance   IV-V AD
unknown

P.Noviomagensis inv. 2.

ED.PR.: R.P.Salomons-K.A.Worp, "Some Nijmegen Papyri. 1: Lychnomanteia," *ZPE* 58
   (1985) 93-95.

COMM.: ed.pr.

PHOTO: ed.pr., plate V b.

DESCR.: papyrus; 8.2 × 4.2 cm. Broken away on both sides and at the bottom. Upper
   margin, 1 cm. The writing runs with the fibers, and the back is blank.

LOC.: Universiteitsbibliotheek, Katholieke Universiteit, Nijmegen.

   Lamp divination. On lychnomancy, see Hopfner, *Offenbarungszauber* II,
§§ 212-227; R.Ganszyniec in *RE* XIII.2, *s.v.* Λυχνομαντεία, coll. 2115-
19; S.Eitrem, *Symb. Osl.* 8 (1929) 49-53; M.Totti, *ZPE* 73 (1988) 297-301;
Merkelbach-Totti, *Abrasax* I, pp. 2-10.
   Dicolon in 4.

1   [   ]. λ[υ]χνε..... χρηϲτὸν ἔλαιον κ[
       [ὑγίαινε,] λύχνε, φαίνων τῷ Ἀρνεχθ[α καὶ τῷ]
       [   ]χθα καὶ τῷ κ(υρί)ῳ θεῷ Ὀϲί[ριδι καὶ]
4   [τῷ ἀρχαγγέ]λῳ Μιχαηλ: τῷ ἐπιτα .[
       [   ]ται τόδε δε[......].. [
                        ]   [
                   ].[.].oc.[
       ─   ─   ─

   1 χρηϲτον: η ex corr. (ex υ?)   2 αρνεχθ[: ρ ex corr. (ex λ?)   4 dicolon in
Pap.   6 spatium vacuum in Pap.

- - - lamp (?) - - - good oil - - - Be well, lamp, who shine upon Harnechtha and Osir-
chentechtha (?) and the lord god Osiris and the archangel Michael who commands (?) - - -;
if this has been granted to me, show (?) - - -.

1 λ[υ]χνε . . . . . : first, either α or λ; then indecipherable traces. The first
editors tentatively suggested: (i) λυχνέαϲε (r. λυχνίαϲε) τὸ; (ii) λυχνέαν
καὶ; (iii) λύχνε, λαβὼν. None of these proposals, however, is wholly satisfactory.

κ[: supplement e.g. κ[ύριε (cf. PGM VII 255, quoted in the next note),
or κ[αίε λέγων (cf. PGM IV 2372), or κ[αὶ λέγε.

1-3. Cf. PGM XXIIb 27-29 κα[ὶ] λ[έ]γε πρὸc τὸν λύχνον, ἕωc
cβεcθῆ· ὑγίαινε, λύχν[ε], παραφα[ί]νων τῷ ['Αρ]cεντεφθα καὶ τῷ
'Αρcεντεχθα καὶ τῷ μεγάλῳ [πα]τρ[ὶ] 'Οcίριδι Μιχαηλ; VII 255-257
κύριε, ὑγίαινε, λύχνε, ὁ παρεμφαίνων τῷ 'Οcίριδι καὶ παρεμφαίνων τῷ
'Οcιρχεντεχθα καὶ τῷ κυρίῳ μου, τῷ ἀρχαγγέλῳ Μιχαηλ. These passages seem to be closely related to Griffith-Thompson, *Demotic Magical
Papyrus*, VI 36 (cf. Betz, *Translation*, p. 206, 185), where the lamp used in
a divination charm is identified with the lamp that shines upon the dead Osiris;
see Hopfner, *Offenbarungszauber* II, § 227.

2 'Αρνεχθ[α: Egyptian Ḥr-nḫt 'mighty Horos'. See J.Spiegel, *Die Götter
von Abydos* (Wiesbaden 1973), p. 76 (cf. also p. 173, *s.v.* Min).

3. The estimated width of the gap makes ['Οcιρχεντε]χθα (cf. PGM VII
257; also III 171) somewhat preferable to ['Αρχεντε]χθα (cf. PGM IV 2003,
2355; VII 252, 362, 403; and see PGM, Vol. 3 [Index], p. 216). The former
is from Egyptian *Wsir-Ḫntj-ḫtj*, the latter from *Ḥr-Ḫntj-ḫtj*. Khenty-Khet
was the major god of Athribis, with whom Horos and Osiris were syncretized; see Bonnet, *Reallexikon*, pp. 131-133; *Lexikon der Ägyptologie* III,
s.v. Horus-Chentechtai, coll. 27-33 (U.Rößler-Köhler); P.Vernus, *Athribis*
(IFAO, Bibliothèque d'étude 74, Cairo 1978), pp. 367-424.

κ(υρί)ῳ: the abbreviation bar is omitted.

4 ἐπιτα .[: ἐπιτάξ[αντι? (ed.pr.).

5. The first editors suggested [εἴ μοι δέδο]ται τόδε, δε[ῖξον, comparing
PGM XXIIb 35 εἰ δέδοταί μοι τόδε τὸ π[ρᾶγ]μα, δεῖξ[ον] κτλ.

5-6. The blank space in 6 suggests that the horizontal stroke probably
separates two different prescriptions. One cannot rule out, however, that it is
the end of a bar over a magical word.

Antinoopolis   Plate XII   VI AD[1]

P.Ant. II 66.

ED.PR.: J.W.B.Barns in: P.Ant. II (London 1960), pp. 47-49, no. 66.

COMM.: ed.pr.

TRANSL.: R.Kotansky in Betz, *Translation*, no. XCIV.

REF.: Pack[2], no. 2391; Marganne, *Inventaire*, no. 43; eadem, "Compléments," p. 177, no. 43; Turner, *Typology*, p. 120, no. 393b (cf. p. 36).

DESCR.: papyrus; 13.3 × 11.8 cm. A fragmentary leaf from a codex that had two columns on each page. Only the upper parts of the columns are preserved. Both sides have an upper margin of 3.3 cm. Side → has a right margin of 2.3 cm; side ↓ a left one of 1 cm. Breadth of the columns 6.7-7.3 cm. Intercolumnium ca. 1 cm. Estimated page breadth 20/21 cm. Estimated breadth of the written area 15/16 cm. The true order of the two sides is uncertain.

LOC.: Ashmolean Museum, Oxford.

Thirteen magico-medical prescriptions, separated by paragraphus (paragraphus with asterisk under 58): lines 1-3 uncertain; 4-6 a drying powder for the eyes; 7-9 for easy childbirth; 10-11 against fever (?); 12-16 uncertain; 17-21 against demonic possession; 22-26 to protect or heal the eyes by means of an inscribed "Gothic" ring; 27-29 against tumors; 30-35 uncertain; 36-38 against strangury; 39-43 against migraine; 44-58 against the effects of a wound; 59-60 uncertain.

Diaeresis on upsilon in 2 and 28; dicola (to close a section in 6 and 21; often after a magical word); stops (3, 11, 52, possibly 1, 2). γρ for γράψον (7); λ̆ό for λόγος (44); ῆ for πρός (7, 10, 17, 22, 39); ō for ὄνομα (24); a raised horizontal for final ν in 36. ∠ for δραχμή in 5 (*bis*), 6.

---

[1] V AD according to the ed.pr.; perhaps somewhat earlier according to Turner, *Typology*, p. 120, no. 393b. A date in the sixth century is suggested by a comparison of the hand with Cavallo-Maehler, *Greek Bookhands*, pl. 31c (mid-sixth century, assigned).

→   col. i

1   [*c.* 7   ] ̣ υνυελ ̣ ̣ [̣]ϲποου ̣

μ[̣] ̣ ̣ [̣]ϲεγειρ ̣ υ ̣ ̣ ϋε ̣

βηθ ̣ ε ̣ [̣]ουχ.

4   ξηρίον ὀξυδορκικόν. κρόκου

(δραχμαὶ) δ̄, ἀλόηϲ (δραχμαὶ) β̄, ϲαρκο ̣ κόλληϲ

(δραχμαὶ) η̄. λιώϲαϲ χρῶ.

π̄ρ̄(ὸϲ) εὐτ̣[ο]κίαν. γρ(άψον) ἐ̣ν̣ περιάπ̣[τ]ῳ·

8   αβραω ̣ αρωνβαρα: βαρ ̣ α ̣

[*c.* 18   ] ̣ ̣ ̣ ω

[φυλακτή]ριον π̣ρ̣(ὸϲ) πυ ̣ ̣ ̣ ̣ ̣ ̣ ν

[*c.* 7   ] ̣ ̣ [̣ ̣] ̣ ̣ ̣ ̣ [̣]ρ̣αρα.

—   —   —

col. ii

12   ̣ ̣ δερματ[̣ ̣ ̣]οντα[*c.* 10   ]

[ἡ]μέραϲ ἑπτὰ [̣]μ ̣ ̣ [*c.* 10   ]

[̣ ̣ ̣ ̣]ιφορου ̣ α ̣ ̣ ̣ ̣ [*c.* 10   ]

[̣] ̣ ⊗⊠ΖϚ ̣ [   ]

16   Ϛ ̣ ̣ ⊗ΝΖ✕ [   ]

π̄ρ̄(ὸϲ) δαιμονιαζομένου[ϲ.   *c.* 9   ]

̣ ̣ ̣ ̣ ̣ ̣ τοὺ ἀπελθε[*c.* 10   ]

̣ υτου ̣ τὰ ὑποκείμεν[α   *c.* 10   ]

20   ̣ ατρ ̣ του Ϲολωμῶ[ν   *c.* 10   ]

τηϲ ἐλούϲατο.   [   ]

π̄ρ̄(ὸϲ) ὀφθαλμούϲ. ποίηϲ[ον δακτύλιον]

Γοθθικὸν καὶ γλύ[ψον ἐν αὐτῷ τὸ]

24   ὑποκείμενον ὄ(νομα) κα̣[ὶ φόρει ἐν τῇ δεξι-]

ᾷ χειρὶ ἐν τῷ μέϲῳ δ̣[ακτύλῳ   *c.* 6   ]

χαχ ̣ [̣]   [   ]

---

3 ουχ· Pap.   5 ∠ (bis) Pap.   6 ∠ Pap.   λειώϲαϲ   χρω: Pap.
7 ↑̣ Pap.   γρ̥ Pap.   8 dicolon in Pap.   10 ↑̣ Pap.   11]ραρα· Pap.
17 ↑̣ Pap.   21 ελουϲατο: Pap., deinde spatium vacuum   22 ↑̣ Pap.   24
ō Pap.   26 post χαχ ̣ [̣] spatium vacuum

[πρ(ὸc)] cκ[ί]ρρου[c] κ̣[c. 14   ]
28 [τὸ] ὑποκείμ[ενον   c. 10   ]
[. . . .] . [. .] . ν̣[   ]

— — —

↓   col. i
[c. 14   ε]ἰc φύλλον ἀμ-
[πέλινον τὰ ὑποκεί]μενα καὶ ζέ-
32 [cαc   c. 12   ]c̣ον τὸ φύλλον
[   ] ⊗ ⊗ B B X̂ X̂
[   ] ⨕ ⧸⧸ cαρχ:
[   ]
36 [πρ(ὸc)   c. 12   κ]αὶ cτρανγουρία(ν).
[c. 10   καc]c̣ιτερίνῳ λαμν̣ί̣[ῳ]
[c. 15   ]μαρωθα: μ . . .
[c. 15   ] ἄλλο πρ(ὸc) ἡμικράν̣ι̣[ον.]
40 [   ]ιυιω ⌉
[   ]υαωω |
[   ]ωυοω |
[   ] . ου ⌋

— — —

col. ii
44 cωcε: λόγ(οc) δὲ τοῦ νηροῦ οὗτοc· [ουρ-]
ουρβεδεραειc: ουρουρβεδερ[αε]ιc[:]
ουρουρουβεδεραειc: ει`c΄θεcαβρ[ ]cα:
ελεχ: β̣ελλενουρε: ουνουρε: βα-
48 φαμμη̣χ: coὶ λέγω, τῷ πλήγμα-
τι· μὴ cφύξειc, μὴ φλεγμάνειc,

28 ὑποκειμ[Pap.   34 dicolon in Pap.   35 post lacunam spatium vacuum   36 cτρανγουριᾱ Pap., l. cτραγγουρίαν   38 dicolon in Pap.   39 ⑂ Pap.   44-48 dicola in Pap.   44 λο̅ Pap.   48 φαμμηχ: α ex ε   49 cφύξῃc   φλεγμάνῃc

μὴ ὀδυνῶν κινήcιc, μὴ ὑγρὸν ποιήcειc, μὴ μελανίαc ποιήcειc, μ[ὴ]
52 [c]φάκελον κινήcειc. ἐὰν γὰρ cφύξειc ἢ φλεγμάνῃc ἢ ὀδυνῶν κινήcειc ἢ ὑ[γ]ρ[ὸ]ν ποιή[c]ειc ἢ μελ[ανίαc]
ποιήcειc ἢ cφά[κ]ελον κ[ι]νήcε[ιc]
56 βω[
γ[
※ —α̣[
χ[
60 α̣[

— — —

50 κινήcῃc	50-51 ποιήcῃc	51 ποιήcῃc	52 κινηcειc· Pap., l. κινήcῃc
52-53 cφύξῃc	53-54 κινήcῃc	54 ποιήcῃc	55 ποιήcῃc κινήcῃc

l4 Dessicative powder promoting sharpness of sight. 4 drachms of saffron; 2 drachms of aloe; 8 drachms of sarcocolla. Pulverize and use.

For easy childbirth. Write on an amulet: l8 abraô arônbara bar- - -.

Protective charm against fever (?) - - -rara.

l12 - - - skin - - - seven days - - - (magical signs) - - -.

For those possessed by evil spirits - - - to go away (?) - - - given below - - - l20 - - - Solomon - - - he (?) bathed.

For the eyes. Make a Gothic ring and inscribe on it (?) the l24 name given below and wear it on the right hand on the middle finger - - - chach- - - .

Against tumors - - - l28 given below - - -.

- - - (write) on a grape-vine leaf what is given below and after boiling it l32 - - - the leaf - - - (magical signs) sarch.

l36 Against - - - and strangury. - - - (write on) a tin plaque - - -marôtha - - -.

Another against migraine. l40 - - - (vowels within a square) - - -.

l44 sôse. This is the formula of the water: ourourbederaeis ourourbederaeis ourouroubederaeis eisthesabr sa elech bellenoure ounoure baphammêch. l48 I say to you, wound, do not throb, do not become inflamed, do not give rise to pains, do not cause humor, do not cause blackening, do not l52 give rise to gangrene. For if you throb or become inflamed or give rise to pains or cause humor or cause blackening or give rise to gangrene, - - -.

1-3 may have consisted entirely of magical words.

1]ϲποου̣ ̣ :]c̣τοου ed.pr. At the end, after υ, a high dot of ink, perhaps too far from it to be a stop; probably remains of a letter.

2 ϋε̣ ̣: a high dot of ink; either a stop or the top of iota.

3 ουχ· : ουχι ed.pr.

4-6. Cf. Alex. Trall. II 17 Puschmann ἄλλο ξηροκολλούριον τὸ διὰ κρόκου πρὸϲ ἀρχομέναϲ ὀφθαλμίαϲ. γλαυκίου, ϲαρκοκόλληϲ, κρόκου, ἀλόηϲ (1 drachm of each). τούτῳ καὶ ὡϲ προφυλακτικῷ χρῆϲθαι δεῖ. Three of these four ingredients are used in the powder prescribed in the papyrus. Cf. also Aëtius VII 100 (CMG VIII.2, p. 348, 11, 18); Paul. Aeg. VII 16, 3; 40; 53 (CMG IX.2, p. 335, 11 f.; 342, 20 f.; 345, 20 f.).

4 ξηρίον: on powders for eye disease, see I.Andorlini, *BASP* 18 (1981) 12 with note 38.

κρόκου : κρόκο(ν) ed.pr. On the ophthalmic application of saffron, see L.C.Youtie in: *Le monde grec. Hommages à Claire Préaux* (Brussels 1975), p. 562 note to line 24; also Till, *Die Arzneikunde der Kopten*, p. 90, no. 130.

5 ∠ δ̄, ἀλόηϲ : κα̣ αλ̣[ ] ̣ ̣ ̣ ed.pr. An initial κ was mistakenly read, because the descender of ξ from the previous line meets the drachm-sign. For aloe as a remedy for eye disease, see Cl.Préaux, *Chron. d'Ég.* 31 (1956) 147; cf. also MPER XIII 3, 11.

ϲαρκοκόλληϲ̣ : ϲάρκα κάπρ[ο]υ ed.pr. For sarcocolla as a remedy for the eyes, cf. Alex. Trall. II 13, 15 and 17 Puschmann (the last of these passages is cited above, 4-6 comm.); Diosc. III 85 (II 102, 8 f. Wellmann); Marcell. Emp., *De medicam.* 8, 163. See also above, 4-6 comm.

6 ῆ. λιώϲαϲ (r. λειώϲαϲ) : ἡλιώϲαϲ ed.pr.

λειώϲαϲ χρῶ: for this sequence at the end of medical prescriptions, cf. e.g. Ps.Gal., *Rem.* III (XIV 523, 6; 536, 2, 8 K.); Alex. Trall. II 93 Puschmann; Aëtius VI 98 (CMG VIII.2, p. 249, 19); Paul. Aeg. III 22, 16 (CMG IX.1, p. 177, 20); Oder-Hoppe, *Corp. Hippiatr. Graec.* II, p. 60, 22.

7 εὐτ[ο]κ̣ίαν : εὐα̣κ̣ίαν ("easy healing") ed.pr. The latter is unattested. After υ the lower part of an upright that cannot be reconciled with α; τ[ο] is quite possible, provided that the omicron was small and high (cf. 44 του). Another charm for easy childbirth is **96 A** 48-50.

8 αβραω̣ : Αβραωθ cannot be read. For αβραω, cf. PGM II 164.

10 πυ ̣ ̣ ̣ ̣ ̣ ̣ ν : π̇'υ̇' ̣ ̣ ̣ ̣ραρα ed.pr., mistakenly incorporating the end of line 11 in line 10.

πυ . . . . υ: after πυ (with high υ) ρ is possible; then the bottoms of two uprights, which seem to exclude πυρετόν. Perhaps πυρ(ετόν) or πυ(ρετόν), as suggested by the first editor.

11 [*c. 7*] .[. . . .] . . . .[.]ραρα :] . .[ed.pr.   See above, 10 comm.

12 . .δερματ[: . . .δερματ[ed.pr.   At the beginning, two letters at most. τ could be ι, in which case read δέρμα ι[.

13 [ἡ]μέρας ἑπτά: a frequent indication of time in PGM. It often indicates the period in which the operator has to keep himself pure; cf. IV 26, 52, 3209; XIII 115 (= 671). For its occurrence in other contexts, cf. I 235; IV 761 f., 1274; VII 527; XII 380; XIII 118 (= 674). On the number seven in magic, see Brashear, *Magica varia*, p. 69 f.

16. Above the sign ✕, a semicircle, probably from a magical sign.

17 πρ(ὸς) δαιμονιαζομένου[c: the same heading in PGM IV 3007; cf. also 86 with app.cr., and see Betz, *Translation*, p. 38 n. 26.

18 . . . . .του ἀπελθε[: . . . . . . .τ[ ]υ ἄπελθε [ed.pr.   Possibly τοῦ ἀπελθε[ῖν (note that lines 17 and 19 belong to a praxis). If ἄπελθε, then a short logos was inserted between two prescriptional sections. For ἀπέρχομαι, in place of the usual ἐξέρχομαι, of the departure of an evil spirit from the possessed, cf. e.g. Joh. Chrys., *De capto Eutr.* 11 (Migne PG 52, 407, l. 12) ἄπελθε ἀπ' αὐτοῦ.

19 .υτου : .υτ. ed.pr.   At the beginning, α is not impossible, though not immediately suggested by the remains.

τὰ ὑποκείμεν[α: after τὰ an unexplained spot of ink, but other forms of the article cannot be read.

ὑποκείμεν[α: above μ an oblique stroke for which we have no explanation.

20 .ατρ.του : ατρ. . .υ ed.pr.   At the beginning, π is possible, but ι cannot be excluded. After the very uncertain ρ, possibly the top of ε or c, certainly not ι. Perhaps ἰατρέ? If τοῦ, restore Coλωμῶ[νος (or -ντος). For Solomon in magic, see *RE Suppl.* VIII, *s.v.* Salomo, coll. 660-704 (K.Preisendanz); cf. also **24** fr. A 4, fr. B 4; **63**, 6.

22-26. The supplements should be regarded as given *exempli gratia*, but in our opinion they are highly probable, at least in outline. It seems certain, however, that the object to be inscribed is a ring. The restoration of line 23 was already given by the first editor; of course, in place of ἐν αὐτῷ a specific part of the ring might have been mentioned. For the reconstruction in general, cf. PGM VII 641 f. καὶ φόρε⟨ι⟩ τὸν δακτύλιον εἰς τὴν δεξιὰν χεῖρα ἐν τῷ λιχανῷ and V 454-456 καὶ εἴρας αὐτὸν (*sc.* τὸν δακτύλιον) εἰς τὸν ἰδαῖον τῆς ἀριστερᾶς coυ χειρὸc δάκτυλον. For the use of rings in medical magic, see *RE* I A.1, *s.v.* Ringe, coll. 837-839 (R.Ganschinietz); also G.Vikan, "Art, Medicine, and Magic in Early Byzantium," *Dumbarton Oaks Papers* 38 (1984) 76 f.

22 ποίηc[ον δακτύλιον] : ποιήc[ειc ζῴδιον?] ed.pr.

23 Γοθθικόν: the mention of a Gothic ring in a magical prescription implies that Goths were well known in Egypt by the time this papyrus was written. In fact, their presence is attested there since the 4th century AD (see H.Kortenbeutel, "Germanen in Ägypten," *MDAI Cairo* 8, 1938, 180-184. For two Gothic helmets of Egyptian provenance, cf. p. 180). A group of papyrus documents from Oxyrhyncos that evidence Goths serving as mercenaries or *bucellarii* is roughly contemporary with **94**: P.Oxy. XXVII 2480, 39 (probably 565-566 AD); PSI VIII 953, 17, 32, 46, etc. (567-568 AD); 956, 26. Like the present text, also the Gothic-Latin Bible fragment P.Giss. Univ. 18 (= van Haelst, *Catalogue*, no. 1205; V or VI AD) came from Antinoopolis. Clear evidence of the familiarity of Egyptians with Goths is provided by the 5th or 6th cent. P.Berol. inv. 13927 (= Pack[2] 2437; text in I.C.Cunningham, *Herodae Mimiambi*, Leipzig 1987, p. 60 f., no. 15); it contains stage directions for the performance of mimes, mentioning a "scene of the Goths" (lines 7, 44) and "customs of Gothic men and women" (lines 47-48).

Gothic rings are reproduced e.g. in G.Becatti, *Oreficerie antiche* (Rome 1955), pl. CLII; M.Degani, *Il tesoro romano barbarico di Reggio Emilia* (Florence 1959), pll. XXI-XXV; V.Bierbrauer, *Die Ostgotischen Grab- und Schatzfunde in Italien* (Biblioteca degli 'Studi Medievali' 7, Spoleto 1975), pll. III.3, XIX.4, XXXIV-XXXV, XLII.3-3a (see pp. 176-180); also R.Harhoiu, *The Fifth-Century A.D. Treasure from Pietroasa, Romania, in the Light of Recent Research* (BAR Supplementary Series 24, Oxford 1977), fig. 10.9-12.

On Germanic barbarians in Egypt since Caesar's age, see Kortenbeutel, *art.cit.*, pp. 177-184. On Barbarian soldiers and mercenaries in Egypt in the Byzantine period, see R.Rémondon, "Soldats de Byzance d'après un papyrus trouvé à Edfou," *Rech. de Pap.* 1 (1961) 41-93, esp. 61, 75, 79 f.; J.Gascou, "Militaires étrangers en Égypte byzantine," *BIFAO* 75 (1975) 203-206; idem, "L'institution des bucellaires," *BIFAO* 76 (1976) 143-156; also E.R.Hardy, *The Large Estates of Byzantine Egypt* (New York 1931), pp. 60-67. For mention of other barbarian artifacts in the papyri, see J.Diethart-E.Kislinger, " 'Hunnisches' auf einem Wiener Papyrus," *Tyche* 2 (1987) 5-10.

24-25 ὄ(νομα) κα[ὶ φόρει ἐν τῆ δεξι]|ᾶ χειρὶ : ὅ κρ[ατήσεις ἀρι-
cτε]ι̣[ρ]ᾶ χειρὶ ed.pr.

ὄ(νομα): for the abbreviation ō and ο for ὄνομα, see the app.cr. to
PGM VII 316 and XIII 965. The ὑποκείμενον ὄνομα survives in part at
the beginning of line 26; it might have begun at the end of 25.

δεξι]ᾶ χειρί: before χειρί is room for one letter only, and there is no
good reason to restore ἀριcτερ]ᾶ with false word division.

δ[ακτύλω : [ed.pr.   The traces suit the lower left corner of δ well. The
beginning of τὸ ὑποκείμενον ὄνομα might have followed in this line.

26 χαχ [ ] : [ ]χαχ [ ] ed.pr., but no letter is missing to the left.

27 [πρ(ὸc)] cκ[ί]ρρου[c]: 'hardened swellings'; see Gal., *De meth.
med.* XIV 6 (X 962, 10 - 963, 5 K.), *Ad Glauc.* II 6 (XI 103, 13 - 104, 2 K.);
Orib., *Syn.* VII 34 (CMG VI.3, p. 235, 14-32; *loci sim.* in app.).

28. [τὸ] ὑποκείμ[ενον or [τὰ] ὑποκείμ[ενα.

32]cον :] ον ed.pr.   Probably the end of an aorist imperative.

36 [πρ(ὸc) *c.* 12 κ]αὶ cτρανγουρία(ν) (r. cτραγγ-): supplements
such as ἰcχουρίαν and δυcουρίαν do not seem to fill the available space,
and so one might consider e.g. πόνουc νεφρῶν or πόνουc κύcτεωc; cf. e.g
Marcell. Emp., *De medicam.* 26, 59 *ad vessicae dolores et strangulia.*

37 κας]cιτερίνω λαμνί[ω]: tin was usually employed for prophylactic
and therapeutic purposes; cf. PGM, Vol. 3 (Index), *s.vv.* λάμνα, λαμνίον,
λεπίc, πλάξ, πέταλον, πτύχιον; also Heim, *Incantamenta*, nos. 11, 66,
115, 193, 194, 213, 214, etc. In PGM VII 417, however, it is used in a
restraining spell.

38 [*c.* 15]μαρωθα : [τὰ ὑποκείμενα] μαρωθα ed.pr., but there is
no cogent reason why τὰ ὑποκείμενα should have been in the lacuna (cf. 7-8).
Probably Μαρ]μαρωθα, as a variant of Μαρμαραωθ, for which see **42**,
52 comm.

39 ἡμικράνι[ον]: the word occurs in PGM VII 199, P.Cair. Masp.
67141 ii recto 20, and (written ἡμικράνιν) lines 1-2 of the silver amulet from
Carnuntum published by A.A.Barb, *Der Römische Limes in Österreich* 16
(1926) 57 f. (= A.Betz, "Die griechischen Inschriften aus Österreich," *Wiener
Studien* 79, 1966, 604, no. 11). Cf. also É.Chassinat, *Un papyrus médical
copte* (MIFAO 32, Cairo 1921), p. 302, line 376 ϩΥΜⲈΚΡⲀΝΙΟΝ.

44 cωcε: a magical word (or the end of one) rather than for cῶcαι.

λόγ(οc) δὲ τοῦ νηροῦ οὗτοc: cf. PGM V 181 λόγοc τοῦ ἀρτοτύρου,
and IV 3260a f. ἔcτιν δὲ ὁ καταγραφόμενοc λόγοc τοῦ [πλιν]θίου

οὗ[τος]. The water becomes magically charged with the logos and then is drunk or applied to the wound.

νηροῦ: see **97** ↓ 29 comm.

44-45 [ουρ]ιουρβεδεραεις (also 45): the beginning of the word might correspond to Egyptian *wr-wr* 'great great', 'twice great'. See PGM, Vol. 3 (Index), p. 266, *s.vv.* ουηρ, ουηρι, ουιηρ, ουρ να ουρ, ουρ ουρ ουηρ, ουραοι ουηρ.

46 ουρουρουβεδεραεις: at the beginning, possibly Egyptian *wr-wrw* 'great one of the great ones'.

ει`ς'θεcαβρ[ ̣]ςα : ει`ς'θεcαβρ[α]ςα ed.pr., which is possible but not obligatory.

47 βελλενουρε: possibly Coptic ΒΕλ-Є(Ν)-ΝΟΥΡΕ 'eye of the vulture'.

ουνουρε: possibly Coptic ΟΥ-ΝΟΥΡΕ 'a vulture'.

48-58. The formula follows a well-known scheme: (i) command (lines 48-52), (ii) "if you do not carry out the command" (52-55), (iii) threat ([56-58]).

48-49 coì λέγω, τῷ πλήγμαιτι· μὴ cφύξεις (r. -ξῃς): cf. PGM IV 2088-90 coì λέγω, τῷ καταχθονίῳ δαίμονι - - -, πορεύου κτλ.; XII 130 f. ὑμῖν λέγω καὶ coí, μέγα δυναμένῳ δαίμον⟨ι⟩· πορεύθητι κτλ.; XXXVI 286 coì λέγω, μήτρα τῆς δεῖνα, χάνε καὶ δέξαι κτλ.; LVIII 8-11 coì λέγω, τῷ ἀώρῳ κτλ.; Joh. Chrys., *Contra Anom.* X 3 (Migne PG 48, 788, l. 3 f.) coì λέγω, τὸ πονηρὸν δαιμόνιον, ἔξελθε ἀπ' αὐτοῦ; *Exposit. in Ps.* 46, 3 (Migne PG 55, 211, l. 53), etc. Cf. also NT Marc. 2, 11 (Jesus to the paralytic) coì λέγω, ἔγειρε (cf. Luc. 5, 24); also Marc. 5, 41; Luc. 7, 14. For commands or adjurations addressed directly to a disease, see **32**, 3 comm.

coì λέγω has a hard and authoritative tone also in other contexts; cf. Headlam's note on Herodas IV 42.

πλήγματι: 'wound' resulting from a strike (so in the papyrus documents P.Cairo Masp. I 67077, 11, 15; P.Lips. 37, 23; 40, 7; P. Herm. 20, 9; SB X 10287, 11; P.Oxy. XLV 3245, 16 (?)), but often used — especially in medical writings — of a wound from serpents, scorpions and other venomous animals; cf. Philum., *Ven.* 7, 4; 11, 2; 14, 1, 4 (CMG X.1, 1, pp. 11, 19; 15, 22; 17, 1, 19); Ps.Diosc., *Ther.* 26 (XXVI 85, 7 K.); Aëtius XIII 12 (p. 268, 14 Zervos); Paul. Aegin. V 8, 2 (CMG IX.2, p. 13, 8, 21); Oder-Hoppe, *Corp. Hippiatr. Graec.* I, p. 309, 6 (also 311, 9; II 209, 24); also Eutecn., *Paraphr. in Nic. Ther.*, pp. 21, 22; 35, 18, 21; 61, 11, 17, 27, 32; 62, 29; 69, 5-6 Gualandri. The latter may well be the case here. Note that the drinking of magically charged water (see above 44 comm.) is frequently prescribed in charms against wounds from poisonous creatures; see A.A. Barb, *Mitteil. d. anthropol. Gesellsch. in Wien* 82 (1953), esp. 17 with notes 116-119. (Charms against the sting of the scorpion are here **16, 17, 89**; see **16**, intr.)

49-55. Much of this section uses concepts and terminology known from medical writers. The symptoms are given in an ascending order of gravity, from throbbing to gangrene. If we are dealing with an ordinary wound (see 48-49 comm. on πλήγματι), they correspond to progressive stages of the resulting infection. If, on the contrary, we are dealing with a wound from a poisonous animal, they rather indicate the effects of different sorts of venom. In this case the envisaged situation could be that of a sting or bite from an unknown or unrecognized animal; hence the need to consider the whole range of possible consequences. For throbbing caused by animal venom, cf. Philum., *Ven.* 33, 7 (CMG XI.1, 1, p. 37, 16); inflammation: e.g. Ps. Diosc., *Ther.* 6, 8 (XXXVI 68, 2, 6 K.); pain: e.g. Philum., *Ven.* 10, 1; 29 (CMG XI.1, 1, pp. 27, 19; 31, 18); humor (ἰχώρ): Philum., *Ven.* 17, 1; 18, 2 (CMG XI.1, 1, pp. 23, 4; 25, 14); blackening of flesh: Philum., *Ven.* 21, 2; 25, 2 (CMG XI.1, 1, pp. 27, 19; 31, 18); decay (cηπεδών): Philum., *Ven.* 26, 2 (CMG XI.1, 1, pp. 32, 13). [Most of these references were kindly supplied by A.Touwaide].

In the app.cr. we 'normalized' the verbs to aorist subjunctives (all but one miswritten). However, in view of the endings (-εις 10×; -ηc 1×; -ιc 1×), future indicatives cannot be ruled out, at least in the protases 52-55. ἐάν with the future can be paralleled (see Radermacher, *Neutestamentliche Grammatik*, p. 200 with n. 3; Blass-Debrunner-Funk, *Grammar*, § 373.2); on the contrary, evidence seems to be quite scanty for prohibitive μή with the future (see Blass-Debrunner-Funk, *Grammar*, § 364.3, who cite J.H.Moulton, *Einleitung in die Sprache des Neuen Testaments* [Germ. transl. Heidelberg 1911], p. 278 f., where the references both to BGU I 197, 14 and to III 814, 27 should be deleted; see BL I, p. 25 and Gignac, *Grammar* II, p. 387.3 respectively).

50 ὀδυνῶν κινήcιc (r. κινήcηc): cf. 53-54. The first editor regarded ὀδυνῶν as a miswriting for ὀδύνην or ὀδύναc, and in fact κινεῖν takes the normal accusative object in 55 and probably 52. On the other hand, the passage of ην (or αc) to ων is not banal, and this writer's misspellings are usually due merely to itacism. κινεῖν takes the genitive object in Thuc. I 143, 1, VI 70, 4 and Isocr., *Pan.* 156. ὀδυνῶν, then, could be correct. Since the

use of the partitive genitive object with verbs that normally take an accusative object becomes increasingly rare after the classical period, it could be that ὀδυνῶν κινεῖν is a linguistic fossil and that the entire charm had a long pedigree.

Apparently, the nexus ὀδύνην κινεῖν (and also cφάκελον κινεῖν) is extraneous to the medical language. It occurs in Soph., *Trach.* 974 f. μὴ κινήσῃς ἀγρίαν ὀδύνην. On the medical usage of κινεῖν, see R.J.Durling in: *Festschrift für N.Mani* (Pattensen 1985), pp. 55-59.

52 [c]φάκελον : [c]φακέλους ed.pr.   After λ the traces are indecisive, but the space can accommodate only two letters; and cf. cφά[κ]ελον in 55, where the ν is certain.

59-60. To the left, paragraphus with asteriscus as e.g. in P.Lond. I 121 (= PGM VII) 466-467, 477-478, 490-491, etc.

Provenance   V AD
unknown

P.Laur. IV 148.

ED.PR.: R.Pintaudi, "PL III/472: frammento magico," *ZPE* 38 (1980) 261-264.

REPUBL.: SB XVI 12640; P.Laur. IV 148 (F.Maltomini).

COMM.: ed.pr.; F.Maltomini, *SCO* 32 (1982) 239 f.; P.Laur. IV 148 (F.Maltomini).

TRANSL.: H.D.Betz, *Translation*, no. CXXVI a-b.

PHOTO: ed.pr., plate XV; P.Laur. IV, plate CV.

DESCR.: papyrus; 21.3 × 24.3 cm. Fragmentary sheet, possibly from a codex. On side →,
   remains of a column damaged at top and right; left margin at least 2.6 cm, right margin
   at least 3.5 cm (line 17), original lower margin 0.7 cm. On side ↓ the column is
   damaged at left, top and right; original lower margin 1.2 cm. On side → original length
   of line was some 15 cm (cf. line 17) containing about 27 letters (cf. the securely
   restored line 15). The true order of the two sides cannot be determined.

LOC.: Biblioteca Medicea Laurenziana, Florence. Inv. PL III/472.

The papyrus preserves spells aimed at separating man and woman
(*diakopoi*). Such spells were used by jealous lovers to win or win back the
beloved from a rival.[1]

---

[1] Other spells intended to upset erotic relationships (certain or probable): PGM XIII
239-242; LXI 39-59, 60-66; O 2; cf. also VII 429. Tablets: Audollent, *DT*, nos. 68, 69,
139, 198; Jordan, "Survey," nos. 30, 31, 32, 57 (see D.R.Jordan, *Hesperia* 54, 1985, 222 f.);
E.Ziebarth, *Sitzungsb. Berlin* (1934) 1040-42, nos. 22 (?) (see C.A.Faraone in: Faraone-
Obbink (edd.), *Magika Hiera*, p. 14), 23 (improved publication of side A by B.Bravo in:
Poikilia. Études offertes à J.-P.Vernant, Paris 1987, p. 202). Gems: Bonner, *SMA*, p. 107 f.
(D. 150). Demotic: PDM xii 108-118, 119-134 (cf. Betz, *Translation*, pp. 170, 171);
Griffith-Thompson, *Demotic Magical Papyrus*, XIII 1-10 (cf. Betz, *Translation*, p. 217).
Coptic: VBP V 123, 85-100; 142; V.Stegemann, *Le Muséon* 51 (1938) 74-82; É.Drioton,
Le Muséon 59 (1946) 479-489; É.Chassinat, *Le manuscrit magique copte n° 42573 du
Musée Égyptien du Caire* (Caire 1955), p. 102. For Byzantine magic, cf. Delatte, *Anecdota
Atheniensia*, pp. 456, 15-22; 619, 15-19. On disjunctive spells that were apparently not
motivated by erotic interest, see **55** intr.

Diaeresis on ι in ↓ 6. Blank space in the line to mark pause in sense (→ 12). Paragraphus under → 20 (and ↓ 2?). κο+ for κοινόν or κοινά (→ 7, 20, ↓ 2); Ⴂ for δεῖνα (→ 7, 14, ↓ 15). καί is abbreviated in → 22.

→   —   —   —

1   [c. 6   ] . [
     [c. 5   ]ατης[
     [c. 6   ] . . [
4   [c. 6   ]μυρικ[
     [c. 5   ] . . ατα[
     [c. 6   ]αccα[
     [c. 7   ] δ(εῖνα). κοι(νόν). [
8   . . κ[. .]β . . βριαψ [ιω Ερβηθ ιω]
     Πακερβηθ ιω Βολχ[οcηθ βαcδουμα]
     Οcεcρω Απομψ Π[αταθναξ κοκκο-]
     λοπτολιν χ . . κ . [c. 5   ιω θαθθα-]
12   βραβο. ἀβιαcτικὸc λ[όγοc· Τυφῶν]
     · Cηθ, πᾶcα`ν′ μαγίαν ἐπιτελ[c. 8   ]
     διάκοψον τὴν δ(εῖνα) [ἀπὸ τοῦ δ(εῖνα), αβεραμενθω-]
     ουθλερθεξαναξεθ[ρελθυοωθνεμα-]
16   ρεβα. καὶ εἰπέ· cίναπι, [οὐκ εἶ cίναπι,]
     ἀλλὰ ⟨ὁ⟩ ὀφθαλμὸ[c τοῦ Α]ἰῶνος, τὰ ἔντερα
     τοῦ ταύρου, τὸ ὑ[
     τοῦ Ἄπιδος . [
20   κοι(νόν). διερχ . . [
     ἀπὸ τοῦ Ὀcίρ[εωc
     κ(αὶ) διάκ[ο]ψ[ον] τὴ[ν δ(εῖνα) ἀπὸ τοῦ δ(εῖνα)

7 Ⴂ κο+ Pap.   12 post βραβο spatium duarum litterarum in Pap.   13 μαγείαν
14 Ⴂ Pap.   20 κο+ Pap.   22 κ̗ Pap.

↓   — — —

1   ] . [.] . ο[
                               ] κοι(νόν). [

                               ] . ἀλλὰ ἡ βλέψιc [
4   τ]οῦ Αδωναι, ἡ δύν[αμιc
                               ]c τοῦ μεγάλου θε[οῦ
                               cίν]απι, ἵνα διακόψ[ηc
                               ] ἔχθραν ἕωc θα[νάτου
8   ] . ν[. εἰ]cέλθηc εἰc τὴν ο[
                               ] . . αὐτοὺc ὡc τὴν [
                               ] ἀκούcαcα περὶ το[ῦ
                               τ]οῦ Ὀcίρεωc ανε . [.] . [
12   ] . [c. 9   ] καὶ φοβερὰ καὶ ε[.] . [
                               ]ν κατεκαυcα[
                               κ]αὶ cύ, cίναπι, α[
                               τὴ]ν οἰκίαν τῆc δ(εῖνα) [
16   ] πάροδον αι . [

2 κο⸓ Pap.   6 ϊνα Pap.   15 Ⳝ Pap.

(→ 7 ff.) - - - NN. Add what you wish. - - - |8 *Iakoubia (?) briaps iô Erbêth iô Pakerbêth iô Bolchosêth basdouma Osesrô Apomps Patathnax kokkoloptolin - - - iô thaththabrabo.* |12 Irresistible formula: "Typhon Sêth, fulfill (?) all magic and (?) separate her, NN, from him, NN, *aberamenthôouthlerthexanaxethrelthuoôthnemareba*." |16 And say: "Mustard, you are not mustard, but the eye of Aion, the innards of the bull, the - - - of Apis - - -." |20 Add what you wish. - - - from Osiris - - - and separate her, NN, from him, NN.

↓ - - -. Add what you wish. - - - (you are not mustard), but the sight - - - |4 - - - of Adônai, the power - - - of the great god - - - mustard, so that you separate - - - enmity until death - - - |8 - - - you enter into the house (?) - - - them as the - - - having heard about the - - - of Osiris - - - |12 - - - and frightful and - - - I (?) burnt - - - and you, mustard - - - the house of her, NN - - - |16 - - - entrance - - -.

→

3. Two specks at upper level on damaged surface. This line was not recorded in the ed.pr.

4]μυρικ[: what survives of the dotted letter is the lower part of an upright with the join of an oblique rising to the right. The only two possibilities in the present hand are η or κ. Probably another instance of μυρικόω in a *diakopos*; see **55** D-G 1 comm.

7] Δ κο†[:]δκc[ed.pr. In magical formularies κοινόν indicates the point of the logos where the operator can speak at will, inserting his wishes or demands without following fixed formulas, i.e. in 'common', 'ordinary', 'profane' language (cf. κοινὸc λόγοc in **82** fr. B 3 and PGM V 435, κοινολογίαι in PGM IV 2080). See E.Kuhnert, *Rhein. Mus.* 49 (1894) 52 n. 5; R.Wünsch, *Aus einem griechischen Zauberpapyrus* (Kleine Texte 84, 1911), p. 26; PGM, Vol. 3 (Index), p. 121, *s.v.* κοινόc. Since κοινόν usually occurs at the end of a section (cf. here → 20, ↓ 2), it is probable that the first *diakopos* (see above, 4 comm.) ended at this line.

8 ͺͺκ[ ]β ͺͺ : first, the foot of an upright; second, probably α; after β a hook on line, probably ι; then a high speck difficult to reconcile with any letter. Ιακ[ου]βια seems a likely restoration. The first editor read ͺ κ[ ]βην.

8-12 ιω Ερβηθ - - - θαθθαβραβο: because the malignant Typhon-Seth is the god usually invoked in disjunctive spells, the Typhonic ιω Ερβηθ logos is frequent in this kind of spell: PGM XII 370-372, 445-452, 459-462, 466-468 (for the last three passages, full contexts and better readings are given by J.H.Johnson, *OMRO* 56, 1975, 38-43; cf. also Betz, *Translation*, p. 169 f.). For the occurrences of the logos, see PGM, Vol. 3 (Index), p. 240 f. and P.Laur. IV 148 *ad loc.* No occurrence is exactly identical with this one; the closest is PGM XII 370-372, on which is based the restoration of 9-11.

In 11 Ιακο[υβια is a possible reading. If so, 10-11 κοκκο]Ιλοπτολινχ.

12 ἀβιαcτικὸc λ[όγοc: apparently, the adjective occurs only here and in Didym., *Gen.* 166, 6 (II 58 Nautin); see J.Rodríguez Somolinos, *Emerita* 56 (1988) 233 f. In both places the meaning appears to be passive, 'irresistible', 'ineluctable'. The expression ἀβιαcτικὸc λόγοc, then, is comparable to ἐπάναγκοc λόγοc in PGM IV 2574 and 3110 f.

12-13 Τυφῶν] Ι Cηθ: for the supplement, cf. PGM III 87; XIV 20.

13 ἐπιτελ[*c.* 8]: possibly ἐπιτέλ[εcον καὶ].

14 διάκοψον: the verb διακόπτω is technical in spells for separation (cf. PGM XII 463, 465; XIII 242). PGM O 2, 38 has ἀπαλλάccω with clear reference to ἀπαλλαγή 'divorce' (see P.Oslo II 15, 38 comm.); XII 459 has διαχωρίζω, and χωρίζω occurs in the gem mentioned by Bonner, *SMA*, p. 107 (see above, footnote 1); cf. also *Test. Sal.* XVIII 22 (pp. 55*, 12 - 56*, 1 McCown), where the daemon Modebel says: γυναῖκα ἀπὸ ἀνδρὸc χωρίζω. The malignity of an 'evil daemon' (πονηρὸc or cκαιὸc δαίμων) is often adduced as a ground for divorce in papyrus divorce agreements of the Byzantine period; cf. e.g. P.Grenf. II 76, 3-5 ἐπεὶ ἔκ τινοc πονηροῦ δαίμονοc cυνέβη αὐτοὺc ἀποζεῦχθαι ἀλλήλων τὴν κοινὴν αὐτῶν cυμβίωcιν; P.Lond. V 1712, 9 f. νῦν δὲ διαφορᾶc ἡμῖν γενομένηc ἐκ cκαιοῦ δαίμονοc ἀπεζύγημεν πρὸc ἀλλήλουc; P.Cair.Masp. I 67121, 9 νυνὶ πονηροῦ δαίμονοc φθονήcαντοc τῷ ἡμετέρῳ cυνοικεcίῳ ἀλλήλων ἀπεζεύχθημεν; other instances, with similar formulae, in R.C.McCail, *Mnemosyne* 21 (1968) 76-78 (he refers also to Justinian, *Nov.* CXL, *praef.* διὸ τοὺc γάμουc εὐτυχεῖc εἶναι τοῖc cυμβάλλουcιν οὕτωc εὐχόμεθα, ὡc μήποτε cκαιοῦ δαίμονοc ἔργον τούτουc γενέcθαι, μηδὲ τοὺc γήμαντας ἀπ' ἀλλήλων χωρίζεcθαι δικαίαν τῆc τοῦ γάμου λύcεωc οὐκ ἔχονταc πρόφαcιν); cf. also SB V 8024, 10 f.; XIV 12043, 5 f.; BGU XII 2203, 11. In these documents the purpose of the evil-daemon clause seems to be to prevent any dispute over liability that might arise between the two parties; see A.Merklein, *Das Ehescheidungsrecht nach den Papyri der byzantinischen Zeit* (Diss. Erlangen-Nürnberg 1967), pp. 73-79.

τὴν Ϟ [Maltomini, *locc.citt.* : τὴν Φ[ed.pr.

14-16 αβεραμεν- - -νεμαρεβα: a well-known palindrome (cf. **48** J 1, and see PGM, Vol. 3 [Index], p. 279), frequently associated with Typhon-Seth (for different contexts, cf. **48** J 1; PGM I 294; II 125 f.; V 178 f.; LIX 6). See Martinez, *P.Mich. 757*, p. 33. On Aberamenthô, see M.Tardieu in: R.van den Broek-M.J.Vermaseren (edd.), *Studies in Gnosticism and Hellenistic Religions, presented to G.Quispel on the Occasion of his 65th Birthday* (EPRO 91, Leiden 1981), pp. 412-418.

16-19. Declaring objects used in rites to be of divine origin or nature is well known in magic. For the formulation used here (and at ↓ 3-5), i.e. denying that a thing is what it seems to be and asserting that it is something else (οὐκ εἶ . . . ἀλλὰ . . .), cf. PGM VII 644-646 cὺ εἶ οἶνοc, οὐκ εἶ οἶνοc, ἀλλ' ἡ κεφαλὴ τῆc 'Αθηνᾶc. cὺ εἶ οἶνοc, οὐκ εἶ οἶνοc, ἀλλὰ τὰ cπλά[γ]χνα τοῦ 'Οcίρεωc, τὰ cπλάγχνα τοῦ Ιαω; LXI 7-9 cὺ εἶ τὸ ἔλαιον, οὐκ εἶ δὲ ἔλαι[ο]ν, ἀλλὰ ἰδρὼc τοῦ ᾿Αγαθοῦ Δαίμονοc, ἡ μύξα τῆc [᾿Ι]cιδοc, τὸ ἀπόφθεγμα τοῦ ῾Ηλίου, ἡ δύναμιc τοῦ Οὐcίριοc, ἡ χάριc τῶν θεῶν; VII 238 f. ἀ[ν]άcτα, δαίμων· οὐκ εἶ δαίμων, ἀλλὰ τὸ ⟨αἷμα⟩ τῶν β᾿ ἱεράκων (also VIII 99 f. and **90** fr. D 14). Further examples and a full discussion in Bell-Nock-Thompson, "Magical Texts from a Bilingual Papyrus," 257-259.

16 cίναπι: to the mustard is assigned the task of causing the separation (cf. ↓ 6). A close parallel is Kropp, *Koptische Zaubertexte* I, M 82-84 (transl. II, p. 46): "Freunde, die du voneinander trennen willst. - - - (Sprich das) Gebet über wilden Senf (cίναπυ). Vergrabe sie an dem Ort, an welchem sie vorüberzugehen pflegen ... " It is probably because of its caustic nature that the plant was thought to be able to arouse the flame of hate (see ↓ 13 comm.). Mustard is used in aggressive magic also in Kropp, *Koptische Zaubertexte* I, M 79-80, 94-95 (transl. II, p. 46 f.). In *Cat. Cod. Astr. Gr.* IV, p. 122, 4 it is connected with Kronos, who had malevolent and unfavourable influences and boded ill for marriage (cf. e.g. Artemid. II 39, p. 176, 4-7 Pack); and it had negative value in dream interpretation; cf. Artemid. I 68 (p. 75, 10-12 Pack) cήcαμον δὲ καὶ λινόcπερμον καὶ cίνηπι ἰατροῖc μόνοιc ἐcτὶν ἀγαθά, τοῖc δὲ ἄλλοιc δριμεῖc ἐπάγει πόνουc καὶ τὰ κρυπτὰ ἐλέγχει; Delatte, *Anecdota Atheniensia*, p. 541, 7 πέπερι ἢ cινάπι ψηλαφᾶν, νόcον, θλῖψιν καὶ κλαυθμὸν cημαίνει.

17 ⟨ὁ⟩ ὀφθαλμὸ[c τοῦ Α]ἰῶνοc : ὀφθαλμ.[ ] . . . . . ed.pr., SB XVI 12640 : ὀφθαλμὸ[c . . .] . . . . . . P.Laur. IV 148. Traces, space and sense considered together make the new reading Α]ἰῶνοc virtually certain. Cf. αἰωνόφθαλμοc said of Aion in PGM V 465 f., and also PGM XIII 570-572 ἐπικαλοῦμαί cε - - - τὸν πάντα ὀρῶντα (cf. 582). In the image of the Aion's eye, the well attested assimilation of Aion with Helios is likely to be at play; cf. PGM IV 1169-1227; 2194-99; SB I 4127, 19 (= Bernand, *Inscriptions métriques*, no. 166); Mesom., *Hymn.* 4, 17 (Heitsch, *Dichterfragmente* I, II); also the inscription published by C.Bonner, *Hesperia* 13 (1944) 34; and see A.D.Nock, *HThR* 27 (1934) 53-104, esp. 84 = *Essays on Religion and the Ancient World* I, pp. 357-400, 383. (In PGM XIII 570-572 quoted above, Aion is distinguished from Helios, but he shows several clearly solar features; see A.J.Festugière, *La révélation d'Hermès trismégiste* IV, Paris 1954², pp. 194, 197 f.). On Aion in the Greek magical papyri, see M.P. Nilsson, "Die Religion in den griechischen Zauberpapyri," *Bull. Soc. de Lettres de Lund* 1947-1948, II, 23-25 (= *Opuscula selecta* III, pp. 153-

155); A.J.Festugière, *op. cit.*, pp. 182-199; on Aion in general, see the literature given in *LIMC* I.1, p. 199 f. and in Merkelbach-Totti, *Abrasax* II, p. 168 f.

17-18 τὰ ἔντερα Ι τοῦ ταύρου: cf., in a similar context, PGM VII 645 f. τὰ cπλά[γ]χνα τοῦ Ὀcίρεωc, τὰ cπλάγχνα τοῦ Ιαω.

18. τὸ ὐ[rather than τοῦ [(ed.pr.).

19 ̣[: horizontal, probably τ (not α, ed.pr.).

20 κο+ Maltomini, *locc.citt.* : μ̣ ed.pr. On κοινόν see above, 7 comm.

διερχ̣ ̣[: a flat base on line; foot of an upright. Probably διέρχετ[αι.

21. Possibly a reference to the enmity between Osiris and Seth, as a paradigm for the enmity to be aroused between the woman and her partner (the same in ↓ 11?); cf. PGM XII 372 f. (a *diakopos*) δότε τῷ δεῖνα τῆc δεῖνα μάχην, πόλεμον, καὶ τῷ δεῖνα τῆc δεῖνα ἀηδίαν, ἔχθραν, ὡc εἶχον Τυφῶν καὶ Ὄcιριc (cf. also LXXVIII 7 f.). Or perhaps the reference was to the adultery committed by Osiris with Nephthys, on which cf. Plut., *De Iside* 356E-F (also 366B-C, 368 E, 375 B) and PGM IV 94-153.

↓

2] κο+ [:] μ̣ [ed.pr. On κοινόν see above, → 7 comm.

2-3. Between these lines is a blank space of 5 cm. At mid-height a very faint and thin horizontal emerges from the lacuna at the left: a long paragraphus?

3] ̣: high horizontal, γ, c, τ possible. Because the practice recognized at → 16-19 seems to be present here too, and because the object in question appears to be once again the mustard (cf. 6, 14), one should probably supplement οὐκ εἶ cίναπι]c (for cίναπιc fem., cf. Anon. Paris. in R.Fuchs, *Rhein. Mus.* 58, 1903, 88; the other occurrences of the word in the present papyrus might not be significant with regard to the gender, as they are probably vocative).

βλέψιc Maltomini, *locc.citt.* : βλάψιc ed.pr.　Perhaps ἡ βλέψιc [τοῦ] Ι [Ὥρου or [τοῦ] Ι [Ἡλίου.

4. E.g. τὸ κράτοc τ]οῦ Αδωναι (cf. PGM XXXV 21).

4-5. E.g. ἡ δύν[αμιc] Ι [τοῦ Cαβαωθ or [τοῦ Ὀcίρεωc or [τοῦ Ιαω as in PGM VII 1019, LXI 9 and XXXV 20 respectively.

5. E.g. ἡ ἰcχὺ]c τοῦ μεγάλου θε[οῦ.

6-7. Possibly [ἐξορκίζω cε, cίν]απι, ἵνα διακόψ[ῃc τὴν] Ι [δ(εῖνα) ἀπὸ τοῦ δ(εῖνα).

7] ̣ : c or ε.

ἔχθραν: cf. PGM XII 372 f. (quoted above, → 21 comm.); O 2, 40-42 δὸς Ἀλλοῦτι ὕβριν, μῖcοc, ἀηδίαν, ἕωc ἀποcτῇ τῆc οἰκίαc Ἀπολλωνίου; Audollent, *DT*, 208, 5-14 Γάϊοc Cτάλκιοc Λειβεράριοc - - - γένοιτο ἐκθρὸc (*sic*) Λολλίαc κτλ.; 198, 30 f., 33.

ἕωc θα[νάτου: cf. μέχρι θανάτου **46**, 24 f.; **48** J-K 25, 39; **50**, 67 f. In the present text, however, ἕωc possibly expresses degree ('a mortal enmity') rather than time; cf. Bauer, *Wörterbuch, s.v.* ἕωc II 4, *in fine*. One might also consider ἕωc θά[νωcι.

3-8. To resume, *exempli gratia*:

[cίναπι, οὐκ εἶ cίναπι]c ἀλλὰ ἡ βλέψιc [τοῦ]
['Ηλίου, τὸ κράτοc τ]οῦ Αδωναι, ἡ δύν[αμιc]
[τοῦ Cαβαωθ, ἡ ἰcχὺ]c τοῦ μεγάλου θε[οῦ].
[ἐξορκίζω cε, cίν]απι, ἵνα διακόψ[ηc τὴν]
[δ(εῖνα) ἀπὸ τοῦ δ(εῖνα) καὶ εἰ]c ἔχθραν ἕωc θα[νάτου]
[αὐτοὺc βάληc

8] ̣ v[̣ : a short horizontal joining v at mid-height; α, ε, c possible. ἵν[α cannot be read.

8-9. Probably εἰc τὴν ο[ἰκίαν] I [τῆc δ(εῖνα); cf. 15.

10. ἀκούcαcα or ἀκούcαc ἄ̣.

11 τ]οῦ 'Οcίρεωc: see above, → 21 comm.

13 κατεκαυcα[: perhaps κατέκαυcα, first person. What survives in 13-14 might suggest something akin to PGM IV 1540-45 ὡc ἐγώ cε κατακάω καὶ δυνατὴ εἶ, οὕτω ἧc φιλῶ, τῆc δεῖνα, κατάκαυcον τὸν ἐγκέφαλον, ἔκκαυcον καὶ ἔκcτρεψον αὐτῆc τὰ cπλάγχνα, or to XXXVI 340 f. ὡc cὺ κάῃ, οὕτωc καὶ cὺ καύcειc τὴν δ(εῖνα). If this is correct, the fire would be that of love which has to seize the woman for the operator, or that of hatred for her partner (cf. Griffith-Thompson, *Demotic Magical Papyrus*, XIII 6 f. "Send the fire towards his heart and the flame in his place of sleeping, the - - - of fire of hatred never [ceasing to enter] into his heart at any time" [cf. Betz, *Translation*, p. 217]).

14-15. A purely illustrative reconstruction: οὕτωc κ]αὶ cύ, cίναπι, α[ὐτὴν] I [κατάκαυcον καὶ τὴ]ν οἰκίαν τῆc δ(εῖνα).

15 Δ [Maltomini (P.Laur. IV 148) : δ[ed.pr.

16 πάροδον: possibly the house entrance (cf. οἰκία in 15); see G. Husson, *OIKIA. Le vocabulaire de la maison privée en Égypte d'après les papyrus grecs* (Paris 1983), p. 69 n. 2. Apparently with another meaning

(stage performance?), the word occurs in a spell that is probably disjunctive in a list of cursed things belonging to the rival: παρατίθομαι Ζοίδα τὴν Ἐρετρικήν, τὴν Καβείρα γυναῖκα, [τ]ῆ Γῆ καὶ τῷ Ἑρμῆ, τὰ βρώματα αὐτῆς, - - - τὸν γέλωτα, τὴν cυνουcίην, τὸ κιθ{φε}άριc[μα] αὐτῆc καὶ τὴν πάροδον αὐ[τῆc], τὴν ἡδον⟨ήν⟩, κτλ.; see E.Ziebarth, *Sitzungsb. Berlin* (1934) 1040, no. 22, 8 (see above, footnote 1).

All of these texts, together with a Coptic codex and some Aramaic fragments (see *SCO* 29, 1979, 19-48 and 125-130), issue from the same magical workshop. Some sections of the major Greek formulary (**96 A**) recur in five other fragmentary papyri (**96 B, C, D, E, F**), suggesting mass production of the texts. This as well as the presence of three languages and a number of different hands bear witness to a workshop or factory of some importance, capable of satisfying a large and diverse clientele.

Provenance is unknown. Linguistic considerations led the editor of the Coptic codex to suppose a provenance from the area in which one now finds the town of Beni Suef (S.Pernigotti, *SCO* 29, 1979, 46).

Because of the irregular way the texts were written, it is not always possible to state if a blank space, even if wide, is to be regarded as margin. In the transcriptions, indication of break is given only when it is certain; absence of such an indication will mean uncertainty, unless the completeness of the papyrus is stated explicitly in the DESCR.

When these papyri were first edited, they did not have inventory numbers. Since the present organisation of the material is somewhat different from the first edition, the following concordance should be useful: **96 A** = Pap. 1 (ed.pr.); **96 B** = Pap. 2; **96 C** = Pap. 3; **96 D** = Pap. 4; **96 E** = Pap. 5; **96 F** = Pap. 6; **97** = Pap. 7; **98** no. 1 = Pap. 8; **98** no. 2 = Pap. 9; **98** no. 3 = Pap. 10; **98** no. 4 = Pap. 11; **98** no. 5 = Pap. 12; **98** no. 6 = Pap. 13.[1]

---

[1] As in the ed.pr., some tiny unplaced fragments bearing only a few letters or traces of drawings (collective inv. no. 1263) are not dealt with here.

Provenance   V/VI AD
unknown

P.Mil. Vogl. inv. 1245, 1246, 1247-1248, 1249, 1250, 1252-1253.

ED.PR.: F.Maltomini, "I papiri greci," in: "Nuovi papiri magici in copto, greco e aramai-
co," *SCO* 29 (1979) 58-93.

COMM.: ed.pr.; (line 72) F.Maltomini, *ZPE* 85 (1991) 244.

TRANSL.: ed.pr.; R.Kotansky in Betz, *Translation*, no. CXXIII a-f.

PHOTO: ed.pr., plates IV-VII and IX-X.

DESCR.: this number consists of a large papyrus (**A**) and five small fragmentary pieces (**B-**
F). Texts **B-E** all repeat material found in **A**; so does **F**, but it also has unique material.

A: 14 × 86 cm. Roll written *transversa charta*. The writing runs against the fibers
on the recto, and the verso is blank. Five kolleseis: cm 15.5 K^1, 17 K^2, 16.5 K^3, 16.5
K^4, 16.5 K^5, 4. The text is probably complete at the bottom, where there is blank
space of 2.6 cm, and possibly at the top, where there is blank space of 1.6 cm. Inv. 1245.

B: 4 × 5.2 cm. Written along the fibers on the recto (= **A** 13-17 left). At the right
top, remains of a magical sign that corresponds with the first one in **A** 12. The verso
is blank. The hand is that of **A**. Inv. 1246.

C: Fr. A 5 × 5 cm; Fr. B 2.7 × 2.2 cm. Written along the fibers on the recto (= **A**
13-18 left; 18-22 right); the verso is blank. The hand is that of **A**. Inv. 1247-1248.

D: 4.6 × 6.3 cm. Written along the fibers on the recto (= **A** 58-59). The hand is not
that of **A**. On the verso, against the fibers, vague traces of two lines in a hand that does
not appear to be the same as that on the recto. Inv. 1249.

E: 8.4 × 10.3 cm. The text begins against the fibers on the verso (= **A** 25-32) in a
hand that may be the same as that of **A**. It continues in a different hand on the recto
along the fibers (= **A** 35-46). At the upper right of the verso are five lines of Coptic,
perhaps from a letter (see S.Pernigotti, *SCO* 29, 1979, 49). We are probably dealing
with a single sheet, not with a page of a codex. There is a kollesis 1 cm from the left
edge of the recto. Inv. 1250.

F: Fr. A 11.9 × 10.6 cm; Fr. B 12.5 × 5 cm. Written along the fibers on the recto
(Fr. A 4-8 = **A** 25-33; Fr. B 2, 3, 4 left = **A** 38, 40, 42); the verso is blank. The hand
is not that of **A**. Inv. 1252-1253.

LOC.: Istituto di Papirologia, Università degli Studi, Milan.

96 A contains fourteen sections separated by long horizontal strokes. Their contents fall into two main categories: (i) lines 1-47, magical words with magical signs, names and drawings; the purpose of this entire section is uncertain; (ii) lines 48-72, ten short prescriptions, eight of them certainly or probably iatromagical, 69-71 a victory charm and 59 a prescription of uncertain nature.

The drawing at lines 2-5 represents a human body. Aside from the position of its arms, it looks like the figure in the Coptic codex (see *SCO* 29, 1979, 24 with plate II) and the one on **97** ↓. A smaller human body or animal appears at lines 7-9. There are several figures at lines 13-22: the group to the left seems to represent a daemon grasping a human body by the hair; the latter has outstretched arms and legs, as though terrified. (If this interpretation is correct, the drawing can be paralleled by some magical figures in PGM XXXVI; see PGM, Vol. 2, Taf. III, Abb. 15-18; also P.Oslo I 1, plates III, IV, VII, X and comm. *ad locc.*). The figure to the right remains mysterious.

B, C, D, E, F repeat some parts of the text of **A** (see intr. to **96-98**). The texts of **A, B, C, D, E, F** are transcribed below, one after the other. In the commentary the lemma is always the reading of **A**, but, when appropriate, the readings of **B-F** are given in parentheses. The parts of **F** which do not occur in **A** are dealt with after the main commentary on **A**.

Diaeresis on iota in **A** 31, 50, 72, **E** ↓ 7 (and often in magical words); dicolon in **F** fr. A 7 after a magical word; double oblique stroke separates words and elements of a series (**A** 1, 23, 63-64, 66; **E** → 4-7; **F** fr. B 2), opens and closes a section (**F** fr. A 4, 8), and terminates a sentence (50). γρα/ for γράψον (23); ▢ for ὀνόματα (23).

A

1   μαρμαριθϊ // μαρμαρϊθε

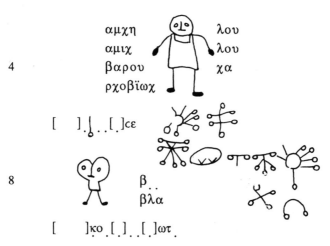

     αμχη   λου
     αμιχ   λου
4   βαρου   χα
     ρχοβϊωχ

[   ].∤..[.]cε

8

     β..
     βλα

[   ]κο.[.]..[.]ωτ.

12   Ευλαμμων
                      φανεμου

καιχαβω
Cαβαϩω
μουcηθ
16   cϊcηθ   λαχαμ
Νεμουηλ   χαμρϊ
α ⚎⚎   χωθ-
                       ϩθωχ
                       χαριωθ
                       αμηϊτηλ̄-
20   αι

                       νεωττασϊα
                       εθοου

γρά(ψον) (ὀνόματα) κασιτέρῳ· κρωμυω// πεγανου // λιβα`νω′.

1, 23 // in Pap.   23 γρα⫽ Pap.   ▱ Pap.   κασσιτέρῳ   κρόμυον?   πήγανον?   λίβανος?

24 ηρυτυλος
    ἡμωφυῆ
    ἡμωχυῆ
    ῥιζωπυέ
28 ἀνδρωγενῆ
    ἀνδρωρ
    ἡμωγενῆ
    κορκωβανϊη
32 χρυcωβελλῆ
    χρυcώκωμε

    κρομύλευκον
    μενουλαθ
36 χαρβαθα
    cθωμβαυλη
    ζανξμνα
    χωνουθα
40 μενουβα
    βελερθϊ
    ζαχθαηρ
    χαλιουβη

44

       ουαμϊραθ   Βριμώ χα
       [αυτ] ⊗ ⊥   υρα ⊥ ⊕
       ζαζεαc   ιτφικαcυ
                     ϊου

---

48 πρὸς γενοῦcαν.
    ἤξερθε ἠκ τοῦ μνεμίου cου· Χριcτόc cε
    καλῖ. // ὢccτρακον δεξιῷ μερῷ.

---

24 Ἐρώτυλος?   25 αἱμοφυῆ   26 αἱμοχυῆ   27 ῥιζοποιέ?   28 ἀνδρογενῆ
29 ἀνδρορρώξ? (cf. F fr. A 6)   30 αἱμογενῆ   31 κροκοφανῆ?   32
χρυcοβελῆ   33 χρυcόκομε   34 an κρόμυ⟨ον⟩ λευκόν?   48 γεννῶcαν   49
ἔξελθε ἐκ   μνημείου   50 καλῖ Pap., l. καλεῖ // in Pap.   ὄcτρακον   μηρῷ

ὑπνοῦν. φύλ⟨λ⟩ῳ δάφνης·

52   ⸎⸎⸎⸎⸎ θαρα θαρω.

ⲥτραγ⟨γ⟩ουρίαν.
μωγιβ ⸎⸎⸎⸎⸎⸎ θθυς
⸎⸎

56   ῥῖγος. χάρτῃ·
λβλαναθαναπαμβαλαναθαναθ . .
ναθαναμαθαναθαναθα.

⸎⸎⸎⸎⸎⸎⸎⸎⸎⸎⸎⸎⸎⸎⸎⸎⸎⸎⸎⸎⸎⸎⸎⸎⸎
Ραφαηλ εϊⲥωϊ ⸎ θνη.

60   λαβὸν ζουδίου μαρμαρίνου ξῦⲥον δεξι-
αc χιρὸc δεξιοῦ μέρου τῆc ψωλῆc· τρῖψον
τῷ τραπεζιν μετὰ κεροῦ.

λαβὸν κωκυμέλου κραδίαc // ξύλον κρά-
64   βηc // ἠρεβίθιν // ⲥκόρδον, ζέⲥαc δὸc
πῖν μετὰ προπώματος.

πύρεθρων // πίπερι κωκία // κγ ⲥτι ̣[]
. . . . [̣]αφνω· τοῦ πιπερίου β̄ τρίψαc
68   μῖξον μετὰ ἀπωπάνακοc.

νικᾶ⟨ν⟩.
ὠδώτα ὑήνα τῆc δεξιᾶc ⲥιαγώνοc
τὸν ἄνω.

72   νάρκ[η] c ὠξ̣ύνγι̣ [χ]ρῖcον ηνπροcτι.

51 an ὕπνον?   60 λαβὼν ζῴδιον μαρμάρινον   60-61 δεξιᾷ χειρὶ δεξιὸν μέροc
62 τραπεζίῳ?   κηροῦ   63-66 // in Pap.   63 λαβὼν κοκκυμήλου καρδίαc   63-
64 κράμβηc   64 ἐρεβίνθιον   65 πεῖν   66 πύρεθρον   κοκκία   ⲥτι []: ad
fin. littera una desit necne, incertum   68 ὀποπάνακοc   70 ὀδόντα ὑαίνηc
70-71 ⲥιαγόνοc τῶν   72 ὀξύγγιον   ηνπροcτï Pap., l. ἔμπροcθε?

B

— — —

1 καιχαβω [
  Cαβαℨω [
  μουcηθ [
4 cιcηθ [
  Ν̣εμουηλ [

— — —

C

Fr. A

— — —

1 καιχαβω [
  Cαβαℨω [
  μουcηθ [
4 cïcηθ [
  Νεμουηλ [
  α ⊿ ⊿ [

— — —

Fr. B

— — —

1] χαρ[ιωθ
  ] αμηι[τηλαι
  ] νεωτ[ταcια
4] εθο̣ο̣[υ

— — —

D

— — —

1   ]̣αθ̣[

Ρα]φαηλ ειc̣[ωι

E

↓   —   —   —

1   ἠμωφυῆ
    ἠμωχυῆ
    ῥιζωπυέ
4   ἀνδρογενῆ
    ἀνδρωρ
    [ἠ]μωγενῆ
    [κορκ]ωβανϊη
8   [χρυϲωβ]ελλῆ

   —   —   —

→   —   —   —

1   μενουλαθ
    χαρβαθα
    ϲθωμβαυλη
4   ζανξμνα //
    χωνουθα // μενου-
    βα // βελερθι // ζαχ-
    θαηρ // χαλιουβη

8   ουαμιραθ
    αυτ ⊗ ⊥
    ζαζηαϲ

    Βριμώ χα
12   υρα ⊥ ⊕
    ιτφικαϲ[υ]

   —   —   —

↓ 1 αἱμοφυῆ   2 αἱμοχυῆ   3 ῥιζοποιέ?   5 ἀνδρορρώξ? (cf. **F** fr. A 6)
6 αἱμογενῆ   7 κροκοφανῆ?   8 χρυϲοβελῆ
   → 4-7 // in Pap.

F

Fr. A

1 ‾ ‾ ‾
        ].̣.[
   [.̣.̣.̣.] υβη εαρ.̣.̣
    [.̣.̣.̣]υρος
4 // ἐμοφηεῖ ἐμοχηῦ .̣[
   ῥ̅υ̅σ̅ο̅π̅ηέ ἀν̅τ̅ρ̅ο̅γύνη
   ἀ̅ν̅τ̅ρ̅ο̅ρ̅οχ ἐμ̅ο̅γ̅ύ̅ν̅ε
   κ̅ο̅ρ̅κ̅ο̅β̅α̅ν̅υ̅η: χρ̅υ̅σ̅ο̅βελῦ
8 χρ̅ο̅σ̅ό̅κ̅ο̅μ̅ε//
   κ̣υνοκεφάλου .̣[

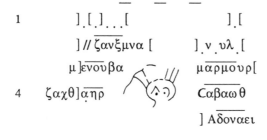

       [.̣.̣.̣]cαι
       [.̣.̣.̣].̣ας
12   [.̣.̣]γοβας
    ε.̣[.̣.̣]νο.̣.̣.̣
      Αδοναει
      Ελοει

Fr. B

1 ‾ ‾ ‾
   ].̣[.̣].̣.̣.[   ].̣[
   ]// ζ̅α̅ν̅ξ̅μ̅ν̅α [   ].̣ν̣.̣υλ.̣[
   μ]ε̅ν̅ο̅ῦ̅βα   μ̅α̅ρ̅μ̅ο̅υρ[
4 ζαχθ]α̅η̅ρ   C̅α̅β̅α̅ω θ
                ] Αδοναει

   ‾ ‾ ‾

Fr. A 4 // in Pap.   αἰμοφυῆ   αἰμοχυῆ   5 ῥιζοποιέ?   ἀνδρογύνη?
6 ἀνδρορρώξ?   αἰμογύνη? an αἰμογενῆ?   7 κροκοφανῆ?   dicolon
in Pap.   χρυσοβελῆ   8 χρυσόκομε   // in Pap.

Fr. B 2 // in Pap.

Marmarithi marmarithe amchê amich barou rchobiôch (drawing) *lou lou cha* - - - (mag. signs, drawing) - - - *bla* - - - (mag. signs) *Eulammôn phanemou kaichabô Sabahô mousêth sisêth Nemouêl* (mag. signs, drawing) *lacham chamri chôthhthôch chariôth amêitêlai neôttasia ethoou.* Write the names on tin. Onion, rue, frankincense. |²⁴ Erotylos (?): "Born of blood, shedding blood, root-maker (?), |²⁸ man-engendered, breaker of men (?), blood-engendered, saffron-colored (?), with golden arrows, golden-haired, onion-white (?), *menoulath* |³⁶ *charbatha sthômbaulê zanxmna chônoutha* |⁴⁰ *menouba belerthi zachthaêr chalioubê.*" |⁴⁴ *ouamirath* - - - *zazeas Brimô cha yra itphikasy iou.* |⁴⁸ For a woman in labor. "Come out of your tomb, Christ is calling you." A potsherd on the right thigh.   To sleep. On a laurel leaf: |⁵² "(mag. signs) *thara tharô.*"   Against strangury. "*môgib* (mag. signs) *ththys* (mag. signs)." |⁵⁶ Against shivering. On papyrus: "*lblanathanapambala-nathanath- - -nathanamathanathanatha.*"   (mag. signs) "Raphael *eisôi* (mag. sign) *thnê.*" |⁶⁰ Take a marble statuette and scrape with the right hand the right side of its penis. Pound on a table with wax.   Take some of the heart of a plum-tree, stalk of a cabbage, |⁶⁴ chickpea, garlic, boil and give it to drink with a before-dinner drink.   Pellitory, pepper: corns, twenty-three - - - laurel (?); pound two of the pepper (corns) and |⁶⁸ mix with opopanax.   To win. A tooth of a hyena, from the right side of the jaw, one of the upper ones. |⁷² Rub with fat of electric ray - - -.

1 μαρμαριθϊ μαρμαρϊθε: a variation of Μαρμαραωθ (on which see **42**, **52** comm.; also **57**, 20 left comm.). For the repetition, cf. Audollent, *DT*, 234, 3 μαρμαρει μαρμαρει; for sequences of two magical words which differ only in the final letter, cf. **52** θαρα θαρω; **14**, 1 coυμα coυμη; **97** ↓ 6 θαθη θαθω; PGM IV 1626 βαθα βαθι; A.Delatte, *BCH* 37 (1913) 271 νχθα νχθω; also Μαcκελλι Μαcκελλω (see **12**, 3-5 comm.; **54**, 27-29 comm.). For similar variations in magical words, see the literature collected by Brashear, *Magica varia*, p. 41 f.

2-4. One might wonder whether the letters to the left of the figurine are to be continued by the letters to the right. αμχηλου might possibly be a corruption of ἄγγελοc, and βαρουχα is attested (cf. **50**, 35; **51**, 3, 12, and see Martinez, *P.Mich. 757*, p. 77). On the other hand, αμιχ is attested, and λου and χα occur as independent words; moreover, the letters to the left and right of the figurine are exactly on the same level only in 2.

2-3 right λου λου: cf. PGM VII 494 λου λου λου, interpreted by K.Fr.W.Schmidt, *GGA* 196 (1934) 175, as Coptic ⲁⲗⲟⲩ 'maiden', with reference to Isis-Kore (see Th.Hopfner, *Archiv Orientální* 7, 1935, 120;

M.Philonenko, *CRAI* 1985, 448 f., with regard to PGM V 487 λαυ λου λου; Merkelbach-Totti, *Abrasax* II, pp. 100, 152; and cf. Crum, pp. 5 *a* and 141 *b*, *s.v.* λελοϒ; Westendorf, p. 78); also **10**, 7; Wessely, *Ephesia grammata*, no. 493 λαλαλου; Wünsch, *Zaubergerät*, p. 12 λουλου; line 5 of the gold amulet published by M.Siebourg, *Bonner Jahrb.* 118 (1909) 158-175 λουλα; Alex. Trall. II 583 Puschmann λου. In Griffith-Thompson, *Demotic Magical Papyrus*, IX 6 (cf. Betz, *Translation*, p. 210) *Loou* is a divine name (see Th.Hopfner, *Archiv Orientální* 7, 1935, 109). For λου in composition, cf. **45**, 25; PGM IV 1705 λουθεουθ; LVII 12 λουβεινε; see also W. Brashear, *Chron. d'Ég.* 58 (1983) 297 n. 1.

3 left αμιχ: a daemon in Delatte, *Anecdota Atheniensia*, p. 437, 33 and in *Cat. Cod. Astr. Gr.* VIII.2, p. 153, 15 (written Ἀμήχ in Delatte, *Anecdota Atheniensia*, p. 72, 11). Cf. also αμιχαμχου in PGM VII 263; Λαμίχ and Ἀλαμίχ in Delatte, *Anecdota Atheniensia*, pp. 36, 5 and 502, 15.

4 left βαρου: probably for βαρουχ, on which see **97** → 6 comm.

4 right χα: cf. PGM I 202; also **42**, 52 χιωχα.

5 left ρχοβϊωχ: cf. PGM XIXa 34 right βιωχ βιωχ.

8 β . : first, ν or κ; then, perhaps ω.

9 βλα: cf. PGM V 477 (but see app.cr. *ad loc.*).

11 Ευλαμμων: see **44**, 17 comm.

12 φανεμου: possibly from Egyptian *p3-ḥr-imj* 'face of a cat' (H.J. Thissen). A reference to Bastet or Sekhmet? Cf. αἰλουροπρόcωποc 'cat-faced' in PGM III 4 f., 13 f., 83, 92. The sequence νεμου occurs in Νεμουηλ in 17 left.

13 καιχαβω (**B** 1; **C** fr. A 1): cf. καχαβ on the amulet published by W.Deonna, *REG* 20 (1907) 366, no. 3, who interpreted it as Hebrew *kōkhabh* 'star'. Cf. also **20**, 2 καιχα.

14 left Cαβαϩω (**B** 2; **C** fr. A 2): for the spelling with hori, cf. *Sabaho* in Griffith-Thompson, *Demotic Magical Papyrus*, XIX 39, XXI 6, *verso* XII 7, 10 (cf. Betz, *Translation*, pp. 227, 229, 245), and cλβλxω in Kropp, *Koptische Zaubertexte* I, G 46. For the omission of -θ, cf. PGM XV 14; LIX 4; P 13a 2; Audollent, *DT*, 241, 27; Bonner, *SMA*, D. 143, 231, 241, 310, etc.

14 right λαχαμ: cf. Delatte-Derchain, *Intailles*, no. 308 λαχαμι (cf. also Bonner, *SMA*, p. 112); Delatte, *Anecdota Atheniensia*, p. 18, 24 λαχα; Griffith-Thompson, *Demotic Magical Papyrus*, XVI 10 (cf. Betz, *Translation*, p. 221) *laikham*. Cf. also -λακαμ- in the cθομβαολη formula (cθομ-

βαοληβαολсθομβαλακαμсθομβλη; see also below, 37 comm.). Finally, -χαμ is a frequent ending of magical words and names; examples in the ed.pr.

15 left μουcηθ (**B** 3; **C** fr. A 3): cf. PGM IV 1625 f. μουcουθι. The possibilities include: (a) a conflation of Μωϋcῆc and Cηθ. (b) Egyptian *m3j*, Coptic моуι 'lion' + снθ (cf. μουωρ in PGM VII 304, interpreted by K.Fr. W.Schmidt, *GGA* 196, 1934, 172 as Egyptian *m3j-Ḥr*, Coptic моуωр "Löwe Hor"). The lion was a solar animal, but Seth was occasionally syncretized with solar deities; see Bonner, *SMA*, p. 152 f.; Merkelbach-Totti, *Abrasax* I, p. 119 on PGM IV 1663; II, p. 25, on PGM III 514. (c) моу-status constructus of мооу 'water' (Crum, p. 197 *b*) + снθ, i.e. 'water (= sperm) of Seth', which would be similar in meaning to the following cïcηθ (H.J.Thissen).

15 right χαμρï: perhaps for χαμαρι, the ending of the well-known Αχραμμαχαμαρι, on which see **10**, 1 comm.

16 left cïcηθ (**B** 4; **C** fr. A 4): Coptic cιcнθ 'son of Seth'. Cf. PGM XIXa 44 right cηι cηθ.

16-17 right χωθ|ₔθωχ: a palindrome, as such unparalleled. For χωθ, cf. PGM VII 753 χοωθ; Wessely, *Ephesia grammata*, no. 488 χωθμαχωθ; Delatte, *Anecdota Atheniensia*, p. 588, 13, 19 κοθ; also PGM VII 554 χινε-χωθ; XXXVI 145 γουνχωθω; **40**, 1 ff. For θωχ, cf. E.Peterson, *Rhein. Mus.* 75 (1926) 402, no. 46 θωχ θωχαω; PGM XII 166 θωχο; in Kropp, *Koptische Zaubertexte* I, R col. 19, 10, θοκ is an angel's name.

17 left Νεμουηλ (**B** 5; **C** fr. A 5): cf. Schwab, *Vocabulaire de l'angélologie*, p. 229 'God has spoken'. The sequence νεμου in φανεμου in 12.

18 left α 𝟺 𝟺 (**C** fr. A 6): what looks like the sign for δεῖνα is used here as a magical sign as in PGM VII 196, where similarly it is preceded by a sign resembling an alpha.

18 right χαριωθ (**C** fr. B 1): cf. PGM XII 338 Χαρεωθ, 341 Χαρ-μιωθ.

19-20 αμηïτηλιαι (**C** fr. B 2): probably Hebrew *'amit(y)- 'el-ḥay* 'my truth is the living God' (A.Vivian, *apud* F.Maltomini in: *Miscellanea Papyrologica* [Papyrologica Florentina VII, 1980], p. 176 f.).

21 νεωττacïα (**C** fr. B 3): possibly based on Greek elements.

22 εθοου (**C** fr. B 4): probably Coptic 'bad' (Crum, p. 731 *b*).

23. For ▯ = ὄνομα/ὀνόματα, see **74**, 1 comm. The ὀνόματα are here the preceding magical words and names.

κασιτέρω (r. κασσιτέρω): the omission of the preposition may be explained by a marked tendency towards brachylogy that appears elsewhere in this text (see also the following note and 50, 51, 56, probably 62). For tin in magic, see **94**, 37 comm.

κρωμυω // πεγανου // λιβα῾νω´: it seems quite unlikely that the three words indicate the substances with which the ὀνόματα are to be written on the tin tablet, or that they are the words that are to be written on it (the latter suggestion in Betz, *Translation*). Rather, they are the ingredients of a burnt offering. If so, the papyrus presents misspellings of κρόμυον, πήγανον, λίβανος. In place of the normally elaborate and complicated ceremonies of the Greek formularies (see Hopfner, *Offenbarungszauber* I, § 544) we then have here a simple indication of the ingredients. Similarly, in some Coptic magical texts the praxeis consist of nothing more than lists of ingredients appended to the end of the spell: cf. e.g. Kropp, *Koptische Zaubertexte* II, XIII 77-79, XIV 10-12, XV 46-48, XXXII 60 f., etc.; W.E.Crum, *JEA* 20 (1934) 196, lines 16-18; cf. however PGM IV 85 ἡ πρᾶξις· κρόμμυον; and P.Carlsberg 52 (inv. 35), line 4 (see Brashear, *Magica varia*, pp. 40 and 53). Frankincense is the most frequently used substance in burnt offerings (see Brashear, *Magica varia*, p. 55); for the onion, cf. PGM IV 85, 2462 f., 2584 f. (= 2650); for rue, cf. Delatte, *Anecdota Atheniensia*, p. 51, 10 and, possibly, PGM IV 1294 and 1990, if αρμαρα is the equivalent of ἁρμαλά, a 'Syrian' name for rue according to Diosc. III 45 [RV] (II 57, 14 Wellmann); but see E.Riess, *JEA* 26 (1941) 53 with n. 1.

24 ηρυτυλος: difficult. Close in spelling is ἐρίθυλος, the name of a bird, but this does not seem to promise much. Of the meanings registered in LSJ *s.v.* ἐρωτύλος, the least unsuitable is perhaps 'sweetheart', 'darling' (cf. Theocr. 3, 7), just possibly here the heading of a love-charm (so Kotansky in Betz, *Translation*, p. 318 n. 9). However, it is tempting rather to compare PGM XIII 946-953, where a series of magical words is quoted from one Erotylos, a compiler of *Orphika*: Ἐρώτυλος ἐν τοῖς Ὀρφικοῖς· υοηεωαι ωαι υοηεαι υοηεω ερεπε, ευα ναρβαρνεζαγεγωη κτλ. = Orph., t. 235 Kern (he is mentioned also by Zosimos; cf. M.Berthelot, *Collection des anciens alchimistes grecs* II, Paris 1888, p. 144, 7, and see O.Kern in *RE Suppl.* IV, *s.v.* Erotylos, col. 386). One might then suppose an analogous situation for the present papyrus: the series of terms in 25-43 might be quoted from a work of Erotylos (the same *Orphika*?). If so, we would have here a third reference to this man.

25-43. A series of adjectives (25-33; on 34 see below *ad loc.*) is followed by a group of magical words (35-43). The first group might be epithets of a god. If so, among the deities of the Graeco-Egyptian pantheon, Hecate (-Persephone-Selene-Artemis) seems to be the one for whom the epithets, on the whole, would be most appropriate (see below).

25 ἡμωφυῆ (**E** ↓ 1; ἐμοφηεῖ **F** fr. A 4): from αἱμοφυής (*addendum lexicis*), 'born of blood'. The case, here as in the whole series 25-33, is probably vocative (cf. 27 and 33). For the vocative ending -ῆ, see **42**, 2 comm. on τρικαρανοστρεφῆ.

26 ἡμωχυῆ (**E** ↓ 2; ἐμοχηῦ **F** fr. A 4): from αἱμοχυής, a new word (now registered for the present text in *DGE Supl.*). No other compound in -χυης is recorded in the lexica. Cf. αἱμοχυσία (see Lampe, *s.v.*) and αἱμόχυτος in *Cyranides* I 1 (p. 21, 12 Kaimakis). The adjective, like the preceding one (cf. also 30), would be appropriate for Hecate: cf. PGM IV 2864 αἱμοπότι; Audollent, *DT*, 242, 41 αἱμοπότι; Hipp., *Refut.* IV 35, 5 (GCS 3, p. 62, 4) χαίρουσα - - - αἵματι φοινῷ; (62, 6) αἵματος ἱμείρουσα; Theocr. 2, 13 ἐρχομέναν νεκύων ἀνά τ' ἠρία καὶ μέλαν αἷμα.

27 ῥιζωπυέ (**E** ↓ 3; ῥυσοπηέ **F** fr. A 5): apparently a new compound, probably one of the following: (i) ῥιζοποιέ (perhaps in reference to the influence of the moon on the growth of plants; see Roscher, *Lexikon* II.2, coll. 3152-54); (ii) ῥοιζοποιέ (of the moon and/or Hecate? Cf. PGM VII 883 δὸς ῥοῖζον, addressed to Selene; Plut., *De facie* 923C τὸ ῥοιζῶδες τῆς περιαγωγῆς; *Orac. Chald.* 107, 5 des Places μήνης ῥοῖζον; Damasc., *De princ.* 282 [II 154, 17-19 Ruelle] ἥ τε μεγάλη Ἑκάτη - - - ζωογόνον ῥοίζημα προΐησι, and 156, 15-17, on which see S.I.Johnston, *Hekate Soteira* [American Class. St. 21, Atlanta 1990], p. 108; see also Index, p. 181, *s.vv.* ῥοιζέω and cognates for their connection with Hecate in the Chaldean Oracles); (iii) ῥυζοποιέ (of Hecate associated with dogs? Cf. PGM IV 2549 κυνολύγματε; 2810 f. ἔχεις σκυλακώδεα φωνήν, and see **57**, 1 comm.).

28 ἀνδρωγενῆ (ἀνδρογενῆ **E** ↓ 4; ἀντρογύνη **F** fr. A 5): in this case the different spellings are real variants: ἀνδρογενῆ (attested in Simpl., *in Phys.* II 8 [CAG IX 372, 2; 381, 7-8], instead of ἀνδροφυῆ in Emp. 31 B 61, 3 D.-K.) and ἀνδρογύνη 'androgynous' (possibly in ΣΤ Hom., *Il.* 13, 289-291, III 454 Erbse). For the latter, cf. PGM IV 2610 ἀρσενόθηλυν ἔρνος (of Hecate); also III 47 f. Ἑρμεκάτη.

29 ἀνδρωρ (**E** ↓ 5; ἀντρορσχ **F** fr. A 6): apparently **F** has the complete form. Possibly ἀνδρορρώξ 'breaker of men' (cf. κυμορρώξ). Cf. the epi-

thets of Hecate δαμασάνδρα, βιασάνδρα, κατανικάνδρα, etc. (see **42**, 30 comm.).

30 ἡμωγενῆ (**E** ↓ 6; ἐμογύνε **F** fr. A 6): probably from αἱμογενής, registered in LSJ *Suppl.* for SEG VIII 374, 8 (= SB V 7804) with the meaning 'related by blood', but the reading is not certain (cf. Bernand, *Inscriptions métriques*, no. 69, *ad loc.*). Here rather 'born of/in blood' or 'producing blood' (for the active meaning, cf. πυρσογενής in Nonn., *Dion.* 2, 495). However, the text of **F** (cf. **F**'s -υ- for **A**'s and **E**'s -ε- also in 28) could be evidence for an elsewhere unattested αἱμογύνης 'woman of blood' (?) (registered for the present text in *DGE Supl.*).

31 κορκωβανϊη (**E** ↓ 7; κορκοβανυη **F** fr. A 7): perhaps κροκοφανῆ. Kotansky (in Betz, *Translation*, p. 319 n. 16) suggests κροκοβαφῆ. Saffron is associated with Demeter and Persephone (see F.Orth in *RE* I A.2, *s.v.* Safran, col. 1730); Hecate is κροκόπεπλος in *Orph. hymn.* 1, 2 (cf. also 71, 1 of Melinoe).

32 χρυσωβελλῆ (**E** ↓ 8; χρυσοβελῦ **F** fr. A 7): χρυσοβελής occurs in Tzetzes, *Alleg. Il.* XX 226, p. 182 Matranga (χρυσοβολίς, p. 274 Boissonade). The adjective is appropriate for Hecate-Artemis; cf. Porph., *De philos. ex orac. haur.* II, *apud* Eus., *P.E.* IV 23, 7 (GCS 8, 1, p. 215, 11) (= p. 151 Wolff) χρυσοβέλεμνος, of Hecate (the same oracle in Lyd., *Mens.* 3, 10, p. 44 Wünsch).

33 χρυσώκωμε (χροσόκομε **F** fr. A 8): read χρυσόκομε, an appropriate epithet for Hecate-Selene; the color of the moon is frequently compared to gold, and moon beams to hair; see Roscher, *Lexikon* II.2, coll. 3130, 3132, and cf. Maxim., περὶ καταρχῶν, 220 χρυσοέθειρα, of the moon.

34 κρομύλευκον: possibly another epithet ('onion-white'), but why is the word placed under the dividing line? Also in view of the desinence, one should perhaps interpret κρόμυ⟨ον⟩ λευκόν, a condensed prescription like the one in 23 (on white onions, cf. Diosc. II 151 [I 216, 3 Wellmann]).

35 μενουλαθ (**E** → 1; **F** fr. B 2 right?): the sequence μενου appears in μενουβα in 40.

36 χαρβαθα (**E** → 2): cf. Delatte-Derchain, *Intailles*, no. 234 χαρβραθι; PGM LXVI 6 χ⟨ο⟩ρβαθ. Based on Hebrew *arba* 'four' (the Tetragrammaton) according to W.Fauth, *Oriens Christianus* 67 (1983) 71 n. 56.

37 cθωμβαυλη (**E** → 3): unattested in the Greek magical papyri, but frequent in gems as part of a longer formula, often connected with solar deities; see Bonner, *SMA*, p. 206, and cf. D. 17, 33, 139, 203, 228, 355;

Delatte-Derchain, *Intailles*, nos. 150, 151; also 83, 84. Cf. Audollent, *DT*, 242, 32 f. ὀρκίζω ϲε τὸν θεὸν τὸν τοῦ ὕπνου δεϲπόζοντα Cθομβλοην.

39 χωνουθα (**E** → 5): unparalleled; cf., however, PGM IV 2017 νουθι; 2020 f. χορτομνουθι; 2024 χιμνουθι; XIXa 4 νουθι νουθι (perhaps equivalent to νουϲι νουϲι in PGM I 240: cf. Moraux, *Une défixion judiciaire*, p. 32). νουθι is interpreted by Hopfner, *Offenbarungszauber* I, § 694 as Coptic ⲚⲞⲨⲦⲈ 'god'.

40 μενουβα (**E** → 5-6; **F** fr. B 3 left): cf. PGM LVII 19 μενδουμβα. The second part of the word occurs in Bonner, *SMA*, D. 175 νουβα and in PGM V 431 f. νουβα⟨χ⟩α. The sequence μενου in μενουλαθ in 35.

42 ζαχθαηρ (**E** → 6-7; **F** fr. B 4 left): perhaps the name of an angel (with change of -ηλ to -ηρ).

43 χαλιουβη (**E** → 7): the same ending in Delatte, *Anecdota Atheniensia*, p. 140, 3 κοθελαουβη.

44 Βριμώ (**E** → 11): see **55**, 1 comm.

χα (**E** → 11): see above, 4 right comm.

45. The lacuna in **A** can be restored with **E** → 9 αυτ.

υρα (**E** → 12): cf. υραμ in PGM XXIIb 8, 9. *Uri* is the name of a *Dekanrichter* (cf. W.Gundel, *Dekane*, p. 75). Cf. Υρο in Schwab, *Vocabulaire de l'angélologie*, p. 423.

46 ζαζεαϲ (ζαζηαϲ **E** → 10): cf. PGM I 218 ζαδηα; VII 819 αζαζειϲθαιλιχ; XIXa 43 left ζαζερ; cf. also *1 Book of Jeu* 7 (p. 264 Schmidt-Till); *2 Book of Jeu* 45 (p. 308, 37-39 Schmidt-Till); and the angel's name Zazean (see Davidson, *Dictionary of Angels*, p. 327).

47 ϊου: cf. PGM II 132; V 141; LXXVII 14, 16; Youtie-Bonner, *Two Curse Tablets from Beisan*, p. 56, line 33; Delatte, *Anecdota Atheniensia*, pp. 16, 16; 416, 7; see also S.Eitrem, *Symb. Osl.* 27 (1949) 144 f. Ιου may be interpreted as a vowel series, but also as a variant of the Tetragrammaton; see L.Blau, *Das altjüdische Zauberwesen* (Budapest 1898), p. 134 n. 3.

48-50. This is the earliest attestation of a specific type of charm for easy childbirth that was often employed in medieval and modern magic; cf. e.g. Heim, *Incantamenta*, p. 550: *Ad difficultatem pariendi probatum. 'Elisabet peperit praecursorem, sancta Maria genuit salvatorem. Sive masculus sis sive femina, veni foras, salvator revocat te. Omnes sancti dei intercedant pro ista femina'. Quod scriptum supra genua tribus digitis ligas. Quod si hoc tam cito non proderit, tunc in alio membranulo scribas: 'Lazare, veni foras, salvator revocat te' et supra pectus feminae mitte (Cod. Bonn.* 218 (66a), fol. 40r;

11th cent.). Similar charms are found in manuscripts of the Latin West since the 9th-10th cent.; see Franz, *Benediktionen* II, pp. 198-201, nos. 1-8; p. 201 f., nos. 1-2; Heim, *Incantamenta*, pp. 550 n. 1; 564, 6-8; *Handwörterbuch des deutschen Aberglaubens* III, *s.v.* Gebärsegen, coll. 344-346. The charm shows many variants, but a constant structure is recognizable: the command of Christ to the baby to be born is preceded or followed by the mention of prior events (often Elizabeth's and Mary's deliveries), which by analogy are to be efficacious in the present. The same kind of charm is also found in late medieval Greek manuscripts. Here the formula to be uttered or written is often inserted in a *historiola*; cf. e.g. Delatte, *Anecdota Atheniensia*, p. 619 f. (= Vassiliev, *Anecdota Graeco-Byzantina*, p. 339, no. 21): Jesus, hearing the cries of a woman in labor, orders an angel to say in her ear (p. 620, 3-5): τέξε, γυνή, ὡς ἡ Μαριὰμ τὸν Χριστόν, ὡς ἡ Ἐλισάβετ τὸν Πρόδρομον· ἔξελθε, τέκνον, καλεῖ σε ὁ Χριστὸς καὶ ἡ γῆ σε περιμένει (further instances: Delatte, *Anecdota Atheniensia*, pp. 114, 25-29; 115, 6-14; 115, 15 - 116, 4; *Cat. Cod. Astr. Gr.* V.4, p. 120, 5-12).

49-50. The birth of the baby is equated with or rather *is* the resurrection of Lazarus; and it is Christ himself who utters the famous words (NT Joh. 11, 43 Λάζαρε, δεῦρο ἔξω). Cf. the end of the charm in *Cod. Bonn.* 218 (quoted above, 48-50 comm.), and *Cat. Cod. Astr. Gr.* V.4, p. 120, 6 f. γράψον μετὰ κινναβάρεως οὕτως· Λάζαρε, δεῦρο ἔξω, ὁ Χριστός σε φωνεῖ; also Delatte, *Anecdota Atheniensia*, p. 115, 30 ἄκουσον, Λάζαρε. Normally, however, the paradigm and the actual situation are not conflated; cf. Franz, *Benediktionen* II, p. 200, no. 4: *Christus quadrinuanum Lazarum vocavit et dixit: Lazare, veni foras. Et ego adiuro te, infans, - - - ut exeas*; Delatte, *Anecdota Atheniensia*, pp. 114, 27 f.; 115, 26 f. - - - ὡς ἐξῆλθεν ὁ Ἰωνᾶς ἀπὸ τοῦ κήτους καὶ ὁ Λάζαρος ἀπὸ τοῦ τάφου, ἔξελθε καὶ σύ, τέκνον, κτλ.

50 ὥσστρακον (r. ὄστρακον) δεξιῷ μερῷ (r. μηρῷ): ⟨write on⟩ a potsherd and ⟨put it on the⟩ right thigh of the woman. The verbs as well as the article and preposition before δεξιῷ μηρῷ have been left out in this compressed Greek (see 23 comm. on κασιτέρῳ); compare the omission of the article and the use of the locative dative in bodily descriptions in documentary papyri (see Mayser, *Grammatik* II.2, pp. 23.1-20; 147.34-45).

ὥσστρακον (r. ὄστρακον): cf. Vassiliev, *Anecdota Graeco-Byzantina*, p. 339, no. 20: πρὸς τὸ γεννῆσαι γυνήν· γράφε εἰς ὄστρακον παλαιὸν κτλ. See **97** ↓ 8 comm.

δεξιῷ μερῷ (r. μηρῷ): cf. the charm πρὸς δυcτοκοῦcαν γυναῖκα in W.Kroll, *Philologus* 57 (1898) 131: γράφε εἰc χάρτην - - - καὶ περίαψον τὸν δεξιὸν μηρόν. For the importance of the right side in magic, see the literature indicated in Brashear, *Magica varia*, p. 43.

51-52. See the similar but more extensive **74**, 1-7.

51 ὑπνοῦν: cf. 69 νικᾶ⟨ν⟩, or else read ὕπνον (cf. 53 cτραγγουρίαν, 56 ῥῖγοc). The latter (as well as cτραγγουρίαν and ῥῖγοc) might be interpreted as free accusatives; cf. Hipp., *Epid.* II 5, 5 (V 130, 2 L.) ἀνεμίην φλεβοτομίη; II 6, 12 (V 134, 2 f. L.) κυνάγχην καὶ ὀφθαλμίην φλεβοτομίη (but II 6, 20 [V 136, 12 f. L.] cτραγγουρίην λύει φλεβοτομίη); also **92**, 14. However, it could also be that πρόc in 48 governs the accusatives in 51 (?), 53, 56 as well.

φύλ⟨λ⟩ῳ δάφνηc: brachylogy; a preposition before φύλλῳ as well as an imperative of γράφω (or the like) are omitted (see 23 comm. on καcιτέρῳ).

52 θαρα θαρω: cf. PGM IV 3178, 3189 αζαραχθαρω; XIII 961 ζαροκοθαρα; Audollent, *DT*, 267, 10 ζαρακ[α]θαρα. Many magical words begin with θαρα (see PGM, Vol. 3 [Index], p. 256), and many end in it: cf. PGM I 153 βαθαρα; II 33 cανκανθαρα; XXXIX 1 ff. θατθαραθαυθωλθαρα. Cf. Θαρα in Delatte, *Anecdota Atheniensia*, p. 496, 12.

53. For another prescription against strangury, cf. **94**, 36; also **8** comm.

56 χάρτῃ: here a piece of papyrus, although normally χάρτηc designates a papyrus roll; see N.Lewis, *Papyrus in Classical Antiquity* (Oxford 1974), pp. 70-78. For the omission of the preposition, see 23 comm. on καcιτέρῳ.

57-58. Variations on Αβλαναθαναλβα, on which see **9**, 1-7 comm.; on the present occurrence, see W.Brashear, *ZPE* 56 (1984) 67, no. 8.

59. The purpose of this recipe is uncertain, possibly iatromagical as in the surrounding ones. Raphael (*rāpha'- 'el* 'God has healed') would be especially appropriate in such a context; see J.Michl, *RAC* V, coll. 252-254; Davidson, *Dictionary of Angels*, pp. 240-242.

60-62. Like most other charms in this text, the present one is probably iatromagical. The mention of marble dust scraped off the penis of a statue suggests perhaps a charm for potency.

Probably to be read λαβὼν ζῴδιον μαρμάρινον ξῦcον δεξιᾷ χειρὶ δεξιὸν μέροc τῆc ψωλῆc· τρῖψον ἐπὶ τῷ τραπεζίῳ μετὰ κηροῦ. But the poor orthography and the lack of parallels leave a wide margin for uncertainty.

60 ζουδίου μαρμαρίνου: for λαμβάνω governing a non-partitive genitive, cf. PGM LII 9 λαβὼ[v i]χνεύμονοc.

ξῦcov: here 'scratch', 'scrape'. The marble dust should be mixed with wax. Marble dust was used especially for the preparation of dentifrices and cosmetics: cf. e.g. Hipp., *Mul.* II 185 (VIII 366, 9 L.); Gal., *Comp. sec. loc.* V 5 (XII 892, 17 K.); Ps.Gal., *Rem.* II 7 (XIV 425, 1 K.); Aëtius VIII 6; 37 (CMG VIII.2, pp. 409, 24; 453, 11, 25 f.); Plin., *N.H.* XXXII 79; Marc. Emp., *De medicam.* XIII 12. Other uses: Aëtius XII 23, p. 108, 16 Kostomiris (against flux in the knees); XVI 23, p. 51, 16 Zervos (for women against excessive lactation). The scraping of statues, stelae and parts of sacred buildings in order to obtain a curative powder is a practice that was wide-spread throughout antiquity and also in later periods; see C.Traunecker, "Une pratique de magie populaire dans le temples de Karnak," in: A.Roccati-A.Siliotti, La magia in Egitto ai tempi dei Faraoni (Verona 1987), pp. 221-242.

60-61 δεξιᾶc χιρόc (r. χει-): 'with the right hand'. The genitive certainly resulted from poor linguistic awareness, and the syntactical coincidence with the isolated μιᾶc χειρόc of Eur., *H.F.* 938 (on which see Wilamowitz *ad loc.*; emended by Bond) is surely fortuitous. The phenomenon of the progressive disappearance of the dative may have been a contributing factor. However, it could also be that a preposition (διά or μετά) has been left out. See Humbert, *La disparition du datif,* esp. pp. 116 ff., 154 ff.; Jannaris, *Grammar,* § 1607, 3.

61 ψωλῆc: see Henderson, *The Maculate Muse,* pp. 35, 110 § 4; in addition to LSJ's references, cf. *Carm. Priap.* 68, 5 (p. 46 Cazzaniga); CIL IV 1363; IV, Suppl. II 4142; P.Oxy. XLII 3070, 2; *Suppl. Hell.* 975, 3.

62 τῷ τραπεζιv: the substantive, as it stands in the papyrus, seems to suggest a direct case, but pulverisation of a table seems an absurd operation. More probably the writer intended τῷ τραπεζίῳ (for the omission of the preposition, see 23 comm. on κασιτέρῳ). τραπέζιον would then indicate the table on which the ritual ceremonies are executed; cf. esp. PGM III 295 f.; IV 1860-63; XII 24, where ζώδια placed on a τράπεζα are mentioned.

63-68. Two apparently medical prescriptions whose aim is not indicated. Typically magical praxeis and logoi are absent.

63 λαβὸν κωκυμέλου κραδίαc (r. λαβὼν κοκκυμήλου καρδίαc): καρδία means here 'pith' (cf. Theophr., *H.P.* I 2, 6; III 10, 2, etc.; also PGM I 245; XII 438; XIII 262). Therefore it is the tree (normally κοκκυμηλέα), not the fruit (κοκκύμηλον), to which the word refers. According

to Pollux I 232, the form κοκκύμηλος is used of the plum tree by a comic poet (probably Araros, fr. 20, II 219 Kock). καρδίας is likely to be partitive genitive rather than accusative plural. On medical properties of the plum tree, cf. Diosc. I 121 (I 111, 14 - 112, 6 Wellmann).

63-64 κρά|βης (r. κράμβης): the same spelling in P.Petr. III 139 b, 9, 14; P.Tebt. III.2, 894 fr. 2, 8; SB XVI 12376, 5 (cf. also SB XVI 12675, 12 κραβίν for κραμβίον). See Gazza, "Prescrizioni mediche" (II), p. 85; L.C.Youtie, *ZPE* 66 (1986) 196.

64 ἠρεβίθιν (r. ἐρεβίνθιον): apparently, the diminutive occurs only in papyri, always in the plural: Stud. Pal. XXII 75, 10, 20, 51; P.Mich. XIV 680, 19; P.Ryl. IV 627, 268; P.Oxy. XVI 1837, 15. Cf. mod. Gr. ρεβίθι. On the properties of chickpea, cf. Diosc. II 104 (I 178, 1-16 Wellmann).

ςκόρδον: the syncopated form is the rule in papyri; see Mayser, *Grammatik* I.1, p. 123; Gignac, *Grammar* I, p. 307. See Gazza, "Prescrizioni mediche" (II), p. 97.

65 πῖν (r. πεῖν): see **43**, 9 comm.

προπώματος: cf. Hdn. Gr., περὶ μονήρους λέξεως II (III.2, p. 935, 22 f. Lentz) πρόπομα, ὅπερ καὶ πρόπωμα λέγεται; also Choerob., *Schol. in Theod.* 1, 339 Hilgard. The spelling with ω occurs in P.Oxy. XVI 2047, 2.

66 πύρεθρων (r. -ον): see Gazza, "Prescrizioni mediche" (II), p. 94; Till, *Die Arzneikunde der Kopten*, p. 47, no. 6; L.C.Youtie, *ZPE* 70 (1987) 82.

πίπερι κωκία (r. κοκκία): a sort of 'partitive apposition'; the quantified and the quantifier are simply juxtaposed. The construction is attested in papyri from the Ptolemaic period as well as in late texts without literary pretensions; cf. e.g. UPZ I 77 ii 12-14 χαλκοῦς στατηριαίους μαρςίπιον πλῆρες; BGU IV 1095, 15 f. ἄρτους ἀρτάβας δύο; further references and secondary literature in P.J.Parsons, *La Parola del Passato* 23 (1968) 289 f. See Gazza, "Prescrizioni mediche" (II), p. 92.

ςτι [] : a round letter, *prima facie* c. P.J.Parsons (*apud* ed.pr.) suggested ςτίβ[ι], and in fact a short β, as in λαβον in 60, is not unsuited to the trace (for the spelling ςτίβι of ςτίμ(μ)ι, cf. P.Ryl. IV 627, 154; P.Haun. III 47, 4 as read by L.C.Youtie, *BASP* 22 (1985) 366; and see LSJ, *s.v.* ςτίμμι. For the pharmacological use of antimony, see the references given in MPER XIII 8, 46 comm.). The sequence κγ ςτίβ[ι], however, is not obvious; perhaps the double oblique stroke is in the wrong position, and one should understand 'pepper corns 23'.

67 ….. [ ]αφνω· τοῦ: first, α or ω; second, κ or ν; then two uprights. Possibly δ]άφνῳ (for the masculine δάφνοc, cf. Diosc. IV 145 [RV], II 288, 13 Wellmann and, probably, PGM III 224). This at any rate is likelier than the adjective δ]αφνωτοῦ, which may possibly occur in *Geopon*. XII 39, 6, p. 383, 11 Beckh (see LSJ, *s.v.*). κοκκ[οδ]άφνῳ does not suit the traces.

πιπερίου: this appears to be the only certain instance of the diminutive πιπέριον. In P.Oxy. XVI 1862, 11c τὸ μικρὸν πίπεριν (registered as πιπέριον in the volume's word-index) one cannot exclude false addition of final -ν, and the same applies to SB XVI 12246, 3 and P.Vindob. G 42011, 1 (ed. J.Diethart, *Tyche* 1, 1986, 90; see note *ad loc*.). Cf. πιπεράδιον in P.Oxy. X 1299, 10 f. and πιπερίδιον in O.Cairo Eg. Mus. JdE 93632, line 7 (ed. R.S.Bagnall, *BASP* 23, 1986, 29, no. 28).

68 ἀπωπάνακος (r. ὀπο-): the spelling *apo*- occurs in Coptic (cf. e.g. Kropp, *Koptische Zaubertexte* I, K 53, 77; see W.C.Till, *Le Muséon* 64, 1951, 79, comm. on line 44; idem, *Die Arzneikunde der Kopten*, p. 107, no. 4) and in late Latin transcriptions (see *TLL* IX 2, 735, 66 f.). The same fluctuation appears in the word ὀποβάλcαμον; cf. BGU I 34 recto, col. 5, 13 (see BL 1, 10); for Latin texts, see *TLL* IX 2, 734, 66-70. The spelling with *a*- was probably caused by an erroneous connection with ἀπό (see W.Heraeus, *Arch. Lat. Lex*. 11, 1900, 63). See Gazza, "Prescrizioni mediche" (II), p. 91; Till, *Die Arzneikunde der Kopten*, p. 82 f., no. 107; PSI Congr. XVII 19, 3 comm.

69 νικᾶ⟨ν⟩: cf. PGM VII 423 κυβεύοντα νικᾶν, as title of the prescription.

70-71. Very close is PGM IV 2897 f. ἔχε δὲ καὶ φυλακτήριον θηλείας ὄνου ὀδόντα τῶν ἄνωθεν δεξιοῦ c⟨ι⟩αγονίου.

70 ὠδῶτα (r. ὀδόντα): a free accusative, characteristic of recipes; cf. e.g. Hipp., *Art*. 86 (p. 243, 21 Kw.) ἴηcιc· ἦν μὲν ἀπύρετοc ἢ ἐλλέβορον; *Mul*. II 158; 181 (VIII 336, 2 f.; 364, 2 L.; see V.Langholf, *Syntaktische Untersuchungen zu Hippokrates-Texten*, Wiesbaden 1977, p. 166); PGM II 141-143 ποίηcιc τῆc πράξεωc· τῇ πρώτῃ ἡμέρᾳ ὄνυχαc προβάτου, τῇ δευτέρᾳ αἰγὸc ὄνυχαc, τῇ τρίτῃ λύκου τρίχαc ἢ ἀcτράγαλον; 75 f.; I 244 f. Comparable is the free accusative that occurs in lists, accounts etc., on which see Mayser, *Grammatik* II.2, pp. 333-336.

ὑήνα: probably a misspelling of ὑαίνηc rather than of ὑηνόν, attested only in Plat., *Leg*. 819D. On the hyena in folklore, see *RE* I.1, *s.v.* Aberglaube, col. 73 (E.Riess); cf. PGM VII 203, 206.

71 τὸν (r. τῶν) ἄνω: as in PGM IV 2898 (quoted above, 70-71 comm.), ἄνω is referred to the teeth rather than, more naturally, to the jaw (cf., e.g., Arist., *H.A.* 536A, 17 ἡ κάτω ciαγών, ἡ ἄνω ciαγών). δεξιὰ ciαγών means here the half of the upper jaw on the right of the vomer. On the role of teeth in magic, see *RE* I.1, *s.v.* Aberglaube, col. 87 (E.Riess); E.Stemplinger, *Antiker Volksglaube* (Stuttgart 1948), p. 102.

72. See F.Maltomini, *ZPE* 85 (1991) 244.

νάρκ[η]c: for the properties of the electric ray, see **76**, 1-2 comm.

ὠξύνγι (r. ὀξύγγιον): for ιον > ι, see Gignac, *Grammar* II, p. 28.

ηνπροcτϊ: read ἔμπροcθε? Or perhaps ⟨τ⟩ὴν πόcθην?

F

Fr. A

2 [. . . .].υβη: perhaps [χαλι]ουβη? (cf. **A** 43). If so, one could consider an inversion of the two groups of names in **A** 25-43. In any case, it is not legitimate to put fr. A above fr. B in such a way as to place the putative [χαλι]ουβη of fr. A 2 in the line below that of ζαχθα]ηρ of fr. B 4 left.

3 [. . .]υροc: before the lacuna, the bottom of a round letter. Perhaps Ἐ[ρώτ]υροc (for Ἐρώτυλοc); see **A** 24 comm.

4 .[: at the edge, remains of a drawing or magical sign.

9 κυνοκεφάλου: the dog-faced baboon was sacred to Thoth (see Hopfner, *Tierkult*, pp. 26-30; idem, *Offenbarungszauber* I, § 428 f.; D. Wortmann, *Bonner Jahrb.* 166, 1966, 99 f.).

10-15. These lines are enclosed by an ouroboros (see **10**, 2 comm.).

Fr. B

In the middle of the fragment is a drawing of the front of a human head wearing a radiate crown.

2 right μ]ενουλα[θ?

3 right μαρμουρ[: variation of Μαρμαραωθ (on which see **42**, 52 comm.; also **57**, 20 left comm.). For the spelling μαρμου-, cf. Kropp, *Koptische Zaubertexte* III, p. 125 n. 9.

Provenance   V/VI AD
unknown

P.Mil. Vogl. inv. 1251.

ED.PR.: F.Maltomini, "I papiri greci," in: "Nuovi papiri magici in copto, greco e aramai-
co," *SCO* 29 (1979) 94-112.

COMM.: ed.pr.

TRANSL.: ed.pr.; R.Kotansky in Betz, *Translation*, no. CXXIV.

PHOTO: ed.pr., plates VII-VIII.

DESCR.: papyrus; 14.7 × 24 cm. The lower part of an opistograph roll written *transversa
charta*. On the verso the text runs with the fibers upside down in relation to the recto,
and it starts two thirds of the way down the sheet. A kollesis 10.4 cm from the upper
edge of the recto. In all likelihood complete at the bottom (of the recto).

LOC.: Istituto di Papirologia, Università degli Studi, Milan.

The recto contains three sections: lines 2-6 a χαριτήϲιον (?); 7-9 a
κατακλητικόν (or rather κατακλιτικόν?); 10-33 a spell whose precise
purpose cannot be determined, but probably an aggressive one. In the third
section the text is written in two columns, the one on the left continuing that
on the right. Between them is a drawing of a human figure, certainly the wax
puppet mentioned in the instructions (lines 12-13). The drawing closely
resembles that in the accompanying Coptic codex (see intr. to **96-98**), where
it represents a worshipper with arms raised in adoration. Above both figures
are the same magical signs and letters.[1] The text on the verso is broken away
at its bottom, and so the specific purpose of the spell cannot be ascertained.
What is preserved contains instructions, and then a logos in which chthonic
powers are commanded to send a corpse-daemon (see 9 comm.).

Dicola (↓ 9, 17, → 6, 7); double oblique stroke (→ 5, 8). καί is often
abbreviated, but the abbreviation mark is sometimes used also with the full
form κε/ (↓ 7, 22, 25).

---

[1] In both cases there is not an exact correspondence between drawing and text: the
Coptic codex does not explain the magical signs and the letters that surround the head; **97**
does not explain the arms raised in worship.

↓

χαρ[. .].

ὀββὰ γραφόμενα κ(αὶ) τὸ ἔναν
4 βάλε εἰς cωτύρια κ(αὶ) τὸ ἔναν
χόϲον εἰς τὸν ὗκον·

θαθη θαθω.

κατακλητικόν. ἐμα ποντυκοῦ κὲ γρά-
8 ψον τρήγονον ὤϲτρακον κ(αὶ) χῶϲον
εἰς τὸν εἶκον· θραξ τραξ: βραξ.

	κυρύον ἀκάπνυϲτον 12
κ(αὶ) κέμυϲον	λάβε κὲ πῆϲον ἀντρηᾶν
28 τὴν κύθραν	κὲ γράψον τοὺς χαρακτῦ-
νερὸν	ροϲ χαρτύου κ(αὶ) βάλε ἔϲωθεν
ἔωϲ τοῦ	τοῦ κυρίου κ(αὶ) γράψον τὰ 16
[. .]υ τοῦ	τρία: ω κ(αὶ) τὰ μετ' αὐτὸν
32 [ἀν]τρηᾶ μο	ἐν τῇ κεφαλῇ τοῦ ἀντρηᾶ
[ ]	κ(αὶ) ὤϲτέα εἰϲφατηϲ τὰ τρήα

κέντηϲον τὸ ἀρηϲτερὸν   20
εἰϲ τὸ ἀρηϲτερὸν ὠπθαρμὸν
τοῦ ἀντρηᾶ κὲ τὸ δεξυὸν
ἐν τοῦ δεξυοῦ, τὸ τοῦ νό-
του ἐπὴ τὴν κεφαλὴν   24
κὲ βάλε αὐτὸν εἰϲ κύθραν κενὴν
κ(αὶ) ἄφηϲ τὴν χίθραν εἰϲ {ει} ϲκότοϲ

3 ᾠὰ   κ/ Pap.   ἔν   4 cωτήρια   κ/ Pap.   ἔν   5 χῶϲον   οἶκον
7 αἷμα ποντικοῦ   κε/ Pap., l. καὶ   8 τρίγονον ὄϲτρακον   κ/ Pap.   9
οἶκον   τραξ: τ ex corr. (ex ο?), dicolon in Pap.   12 κηρίον ἀκάπνιϲτον   13 καὶ
ποίηϲον ἀνδριάντα   14 καὶ   14-15 χαρακτῆραϲ χαρτίῳ   15 κ/ Pap.   16
κηρίου   κ/ Pap.   17 dicolon in Pap.   κ/ Pap.   αὐτῶν   18 ἀνδριάντοϲ
19 κ/ Pap.   ὀϲτέα   εἰϲφατηϲ quid significet obscurum   τρία   20 ἀριϲτερὸν
21 τὸν ἀριϲτερὸν ὀφθαλμὸν   22 ἀνδριάντος   κε/ Pap., l. καὶ   δεξιὸν
23 τῷ δεξιῷ   23-24 νότου ἐπὶ   25 κε/ Pap., l. καὶ   καινὴν   26
κ/ Pap.   ἄφεϲ   κύθραν   27 κ/ Pap.   γέμιϲον   32 ἀνδριάντος

→   1   ῥοδοδάμνα τρῆψον μετὲ ὦξου
        κὲ ῥάντυσον τὰ πρόθυρα τοῦ μνη-
        μύου κ(αὶ) φόρηει ϲτέμμα ἀπὸ αὐτô⟨ν⟩
    4   κὲ ὑπέντουϲ λόγου ἔξαψ[ο]ν τοῦ
        μνημύου· // πρôτε ἄνκε[λε τ]ôν
        καταπθωνύον B‾α‾ρ‾ο‾υ‾χ: κὲ ϲέ, πορύ-
        μορφε ἄγγελε Ολ‾α‾μ‾τ‾η‾ρ: ταύ[τ]η τῦ
    8   ὥρᾳ μή μου παρακούϲατε, // ἀλλὰ
        [ἐ]κπέμψατέ μου . . . ἀφόβοϲ ἀβαλ . οϲ
        πηοῦντά μου πᾶϲαν τὴν . . . ουτην‾
        [.]υ[c. 20   ] . [.] . . [.]

_____   _____   _____

1 ῥοδοδάφναϲ?   1-2 τρῖψον μετὰ ὄξουϲ καὶ ῥάντιϲον   2-3 μνημείου
3 κ/ Pap.   primitus φορηεϲτεμμα exaratum, deinde ι insertum   φόρει   αὐτῶν
4 καὶ εἰπόντοϲ λόγον?   5 μνημείου   // in Pap.   5-6 πρῶτε ἄγγελε τῶν
καταχθονίων   6, 7 dicola in Pap.   6-7 καὶ ϲύ, πολύμορφε   7 τῇ   8 // in
Pap.   9 μοι   ἀφόβωϲ   10 ποιοῦντά μοι

↓ (mag. signs) Spell to secure favor (?). Written eggs, and the one |⁴ put in a latrine,
the other bury in the house: (mag. signs) thathê thathô.   Spell for calling in customers (?).
Blood of a mouse, and write |⁸ on a triangular potsherd and bury it in the house: thrax trax
brax (mag. signs).   (Drawing) |¹² Take unsmoked wax and make a figurine. Write the
magical signs on a small piece of papyrus and place it inside |¹⁶ the wax and write the three
ô's and the letters with them on the head of the figurine, and the three bones of a - - - |²⁰
stick the left one into the left eye of the figurine and the right one into the right eye, and
the dorsal one |²⁴ into the head, and put it (the figurine) into a new earthenware pot and
leave the pot in the dark and fill |²⁸ the pot with water, only (?) up to the shoulder (?) of
the |³² figurine.

→ Crush rhododendron leaves with vinegar and sprinkle the entrance of the tomb, and
bring a wreath made of them |⁴ and, while pronouncing the formula, attach it to the tomb:
"First angel of those in the underworld, Barouch, and you, many-formed angel, Olamtêr, in
this |⁸ hour do not disobey me, but send to me - - - without fear, without harm (?), doing
me every - - -.

↓ 1-2. For the zeta with the stroke through it, see **10**, 4 comm. The last sign in 2 looks like the Hebrew letter *lamed* within a circle.

2 χαρ[ ] : what emerges from the lacuna is a 6 mm oblique rising to the right. E.G.Turner (*apud* ed.pr.) proposed χαρ[τί]α (the stroke could indeed be the prolonged tail of alpha), but it is difficult to provide this with a context. Perhaps we are dealing with an abbreviation stroke: χαρ[ιτ](ήϲιον)? If so, the prescription would have exactly the same structure as the following one (lines 7-9): (a) heading (κατακλητικόν 7 ~ χαριτήϲιον 2); (b) indication of an ingredient (αἷμα ποντικοῦ 7 ~ ᾠὰ γραφόμενα 3); (c) καὶ + indication of the other operations; (d) magical signs and words to be written.

3 ὀββά: r. ᾠά (so also H.C.Youtie [*apud* ed.pr., p. 123], who compared Hesych. *s.v.* ὤβεα· τὰ ᾠά. Ἀργεῖοι [IV, p. 317, 13 Schmidt]; and more recently F.Th.Gignac, letter of 9 May 1991). The spelling with -β(β)- appears to reflect a pronunciation of ᾠά with a [w] glide between the two vowels. The same pronunciation seems to be rendered by ὀουῶν for ᾠῶν in BGU XIII 2358, 4, 6 (early 4th cent.). Influence of Latin *ova*, however, cannot be excluded. For writing on eggs, cf. PGM XII 100 (a χαριτήϲιον!); PGM VII 521 f.; Delatte, *Anecdota Atheniensia*, pp. 462, 2; 466, 22; 596, 16; also the Aramaic charms in Naveh-Shaked, *Amulets*, pp. 233 (p. 2, l. 16 f.), 235 (l. 9 f.); *Handwörterbuch des deutschen Aberglaubens* II, *s.v.* Ei, coll. 629, 640 note 527.

3-4 τὸ ἔναν - - - τὸ ἔναν: for neut. ἔναν, see Gignac, *Grammar* II, p. 184; Jannaris, *Grammar*, p. 550, § 25. For the repetition of εἷϲ preceded by the article to mean 'the one ... the other', cf. LXX Is. 6, 2 ἒξ πτέρυγεϲ τῷ ἑνὶ καὶ ἒξ πτέρυγεϲ τῷ ἑνί; *Epist. Barn.* 7, 9 (cf. also 7, 6 f.); *Anth. Pal.* XI 381, 2 (Palladas); Palladius, *Hist. Laus.* 35 (100, 12 f. Butler); Chrest.Mitt., 372 v 14; also PGM XIII 131-133 γράψαϲ οὖν εἰϲ τὰ δύο μέρη τοῦ νίτρου τὴν ϲτήλην, ἀπόλειξον τὸ ἓν μέροϲ καὶ τὸ ἓν μέροϲ βρέξαϲ εἰϲ τὸν κρατῆρα ἀπόπλυνε, where the second τὸ ἓν μέροϲ of the papyrus was wrongly changed into τὸ ἕτερον by Preisendanz (see F.Maltomini in: *Miscellanea Papyrologica* [Papyrologica Florentina VII, 1980], p. 175).

4 ϲωτύρια (r. ϲωτήρια): 'latrine'; cf. *Anth. Pal.* IX 642 *in lemm.*; Suid., *s.v.* ἀφ' ἑδρῶν: ἀπὸ τῶν ἑδρῶν. ἕδραι γὰρ λέγονται αἱ ϲέλλαι, ϲελλάρια, ϲωτήρια (I, p. 427, 14 f. Adler); cf. also Hesych., *s.v.* ἀφεδρῶ-νεϲ (I, p. 290, 86 Latte); *Lex. Seguer. Synag.*, p. xxvii Boysen (= *Lex. Gr. min.*, p. 36); Byzantine attestations in Ducange, *Glossarium*, *s.v.* The use of a latrine for the performance of magical practices has no parallel in the

Greek magical papyri. It is widespread, however, in medieval magic (latrines were believed to be haunted); see *Handwörterbuch des deutschen Aberglaubens* I, *s.v.* Abort, coll. 93-95. For the Jewish and Muslim world, see e.g. A. Cohen, *Everyman's Talmud* (London 1932), pp. 278-280.

5 χόcον (r. χῶcον): 'bury', as in 8 and in PGM V 337, 343; LXII 106.

6 θαθη θαθω: these words together with the preceding magical signs are what is to be written on the eggs. The sequence is unparalleled as such, but cf. PGM IV 2414 φθουθο οθομ μαθαθου; XIII 919 θαφθω; lines 2-3 of the silver tablet from Antioch (Pisidia) edited by D.M.Robinson, *Hesperia* 22 (1953) 172-174 (= SEG XII 484) θαθωαθφρο; also **63**, 12-14. For sequences of magical words which differ only in the final letter, see **96 A 1** comm. θαθω however might be equivalent to Θωθω (PGM XIII 810, etc.), Egyptian *Ḏḥwtj-ᶜ3* 'great Thoth'. For Θαθ = Θωθ, see PGM, Vol. 3 (Index), p. 222, *s.v.* Θαθ.

7 κατακλητικόν: the word occurs only in PGM IV 2373 as title of a spell: καταπρακτικὸν καὶ κατακλητικὸν ἐργαcτηρίου ἢ οἰκίαc ἢ ὅπου ἐὰν αὐτὸ ἱδρύcῃc. LSJ glosses 'invocatory spell', but the context suggests rather a spell for 'calling in', 'attracting' customers, business, etc. ("Umsatz förderndes Mittel" Preisendanz; "Kundschaft ladend" Eitrem; cf. app.cr. *ad loc.*). Our papyrus, however, might also present a misspelling of κατακλιτικόν, a spell for causing illness. In all likelihood the word occurs in PGM VII 430 (cf. app.cr. *ad loc.*); and cf. κατακλίνω in PGM IV 2076, 2450, 2497, 2624; LXIV 1 f.; O 2, 31 f.; Bonner, *SMA*, D. 156 and p. 118; see also Jordan, "Survey," nos. 146 and 163.

ἔμα (r. αἷμα): for blood used as ink, see P.Oslo I 1, 72 comm.; S.Eitrem, *Opferritus und Voropfer der Griechen und Römer* (Oslo 1915), p. 448 f.; N.G.Politis, *Byz. Zeitschr.* 1 (1892) 562 f.

ποντυκοῦ (r. ποντικοῦ): 'mouse', as in modern Greek. For writing with the blood of a mouse, cf. Delatte, *Anecdota Atheniensia*, p. 73, 32.

7-8 γράλψον τρήγονον ὤcτρακον: standard Greek would require γράψον εἰc (or ἐπὶ). This transitive use of γράφω appears to be a popular extension to the active of a use which is normal in the passive: cf. LXX Ez. 2, 10 ἐν αὐτῇ (a roll) γεγραμμένα ἦν τὰ ὄπιcθεν καὶ τὰ ἔμπροcθεν; NT Apoc. 5, 1 βιβλίον γεγραμμένον ἔcωθεν καὶ ὄπιcθεν; also above, line 3 ὠὰ γραφόμενα; PGM XIII 133 f. (= 692) γραφέcθω δὲ τὸ νίτρον.

8 τρήγονον ὤcτρακον (r. τρίγωνον ὄcτρακον): cf. PGM XXXVI 256 ὄcτρακον ἀπὸ τριόδου τρίγωνον. In these passages ὄcτρακον means

'sherd', as in **96 A** 50; PGM XXXVI 189; XLVI 5. In PGM IV 2218; VII 300a, 374, 467 (also Audollent, *DT*, 234, 32) the word means 'shell' (see O.Wilcken I, p. 7). On ταρίχου ὄςτρακον in PGM XII 366, see K. Preisendanz, *Phil. Wochenschrift* 53 (1933) 1033 f. On triangularity in magic, see P.Oslo I 1, 256 comm.; L.Deubner, *Gnomon* 2 (1926) 410; *RAC* IV, *s.v.* Dreieck, col. 311 f. (A.Stuiber). Cf. also the shape of **41**.

9 θραξ τραξ βραξ: the sequence is unparalleled as such. τραξ recalls τετραξ, one of the "original" *Ephesia grammata* (αςκι κατασκι λιξ τετραξ δαμναμενευς αιςια; see K.Preisendanz, *RAC* V, col. 516); cf. τραξ τετραξ in I.Cret. II, XIX 7, 15 (4th cent. BC); *Test. Sal.* XVIII 20 (p. 55*, 2 McCown) Κατράξ, *vv.ll.* ᾽Ιατράξ, ᾽Ατράξ (all of which, however, may be corruptions of κ(ύρι)ε ῥήξ; see P.Reiner Cent., p. 304 Appendix); *Cat. Cod. Astr. Gr.* VIII.2, p. 175, 34 Πόβραξ. Sequences of magical words which differ only in the first letter are frequent, cf. e.g. **6**, 2 ιβει αβει, ςελτι βελτι; PGM III 484 ξιχα μιχα; IV 1805 f. μαρβα καρβα; XII 112 νεννανα ςεννανα; XIII 809 τουχαρ ςουχαρ; and see A.Dieterich, *Papyrus magica musei Lugdunensis Batavi*, Jahrb. cl. Phil. Supplbd. 16 (1888) 769 (= *Kleine Schriften*, p. 23); idem, *Rhein. Mus.* 56 (1901) 90 f. (= *Kleine Schriften*, p. 214 f.); A.Jacoby, *ARW* 29 (1931) 205; W.Deonna, *Genava* 22 (1944) 128.

12 κυρύον (r.κηρίον): honeycomb, i.e. the rough wax of the honeycomb.

ἀκάπνυςτον (r. -ιςτον): the adjective indicates wax taken from hives that had not been smoked out when the honey was extracted (for technical details, see the ed.pr.; also H.Chouliara-Raïos, *L'abeille et le miel en Égypte d'après les papyrus grecs*, Jannina 1989, p. 108). What mattered was the purity of the wax; cf. PGM IV 2378, 2945 (κηρὸς ἄπυρος); Delatte, *Anecdota Atheniensia*, pp. 16, 12; 77, 8; 410, 2; 416, 2, etc. (παρθένος); 406, 2 (καθαρός); 646, 11 (νέος); 648, 3 (καινός).

13 πῆςον (r. ποίηςον): the same spelling in P.Herm. 15, 6.

ἀντρηᾶν: for ἀνδριᾶν, accusative of ἀνδριάς declined -ᾶς, -ᾶ, -ᾷ, -ᾶν (cf. genitive ἀντρηᾶ in lines 18, 22, 32).

14-15 χαρακτῦ|ρος (r. χαρακτῆρας): the magical signs in 10.

15 χαρτύου (r. χαρτίῳ): the verb γράφω is constructed with the dative without preposition also in **96 A** 23 (cf. also 51 φύλλῳ, 56 χάρτῃ).

βάλε ἔςωθεν: -θεν is here completely stereotyped and meaningless; cf. PGM XXXVI 369 βαλὼν ἔςωθεν. On the inserting of written objects into figurines, cf. PGM IV 2359-72, 1846 f., 3143; V 384. In all of these passages the intention was to animate the statuette so as to gain its services (see Dodds, *The Greek and the Irrational*, p. 293 f.). Closer to the present text is VPB V 142, 16 f., where the procedure is prescribed in a disjunctive spell.

17 τὰ μετ' αὐτόν (r. αὐτῶν): the three iotas and the three sigmas which appear above the head of the figurine (line 11).

18 ἐν τῇ κεφαλῇ: on the inscribing of parts of the body in magic, see P.Oslo I 1, pp. 38-42.

19 ὠcτέα (r. ὀcτέα): bones play an important role especially in aggressive magic: cf. e.g. Tac., *Ann.* II 69, 5; Horat., *Sat.* I 8, 22; PGM IV 1886.

εἰcφατηc: the bones of what or whom? Perhaps cφα⟨κ⟩τῆc? (if so, ει- is prothetic *i-* before c + consonant; see Gignac, *Grammar* I, p. 312; cf. e.g. l. 5 of the inscription from Kara-aga (Lykaonia, III AD) published by J.R.S. Sterrett, *An Epigraphical Journey in Asia Minor*, Boston 1888, p. 166, no. 156 (also in L.Robert, *Études Anatoliennes*, Paris 1937, p. 96) ἰcφαγέντι; Delatte, *Anecdota Atheniensia*, p. 82, 4 αἷμαν - - - κτήνου ἠcφακτοῦ). But referred to what? Or rather φά⟨τ⟩τηc? (but what to make of εἰc- ?).

20 κέντηcον: the verb seems to be used here in the sense of 'stick', not in the usual one of 'prick'.

20-23 κέντηcον - - - εἰc - - - ἐν - - -: it is difficult to appreciate the difference in meaning of the two constructions. In all likelihood, only an example of the indifference to or uncertainty about the use of ἐν and εἰc (see Mayser, *Grammatik* II.2, pp. 371-373; Blass-Debrunner-Funk, *Grammar*, §§ 205-206, 218; Bauer, *Wörterbuch*, *s.vv.* εἰc 9, ἐν I 6).

23-24 τὸ τοῦ νόἰτου ἐπὶ (r. νώτου ἐπὶ) τὴν κεφαλήν: the interpretation offered here is by H.C.Youtie (*apud* ed.pr., p. 124).

24 ἐπή: so spelled in BGU IV 1185, 18 and, possibly, P.Lond. V 1660, 27.

25 βάλε αὐτὸν εἰc κύθραν: also the little dog made of flour or wax in PGM IV 2943 ff. is to be placed εἰc κωθώνιον καινόν (2952). The wax figurines that accompanied **45** and **47** were found in vessels.

κύθραν: spelled χίθραν in 26. On the fluctuation κύθρα, χύτρα, χύθρα, see Gignac, *Grammar* I, p. 94.

κενήν: in all likelihood an error for καινήν (in *Cat. Cod. Astr. Gr.* IV, p. 132, 2 f. ἔπαρον λεκάνην καινήν, ὁμοίωc κενήν we are probably dealing with variants and, if so, καινήν is the correct one). Everything new is ritually clean and in possession of all its magic power; see P.Oslo I 1, 266 comm.; Pradel, *Gebete*, p. 128 n. 4. The use of a 'new earthenware pot' also has a long history in scientific writings. It is prescribed frequently in medical texts as early as in the *Corpus Hippocraticum*: cf. *Morb*. III 17 (VII 156, 12 L.), *Mul*. II 140 (VII 314 L.) and the other passages quoted by J.Jouanna in his edition of Hipp., *Morb*. II (Paris 1983), p. 195 n. 4 (Jouanna refers also to the ancient Egyptian Papyrus Ebers 325 von Deines-Grapow-Westendorf; cf. also 305, 642, 786+787); cf. also Diosc. II 70, 4; 76, 6 (I 144, 15; 153, 13 Wellmann), etc.; Gal., *Alim. fac.* II 9 (VI 576, 11 K.); *Simpl. medic.* I 3 (XII 244, 13), etc. For alchemical writings, cf. P.Leid. X 442 Halleux; P.Holm. 299, 477, 486 Halleux. In such texts, however, what matters is not the ritual purity but the need of complete cleanness, which, for earthenware, could be guaranteed only if it was new; see G.Björck, *Apsyrtus, Julius Africanus et l'hippiatrique grecque* (Uppsala 1944), p. 61; R.Halleux, *Les alchimistes grecs* I (Paris 1981), p. 34.

27-29 κέμυϲον (r. γέμιϲον) | τὴν κύθραν | νερόν: for γεμίζω taking two accusatives, cf. P.Flor. II 195, 4-6 ἵνα - - - αὐτὸν γεμίϲῃϲ ἄρτων ἀρτάβαϲ δύο; SB VI 9074, 5 f. γεμίϲαι αὐτοὺϲ ξύλα καύϲιμα (cf. also LSJ, *s.v.*, II).

29 νερόν: 'water'; cf. mod. Gr. νερό. The form with epsilon occurs in another 6th century papyrus, SB XVI 12703 ii 2, iii 2, v 4. The earliest attestations of νερόν in literature are roughly contemporary; see Sophocles, *Lexicon, s.v.* νηρόϲ. For the form with eta in papyri, cf. **94**, 44 and the occurrences indicated in P.Oxy. LVI 3865, 35 comm.; also P.Monac. III 131, 12, 13; P.Haun. III 58, 8, 13 (written νειρῶν). For the history of the word, see A.Thumb, *Die griechische Sprache im Zeitalter des Hellenismus* (Strasbourg 1901), pp. 94 f., 97, 99; esp. H.Eideneier, *Sogenannte christliche Tabuwörter im Griechischen* (Miscell. Byz. Monacensia 5, Munich 1966), pp. 104-119 (with further literature).

The use of dipping statuettes in water is unparalleled in the Greek magical papyri, but see *Handwörterbuch des deutschen Aberglaubens* VII, *s.v.* Rachepuppe, col. 459; J.Grimm, *Deutsche Mythologie* II (Berlin 1876), p. 913 ff.

30-33. P.J.Parsons (*apud* ed.pr.) restored *exempli gratia* ἕωϲ τοῦ | [ὤμο]υ τοῦ | [ἀν]τρηᾶ μόl[νον].

→ 1 ῥοδοδάμνα: probably from ῥοδοδάφνη (cf. PGM VII 150-152 ῥοδοδάφνην μεθ᾽ ἅλμηϲ βρέξαϲ καὶ τρίψαϲ ῥᾶνον). If so, the ending seems to suggest ῥοδοδάφναϲ (cf. also 3 ἀπὸ αὐτῶν) rather than ῥοδοδάφνην (for the plural, cf. Gal., *Protr.* 11, p. 112, 19 Wenkebach; Oder-Hoppe, *Corp. Hippiatr. Graec.* I, p. 167, 6 ἐὰν φάγῃ ῥοδοδάφναϲ).

2 ῥάντυϲον (r. ῥάντιϲον): sprinkling of liquids is mentioned also in **100**, 5; PGM II 177; III 41; IV 2158.

3 ἀπὸ αὐτô⟨ν⟩ (r. αὐτῶν): i.e. ῥοδοδαφνῶν (see 1 comm.), rather than προθύρων (cf. e.g. Joh. Malal., *Chronogr.* XI 272, 21 Dindorf [p. 44 Schenk = Migne PG 97, 413 A] ϲτέφανοϲ ἀπὸ ἐλαιοκλάδων). For wreaths placed on tombs, see K.Baus, *Der Kranz in Antike und Christentum* (Theophaneia 2, Bonn 1940), pp. 118-124, 128-132, 136 f. Cf. PGM IV 333 f.

4 κὲ ὑπέντουϲ λόγου: if καὶ εἰπόντοϲ λόγον is the correct interpretation of the sequence, the subject of the genitive absolute is the same as the subject of the main sentence (see Mayser, *Grammatik* II.3, pp. 68-70; Mandilaras, *Verb*, § 909 f.; for λόγον without the article, cf. PGM III 699 and XII 366). But two other possibilities may be entertained: (i) καὶ εἰπὼν τοὺϲ λόγου⟨ϲ⟩ (for the plural, cf. PGM II 146); (ii) καὶ εἰπὲ τοὺϲ λόγου⟨ϲ καὶ⟩ (suggested by H.C.Youtie, *apud* ed.pr., p. 124).

5-6 πρôτε ἄνκε[λε τ]ὸν | καταπθωνύον: r. πρῶτε ἄγγε[λε τ]ῶν καταχθονίων. For πρῶτοϲ ἄγγελοϲ, cf. PGM XIII 147 f. (= 455); possibly P.Carlsberg 52 (inv. 35), 1 (see Brashear, *Magica varia*, pp. 40 and 53); also VII 261 f. For ἄγγελοϲ τῶν καταχθονίων, cf. Audollent, *DT*, 74, 1 f.; 75, A 1-3 καταγράφω καὶ κατα[τί]θω ἀνγέληϲ (*sic*) καταχθονίοιϲ. On these infernal angels, see J.Michl, *RAC* V, col. 55 f.; also J.M.R.Cormack, *HThR* 44 (1951) 31; M.Guarducci, "Gli 'angeli' di Tera," in: *Mélanges helléniques offerts à G.Daux* (Paris 1974), pp. 147-157 (= M.Guarducci, *Scritti scelti sulla religione greca e romana e sul cristianesimo* [EPRO 98, Leiden 1983], pp. 60-70). A less probable interpretation: πρῶτον (or πρῶτα) κα[λῶ τ]ὸν | καταχθόνιον Βαρουχ καὶ ϲέ, κτλ.; cf. PGM XIII 139 f.; Delatte, *Anecdota Atheniensia*, p. 51, 8 f. ἐπικαλοῦ πρῶτα τοὺϲ ἀγγέλουϲ; and see Keyßner, *Gottesvorstellung*, pp. 9-13.

6 Βαρουχ: Hebrew *bārûkh* 'blessed' (cf. here **47**, 15; **49**, 3, 34; **50**, 35, 36; **51**, 3; **75**, 21; **96** A 4; and see Martinez, *P.Mich. 757*, p. 77). As in the present papyrus, however, the word appears as the name of a daemon in some Coptic magical documents: Kropp, *Koptische Zaubertexte* I, M 108; Stegemann, *Zaubertexte*, XXVIII 1; VBP V 140, 3 (cf. also 139, 28).

7 Ολαμτηρ: possibly a conflation of Hebrew *'ôlām* 'eternity' and Coptic ⲉⲛⲧⲏⲣ 'gods'. For the occurrences of *'ôlām* in magical words, see especially A.Jacoby, *ARW* 28 (1930) 276-285; see also **10**, 4-5 comm. and **44**, 17 comm.

8 μή μου παρακούσατε, ἀλλὰ κτλ.: cf. e.g. **42**, 43; **45**, 22 f.; PGM IV 367-369 (and the parallels **47**, 17 f.; **48** J 19 f.; **50**, 49 f.); XIVa 10; P.Carlsberg 52 (ed. Brashear, *Magica varia*, pp. 16-62), lines 21-23 μὴ γενοῦ μοι παρήκοος, [ἀλ]λὰ γενοῦ μοι ὑπήκοος. For μή and the second person aorist imperative, see Mandilaras, *Verb*, § 568.

9 [ἐ]κπέμψατέ μου (r. μοι) . . : the magician asks for the dispatch of the spirit of the dead man buried in the tomb, who will have to serve as ὑπηρέτης (cf. PGM IV 1467-69 ἀναπέμψατέ μοι τῶν νεκύων τούτων εἴδωλα πρὸς ὑπηρεσίαν; 1328 etc.). But where is the object of [ἐ]κπέμψατε? After μου one might guess τὸν or τὰ, but the traces are too scanty for any interpretation.

μου: for the frequent, probably syntactical, confusion μου/μοι, cου/cοι (cf. also 10), see Gignac, *Grammar* I, p. 215 n. 1; see also Humbert, *La disparition du datif*, p. 166 ff.

ἀφόβος (r. ἀφόβως): the magician protects himself against possible dangers connected with the daemon's apparition; see **66**, 22 comm.

ἀβαλ . ος: the unread letter is perhaps β, though ρ or c are also possible. Another adverb is likely: ἀβαλβὸς for ἀβλαβῶς?

10 τὴν . . . . ουτην: first, the base of a round letter; second, a speck at mid-level at the edge of a hole; third, two converging obliques, as of χ or κ; fourth, π? (ex corr.?). We can make nothing of this. In all likelihood, the object of ποιοῦντα.

98

Provenance   V/VI AD
unknown

P.Mil. Vogl. inv. 1258-1259-1260, 1262, 1261, 1254-1255, 1256, 1257.

ED.PR.: F.Maltomini, "I papiri greci," in: "Nuovi papiri magici in copto, greco e aramai-
co," *SCO* 29 (1979) 113-120.

COMM.: ed.pr.

TRANSL.: Betz, *Translation*, no. CXXV a-f.

PHOTO: ed.pr., plates VIII, XI, XII.

DESCR.: six papyri are grouped under this number.

No. 1: three fragments (A 9.5 × 3.7 cm; B 2.2 × 2.1 cm; C 11.7 × 9.4 cm) written
against the fibers on the recto; the verso is blank. Fr. A is broken away on both
sides; above and below the four preserved lines of writing is a space of some 0.5 cm.
Fr. B is broken away on all sides. Fr. C is broken away at the bottom; near the edge
are remains of a magical sign or drawing. There is a kollesis ca. 2 cm below the
upper edge. Inv. 1258-1259-1260.

No. 2: 4.9 × 9.2 cm. The Greek text runs with the fibers on the verso (?) (on the other
side, also with the fibers, an Aramaic text; see *SCO* 29, 1979, 128, fr. 1). Broken away
on both sides and at the top; below the text, blank space of 2.5 cm. Inv. 1262.

No. 3: two fragments (A 3.5 × 5.8 cm; B 5.3 × 7.5 cm) broken away on all sides. The
writing runs with the fibers on the recto; the verso is blank. Parts of the same lines
appear to be preserved on the two fragments, probably in the order A-B. Inv. 1261.

No. 4: two fragments (A 5.5 × 6.2 cm; B 5.9 × 6.7 cm) broken away on both sides and
at the top; below the text, blank space of 4 and 6.1 cm respectively. The writing
runs with the fibers on the recto; the verso is blank. Inv. 1254-1255.

No. 5: 6 × 11.2 cm. Broken away at left, top and right; below the text, blank space of
1.5 cm. The writing runs with the fibers on the recto, and the verso is blank. There
is a kollesis ca. 3 cm from the left edge. Between lines 4 and 5 is a blank space of
5.5 cm. The hand could be the same as that of **96 A**. Inv. 1256.

No. 6: 14.5 × 2.7 cm. Broken away at top and bottom. The Greek text runs with the
fibers on the verso; on the recto, also with the fibers, an Aramaic text (see *SCO* 29,
1979, 129, fr. 3). The strip coincides exactly with the overlap of a kollesis join.
Inv. 1257.

LOC.: Istituto di Papirologia, Università degli Studi, Milan.

No. 1

Fr. A   Fr. B

1   ]λακαλου: σαλακαλου: πμα[1   ]αυνᾱν[
     ]η̄νενμαυ κερκηβι: cινα ̣[   ] αὐτὸς [
     ]οαυ[̣]ν καυ Καυλυουκαυ [
4   ]ο̣ αὐτοῦ ξύλα θ[̣ ̣ ̣ ̣ ̣] ̣ ̣[

Fr. C

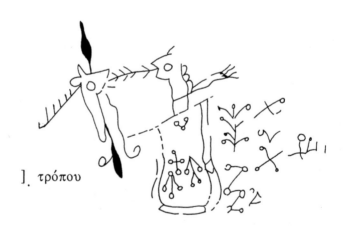

]̣ τρόπου

Fr. A 1-2 dicola in Pap.

No. 2

```
        —   —   —
1       ]οιον υνου αδ[
        ] ἀλυλούια το .[
        ] C̅α̅β̅α̅ω̅θ̅ τὸν ο[
4       ]. . . . ξ . . . . . [
        ] μὴ παρακούς[ης
        ]ου . ουγαν[
            ]αει Αδο̅ν̅ο̅[
8           ] . . . . . νον[
            ] ἄκουϲον [
```

No. 3

Fr. A

```
        —   —   —

        (remains of drawings)

1       ] . [ . ]βιν . α . [
        ]λιβωνοϲ̣ν[
        ] . ϲ̣υ . . υν . [
4       ] . . . . . . [
        —   —   —
```

Fr. B

```
        —   —   —

        (remains of drawings)

1       ]ω
        ]ϩ̣ο̅ϒ̅ τε4ΒΡΙΜ[
        ]ευκο̣ν[
        —   —   —
```

No. 4

Fr. A

```
1       ]ριου ανο[
        ] . υυπ[ . ]λυμο[
```

Fr. B

```
1       ] . . . . τοι[ . . . ] . . . . [
```

No. 2, 1 οἴνου?   2 ἀλληλούια

No. 5

— — —

1   ]η̣ [
         ]ηλ[
         Αδονα[
4   Cυβα͞ωθ̣ [

]ρ̣οc

No. 6

— — —

1   [̣]. . . . ξ ̣ρ ̣. . . cὲ ὡρκύζω [κ]α̣[τ]ὰ
     τὸν ἁγίον ὀνομ[ά]τ̣[ων] ̣[̣ ̣] traces
     βαροχ c͞ημο   traces
4   . . .[

— — —

No. 6, 1 ὀρκίζω   2 τῶν ἁγίων

No. 1, Fr. A - - -*lakalou salakalou pma*- - -*ênenmau kerkêbi sina*- - -*oau n kau Kauly-*
oukau - - - of it pieces of wood - - -. Fr. B - - -*aunan*- - - he - - -. Fr. C (drawing) - - -
manner.

No. 2 - - - of wine (?) - - - hallelujah - - - *Sabaôth* the - - - do not disobey me - - -
Adonoei (?) - - - hear - - -.

No. 5 - - - *Adonai (?)* - - - *Sybaôth* - - -.

No. 6 - - - I adjure you by the holy names - - - *baroch sêmo* - - -.

No. 1. Fr. A.

1 cαλακαλου: for cαλα cf. Schwab, *Vocabulaire de l'angélologie*,
p. 418, who interpreted it as Hebrew *Selāh*, "terme fréquent dans les Psaumes

et constant dans les formules de conjuration"; see also *DACL* 1.1, col. 149; Naveh-Shaked, *Amulets and Magic Bowls*, p. 36. Many magical words begin with ϲαλα; see PGM, Vol. 3 (Index), p. 269, and the indications given in the ed.pr. For καλου, cf. PGM VII 558 (but see app.cr. *ad loc.*); Kropp, *Koptische Zaubertexte* I, H 79 (see Müller, *Engellehre*, p. 300).

2 κερκηβι: cf. PGM III 104 κερκερυμι. Perhaps Egyptian *grg* (cf. Erman-Grapow, *Wörterbuch* V, pp. 185-190: 'hunting-net'; 'preparation', 'foundation'; 'lie') and *b3/bj* (Coptic ⲃⲁⲓ) 'soul'?

ϲινα [: cf. ϲιναφ (PGM XIXa 5); κιραϲινα (V 62); ϲινα (Delatte, *Anecdota Atheniensia*, pp. 35, 18; 66, 11); Ϲιναηλ (*ibid.*, p. 69, 38).

3 Καυλυουκαυ: according to Epiphanius, *Panar.* 25, 3, 6 (GCS 1, p. 270 f.) Καυλακαυ is the name the Nicolaitans gave to one of the archons (cf. Filastr., *Haeres.* 33, 3, p. 18, 8 Marx). On the other hand, Hippolytus, *Refut.* V 8, 4 (GCS 3, p. 89, 20 f.) implies that the Naassenes or Ophites called the Saviour by the same name (see Harvey *ad* Iren., *Haeres.* I 24, 5 f. [Vol. I, p. 201 n. 4]); likewise the Basilidians according to Theodoretus, *Haer. fab.* I 4 (Migne PG 83, 349 C) and probably Iren., *loc.cit.* (see Harvey, *ad loc.*). In Epiphanius, *Panar.* 25, 4, 3-5 (GCS 1, p. 271, 12-25) it is stated that Kaulakau is Hebrew *qaw lāqāw*, occurring in OT Is. XXVIII 10, 13 (on this, see J.N.Oswalt, *The Book of Isaiah, Chaps. 1-39*, Grand Rapids 1986, p. 512).

Fr. C

Two figures in profile, facing each other. The figure to the left seems to have an animal head, with a large circular eye. A wavy line ending in a spiral comes down from the mouth. A herring-bone-like element projects from the snout to the right connecting with the face of the other figure; another similar element, without the lower row of barbs, projects to the left. Above the head a small segment turns into a lance-shaped blot, and something similar appears below the trunk. The second figure seems to be a woman, if the wavy line on the back represents long hair. Its mouth is open, its left arm (the right is not represented) stretched out, hand wide open. The trunk is cut across by a long oblique stroke; the space below is surrounded by a double line and filled with magical signs. Other magical signs appear to the right of the figure. The drawing might represent an attack by the figure on the left against the other.

No. 2

2 ἀλυλούια (l. ἀλληλούια): cf. **34**, 12 f.; PGM VII 271; P 10, 33 (probably also IV 3032 αλληλου); see also Peterson, ΕΙΣ ΘΕΟΣ, p. 42 n. 1 and p. 233.

6]ου̣ : a well preserved but anomalous letter, possibly a poorly made δ.

7 Αδονο̣[: possibly Αδονο̣[ει; cf. Delatte-Derchain, *Intailles*, no. 364 Αδωνοει.

9. ἄκουcον or a compound (ἐπ-, εἰc-).

No. 3. Fr. A

2. -θ]λι̣βων? Misspelling of λίβανοc?

Fr. B

2 ⲧⲉϥⲃⲣⲓⲙ[: if ⲧⲉϥ- is the possessive, one expects a common noun: Greek βριμή?

3. λ]ευκόν̣?

No. 4. Fr. A

2]̣ : a round letter.

π[ο]λυμ̣ο[ρφ-?

No. 5

1-2. Probably angels' names; with Cαβαωθ, Αδωναι also in PGM X 42-48; XLIII 1-23.

1]η̣ [: perhaps]ηλ[as in 2, but only a dot of ink is preserved at the edge.

3 Αδονα[: Αδονα̣[ι or Αδονα[ει (cf. e.g. **96 F** fr. A 14, fr. B 5; **10**, 10).

4 Cυβαωθ̣: for Cαβαωθ.

No. 6

3 βαροχ cημο: Hebrew *barûk šᵉmô*, 'blessed be his name'. For *barûk* in magical texts, see **97** →6 comm. For the spelling -οχ (-ωχ), cf. e.g. **2**, 6; PGM XII 155 βαρωχ; E.Peterson, *Rhein. Mus.* 75 (1926) 400, no. 31 βαρωχθα; G.S.Chiesa, *Gemme di Luni* (Roma 1978), p. 129, no. 173 βαρωχ; W.H.Worrell, *Orientalia* 4 (1935) 25, line 173 ⲭⲟⲩⲃⲁⲣⲱⲭ.

Antinoopolis   Plate XIII   V-VI AD

P.Ant. III 140.

ED.PR.: J.W.B.Barns, P.Ant. III (London 1967), p. 71, no. 140.

COMM.: ed.pr.

TRANSL.: R.Kotansky in Betz, *Translation*, no. XCV.

REF.: Marganne, *Inventaire*, no. 62.

DESCR.: papyrus; 12 × 5.5 cm. A fragment from the top of a sheet inscribed along the fibers on the recto and against the fibers on the verso. On each side, an upper margin of 3-3.5 cm. On the recto, intercolumniation of 1 cm. The same hand probably wrote both front and back, though it is relatively cramped in recto col. i.

LOC.: Ashmolean Museum, Oxford.

Recto i 1-2, subjugation spell (?); i 3-6, for successful operation of a workshop; ii 1 ff., on uses of the blind-rat. Verso: iatromagical charm of diverse nature; among other things it cures lunatics (line 3) and lung patients (line 5). The text on the verso might continue the second column of the recto.

Diaeresis on upsilon (R° i 2, ii 3). High stop (R° i 4). A raised horizontal for final ν (R° i 4). ϗ for καί (V° 3 *bis*).

Recto.

              col. i   col. ii

                                         1   περὶ ἀcπ[άλακοc
1   ] .. τῷ εὐωνύμῳ πέλματι προc   ᾱ   ἀcπάλαξ ζῷον [
     ] ορῳ ὑποταcαc —   ↘   τῆc ἱερᾶc λυc[
     ]δωρ .. επ .... μιcθὸc δὲ τοῖc   4   τὴν νεομηνί[αν
4   ]cται· δέρμα μυὸc λαβὼ(ν)   βωμ[..] ... [
     ] .δε ἔχε ἐν ἐργαcτηρίῳ ὑπο   πων[
     ] ... μενον [.] ....   [.] ... [

i 2 ϋποταcαc Pap.   i 4]cται· Pap.   λαβῶ Pap.   ii 3 ϊερᾱc Pap.

Verso.

1   ] τόδε coι ἔcται βοήθημα κατὰ πάντων ῥω[
     ] ̣αθου τρὶc μὲν τοῦ μηνὸc δοθὲν c ̣ῴζει ̣ ̣[
     ] τῷ αὐτῷ τρόπῳ κ(αὶ) cεληνιαζομένουc κ(αὶ) ̣ ̣ ̣ ̣[
4   ] ̣[̣ ̣ ̣ ̣]υτωc κατ' ἀμοιβὰc δίδομεν ̣[
          ο]υc πνευμονικοὺc π ̣ ̣ ̣ ̣ ̣ου ̣[
                    ] ̣ ̣]
          —   —   —   —   —

4 κ̣ Pap. (bis)

Recto: (i 1-2) - - - under the left sole - - - subjugating (?). (i 3-6) - - - reward for the - - - will be (?); take the skin of a mouse - - keep it (?) in the workshop under (?) - - -. (ii 1-6) About the blind-rat. The blind-rat is an animal - - - of the holy, to deliver (?) - - - the new moon - - -.

Verso: - - - this will be a remedy for you against all - - - given three times in the month it saves - - - in the same way both lunatics and - - - in turns given - - - lung patients - - -.

Recto.

i 2 first letter: perhaps κ or χ.

We see ὑποταcαc ̣ — where the ed.pr. gave ὑ ̣π ̣οταcαc:—, but what was regarded as a dicolon on the papyrus could be traces of a letter. Much is uncertain in the reading, but ὑποτα- seems fairly secure. In a magical text this suggests in the first place a form of ὑποτάccω or ὑποταγή. It becomes all the more tempting to recognize a form of one of these words in light of the preceding τῷ εὐωνύμῳ πέλματι; cf. PGM VII 925-929 ἄλλο (sc. νικητικόν), καὶ ὑποτακτικόν. λαβὼν λεπίδα μολιβῆν ἀπὸ ζυγοῦ μούλων καὶ γράψον χαλκῷ γραφείῳ τὰ ὑποκείμενα ὀνόματα καὶ τοὺς χαρακτῆρας καὶ θὲc ὑπὸ τὸ πέλμα cου τοῦ εὐωνύμου ποδὸc κτλ. (see the similar passages cited in **54**, 25-26 comm.). Possibly a form of ὑποταξ- was spelled here ὑποταc-; though the interchange of c and ξ is not indicated in Gignac, *Grammar* I (cf. p. 141 note 3), it is not unparalleled: cf. Mayser, *Grammatik* I.1, p. 184; A.Wilhelm, *SB Berlin* 1932, p. 802 (= *Akademieschriften zur griechischen Inschriftenkunde* 2, p. 346); L.Robert, *REG* 70

(1957) 366 f. with note 3, and idem, *Gnomon* 31 (1959) 26 (= *Opera minora selecta* III, pp. 1483 f. and 1665 f. respectively).

i 3-6. Apparently a charm for the prosperity of a workshop (cf. 3 μιϲθόϲ and 5 ἔχε ἐν ἐργαϲτηρίῳ). Similar are PGM IV 2359-72; 2373-2440 (title cited in **97** ↓ 7 comm.); VIII 57-63; XII 99-106 (99 f. cited in **100**, 2 comm.); also possibly **97** ↓ 7-9 (see comm.).

i 3]δωρ. or]δωρ... . If the former, perhaps]δωρῳ.

επ.... (the last three letter possibly deleted) : επ...... ed.pr. For the traces after π, the ed.pr. suggested the possibility of μφαλω, noting that the first of these letters seems too narrow for ο.

i 5-6 ὑπὸ | [τὸν οὐδόν?

ii 1-2. Cf. *Cyranides* II 3 (p. 117, 1-9 Kaimakis) Περὶ ἀϲφάλακοϲ (var. ἀϲπάλακοϲ). ἀϲφάλαξ (var. ἀϲπάλαξ) ζῷόν ἐϲτιν τυφλόν, ὑποκάτω τῆϲ γῆϲ τὴν οἴκηϲιν ποιούμενον, ἐν ᾗ καὶ φωλεύει καὶ βαδίζει. - - - τούτου οὖν ἡ καρδία ἐν ἐλαφείῳ δέρματι περιαπτομένη ϲεληνιαζο-μένουϲ ἰᾶται. The text of the papyrus will have been much shorter. What survives in lines 3-6 does not resemble anything that follows the beginning of *Cyranides* II 3. Possibly the verso (cf. line 3 ϲεληνιαζομένουϲ) continues the present column.

ii 2. The ᾱ to the left of the line is probably not a numeral letter, but rather indicates that we are dealing with animals whose names begin with alpha. Works such as *Cyranides* were arranged alphabetically.

ii 3. To the lower left of this line, a sign the significance of which is obscure.

ii 4 νεομηνί[αν: probably νεομηνί[αν κατὰ θεόν 'the new moon' rather than 'the first day of the month'. In the magical papyri the word regularly occurs with κατὰ θεόν *vel sim.*; PGM IV 787 τῇ ἐν λέοντι κατὰ θεὸν νεομηνίᾳ; 2389 κατὰ θεὸν νεομηνίαν; XIII 29 f. οἵᾳ δήποτ' οὖν νεομηνίᾳ κατὰ θεόν; 387 f. ταῖϲ τῶν θεῶν αὐθεντικαῖϲ νεομηνίαιϲ.

Verso.

1-4. Possibly the continuation of recto ii.

2 first letter: perhaps η, μ, ν, π or υ.

4 first two letters: perhaps εδ. After διδομεν, probably α or ο.

5. After π, perhaps λην.

6 [ ] : not indicated in the ed.pr.

100

Antinoopolis   Plate VIII (side ii)   V AD

P.Ant. II 65.

ED.PR.: J.W.B.Barns, P.Ant. II (London 1960), pp. 45-47, no. 65.

COMM.: ed.pr.

TRANSL.: Betz, *Translation*, no. XCIII.

REF.: Turner, *Typology*, p. 120, no. 393a.

PHOTO: P.Ant. II, plate III (side i).

DESCR.: parchment; 6.6 × 4.6 cm. A leaf from a codex inscribed on both sides. The parchment is of fine quality and tends to show the writing on the other side (esp. side i, between lines 6 and 8). In places the ink has corroded the parchment.

LOC.: Ashmolean Museum, Oxford.

Fragmentary prescriptions of uncertain purpose. Much if not all deals with the sacrifice of animals. The true order of the two sides cannot be determined. A new section begins at i 7; it is separated by space and apparently numbered. Raised horizontal for final ν (ii 13, 14, 15, 19). Iota adscript twice in 6.

Side i

```
      —    —    —    —

1     [              ]ν θῦε δ [
      [ . . . . κα]τόρυξον π[
      τὸ αὐτὸ παντακα    [
4     αἷμα ἔγχεον εἰc ἀγγ[εῖον
      καὶ ἔξω κατάρανον τ[
      ειν τῆι Ἑκάτηι ω[
   μγ̄                  [


8     ἦν δὲ θέλῃc  . . [
      τυφ[λ]ὸν επ[
      [ . . . . . ]υ [
```

Side ii

— — —

]αϲτριμ[
12   ] ἀλέκτορα ζ[
] ἐνεγκαϲ θὲϲ ἐπὶ τὴ(ν)
] τὸ χοιρίδιον καὶ τὸ(ν)
]ω φέρων ἔξω πολλῷ(ν)
16   ]νον τὴν οἰκ[ί]αν
] μετὰ δὲ ταῦτα κα
γ]υναῖκαϲ· ἐννέα
] πρὸ τῶν θυρῷ(ν)
20   ] ομιζ[ε]ται
] [

— — —

13 τῇ Cod.   14 τō Cod.   15 πολλ͞ω Cod.   19 θυρ͞ω Cod.

(Side 1) - - - sacrifice (?) - - - bury - - - the same - - - |⁴ pour the blood into a vessel - - - and outside sprinkle - - - sacrifice (?) to Hekate - - - 43. |⁸ If you wish - - - blind - - -.

(Side ii) - - - belly (?) - - - |¹² live (?) cock - - - having carried put it on the table (?) - - - the piglet and the - - - carrying aside from many - - - |¹⁶ - - - the house - - - after these things - - - women. Nine - - - before the doors - - - |²⁰ is customary (?) - - -.

2 κα]τόρυξον: cf. PGM IV 2215 f. κατορύξειϲ δὲ ἐπὶ ἀώρου θήκην τὴν λεπίδα ἐπὶ ἡμέραϲ γ´; XII 99 f. ἐργαϲτήριον εὖ πράϲϲειν· ἐπὶ ὠοῦ ὄρνιθοϲ ἀρϲενικοῦ ἐπίγραφε καὶ κατόρυξον πρὸϲ τὸν οὐδόν; also VII 450 κατορυκτικόν.

π[: π[ed.pr.
3 παντακα [: πανταχ [ed.pr.

4-5 αἷμα ἔγχεον εἰς ἀγγ[εῖον - - -] ǀ καὶ ἔξω κατάρανον: cf. PGM II 177 f. ῥάνας αἵματι περιστερᾶς καὶ ἐπιθύσας ζμύρναν κτλ. For sprinkling, see also **97** → 2 with comm.

4 ἀγγ[εῖον : αγγε[ιον ed.pr., but no ink is visible before the break.

5 κατάρανον : καταρανον ed.pr.

5-6. Perhaps θύ]ǀειν τῆι Ἑκάτηι as suggested in the ed.pr.

7 μ͞γ: regarded as numbering of the procedures in the ed.pr., where it is pointed out that this is atypical of magical texts; cf. here **86** fr. A ii 9 comm.

[: before the break, perhaps a trace of ink.

8 ἢν δὲ θέληις: frequent at the beginning of prescriptions. Cf. PGM XIII 261 f. ἐὰν θέληις ὄφιν ἀποκτεῖναι, λέγε κτλ.; 282 f. ἐὰν θέληις ἐπάνω κορκοδείλου διαβαίνειν, καθίσας λέγε κτλ.; 320 ἐὰν θέληις γυναῖκά σου μὴ σχεθῆναι ὑπὸ ἄλλου ἀνδρός, λαβὼν κτλ.; LXXVII 1 f. ἐὰν θέληις χρηματισθῆναι περὶ οὗτινος θέλεις πράγματος, λέγε κτλ. Further references in PGM, Vol. 3 (Index), p. 106, s.v. θέλειν.

[: [ed.pr.

10]υ [or]χ [:]υ [ed.pr. Before the break, perhaps π or τ.

11]αστριμ[: probably γ]αστρὶ μ[as suggested in the ed.pr., where consideration is also given to the possibilities of γ]αστριμ[αργ- (E.G.Turner) and ἐγγ]αστριμ[υθ-. Also possible: ἐγγ]αστριμ[αντ-.

12 ἀλέκτορα ζ[: perhaps ἀλέκτορα ζ[ῶντα; cf. PGM XII 312 f. ζῶντα τὸν ἀλέκτορα ἀνάπτυξε. For other occurrences of sacrificed cocks, see PGM, Vol. 3 (Index), p. 53 s.vv. ἀλεκτρυών and ἀλέκτωρ.

13] ενεγκας :] ε[ν]εγκας ed.pr. Either ἐνέγκας or one of its compounds.

13-14 θὲς ἐπὶ τὴ(ν) ǀ [: at the beginning of 14, perhaps [τράπεζαν, less likely [ἑστίαν or [ἐσχάραν as suggested in the ed.pr. Cf. PGM IV 2188-90 θήσεις τράπεζαν, ἐν ᾗ ἤτω σινδὼν καθαρὰ καὶ ἄνθη τὰ τοῦ καιροῦ, καὶ θύσεις ἀλέκτορα λευκόν; for other occurrences of τράπεζα in PGM, see Vol. 3 (Index), p. 189 s.v.

14 τὸ χοιρίδιον: see **75** intr., 8-11 comm. The article suggests that the piglet was mentioned earlier.

] τὸ χοιρίδιον καὶ :] ω το χοιριδιον κ[αι] ed.pr.

18 γ]υναῖκας· ἐννέα: punctuation was not supplied in the ed.pr. 'Nine women' might call to mind the *novem glandulae sorores* that figure in the logos of the charm against tonsillitis in Marcell. Emp., *De medicam.* XV 102 (= Heim, *Incantamenta magica*, no. 96) or the seven maidens mentioned in

the hexameters of the Philinna papyrus PGM XX (cf. **88** intr. and 2-3). However, here in the midst of instructional material, a reference to a specific number of women (or men) is hardly to be expected. 'Nine', then, may refer to a number of days over which the rite is to be carried out, or to a number of things. For what preceded, perhaps πρὸc ἄνδραc καὶ γ]υναῖκαc or πρὸc πάcαc γ]υναῖκαc etc. On the number nine, see W.H.Roscher, *Die enneadischen und hebdomadischen Fristen und Wochen der ältesten Griechen* (Abh. König. Sächs. Ges. Wiss. XXI.4, Leipzig 1903), esp. pp. 14-28; idem, *Die Sieben- und Neunzahl im Kultus und Mythus der Griechen* (Abh. König. Sächs. Ges. Wiss. XXIV.1, Leipzig 1904), esp. pp. 54-67; *Lexikon der Ägyptologie* IV, *s.v.* Neunheit, coll. 473-479 (H.Brunner).

19] . . πρὸ : π]ρο ed.pr.

20. Probably νομίζ[ε]ται as suggested in the ed.pr. Directly before ο, a vertical, and so κομίζ[ε]ται can be ruled out.

INDEXES

I. PERSONAL NAMES

An asterisk * indicates that a name is listed neither in Preisigke, *Namenbuch*, nor in Foraboschi, *Onomasticon*.

d. = daughter   f. = father   h. = husband   m. = mother   s. = son   w. = wife

*Ἀδώνη m. of Amatis **19**, 18, 25

Ἀθανάςιος f. of Phoibammon **26**, 5-6

Ἀϊᾶς m. of Ptolemais and w. of Horigenes **47**, 8, 20, 25

Αἰλουρίων s. of Kopria **48** J-K 7, 9, 10, 11, 13, 21, 24, 25, 34-35, 38

Ἀλέξανδρος s. of Didyme **66**, 20

*Ἀλθέα **4**, 4-5?, 6?

Ἀμᾶτις d. of Adone **19**, 17, 24

Ἄμμων **12**, 5

Ἀμμωνίων s. of Hermitaris **38**, 6, 10, 11

Ἀνατόλιος s. of . . . η **18**, 14

Ἄνιλλα m. of Eremega **22**, 3

Ἀννιανός **54**, 1, 9, 20, [38]

Ἀντίνοος **47**, 6, 12, 14, 18

Ἀπλωνοῦς d. of Arsinoe **39**, 2, 11

Ἀπολλωνοῦς m. of Nike **37** A 5-7, B 1-2

Ἀρέα m. of Sarapammon **47**, 10, 11, 21, 24

Ἀρcινόη m. of Aplonous **39**, 3, 11

Ἀρτεμιδώρα **7**, 14

Αὐρήλιος: *see* Ἰcίδωρος, Αὐρ.

Ἀφοῦς s. of Taeis **53**, 16, [24]

Ἀχιλλᾶς s. of Helene **44**, 12, 18

*Γενναδία (-τια Pap.) **25**, 7-8

Γενναία m. of Vibios **35**, 9

Γοργονία d. of Nilogenia **42**, 12, 13, 16, 34, 36, 37, 39, 43, 45, 47, 50-51, 55, 58, 60

Δημητρία m. of Tapias **44**, 11-12

*Διᾶς s. of Sophia **11**, 11

Διδύμη m. of Alexandros **66**, 21

Διδύμη m. of Hermias **55** D-G 4, 6

Διδύμη m. of Ptolemaios **40**, 14-15, 21

Δίδυμος h. (?) of Severine **59**, 3, [12]

Διόcκουρος s. of Thekla **43**, 10-11

*Δροcερ m. of Zoel **41**, 12

Δωροθέα m. of Euphemia **45**, 5, 11-12, 30

Ἑλένη d. of [m.] **3**, 3

Ἑλένη m. of Achillas **44**, 13

Ἑλένη m. of Ptolemais **40**, 13, 20

*Ἐρεμέγα (perhaps = Ἰερεμίας or Ἐρμείας) s. of Anilla **22**, 2

Ἐρμείας?: *see* Ἐρεμέγα

Ἐρμίας s. of Didyme **55** D-G 3, 5

*Ἐρμιταρίς m. of Ammonion **38**, 6, 11

"Εὖα": *see* Index VII

Εὖς m. of Theodotis **38**, 1, 9

Εὐφημία d. of Dorothea **45**, 5, 11, 17, 29, 36, 43

II. GEOGRAPHY, ETHNICS

III. DATE

IV. MEASURES

V. GREEK WORDS

An asterisk * denotes a word not recorded in LSJ or *Suppl.*

α (alphabetical indication) **99** R° ii 2

α and ω (in Christian monograms) **22**, 1 (*ter*); **27**, 6 (*ter*)

*ἀβιαστικόc **95** → 12

ἀβλαβῶc **97** → 9?

ἀγαθόc **11**, 10; **63**, 3
- ἐπ᾽ ἀγαθῷ **42**, 46

ἀγάλλεcθαι **49**, 72

ἀγαπᾶν **45**, 51

ἀγγεῖον **100**, [4]

ἄγγελοc **10**, 10; **11**, 9; **14**, 7; **97** → [5], 7

ἄγγοc **86** fr. A ii 13, [14?], [15?]

ἄγειν **40**, 12; **41**, 10; **42**, 15, 16, 37, 57?, 58; **44**, 10, 17; **45**, 6, 11, 29, 43; **47**, 19; **48** K 33; **49**, 19, 62, [65], 76; **71** fr. 14, 4; **72** ii 21; **73** ii [4?]

ἁγιάζειν **29**, 14

*ἁγιαcτί **87**, 6?

ἅγιοc **49**, [66]
- ἅ. ἅ. κύριοc Cαβαωθ **29**, 15-16
- ἅ. ἅ. ἅ. κύριοc Cαβαωθ **25**, 5-6; **32**, 6
- ἅ. ἅ. ἅ. **32**, 1
- ἁ. δόξα **29**, 17
- ἅ. θεόc **6**, 2; **61**, 1; **89**, 4
- ἅ. ὄνομα **45**, 52; **50**, 15; **57**, 16; **98** no. 6, 2
- ἅ. πνεῦμα **21**, 2; **31**, 4
- ἁ. cτήλη **23**, 10

- ἅ. χαρακτῆρεc **21**, 10

ἁγνόc **49**, 71; **79**, 14

ἄγνωcτοc **87**, 5

ἀγριαίνειν **39**, 3

ἄγριοc **88**, 3

ἀγριοῦν **42**, 4, 65

ἀγρυπνεῖν **49**, 77; **53**, [18]; **74**, [2]; **90** fr. D [16-17]

ἀγρυπνία **71** fr. 22, 4; **72** ii 2

ἀγύναιοc **52**, 22

ἀγώγιμον or ἀγωγή **82** fr. A (4)

ἀδαμάντινοc **45**, 44

ἀδελφή **45**, 48

ἀδελφόc **45**, 13, 47; **72** ii 5

ἄδημοc **72** ii 16

ᾅδηc: *see* Index VII Ἅιδηc

ἀδιάλειπτοc **48** J 12

ἀδιαλύτωc **54**, [38]

ἀδιαχώριcτοc **46**, 24

ἄδυτον **45**, 18-19; **72** i 3

ἀεί **38**, 12 (*bis*)
- αἰεί **72** i 7, ii 22

ἀέναοc **71** fr. 19, [1]

ἀεροπετεῖν **43**, 6

ἀεροποτεῖcθαι (for ἀεροπετ- ?) **38**, 11

ἀήρ **45**, 39

ἀθάνατοc **14**, 7; **42**, 20; **71** fr. 18, 3; **72** i 8

ἀθλητήc **53**, 17

αἴγειοc **78** ii [5], [13-14?]

Αἰγύπτιοc: *see* Index II

ἄμφοδον

- εἰς πᾶν ἄμφοδον **46**, 8, 19-20;
  47, 7, 19; **48** J-K 7, 20, 32; **49**,
  18; **50**, 18

ἄν **32**, 1; **40**, 18; **42**, 61; **72** i 8, ii 16,
  19

- *see also* δάν, ἐάν, ὁπουδάν, ὅταν

ἄν (= ἐάν)

- c. subj. **2**, 14; **50**, 71

ἀναγκάζειν **37** A 2-3; **45**, 29

ἀνάγκη **42**, 6; **49**, 66

- *see also* Index VII

ἀνακύπτειν **76**, 1

ἀναλαμβάνειν **31**, 1; **35**, 6; **90** fr. D 3

ἄναξ **42**, 20, **90** fr. D 13

ἀναπαύειν **45**, 13

ἀνάπαυcιc **49**, 17; **50**, 14

ἄναccα **54**, 27

*ἀναcτάτειρα **71** fr. 13, 2

ἀνατέλλειν **72** ii 9 (*bis*)

ἀνατολή **72** ii 14; **80**, [3?]

ἀναφαίνεcθαι **87**, 1

ἀνδριάc **97** ↓ 13, 18, 22, 32

*ἀνδρογενήc **96 A** 28?; **96 E** ↓ 4?;
  96 F fr. A 5?

*ἀνδρογύνηc **96 A** 28?; **96 E** ↓ 4?;
  96 F fr. A 5?

*ἀνδρορρώξ **96 A** 29?; **96 E** ↓ 5?; **9 6**
  F fr. A 6?

ἀνεγείρειν **35**, 5

ἄνεμος **45**, 22

ἀνενέγκαcθαι **54**, 11-12

ἀνήρ **38**, 4, 10; **46**, 10, 21; **47**, 9, 22;
  48 J 8, 22; **49**, 23; **50**, 59; **59**, 13;
  60, 3

- ('husband') **71** fr. 2, 3; **72** ii [5]

ἄνθρωπος **38**, 5; **54**, 10-11; **60**, 5; **70**,

8; **72** i 7-8; **89**, [3?]

ἀνίκητοc **45**, 3-4

ἀνιcτάναι **23**, 4; **31**, 1

ἀνοίγειν **46**, 13; **47**, 13; **48** J 15; **49**,
  29, {30}

ἀντειπεῖν **57**, 42

ἀντίδικοc **79**, 26, 31

ἀντιλαμβάνεcθαι **59**, 2

ἀντίοc **54**, 24

ἄνω **96 A** 71

ἀξιοῦν **41**, 6

ἀπαλλάccειν **7**, 13; **9**, 8; **12**, 5; **18**,
  5; **29**, 8; **74**, 17; **84**, [1?]

ἀπαντᾶν **71** fr. 7, 4?

ἀπάντῃ **60**, 5; **71** fr. 7, 4?

ἀπαραίτητοc **45**, 41-42

ἄπαc **42**, 7

- εἰς (ἐπὶ) τὸν ἄπαντα χρόνον **14**,
  10; **39**, 13, 17; **46**, 26; **47**, 26;
  49, 5; **51**, 9

ἀπελθεῖν **31**, 2; **50**, 54; **51**, 5; **94**, 18

ἀπό **2**, 10; **3**, 4 (*bis*); **4**, 7; **6**, 8, 9; **9**,
  9; **10**, 7; **11**, 13; **14**, 4, 8; **19**, 18,
  25; **21**, 14; **22**, [3]; **23**, 7, 15; **24** fr.
  B 6; **30**, 6; **31**, 3, [3], 4 (*quater*); **32**,
  7, 8, 11; **35**, 10; **45**, 46; **49**, [17];
  50, 13; **71** fr. 12, 1; **81**, 3; **84**, [1],
  [2], 4, [7], [8], [10]; **89**, 8; **90** fr. C
  1; **95** → [14], 21, [22]; **97** → 3

- ἀπὸ cήμερον **45**, 37

- ἀπὸ τῆς cήμερον ἡμέρας **14**, 9; **48**
  J 13; **54**, [39]

- ἀφ' ἧς ἡμέρας **72** i 23

- ἀπὸ τῆς ἄρτι ὥρας **48** J 13; ἀπὸ
  ἄρτι ὥρας **14**, 9

ἀποβάλλειν **53**, 19

ἀποβλέπειν **79**, 27

ἄφωνος **58**, 8, 10

αχαβιccος (?) **52**, 23

ἀχώριστος **50**, 66

ἄωρος **44**, 14; **45**, 3; **46**, 4 (bis); **47**, 4
(bis); **48** J 4 (bis); **49**, ⟨12⟩, 12; **50**,
⟨9⟩, 9-10; **52**, 20; **54**, 22

β (numeral letter) **45**, 37; **92**, 18 (bis);
94, 5; **96** A 67
- see also δύο

βαίνειν **49**, 60

βαίτιον **67** B 3?

βαλανεῖον **42**, 14, 35, 44, 51, 62; **76**, 3

βαλάνιccα **42**, 14, 62

βάλλειν **42**, 14, 34, 44, 51, 61; **72** i 6,
9; **73** ii 14; **76**, 8, 10; **78** ii [1?], [4-
5?]; **86** fr. A i 7, ii 9, 12; **91**, 2?; **9** 7
↓ 4, 15, 25

βάρβαρος **49**, 69?

βασανίζειν **42**, 16, 37, 60; **72** ii 19

βασιλεύειν **35**, 7; **45**, 38; **72** ii [13?]

βασιλεύς **24** fr. B 4; **42**, 35, 40; **72** ii
[13?]

βάσκανος **6**, 9

βασκοσύνη **31**, 4

βαστάζειν **72** ii [13?]

βῆμα **59**, 8

*βιάρπαγος **42**, 21

βιασάνδρα **49**, 52; **57**, 2

βιβρώσκειν **72** ii [15?]

βινεῖν **38**, 4; **46**, 9; **47**, 8; **48** J 8, 22;
49, 21; **76**, 11

βλάπτειν **24** fr. B 5

βλέπειν **54**, 25; **55** D-G 16

βλέψις **95** ↓ 3

βλώσκειν **42**, 3, 5, 64

βοήθεια **26**, 6-7; **29**, 10

βοηθεῖν **13**, 5

βοήθημα **99** V° 1

βοηθός **28**, (2?); **29**, 12

βοτάνη **67** B 2

βούλεσθαι **75**, [20]

βοῦς **70**, 3; **71** fr. 4, 2; **78** ii 13

βρέχειν **86** fr. A ii [13]

*βριττάνδρα **42**, 30

βροντάζειν **90** fr. D [6]

βρωτός **72** i 7
- τὸ βρωτόν **46**, 21; **47**, 20; **50**, 56-
57

βύβλος **72** i 2

βύθιος **57**, 18

γ (numeral letter) **75**, 1
- see also τρεῖς; τρίς; τριταῖος; τρίτος

γαῖα **42**, 8, 23
- see also γῆ

γάλα **49**, 68; **82** fr. A [2?]

γάρ **32**, 8; **38**, 6; **42**, 8, 23; **45**, 7;
50, 14, 32; **54**, 27; **62**, 8; **71** fr. 23,
3; **74**, 2; **86** fr. A ii 15; **94**, 52

γαστήρ **100**, 11?

γαστριμαργ- **100**, [11?]

γελᾶν **45**, 46

γεμίζειν **97** ↓ 27

γένεσις **57**, 37

γεννᾶν **23**, 1; **31**, [1?]; **96** A 48

γεύεσθαι **72** i [17?]

γῆ **29**, 4, 17; **30**, [2?]; **45**, 10, 16; **46**,
12; **47**, 12; **48** J 15; **49**, 29; **53**, 2;
71 fr. 2, 5; **75**, 17
- see also γαῖα and Index VII Γῆ

γίνεσθαι **42**, 14, 62; **57**, 43; **58**, 11;
72 i 21-22; **76**, 7; **87**, 6

γινώσκειν **59**, [1?]

- - διὰ μιᾶς (sc. ἡμέρας) 34 A 11
- - δι' ὅλης νυκτός 45, 6; 53, 19
- - διὰ παντός 48 J 9, 23; 90 fr.
  D [7]
- c. acc. 57, 16
διακονεῖν 39, 2; 81, 7
διακόπτειν 95 → 14, 22, ↓ 6
διάκτωρ 42, 23
διαλείπειν 72 ii 19
διάνοια 48 J 23; 53, 14; 56, 5-6
διατάccειν 75, 18
διατελεῖν 75, [19?]
διατρέφειν 45, 2
διατρίβειν 45, 2-3
διαφυλάccειν 6, 7
διδόναι 45, 12; 59, 14; 60, 4; 63, 3,
    14; 64, 3; 71 fr. 22, 4; 72 i 6?, 8, ii
    5, 6; 79, 7; 93, [5?]; 96 A 64; 99
    V° 2, 4?
- δοῖ (subj.) 39, 14
διεγείρειν 39, 1
- διέγειρέ μοι cεαυτόν 46, 6-7; 47, 6
διερμηνεύειν 72 i 4
διέρχεcθαι 95 → [20]
διό 42, 43
διώκειν 32, 8
δόξα 29, 17; 63, 15
δορκ- 49, 71
δουλαγωγεῖν 38, 10
δούλη 24 fr. B 5; 25, 9; 31, 3; 42, 18,
    39
*δρακοντέλιξος (for *δρακονθελικτός?)
    42, 2, 63-64
δράκων 42, 4, 65-66
δραμεῖν 53, [17-18?], [21-22], 29
δρᾶν 42, 7
δραχμή: see Index IV

δριμύς 76, 9
- δριμύτατος 32, 5
δρομεύς 53, 17
δύναμιc 6, 1; 22, 1; 41, 7-8; 45, 52;
    53, 31; 54, 21; 59, 6; 88, [15]; 95
    ↓ [4]
δύναcθαι 38, 3-4; 45, 6; 46, 10; 48 J
    9, 23; 49, 24; 53, [17?]; 54, 24
δυνάcτειρα 54, 11
δύνεcθαι 45, 10
δύο 70, 3; 71 fr. 10, 1
- see also β
δύcιc 72 ii [13?], 14
δώδεκα: see ιβ
*δωδεκακίcτη: see Index VIII

ε (numeral letter) 37 B 5
ἐάν 45, 9, 11, 14; 46, 27; 47, 27; 72
    ii 18, fr. 2; 73 ii 5, [5], 6; 74, [1?]; 86
    fr. A ii 11; 94, 52
- ὃ ἐάν 39, 6, 14
- c. opt. 72 ii 19
- see also ἤν
ἐᾶν 43, 8; 45, 45; 46, 21; 47, 22
ἑαυτοῦ
- ἑαυτῆc 42, 18, 39; 48 J 24-25
- - τὰ ἑαυτῆc 51, [5]
- ἑαυτήν 42, 18, 39
Ἑβραϊκόc: see Index II
ἐγγαcτρίμυθος 100, [11?]
ἐγγαcτρίμαντιc 100, [11?]
ἐγγράφειν 42, 40
ἐγείρειν 23, 5
- ἔγειρέ μοι cεαυτόν 47, 18; 48 J-
    K ⟨6⟩, 20, 31; 49, 16, 39; 50,
    12-13; 51, [4]
- ἐγείρεcθε 45, 4

ii 5; **73** ii [3], 12; **74**, 5, [8?], [9?];
76, 4, 8; **78** ii [1?]; **79**, 4, 25; **85**,
42, 43; **86** fr. A ii 1, 2, 9, 12, 14;
94, 30; **95** ↓ [7?], 8; **97** ↓ 4, 5, 9,
21, 25, 26; **100**, 4
- εἰc αἰῶνα **49**, 74
- εἰc ὂν πάντα χρόνον **19**, 20
- εἰc τὸν ἄπαντα χρόνον **14**, [9?];
 39, 13, 17; **46**, 26; **47**, 26
- εἰc τὸν ἀεὶ χρόνον **38**, 12
- εἰc τὸ c. inf. **39**, 4
- ἐναρῶ ὑμῖν εἰc **45**, 18
εἷc, μία, ἕν **42**, 41; **59**, 17; **60**, 2
- διὰ μιᾶc (sc. ἡμέρας) **34** A 11
- εἷc θεόc **33** R° 2
- εἷc πατήρ, εἷc υἱόc, ἓν πνεῦμα
 ἅγιον **21**, 1
- μίαν παρὰ μίαν (sc. ἡμέραν) **10**,
 9; **19**, 20, 27-28; **21**, 16-17
- μίαν ὥραν **39**, 15
- τὸ ἕναν ... τὸ ἕναν **97** ↓ 3, 4
εἰcακούειν **52**, 18; **87**, 11
εἰcελθεῖν **95** ↓ 8
εἰcκρίνειν **66**, 19
εἴτε
- εἴτε ... εἴτε **13**, 26-27; **42**, 23;
 46, 7, 15; **48** J 6, 20; **49**, 33
- εἴτε ... εἴτε ... εἴτε **13**, 11-14;
 32, 5
- εἴτε ... ἤ **72** i 11
ἐκ, ἐξ **26**, 1; **31**, [1?]; **42**, 17, 38; **48**
 J 11; **49**, 65; **70**, 7; **72** i 1; **73** ii 3;
 96 A 49
- ἐξ ὅλης καρδίας **48** J 24
- ἐξ ὅλης ψυχῆς **48** J 12
- ἐξ ὅλου πνεύματος **48** J 12, 24
- ἐνιαυτοὺς ἐξ ἐνιαυτῶν **46**, [4];

 47, 4; **48** J 5; **49**, 13
- ἡμέρας ἐξ ἡμερῶν **46**, 5; **47**, 5;
 48 J 5; **49**, 14
- μῆνας ἐκ μηνῶν **46**, 5; **47**, 5; **48**
 J 5; **49**, 13
- νύκτας ἐκ νυκτῶν **46**, 5; **47**, 5;
 48 J 5; **49**, 14
- ὥρας ἐξ ὡρῶν **46**, 5; **47**, 5; **48** J
 5; **49**, [14]
ἑκάτεροc **70**, 7
ἑκατὸν τέccαρεc: *see* ρδ
ἐκβάλλειν **86** fr. A ii 3, [5?]
ἐκγ[**71** fr. 17, 2
ἐκδικεῖν **59**, 19 (*bis*)
ἐκδίκηcιc **59**, 11
ἔκδοτοc **42**, 17, 39
ἐκεῖνοc **45**, 50
- ἐπ' ἐκείνῃ τῇ ἡμέρᾳ **72** ii 6
ἐκκόπτειν **78** ii 4
ἔκκριμα **79**, 1
ἐκλείχειν **75**, 3
ἔκλευκοc **67** B 3
ἐκπείθειν **42**, 6
ἐκπέμπειν **97** → 9
ἐκπηδᾶν **40**, 18; **42**, 17, 38; **45**, 46;
 48 J 10
ἐκπλήκτωc **74**, 7
ἐκπυροῦν **86** fr. A ii 15
ἐκτόc **46**, 11; **47**, 11; **49**, 81; **50**, 25
ἐκχεῖν **71** fr. 7, 5; **79**, 3
ἐλαία **82** fr. B 4
ἔλαιον **86** fr. A ii 7; **93**, 1
ἐλεεῖν **61**, 4
ἐλεύcεcθαι: *see* ἔρχεcθαι
ἐλθεῖν: *see* ἔρχεcθαι
ἕλκειν **46**, 22; **47**, 23; **50**, 62
Ἑλληνικόc: *see* Index II

ἐπαοιδή: see ἐπῳδή
ἐπαφροδιcία 64, 4-5; 72 ii [6?]; 82 fr.
 A 11
ἐπεί 42, 25; 79, 31
ἐπερεῖν 86 fr. A ii [4?]
ἐπέχειν 39, 15
ἐπήκοος 39, 6; 58, 11
ἐπί
  - c. gen. 6, 1; 42, 58; 45, 22; 72 i
    5; 79, 1, 26, 33; 90 fr. C 2, fr. D
    [3], [7]
  - c. dat. 2, 2; 26, 6; 42, 13, 15, 22,
    36, 45, 47, 55; 49, [56], 60; 50,
    22; 53, 20; 72 i 10; 90 fr. D [5?],
    [10]
    - - ἐπ' ἀγαθῷ 42, 46
    - - ἐπ' ἐκείνῃ τῇ ἡμέρᾳ 72 ii 6
  - c. acc. 29, 13; 31, 1; 45, 36; 97 ↓
    24; 100, 13
    - - ἐπὶ ε' μῆνας 37 B 5
    - - ἐπὶ τὸν ἅπαντα χρόνον 14,
      [9?]; 49, 4; 51, 9
    - - ἐπὶ τὸν λοιπὸν χρόνον 48 J
      14
    - - ἐφ' ὃν ἔχει χρόνον 6, 8
  - case uncertain 19, 22; 73 ii 17; 82
    fr. A 4; 90 fr. E 1; 91, 6
ἐπι(-) 85, 43; 89, 6
ἐπιβουλή 59, 6
ἐπιγράφειν 74, [3-4], 10; 82 fr. B 4
ἐπιδιδόναι 59, 10
ἐπιζητεῖν 48 J 10, 23
ἐπίηρα c. gen. 59, 17; 60, 2
ἐπικαλεῖν 56, 6-7
  - ἐπικαλοῦμαι 2, 1; 53, 1; 54, 10;
    57, 36; 75, 12; 87, 4; 88, 10,
    [11-12]; 90 fr. D [4], 8

ἐπικλώθειν 54, 26
ἐπιλαμβάνεcθαι 2, 15
ἐπιλανθάνεcθαι 45, 50; 54, 9
ἐπίληψιc (-λημ- Pap.) 84, 8
ἐπιούcιος 29, 15
ἐπιπομπή 84, 11
*ἐπιcχυρίζειν 45, 53
ἐπιτάccειν 42, 18; 45, 23; 93, [4?]
ἐπιτελεῖν 49, 22, 61; 51, [5?]; 53,
  [1?]; 95 → [13]
ἐπιτολή 80, [3?]
ἐπιτυγχάνειν 79, 16
ἑπτά 45, 40; 88, 2, [2], 6, [6?], 7
  (bis); 94, 13
  - see also ζ
ἐπῳδή 72 i 1, 5
  - ἐπαοιδή 42, 5; 45, 53; 71 fr. 21 i
    3 + fr. 2, 6; 72 i 14, 27, ii 8, 25;
    73 ii [18]
ἐρᾶν 45, 7, 48; 47, 27; 48 J-K 12, 24,
  38
ἔραcθαι 37 A 7-9, B 3
ἐργαcτήριον 99 R° i 5
ἐρεβεννός 54, 13
ἐρεβίνθιον 96 A 64
ἔρεβος 49, 70
ἐρεῖν: see λέγειν
ἐρίθυλος 96 A 24?
ἑρμηνεία 70, [15?]
ἑρμῆc (rotating part of a mill) 56, 1
ἐρυθρόν 88, 6, [13-14?]
ἐρυcίπελας 88, 1
ἔρχεcθαι 13, 9, 22
  - ἐλεύcεcθαι 31 [1?]
  - ἐλθεῖν 27, 2; 32, 8-9; 39, 15; 40,
    19; 42, 24; 43, 10; 45, 6, 32,
    48; 47, 21; 48 J 11; 50, 27, 65;

[27]; **50**, 2-3, 21-22; **51**, [2]; **70**, 8,
9; **72** ii 26, 27 (*bis*), 28 (*bis*), 29; **73**
ii [7-8? *bis*]; **74**, 5; **90** fr. D 11, 15-
16; **97** ↓ 18, 24
- ἀπὸ κεφαλῆς μέχρι ὀνύχων **32**, 11
κς (numeral letters) **52**, 24
κῆπος **49**, 65
κηρίον **97** ↓ 12, 16
κηρός **96 A** 62
κηρύκειον **49**, 57-58
κῆρυξ **42**, 24
κινεῖν **94**, 50, 52, 53-54, 55
κλαίειν **59**, 9
κλείς **46**, 3; **47**, 3; **48** J 4; **49**, 11, 57
κλέπτειν **86** fr. A ii 4, 5, [6?], 10
κλέπτης **86** fr. A i [8]
κλήζειν ('call') **42**, 25
κλίνειν **39**, 4-5
κλίνη **59**, 4
κλύζειν **86** fr. A ii 8
κοιλία **79**, 10
κοιμᾶσθαι **79**, 13
κοιμίζειν **88**, [7-8?]
κοινός
 - κοινόν, κοινά **9 2**, (12), (13), (15);
  95 → (7), (20), ↓ (2)
 - κοινὸς λόγος **82** fr. B 3
κοκκίον **96 A** 66
κοκκύμελος **96 A** 63
*κολάσιμος **62**, 5-6
κολλᾶν **71** fr. 5, 2; **73** ii [7?]; **88**, 13
κόλπος **45**, 49-50; **72** i 12, ii 5
κόνδυ **71** fr. 10, [1?]
κονδύλιον **71** fr. 10, [1?]
κόπρος **83**, 2
κόρη **42**, 5; **49**, 61; **71** fr. 13, 1?
κορυφή **75**, 15

κόσμος **42**, 23, 41; **45**, 11; **48** K 42
κοῦρος ('boy') **45**, 3
κράζειν **49**, 69; **52**, 9
κράμβη **96 A** 63-64 (κραβη Pap.)
κρανίον **53**, 27?
κρατ- **60**, [6]
κραταιός **45**, 1, 33; **46**, 3; **47**, 3; **48** J 4
κρατεῖν **48** K 42
κράτος **63**, 3
κρεμαννύναι **72** ii 2?
κρήνη **8**
κρίνειν **23**, 5; **59**, [8?]
κριός **38**, 2
κροκόδιλος **38**, 2
κρόκος **94**, 4
*κροκοφανής **96 A** 31?; **96 E** ↓ [7?];
  96 F fr. A 7?
*κρομύλευκος **96 A** 34?
κρόμ(μ)υον **86** fr. A ii 9 (κρομβυον Pap.),
  [10?]; **96 A** 23, 34?
κρόταφος **22**, 4 (κοτρ- Pap.); **31**, 4;
  72 ii 26, 28
κροτών **76**, 4; **78** ii [12-13]
κρούειν **86** fr. A ii 3
κρύβειν **48** K 41
κρυπτός **42**, 25; **63**, 11
κρύφιος **65**, 36
κτῆμα **42**, 18, 39
κύθρα **97** ↓ 25, 26, 28
κυνόδηκτος **76**, 7-8
κυνοκέφαλος **96 F** fr. A 9
κυρία **49**, 39; **57**, 1
κύριος **42**, 35, 40; **53**, 31; **57**, 14; **59**,
  [1?], 5; **61**, 4; **84**, (1); **86** fr. A i 6;
  87, 4; **92**, 1, 2; **93**, [1?]
 - ἅγιος ἅγιος ἅγιος κύριος Σαβαωθ
  25, (6); **32**, (6); ἅ. ἅ. κ. C. **29**,

μηκέτι 29, 6; 38, 9

μῆλον 72 i 5, 6, 9 (bis)

μήν ('month') 37 B 6; 45, 37; 99 V° 2
 - μῆνας ἐκ μηνῶν 46, 5; 47, 4-5;
 48 J 5; 49, 13

μῆνις 6, 9

μηρός 38, 12 (bis); 73 ii [7? bis]; 96 A
 50

μήτε 24 fr. B 5; 38, 4-5 (ter); 43, 9
 (bis); 47, 10 (bis); 48 J 8, 9-10
 (quater), 22, 23 (quater); 49, 22; 72 ii
 14 (bis), [14]-15 (bis)

μήτηρ 8, 1; 45, 30, 47; 48 J-K 7, 8, 9,
 10, 11, 12, 13, 21, 22, 24, 25, 34,
 35, 39

μήτρα 43, 7

μιγνύναι 96 A 68
 - see also μίςγειν

μικρός 13, 5, 10, 23

μίςγειν 82 fr. B 3
 - see also μιγνύναι

μιςεῖν 45, 50; 55 D-G 4, 5, 13

μίςημα 55 D-G 14

μιςθός 99 R° i 3

μνημεῖον 31, 1; 96 A 49; 97 → 2-3, 5
 - μνημήϊον 59, 16

μνήμη 54, 9

μνημήϊον: see μνημεῖον

μνημονεύειν 54, 10

μολιβοῦς 81, [3?]

μολύνειν 86 fr. A ii 16?

μονογενής 26, 2

μόνος 38, 6 (bis), 10; 46, 10, 22; 47, 9,
 22; 48 J 9; 54, 9-10
 - μόνον (adv.) 97 ↓ [32-33?]

μόριον 75, 1

μορφή 70, 11, 13

μοῦλος 81, [3?]

μυλαῖον 56, 2

*μυρικοῦν 55 D-G 1, 8-9; 95 → [4?]

μύρον 72 ii 4 (bis)

μῦς 99 R° i 4

μωλύειν 86 fr. A ii 16?

ναί
 - ναί, κύριε 42, 35, 40; 57, 14

νάρκη 76, 1; 96 A 72

ναςμός 49, [67]

νεανίςκος 48 J 8, 22

*νειχαροπλήξ: see Index VIII

νεκρός 23, 6; 29, 8; 50, 9; 76, 3-4

νεκυδαίμων 39, 1; 42, 12 (νεκυοδαί-
 μων?); 47, 11, 14, 18; 48 J-K 6, ⟨6⟩,
 14, 20, 31; 49, 28, 33, 38, 53; 50,
 12; 51, [2?], [4?]; 57, 1

νέκυια 54, 14

νέκυς
 - νέκυς δαίμων 46, 7, 15, 19

νεομηνία 99 R° ii 4

νερόν: see νηρόν

νεῦρον 53, 13, 15; 54, 23; 74, 19

νή 79, 15

νηρόν 94, 44
 - νερόν 97 ↓ 29

νήςτης 83, 8,

νικᾶν 7, 8; 25, 1, 10; 54, 26; 96 A
 69

νίκη 63, 14

νικητικόν 58, 2; 79, 26

νομίζειν 100, 20?

νόος, νοῦς 47, 27; 49, [63], 78; 53, 13;
 57, 41; 72 ii [15?]

νόςος 3, 4; 18, 6; 22, 3; 30, 3; 31, 2,
 3; 33 R° 4; 34 A 8; 74, [18?]; 78 ii

25, 26; **47**, 8, 9, 11 (οὖ), 20, 21, 24 (οὖ), 25; **48** J-K 7, 8 (ᾧ), 9 (ᾧ), 10, 11, 12, 13, 21, 21 (ᾧ), 24, 25, 33, 35 (ᾧ), 38; **49**, 2, 4, [20], 23, 26, 27, 55, 56, [62], 64, 77, 79; **50**, 1, 4, 20, 23, 30, 52, 58, 61; **51**, [1?], 2; **53**, [15], 16, 24, [24]; **55** D-G 1, 2, 3, 5, 7, 11; **57**, 4, 30, 32, 35, 41, 42; **66**, 20; **73** ii [11]; **80**, 1
- ἕως οὖ **48** J 10
- μέχρι οὖ **46**, 24
- ὃ ἐάν **39**, 5, 14
- ὅν for τόν **19**, 20
ὅcτε **71** fr. 18, 2
ὀcτέον, ὀcτοῦν **74**, 19; **88**, 4; **97** ↓ 19
ὅcτιc **45**, 37
- ὅcτιc ποτὲ (ποτ') εἶ **46**, 7, 15, 19; **48** J-K 6, 20, 31; **49**, 38; **50**, 12; **51** [4?]; **57**, 1
ὀcτράκινοc **82** fr. A [4?]
ὀcτράκιον **82** fr. A [4?]
ὅcτρακον **96** A 50; **97** ↓ 8
ὀcφῦc **76**, 2, 4
ὅταν **42**, 22; **86** fr. A ii 6
ὅτι **31**, 2, 2; **39**, 7; **42**, 18, 40, 47; **45**, 1, 23, 33; **46**, 12; **48** J 14; **49**, [28], 39; **51**, 6; **52**, 19; **57**, 36; **59**, 2; **72** ii [14?]; **89**, [3?]
- recitativum **86** fr. A ii 10
οὐ, οὐκ **45**, 10-11 (*bis*); **72** ii 10 (*bis*), fr. 1?; **90** fr. D [14]; **95** → [16]
- οὐ μή c. subj. **72** ii 27, 28, 29
οὐάτιον **86** fr. A ii 17
οὐδέ **72** ii 10
οὐδέποτε **59**, 13; **60**, 3
οὐρά **38**, 1

οὐρανόc **26**, 8; **29**, 11, 14, 16; **30**, [2?]; **31**, 1; **48** K 41-42; **71** fr. 2, [5], fr. 18, 2; **72** i 21; **75**, [17]; **79**, 23
οὐcία **49**, 4, 20, 55-56, 63, 78; **50**, 53-54, 59; **51**, [1?]
οὔτε **45**, 10-11 (*bis*)
οὗτοc **23**, 9, 16; **38**, 9, 13; **42**, 6, 11, 18, 40, 47; **45**, 52, 53; **46**, 6 (*bis*), 27; **47**, 1, 6 (*bis*), 27; **48** J 2, 6; **49**, 6, 15, 16, 21, 62, 74; **50**, 6, 11, 71; **51**, [5?]; **54**, 15, 19, 27, 31, 32, 36, 37; **56**, 2-3; **58**, 8; **74**, 1, 4; **85**, [42]; **88**, 5; **90** fr. D 4; **94**, 44; **97** → 7; **100**, 17
οὕτω, οὕτωc
- ὡc . . . οὕτωc **51**, [8?]; **58**, 9
- ὥcπερ . . . οὕτωc **56**, 3
ὀφθαλμόc **26**, 4; **32**, 7; **53**, [28]; **78** ii [3?]; **86** fr. A ii [2], 4, 6, [9?]; **94**, 22; **95** → 17; **97** ↓ 21
ὄφιc **38**, 1; **70**, 6

πάθος **19**, 18, 25
παιδίον **68**, 4
παίζειν **45**, 46
παῖc **42**, 24; **49**, [66]
πάλαι **59**, 4
πάλιν **45**, 29, 38, 39, 40
παλλακίc **83**, 1?
παμφόρβα **54**, 11
πανδυνάcτειρα **54**, 27
πανεργέτηc **66**, 11
παντεπόπτηc **45**, 19
παντοῖοc **32**, 1?, 7
παντοκράτωρ **24** fr. A [4?], fr. B [3?]; **29**, 5-6; **87**, [4?]
παρά

- c. gen. 52, 7; 72 ii 10 (bis), 11
  (bis); 81, [2?]; 95 ↓ 10; 99 R° ii
  1
- c. acc. 80, 2
  - - οἱ περὶ + nomen proprium 53,
    15, 23
περίαμμα 5, 1
περιάπτειν 78 ii 12; 80, 2
περίαπτον 94, 7
περιέχειν
  - ὡς περιέχει 5, 4
περίμετρον 72 ii 27, 29
περιχρίεσθαι 83, [4]
πέταλον 5, 2; 42, 40; 81, 3
πέτρα 46, 14; 47, 14; 48 J 16; 49, ⟨32⟩
πήγανον 96 A 23
πηγνύναι 32, 9
πικρός 12, 2; 42, 4, 21, 65
πίνειν 43, 9; 45, 45; 46, 11; 47, 10;
  48 J 9, 23; 72 ii 14; 73 ii 6, [6];
  83, 9; 96 A 65
πίπερι 96 A 66
*πιπερίον 96 A 67
πιcτεύειν 31, [2?], 2; 44, 16-17
πιττάκιον 5, 3; 56, 3
πλάcμα 24 fr. B 6
πλάccειν 70, 3
πλάcτης 70, 2
πλειcτάκις 81, [7?]
πλῆγμα 94, 48-49
πλήρης 29, 16
πνεῦμα
  - ('air') 2, 3-4
  - ('demonic spirit') 24 fr. A 1; 31, (4)
  - ('soul') 30, (5); 40, 16; 42, 12, 15,
    36, 45, 46, 54-55, 60; 48 K 37
    - - ἐξ ὅλου πνεύματος 48 J 12,

24
- (Christian) πνεῦμα ἅγιον 21, 2;
  ἅγιον πνεῦμα 31, (4)
*πνευματηλάτης 42, 3, 64-65
πνευμονικός 99 V° 5
ποθεῖν 42, 22
πόθος 42, 52, 55; 45, 30-31, 36
ποιεῖν 30, 2; 37 A 2, B 1; 38, ⟨5⟩;
  39, 11; 42, 6, 7, 43; 45, 23, 46; 46,
  10, 24, 27; 47, 9, 28; 48 J 8, 22;
  50, 23, ⟨29⟩, 67; 54, 30, 32; 59,
  [7?]; 72 i 20, ii 13; 74, 1; 76, 9;
  94, 22, 50-51, 51, 54, 55; 97 ↓ 13,
  → 10
  - τὸ ἱκανόν τινι ποιεῖν 61, 1
πόλις: see Index II Ἡλίου πόλις
πολύϊδρις 71 fr. 18 [1?]
πολύμορφος 97 → 6-7; 98 no. 4 fr. A
  [2?]
πολυπενθής 60, 1
πολύς 60, 2; 100, 15
  - πολλά (adv.) 76, 11; 83, 5
πονεῖν 72 ii 26 (bis), 27, 28 (bis), [29]
πονηρός 31, 4; 84 [2]
πόνος 22, 4; 26, 4; 32, 12; 74, 18
ποντικός ('mouse') 97 ↓ 7
πορεύεσθαι 72 ii 5, 19
πόσθη 96 A 72?
ποταμός 8; 32, 9; 46, 13; 47, 14; 48 J
  15; 49, 31
ποτέ
  - ὅcτιc ποτὲ (ποτ') εἶ 46, 7, 15, 19;
    48 J-K 6, 20, 31; 49, 38; 50, 12;
    51, [4?]; 57, 1
πότνια 54, 29; 71 fr. 18, 3; 72 i 26, ii
  24
ποτόν 46, 21; 47, 21; 50, 56

ῥιγοπυρέτιον 23, 7; 82 fr. B [4?]

ῥιγοπύρετον 4, 5, 7-8; 23, 14; 34 C 5-6

- gender uncertain (-οc?) 9, 11-12; 22,
5; 25, 2-3; 29, 3; 31, 4

ῥῖγοc 3, 4; 10, 8; 12, 6; 13, 12, 26;
14, 3, 4, 8; 18, 7, 9; 19, 18, 26; 21,
14; 25, 1; 34 A 4; 35, 11; 92, 14;
96 A 56

*ῥιζοποιόc 96 A 27?; 96 E ↓ 3?; 9 6
F fr. A 5?

ῥοδοδάφνη 97 → 1?

*ῥοιζοποιόc 96 A 27?; 96 E ↓ 3?; 96 F
fr. A 5?

ῥοπή 42, 6

*ῥυζοποιόc 96 A 27?; 96 E ↓ 3?; 9 6
F fr. A 5?

ῥύμη 71 fr. 7, 3

cάνδαλον 49, 58, 59

cαρκοκόλλα 94, 5

cαρκοφάγοc 52, 4-5

cάρξ 54, 23

cαύρα 78 ii 3

cεαυτοῦ

- (δι-), (ἐξ-)ἔγειρε cεαυτόν 46, 7;
47, 6-7, 18; 48 J-K ⟨6⟩, 20, 31;
49, 16, 39; 50, 13, 50-51; 51, 5

- τὰ cεαυτῆc 72 ii [6?]

cεληνιάζεcθαι 99 V° 3

cεληνιαcμόc 84, 9

cέλινον 76, 11

cήμερον

- ἀπὸ cήμερον 45, 37

- ἀπὸ τῆc cήμερον ἡμέραc 14, 9; 48
J 13; 54, 39

- ἐν τῇ cήμερον 12, 7

- ἐν τῇ cήμερον ἡμέρᾳ 9, 12; 11,

16; 13, 25; 55 D-G 18; 79, [30]

- ἤδη ἤδη, ταχὺ ταχύ, cήμερον 51,
10

cιαγών 96 A 70

*cιδηροcάνδαλοc 49, 59-60

cίναπι 95 → 16, [16], ↓ [3?], 6, 14

cκέπη 26, 7; 29, 10-11

cκῆπτρον 42, 20

cκιά 13, 13; 24 fr. A 2

cκιερόc 49, [64]

cκίρροc 94, 27

cκόρδον 96 A 64

cκορπίοc 16, 8; 17, 3; 89, 6

cκότιοc 49, 70

cκότοc 42, 1, 63; 97 ↓ 26

cκύλαξ 42, 2, 63

cμερδαλέοc 69, 1

cμύρνα 67 B 2

cμυρνόμελαν: see ζμυρνόμελαν

cορόc 90 fr. D [10]

cόc 42, 22, 23, 24; 53, 31; 54, 30

cπέρμα 76, 12; 83, 6

cπλάγχνον 46, 23; 47, 23; 50, 64;
75, 10

cτάcιc 72 ii 2

cταυροῦν 23, 2; 31, (1); 32, 10

*cταφυλοτόμοc 1, 1 ff.

cτέγειν 47, 10

cτέμμα 49, [57]; 97 → 3

cτένειν 59, 9

cτέργειν 46, 11

cτερεόc 59, 18; 60, 7

cτήλη 23, 11; 45, 18; 60, 1

cτήριγμα 75, [12-13?]

cτηρίζειν 75, 13

cτίβι 96 A [66?]

cτόμα 38, 2; 90 fr. D 7

cωματοειδής **57**, 36

*cωcίκοcμοc **49**, 61

cωτήρ **31**, 2

cωτήρια ('latrine') **97** ↓ 4

ταράccειν **48** J 16

ταῦρος **95** → 18

ταφή **52**, 13

ταχέως **44**, 10; **45**, 9-10; **50**, 72

τάχος

- ἐν τάχει **10**, [10?]; **42**, 7

*ταχύειν **34** A 12, C 7

ταχύς **59**, 6

- τάχιον **45**, 23

- ταχὺ ταχύ **28**, 3; **51**, [7?]

- ἤδη, ταχύ **40**, 21; **41**, 13; **50**, 4

- ἤδη ἤδη, ταχύ **32**, 12; **51**, 6

- ἤδη ἤδη, ταχὺ ταχύ **9**, 14; **11**, 18-19; **12**, 7; **14**, 6, 11; **18**, 16-17; **19**, 29; **20**, 7; **35**, 14; **43**, 12; **44**, 19; **45**, 53; **46**, 27; **48** J-K 26, 40; **49**, 5; **55** D-G 15; **56**, 8; **57**, 5, 32, 33, 43

- ἤδη β', ταχὺ β' **92**, 18

- ἤδη ἤδη, ταχὺ ταχύ, ἄρτι ἄρτι **49**, 82; **50**, 70

- ἤδη ἤδη, ταχὺ ταχύ, cήμερον **51**, 10

- ἤδη ἤδη ἤδη, ταχὺ ταχὺ ταχύ **23**, 17

τε **42**, 6?; **71** fr. 18, 3, fr. 19, 2 (bis?)

- τε . . . τε **42**, 21; **72** i 9

- τε καί **46**, 4 (bis); **47**, 4; **48** J 2, 4 (bis); **49**, 12 (bis); **50**, 9

τέκνον **59**, 7; **61**, 2

τελεῖν **42**, 25; **45**, 10, 14, 53; **50**, 71; **51**, 7; **71** fr. 8, [3?]; **72** i 13, 27, ii

8, 25; **75**, [19?]

τέλειος **45**, 53; **73** ii [18?]

- τέλεος **71** fr. 21 i [3]; **72** i 14, 27, ii 8, 25; **73** ii [18?]

τελειοῦν **38**, 8; **54**, 14-15, [36-37]

τέλεος: see τέλειος

τελετή **82** fr. A [10?]

τέρπειν **42**, 22

τεccαράκοντα τρεῖc: see μγ

τέccαρεc **45**, 22

- see also δ

τεταρταῖος **3**, 5; **10**, 8-9; **14**, 6; **18**, 10-11; **19**, 19-20, 27; **21**, 15; **29**, 5

τετραβάμων **49**, 66, 71

τέωc **71** fr. 2, 5?

τήκειν **48** K 36

τηρεῖν **32**, 2?; **54**, 31

τιθέναι **24** fr. B 3; **100**, 13

(-)τιθέναι **72** ii 13

τίκτειν **71** fr. 22, [3]

- ἣν (ὃν) ἔτεκε **3**, [3]; **9**, 9; **10**, 7; **11**, 12; **18**, 15; **21**, 11-12; **22**, 2-3; **35**, 9; **37** A 11-12, B 4; **39**, 3, 7, 11, 12-13, 16; **40**, 13, 14, 19-20, 21; **41**, 11 (bis); **42**, 12, 13 (bis), 14, 15, 16, 17, 34, 35, 36, 37, 38-39, 43-44, 44, 45, 45-46, 47 (bis), 51 (bis), 55 (bis), 58, 59, 61 (bis); **43**, 7, 11; **44**, 11, 13; **45**, 5 (bis), 11, 12, 29, 30; **46**, 8, 9, 20, 22, 25, 26; **47**, 8, 9-10, 11, 20, 21, 24, 25; **48** J-K 7, 8, 9, 10, 11, 12, 13, 21 (bis), 24, 25, 33-34, 35, 38; **49**, 2, 4, 20, 23, 26, 27, 55, 56, [62-63], 64, 77, 79; **50**, 1, 4, 20, 23, 30, 52-53, 58, 61-62; **51**, [1?], 2; **53**, 16 (bis),

ὕπνος 43, 9; 45, 6, 45; 46, 11; 47, 11;
  48 J 9, 23; 49, 25; 50, 26, 55-56;
  74, 1; 82 fr. A 1; 96 A 51?
ὑπνοῦν 74, 7; 96 A 51?
ὑπνοφανής 84, [6?]
ὑπνοφόβης 84, [6?]
ὑπό
  - c. gen. 31, 1; 53, 26; 71 fr. 2, 4
  - c. acc. 45, 10; 53, 2; 54, 26; 74,
    [4?]
  - case uncertain 71 fr. 11, 2
ὑπο(-) 99 R° i 5
ὑποκάτω 71 fr. 9, [1?]
ὑποκεῖσθαι 71 fr. 9, [1?]; 94, 19, 24,
  [28], [31]
ὑπομένειν 59, 17; 60, 2
ὑποπίπτειν 54, 25-26
ὑποταγή 99 R° i 2?
ὑποτακτικόν 82 fr. A 7
ὑποτάσσειν 46, 25; 47, 26; 50, 24; 82
  fr. A 8; 99 R° i 2?
ὑποτιθέναι 74, [4?]
ὑποχόνδριον 45, 8
ὑστερεῖν 53, 22 (bis?)
ὑφάπτειν 91, 3?
ὕψιστος 26, 7; 29, 10

φαγεῖν 43, 8; 45, 45; 46, 11; 47, 10;
  48 J 9, 23; 72 i 11; 73 ii [5], 6; 79,
  14
φαίνειν 35, 2; 66, 21; 93, 2
φαντασμός 84, [4-5?]
φάος: see φῶς
φάρμακον 72 i 6-7
φάσσα 97 ↓ 19?
φέρειν 100, 15
  - ἐνεγκεῖν 46, 20

- (-)ἐνέγκαι 100, 13
φεύγειν 23, 6; 49, 59; 72 ii 12
*φθιςίκηρε: see Index VIII
φθιτός 42, 24
φιλεῖν 39, 5, 12, 14; 42, 17, 38, 51;
  45, 30, 32, 43, 48, 51; 47, 27; 48 J-
  K 12, 24, 25, 37; 49, 2, 79; 50, 1, 3,
  29; 51 [1?], [8 bis]; 71 fr. 9, 2; 72 i
  13, fr. 1
φιλία 42, 13, 37, 45, 47, 55; 45, 9,
  17, 36, 45, 49; 49, 56; 50, 22, 60;
  54, 37; 64, [3]; 72 i 25
φίλος
  - φίλτατος 59, 7; 73 ii 9
φιλότης 72 i 11
φιλτροκατάδεςμος 38, 8
φίλτρον ('love') 42, 51, 55; 48 J 12
φλέγειν 42, 12, 15, 36, 45
φλεγμαίνειν 94, 49, 53
φοβεῖσθαι 46, 14; 47, 13; 63, 2
φοβερόμματος 66, 11
φοβερός 42, 21; 46, 12; 47, 12; 48 J
  14; 49, 29; 95 ↓ 12
φοινικοῦς 78 ii [1-2?]
φοιτᾶν 54, 36
φορεῖν 94, [24?]; 97 → 3
  - ὁ φορῶν, ἡ φοροῦσα 2, 9; 15, 7;
    23, 8, 15; 29, 7; 30, 4, [4]; 31,
    3; 34 A 9-10; 64, 5-6
(-)φορεῖν 71 fr. 3, 4
φρήν 42, 22; 48 J 10; 53, 13; 57, 41;
  72 ii [15?]; 82 fr. A 6
φρικτός 42, 5; 49, 49
φρικώδης 49, 69
φρίσσειν 50, 15-16
φυλακτήριον 23, 8-9, 16; 28, 1; 34 A
  10; 64, 6-7; 92, (14); 94, [10]

φύλαξ **87**, 4

φυλάccειν **2**, 8; **10**, 7, 10; **15**, 6; **49**, 73

(-)φυλάccειν **80**, 1; **84**, [1?]

φύλλον **74**, 3; **82** fr. B 4; **85**, 43; **94**, 30, 32; **96 A** 51

*φυcιδρόμοc **49**, 57?

φύcιc **70**, 4

- ('sex') **87**, 2

- ('sexual organ') **38**, 12 (*bis*); **45**, 8; **48** K 37; **79**, 5

*φυcιτρόμοc **49**, 57?

φωνή **49**, 69; **63**, 7; **66**, 22

φώρ **86** fr. B [2?]

φῶc **57**, 37; φάοc **49**, 71; **59**, 14; **60**, 4

χαίρειν **72** ii 9 (*ter*), 10

χαίτη **42**, 21

χαλᾶν **86** fr. A ii 11

χαλεπόc **71** fr. 19, [2]

χάλκεοc: *see* χαλκοῦc

χαλκοῦc **24** fr. B [2?]

- χάλκεοc **49**, 58

χαλκόc **24** fr. B [2?]; **72** ii [23?]

χαρακτήρ **19**, [16]; **21**, 11-12; **23**, 13; 92, 16?; **97** ↓ 14-15

χαράccειν **86** fr. A ii 17

χαρίζειν **45**, 51; **51**, [5?]; **63**, 11

χάριc **26**, 1; **63**, 8; **64**, 3; **72** ii 6

- χάριν c. gen. **63**, 1

χαριτήcιον **97** ↓ [(2?)]

χαρτάριον **85**, 42

χάρτηc **96 A** 56

χαρτίον **97** ↓ 15

χεῖν **79**, 10

χείρ **31**, [3?]; **45**, 8; **59**, 18; **60**, 7; **72**

i 11, ii 1; **86** fr. A ii 14, [15?]; **94**, 25; **96 A** 61

χελιδών **83**, 3

χηναλώπηξ **70**, 9

χθόνιοc **42**, 35, 40; **45**, 1; **48** J 4; **54**, 2, 6, 15-16, 29

χοιρίδιον **100**, 14

χοῖροc **75**, 9

χοῦν **97** ↓ 5, 8

χρᾶcθαι **38**, 9; **72** i 18, ii 3; **94**, 6

χρηcτόν or χρήcιμον **82** fr. A (9)

χρηcτόc **93**, 1

χρίειν **72** ii 2 (*bis*); **75**, 5; **76**, 2, 6; **96 A** 72

χρόνοc **6**, 8; **14**, 10; **19**, 21; **38**, 12-13; **39**, 13, 17; **45**, 37; **46**, 26; **47**, 26; **48** J 14; **49**, 5; **51**, 9

χρύcεοc: *see* χρυcοῦc

χρυcοβελήc **96 A** 32; **96 E** ↓ [8]; **96 F** fr. A 7

χρυcοειδήc **70**, 10

χρυcόκομοc **96 A** 33; **96 F** fr. A 8

χρυcοcάνδαλοc **49**, 60

χρυcοῦc **5**, 2

- χρύcεοc **49**, 59

χυλόc **76**, 5

χωρεῖν **42**, 23

χωρίc **49**, 24, 27

χῶροc **49**, 65

ψῆφοc **76**, 9

ψύχειν **89**, 9

ψυχή **29**, 6; **30**, 5; **39**, 3, 4, 5; **40**, 17; **42**, 15, 36, 46, 54, 59; **43**, 6; **44**, 14; **45**, 14; **48** J-K 10, 23, 25, 36; **50**, 64; **54**, 23; **72** i 17

- ἐξ ὅλης ψυχῆc **48** J 12

- καθαρᾷ ψυχῇ 87, 5
- κατὰ ψυχήν 72 i 22

ψυχρός 45, 13

ψωλή 96 A 61

ὦ 59, 8; 72 i [26]; 88, 5

ὧδε 44, 10

ὠκεανός 2, 2-3

ὦμος 97 ↓ [31?]

ᾠόν 38, 8?; 97 ↓ 3

ὥρα 80, 4
- ἀπὸ τῆς ἄρτι ὥρας 48 J 14; ἀπὸ ἄρτι ὥρας 14, 9
- ἀφ' ἧς ἡμέρας καὶ ὥρας 72 i 23
- ἐν τῇ ἄρτι ὥρᾳ 9, 13; 11, 17; 55 D-G 19

- μίαν ὥραν 39, 15
- πᾶσαν ὥραν 46, 23
- πάςῃ ὥρᾳ 49, 80; 50, 28, 69
- ταύτῃ τῇ ὥρᾳ 97 → 8
- ὥρας ἐξ ὡρῶν 46, 5; 47, 5; 48 J 5; 49, 14

ὡς 95 ↓ 9
- (adv.) 42, 18, 39; 48 J 24; 59, 4, 15; 71 fr. 2, 5?
- - ὡς . . . οὕτως 51, 8; 58, 8
- - ὡς περιέχει 5, 4
- (conj.) 32, 2?, 3

ὡςεί 71 fr. 23, 2

ὥςπερ
- ὥςπερ . . . οὕτως 56, 1

VI. LATIN (36)

VII. GODS, DAEMONS, ANGELS, MYTHOLOGICAL NAMES, AND NAMES FROM THE OLD AND NEW TESTAMENT

Damaged at the beginning

VIII. MAGICAL WORDS

It is a well-known fact that editorial division and analysis of magical words is often nothing other than guess work, among other reasons because so many are unparalleled, because the ancient texts for the most part lack word division, and because much is meaningless gibberish that cannot be explained by Egyptian, Hebrew and other languages. A number of the shorter "words" listed below will of necessity be wrong divisions. Also a number of the longer "words" must occasionally contain shorter, meaningful elements that have not been correctly isolated. For the longer "words" we considered analytical cross-referencing of possible parts — e.g. "φαμμιεαρθειαηαιμα in τοφαμμιεαρθειαηαιμα (42, 26)," "μιεαρθειαηαιμα in τοφαμμιεαρθειαηαιμα," etc. — but have by and large refrained from doing so, finding that such a system would usually also present wrong information and so unnecessarily encumber the index, and because computer readability of texts should soon render this superfluous for future study.

ααλω **43**, 3

αβαδαωτ[. .] **42**, 32

αβαρι **42**, 56

αβει **6**, 2

αβεραμενθωου(θ)λερθεξαναξεθρελ-
(θ)υοωθνεμαρεβα **48** J 1; **95** →
[14-16]

αβι **6**, 5 (*bis*)

αβλαναθαναλβα: *see* Index VII

αβρα **19**, 10

αβραμ **75**, [21]

- *see also* Index VII Αβρααμ

αβρασι **13**, 3, 18-19

αβραω (for Αβραωθ?) **94**, 8

αγατα **66**, 4

αγραμμη **3**, 1, 6

αδεφαπαβα **92**, 6

αδυναισα **66**, 15

αεοωοθ **4**, 1

- *see also* Index VII Αεωθ

αεριβης **18**, 2

αζαθοαθαγενγη **66**, 16

αθβιπ . ω . ς **19**, 13

αθερεοφιλαυω **48** K 47

αθθα **49**, 49

αθινεμβης **42**, 9

αιαναφα **48** K 46

αιφνωσαβαω **38**, 7

ακραχαμιφωνχωωθψαυς **40**, 1-10 (in Schwindeschema)

ακρουβορερα **49**, 47-48

- *see also* Index V ἀκρουροβόρε

αλαλαχος **42**, 8

αλεου **66**, 9

αλιλαμψ: *see* Index VII Λαιλαμψ

αλις **42**, 30

αλληχ **42**, 8

αμαζε **50**, 48

αμαζων in λαμψαμαζων

αμαρδα **48** J 19

αμαρζα **46**, 18

   - *see also* μαρζα

αμαρχεθυ **19**, 11

αμαψουουρου **66**, 4

αμβρα: *see* βαρουχαμβρα

αμεν **42**, 26

αμερω in λαμψαμερω

αμητηλαι **96** A 19-20; **96** C fr. B [2]

αμιμ **43**, 2

αμιχ **96** A 3 ?

αμιχλου **96** A 3 ?

αμου **42**, 31; **43**, 2

αμου νηι **6**, 3

αμουραχθη **48** K 46

αμχη **96** A 2 ?

αμχηλου **96** A 2 ?

ανααπαντο **66**, 5

αναξ **16**, 4 ?

αναξαρναξα **57**, 27

αναχαζα **57**, 25

ανιααδαιια **29**, 17-18

αννε **42**, 28

αννουχεω **42**, 20

ανοχ ανοχ **42**, 30

αορκαχ **28**, 3

αοστραχιν **42**, 31

απτουμι **42**, 48

αραμε **42**, 27

αραχα: *see* ερηκισιθφηαραχαραραηφ-
   θισικηρε

αρι χ **4**, 2

αρμαριννε **4**, 2

αρμαχα **49**, 51

αρουηου (for Ἀρουηρ?) **57**, 34

αρταζαβαθος **42**, 9

αρχεδαμα **54**, 2, 6, 16, 32

αρχις[ ] **49**, 53

ασαρα[in ιρααασαρα[

ασκατανθιρι **41**, 9

ασκι **49**, 64

ασταζαβαθος **42**, 9

ασωρ **41**, 9

αθεραθιωθ **6**, 4

αθουεινι αθουιν **6**, 3

αυτ **96** A [45]; **96** E → 9

αφανθ[**19**, 10

αχαιφωθωθωαιηιαηαιιαηαιηιαωθω-
   θωφιαχα **42**, 25

αχαλ **42**, 31

αχεωπηθιθου **49**, 44

αχλαλ **45**, 40

αχχαχ **42**, 48

αχχωρ αχχωρ **42**, 48

αχωρ **42**, 27

αχ [ ] **79**, 24

βααρα **43**, 3

βαβαραθα **49**, 49

βαβαρβαριαωθ **49**, 35

βαβριθηεαθ **49**, 50

βαδητοφωθι **53**, [10]

βαθα: *see* φρεννωβαθα

βαθαραρ **42**, 33

βαθος: *see*
   αρταζαβαθος
   ασταζαβαθος

βαθραηλ **42**, 31

βαιζαχα **4**, 3

βαιν **43**, 3

βαινααρα **43**, 3 ?

βαιωθ **46**, 18

βακα **53**, 7

βακαω **43**, 1

βαλ (= Βαλ ?): *see*

   βαρβαλ

   φθωβαλ

βαλεω **45**, 41

βαλοχρα **12**, 1

βαμεα **10**, 5

βαρα: *see* αρωνβαρα

βαραθαθ **49**, 50

βαραι **39**, 9

βαρασθρομουαι **42**, 26

βαρβαλ **42**, 32

βαρβαραρα **49**, 50

βαριαμβω: *see* ιωβαριαμβω

βαριοθ **50**, 48

βαριχαμω **42**, 50

βαριωθ **49**, 37-38

βαρου **96 A** 4 ?

βαρουχ **47**, 15; **49**, 3, 34; **50**, 35, 36;

   51, 3; **75**, [21]; **96 A** 4 ?

   - *see also* Index VII Βαρουχ

βαρουχ[**51**, 12

βαρουχα **50**, 35; **51**, 3, 12; **96 A** 4 ?

βαρουχαμβρα **46**, 16; **48 J** 17

   - *see also* Index VII

     Αβραθ

     Αμβραθ

βαροχ **2**, 6; **98** no. 6, 3

βαρ α **94**, 8

βασαρα **42**, 33

βασδουμα **95** → [9]

βασυμ **57**, 23, 30; **87**, 10

βαυζαχαμ **42**, 11

βαφαμμηχ **94**, 47-48

βαφαρ **51**, 7

βαφρενεμουν: *see* ιαεωβαφρενεμουν

   palindrome

βαχαμ **42**, 50

βαχυχ **53**, 7

βαψι **53**, 11

βββ **92**, 12

βββββ (an oblique through the last four

   β's) **20**, 6

βεζεβυθ: *see* Index VII Ιωβεζεβυθ

βελερθι **96 A** 41; **96 E** → 6

βελιας **57**, 34

   - *see also* Index VII βελιαμ

βελιωας **57**, 34

βελλενουρε **94**, 47

βελτι βελτι **6**, 2 (*bis*)

βερβαισω **42**, 33

βερωουνηρ **66**, 12

βεωθ **48 J-K** 19, 30

βηθ ε [ ]ουχ **94**, 3

βηι **6**, 5

βηχε **92**, 9

βι **6**, 5

βιασάνδρα: *see* Index V

βιβιβε **48 K** 45

βιβιουθ **48 K** 45

   - *see also* Index VII

     Βιου

     Βιβιου

βιβιωθ **53**, 11

βιλλακου **6**, 3

βιρααριν **66**, 15

βλα **96 A** 9

βοασαραουλ **42**, 32

βοζο[**4**, 3

βολβεσρω **45**, 41

βολβεω **45**, 41

βολβεωχ **45**, 41

fr. B [4]

ζθο **66**, 7

ζοχ[**4**, 2

ηϊ **44**, [8]

ηθουατ **6**, 4

ηκιαεου **41**, 9

ηλο . . ουεα **20**, 5

ηνωρ **42**, 56

ηρερε **42**, 53

ηχβερηχ **42**, 53

θαβαψραβου **42**, 27

- see also Index VII Θωβαραβαυ

θαθ: see Index VII

θαθη θαθω **97** ↓ 6

θαθθαβραβο **95** → [11-12]

θαμβαμι **66**, 13

θαμρα **12**, 1

θανωαμα[**87**, 8

θαρα θαρω **96 A** 52

θαccουθο **42**, 42

θεcμαοαθαα **66**, 18

θεχθει **82** fr. A 3 ?

θηνωρ **42**, 52, 56

θηνωρθcι **42**, 52

θηcααρcαc **19**, 8

θθυc **96 A** 54

θι **48 G** 2

θι[**73** ii 15

θιανοηρ **79**, 29

θλιβαρφιξ **42**, 27

θνη **96 A** 59

θοαθοηθαθοουθαεθωυcθοαιθιθηθοινθω
63, 12-14

θονινευκτευ **66**, 7

θοου **42**, 43

θοραξ **58**, 6

θου **42**, 10

θουφ **66**, 6

θραξ **97** ↓ 9

θυ **19**, 9, 11 ?, 12 ?

θυηοηω **42**, 42

θυρcερψε αμαχθεν **66**, 6

θωβαυcθω **42**, 43

θωβαφ **66**, 13

θωβωθ **42**, 54

θωθω: see

αχαιφω palindrome

Index VII Θωουθ

ι **79**, 15

ιαεωβαφρενεμουνοθιλαρικριφιαευεα-
ιφιρκιραλιθοννομενερφαβωεαι **49**,
1+3; **74**, 11-16

- in Schwindeschema **48 A** 1-30; **65**,
[1-30]

ιακινθου (Ιακιν θ⟨ε⟩οῦ?) **57**, 30

ιαλφηc **73** ii 15

ιαμβω: see ιωβαριαμβω

ιαμελου **39**, 8

ιανβελαχι **39**, 9

ιαρτανα **42**, 19 (bis)

ιατθεουν **48 K** 43

ιατθεραθ **48 K** 44

ιατρεουν **48 K** 43

ιαφθω **42**, 43

ιαχα **10**, 5

ιβεαλη[**82** fr. A 3 ?

ιβει **6**, 2

ιβιβι **42**, 32

ιθελ **16**, 6 ?

ιοελ **16**, 6 ?

ιοιναθαψαωcευ **66**, 15

σαβαρααμ 2, 7; **50**, 37, 39

σαβαρβαριαωθ **46**, 17; **49**, 36

σαβαρβατιανη **48** J 18

σαβαρβατιαωθ **48** J 18

σαβαρβαφαει **47**, 16

σαβαρβαφαι **48** J 18

σαλακαλου **98** no. 1 fr. A 1

σαλαμαξα **10**, 3

σαλβαναχαμβρη **49**, 46

σαλβιουθ **48** K 43

σαληνασαυ **42**, 31

σαμουσουμ **14**, 1

σανβαλχανβαλ **87**, 8

σανκιστη **38**, 8; **49**, 47

σαξα **51**, 7

σαοραυινιενουτιο **52**, 1

σαραηφθω **42**, 41

σαρερταθου **54**, 2, 6, 16, 33

σαριχ **28**, 2

σαρουχα **42**, 32

σαρχ **94**, 34

σασιβηλ **42**, 41

σαταμα **48** K 46

σεβαων **16**, 2

σελτι **6**, 2

σεπανσασε **42**, 43

σερπωτ **44**, 7

σερφουτ **44**, 9

σετωνεκοιι **41**, 10

σημο **98** no. 6, 3

σθομψιμ **66**, 14

σθωμβαυλη **96** A 37; **96** E → 3

σιελβιουχ **6**, 3-4

σιερσειρ **42**, 29

σιμ **44**, 1

σινα [**98** no. 1 fr. A 2

σιουσιου: *see* ουσιουσιου

σισεμβρηχ **42**, 53

σισηθ **96** A 16; **96** B 4; **96** C fr. A 4

σισι **42**, 49; **57**, 14

σισιςρω **42**, 32, 49; **57**, 14; **79**, 28

　　- *see also* σρο

σιτ **41**, 1

σκυλμ[ ] **42**, 30

σοβουχ **42**, 32

σοζοχα **4**, 3

σοζοχαμ **42**, 11

σομοχαν **42**, 11

σου **42**, 43

σουμα σουμη σουμηια **14**, 1

σουχιαρ **42**, 30

σοχσοχαμ **42**, 11

σρο **44**, 8, 9

　　- *see also* σισιςρω

σρουατ **14**, 2

σσσ **97** ↓ 11

σσσσσ **23** (in drawing)

στησεων **38**, 7

συιε **49**, 47

συμμυθα **42**, 29

συρια **48** K 45

σωθαλις **42**, 27

σωθαρα **42**, 29

σωθεωθ **42**, 30

σωθη **42**, 27

σωκ ̤ ρουμε **42**, 30

σωρσανγαρ **42**, 31

σωσε or]σωσε **94**, 44

ταατ (Thoth?) **42**, 31

τειλουτειλου: *see* Index VII

τευθραιαιαιαω **43**, 1

τεφρεωθι **50**, 42-43

τεωαντισιρονμυραε **66**, 8?

IX. VOWEL COMBINATIONS

A. The Seven Vowels

ααααααα εεεεεεε ηηηηηηη ιιιιιιι οοο-
οοοο υυυυυυυ ωωωωωωω **43**, 4-5

α εε ηηη ιιιι οοοοο υυυυυυ ωωωωωωω
3, 2; **7**, 1-7 (upright isosceles tri-
angle); **20**, 1

αεηιουω **10**, 2, 3, 6-7; **42**, 19, 20, 42;
48 D 1-4 (in Schwindeschema); **64**,
1; **66**, 17

αεηιουωωυοιηεα (in Schwindeschema)
3, 7-13

ωυοιηεα (in Schwindeschema) **48** F 1-4

B. Other Combinations

αα **48** G 12, 22, H 6

αααα **6**, 7

ααααααα **48** J 28

αααααααα **15**, 2-3

αε **48** G 3; **87**, 12

αειω **48** J 28

αευια **41**, 5

αεο . . . ωαηω **48** K 29

αεωαεαεω **48** J 28

αη **6**, 6

αηαη 48 B 11

αηι **6**, 6

αιεουω **41**, 2

αιηιαηαι: *see* Index VIII αχαιφω palindrome

αιηου **41**, 4

αιυαυεω **48** K 29

αυ **48** H 9

αω **48** B 1, H 14

αωοε **48** B 14

εα **48** B 2, H 11

εαω **10**, 2

εε **48** G 14, H 8

εεεεεε **68**, 3

εο **48** B 6, H 2

εοαωα **48** B 16

εοηι **48** B 8

ευ **41**, 4

εω **48** G 9, H 1

ηα **41**, 6

ηε **48** G 20

ηει **15**, 4

ηη **48** G 11, 15, 19

ηηη **23** (in drawing)

ηηηη **6**, 7

ηϊ **48** G 16, 18, 21, H 16
    - *see also* Index VIII

ηια **45**, 16

ηιου **48** B 12

ι: *see* Index VIII

ια **42**, 42; **45**, 19-20 (ια ια ια); **48** H
12, 21

ια[**64**, 1

Ιαεουωι: *see* Index VII

Ιαεω: *see* Index VII

ιαη **41**, 4; **45**, 16

ιαηαιηια: *see* Index VIII αχαιφω palindrome

X. ABBREVIATIONS, MONOGRAMS, SYMBOLS

Christian	Others

Christian

θ͞c͞ 27, 7?; 32, 6 (*bis*); 33 R° 2

θ͞υ͞ 24 B, 3, 6; 25, 4; 29, 11, 12

θ͞ε͞ 20, 3

ι͞c͞ 25, [1], 9; 34 A 1

ι͞η͞υ͞ 20, 5

υ͞υ͞ 28, 2

υ͞υ͞ (voc.) 30, 4; 31, 2 (*bis*), 3

κ͞c͞ 25, 6; 29, 16; 32, 6

κ͞υ͞ 32, 10

κω 93, 3

κ͞ν͞ 29, 18

κ͞ε͞ 84, 1

και = κ(ύρι)ε 20, 3

π͞ν͞α͞ 30, 5

π͞ν͞α͞ (gen.) 31, 4 (*bis*)

π͞ρc͞ 31, 4

υ͞υ͞ 31, 4

χ͞c͞ 25, [1], 10; 34 A 1; 35, 1-8 (*octies*)

χ͞ρυ͞ 20, 6; 28, 2

χ͞ε͞ 30, 4

εcτ͞θ͞η͞ = έcταυρώθη 31, 1

χμγ 62, 2

† 23, 1; 29, 1; 31, [1?]; 34 B (*ter*), C
    7 (*bis*); 35 top (*quater*), bottom
    (*septies*); 36, 1; 61, 1 (*ter*)

⳨ 25, [1?], 10; 26, 1; 59, 19 (*sexies*);
    62, 1

♀ 33 V°

⳩ 21, 1 (*ter*)

α͞ω͞ 22, 1 (*ter*)

⊕ / α͞ω͞ 27, 6 (*ter*)

᷍ο͞ᖯᖇ = βοηθ(οῦ) 28, 2

Others

αγω^γ = ἀγώγιμον or ἀγωγή 82, 4

α᷍ᶜ = ἄλλο 79, 6

βα(cι)λεῦ (?) 42, 40

γ^ρ = γράψον 85, 42

γᵖ = γράψον 94, 7

γρ/ = γράψον 92, 14

γρα/ = γράψον 96 A 23

δ = δεῖνα 71 fr. 14, 2?

Ⴃ = δεῖνα 73, 7; 74, 17 (*bis*); 79, 5?,
    9, 21, 25 (*bis*), 31; 80, 1; 87, 11; 95
    → 7, 14, ↓ 15

Ⴃ = δεῖνα 89, 3

Ⴃ̄ = δεῖνα 72 i 19 (*bis*), 20, 23, ii 22

Ⴃνα = δεῖνα 79, 8

∠ = δραχμή 94, 5 (*bis*), 6

⟨ἰ⟩νδικ(τίωνος) 45, 37

κ/ = καί 97 ↓ 3, 4, 8, 15, 16, 17, 19,
    26, 27, → 3

κ͜ = καί 30, 5 (*bis*); 31, 1 (*quinquies*), 2,
    3 (*ter*), 4 (*septies*); 72 ii 13, 16, fr. 3,
    1; 74, 4, 6, 7, 18, 19; 77 fol. 6v, 6;
    82 fr. B 3, 5; 95 → 22; 99 V° 3 (*bis*)

κο† = κοινά, κοινόν 95 → 7, 20, ↓ 2

κο‡ = κοινά, κοινόν 92, 12, 13, 15

λ᷍ο͞ = λόγος 94, 44

ō = ὄνομα 94, 24

ονō = ὄνομα 85, 42

ō͞ = ὄνομα 74, 1, 4, 7

⊡ = ὄνομα 96 A 23

ꝑ = πρός 88, 1, 6; 94, 7, 10, 17, 22, 39

φυλ/ = φυλακτήριον 92, 14

✳ = χρηcτόν or χρήcιμον 82 fr. A 9

Final ν indicated by supralinear stroke
    79, 7 ηδον͞η; 94, 36 cτραγγουρι͞α;
    99 R° i 4 λαβ͞ω; 100, 13 τ͞η, 14 τ͞ο,
    15 πολλ͞ω, 19 θυρ͞ω

XI. INDEX LOCORUM

A. Ancient Writings Referred to in the Texts.
B. Ancient Writings Referred to in the Discussions.
    1. Authors and Writings. 2. Papyri, Ostraca and Inscriptions.

An asterisk * before an entry indicates that the passage is treated critically.

A. Ancient Writings Referred to in the Texts
(by quotation, allusion or mention of author's name)

B. Ancient Writings Referred to in the Discussions

(a selection)

2. Papyri, Ostraca and Inscriptions

XII. GREEK LANGUAGE

comm.

- κατας βένω **2**, 17-18 comm.
- κατάσχησον **13**, 7 comm.
- κεντέω τι εἴς τι **97** ↓ 20
- κράζω 'cry out in accusation' **52**, 9 comm.
- μολύνω, forms of confused with μω- λύω **86** fr. A ii 16 comm.
- παρακατατίθομαι (thematic) **46**, 1
- πατάξησον for πάταξον **61**, 2, 3

- πεῖν **43**, 9 comm.; **45**, 45; **46**, 11; **47**, 10; **48** J 9, 23
- ποιεῖν τὸ ἱκανόν τινι **61**, 1 comm.
- coὶ λέγω, authoritative tone of **94**, 48-49 comm.
- cυμπαράcτατε impt. **46**, 6
- cυνέχω of fever **9**, 9-10 comm.
- ὑπερτίθεμαί τινα 'put someone off' **45**, 50; **72** i 10?
- *see also* Nouns: cases

XIII. SUBJECT INDEX

intr. with n. 5

- *see also* Disjunctive spells

Dates, applied charms provided with **45**, 37 comm.; **52**, 24 comm.

Dawn, magical actions performed at **72** ii 3 comm.

Death as robber **42**, 21 comm.

Decans **44**, 3-4 comm., 4-6 comm.

Disjunctive spell(s)
- motivations of
- - erotic jealousy **95** intr.
- - other **55** intr.
- possible example of **69** intr.

Divination: *see*
Bes
Child mediums
Dream oracles and requests
Homer oracle
Lamps
Necromancy
Vessels

Divorce, cause of, ascribed to an evil demon in documentary papyri **95** → 14 comm.
- *see also* Legal matters

Dream oracles and requests: *see under* Formularies, contents of

Drowning or immersion, divinity resulting from **71** fr. 7, 4 comm.

Egyptian god(s)
- blood of **79**, 1-11 comm.
- sleep of **52**, 10-13 comm.
- water of **79**, 1-11 comm.

Egyptian words
- ovϩ 'life' **63**, 10

- ωαπ 'holiness, purity' **45**, 20

Erichthonios **1** comm.

Erotic charm(s)
- Anubis invoked in **71** fr. 9, 2 comm.
- apples in **72** i 5-14 comm.
- for either a woman or a homosexual to win a man **72** ii 1-25 comm.
- love for beloved explicitly mentioned in **71** fr. 9, 2 comm.; **72** ii 1-25 comm.
- occasionally limited to a fixed period of time **37** B 5-6 comm.
- used to mollify a legal adversary **54** intr.
- *see also*
Ointments
Ousia

Falcon, animal of Horos, statuette of inscribed with protective charm **6** intr.

Figurines, wax
- in aggressive spell **97** ↓ 15 comm.
- in erotic spells **45** intr.; **46** intr.

Formularies, Christian: *see* Christian formulary

Formularies, contents of (texts and passages of uncertain nature are omitted)
- aggressive spell **97** ↓ 12-33
- blind rat, uses of **99** R° ii 1 ff.
- charitesion **82** fr. A 10-11?; **97** ↓ 2-6?
- charms for successful business **97** ↓ 7-9?; **99** R° i 3-6
- disjunctive spells **95**

stones **56**, 1 comm.
- detector of thieves **86** fr. A i 6 comm.

Historiola(e) and mythical paradigm(s)
- Isis' love for Osiris **38**, 9 comm.; **71** fr. 7, 3-4 comm.; **72** ii 4-6 comm.
- Jesus stopping the Euphrates **32** intr.
- obscure **72** i 15-27 comm.
- Osiris and Seth, enmity between **95** → 21 comm.
- Solomon's binding of the daemons and placing them under oath **24** fr. B 1-3 (see intr. and comm.)

Holy books, Egyptian, true and purported sources of Greek magical and religious texts **72** i 1-5 comm.

Homer oracles **77** intr.

Homosexuality **42** intr.; **54** intr.; **72** ii 1-25 comm.

Horos
- 'Horos the great' **42**, 49-50 comm.
- 'Horos on the horizon' **42**, 8-9 comm.
- identified with Khenty-Khet **93**, 3 comm.
- identified with Min **92**, 9-10 comm.
- *see also*
  Athribis
  Chnum-Horos
  Falcon

Horos-Apollo as white wolf **34** C comm.

Horses, therapeutic and protective charms for **92**, 11 comm.

Human body, 365 (also 36 and 12) members of **53**, 14-15 comm.

Ibis **3**, 1 comm. on φιβλω; **6**, 2 comm. on ιβει αβει.

Illness, personified, directly adjured **32**, 3 comm.; **94**, 48-49 comm.

Ink: *see under* Palaeography

Inscription, magical, licked, or dissolved and drunk **75**, 3 comm.
- *see also under* Water

Isis **72** ii 27 comm.
- and Nephthys as birds lamenting the corpse of Osiris **90** fr. D 14-15 comm.

Jordansegen **32** intr.

Khenty-Khet **93**, 3 comm.

Kneph **66**, 5 comm.; **70**, 2 comm.

Kronos **95** → 16 comm.

Lamellae, gold and silver **64** intr.
- *see also* Survey C *under* Silver tablets

Lamps, divination with **93** intr.

Laurel-leaf **85**, 43 comm.

Lead tablet(s)
- pierced by nails **37** descr.; **39** descr.
- *see also*
  Lamellae
  Survey C *under*
    Lead tablets
    Silver tablets

Legal and quasi-legal matters
- crying out in accusation (βοᾶν, κράζειν) **52**, 9 comm.

SURVEYS AND CONCORDANCES

A. CHRONOLOGICAL TABLE

(all dates assigned unless otherwise indicated)

II-I BC: **70**

I BC: **71**

Augustan Age: **72**

Roman Period: **6**

I AD: **52, 73**

I/II: **67**

II: **37, 38, 74, 75**

II-III: **46, 47, 48, 54, 64, 77**

II/III: **49, 50, 51, 76, 78**

II-V: **69**

Early III: **63**

III: **1, 2, 3, 4, 5, 7, 39, 40, 53, 55,
65, 68, 79, 80, 81, 82, 83, 91**

Later III (terminus post quem 249/50):
85

III or early IV: **86**

III-IV: **8, 9, 10, 11, 41, 42, 44, 84,
87**

III/IV: **12, 56, 66**

IV: **13, 14, 43, 57, 88, 89, 90**

IV-V: **15, 16, 22, 58, 93**

IV/V: **20, 21, 92**

V: **17, 18, 23, 24, 25, 26, 27, 28,
45, 95, 100**

V or V/VI: **36**

V-VI: **29, 32, 33, 62, 99**

V/VI: **31, 96, 97, 98**

Late V or VI: **30**

VI: **19, 34, 35, 59, 60, 61, 94**

B. PROVENANCES

(known or surmised)

Aboutig **84?**

Abusir el Melek **72**

Alexandria **54**

Antinoopolis **65, 94, 99, 100**

Assiut, north of **45**

Athribis **6**

Fayum **10?, 66?, 69, 81?**

Fustat **32, 36**

Hawara **46**

Hermopolis **42**

Karanis **68**

Middle Egypt **47?**

Narmouthis **67**

Oxyrhynchos **2, 5, 7, 16** (see Vol. II,
p. xiii), **49-51, 53, 55, 56, 64, 70,
78, 79, 85, 86, 88, 90**

Panopolis **37?, 59-60**

Saqqara **52?**

Tebtunis **76**

Thebes **58**

C. INSCRIBED MATERIALS

(other than papyrus)

Earthenware vessels
- incised into still moist clay **65**
- inscribed with ink **51**

Lead tablets
- incised **37** A and B, **38, 41, 42, 46, 47, 48, 49, 50, 53, 54, 55, 57, 66**
- inscribed with ink **39**

Linen cloth **44**

Ostraca **58, 67, 68, 89**

Parchment **100**

Silver tablets **2, 64**

Stone (haematite) statuette of a falcon **6**

Wooden tablet **52**

D. PREVIOUS PUBLICATIONS

1. Papyrological Text-Editions.   2. Editions in Periodicals.   3. Other Publications.
An asterisk * indicates that a publication is a first edition.

1. Papyrological Text-Editions

SB XIV 11493	10	*57-80, no. 2	50
11494	26	*80-84, no. 3	51
11495	31	*85-102, no. 4	45
11534	43	*102-104, no. 5	20
11535	44	*104 f., no. 6	2
11909	76	*105, no. 7	33
12103	41	*106, no. 8	64
12113	84	*107 f., no. 11	7
12114	15	*108 f., no. 12	53
12115	12	*109-111, no. 13	78
12184	62	*Bull. Soc. Arch. Alex. 21 (1925)	
SB XVI 12640	95	42-47	46
12719	32	*Chron. d'Ég. 43 (1968) 111-113	15
13019	3	*Genava 6 (1928) 56-64	38

* * *

Hellenika 27 (1974) 251-253　　76

*Kungl. Humanistiska vetenskapssam-
fundets i Lund, Årsberättelse 1945-
1946 III (Lund 1946), p. 12 f.,*

2. Editions in Periodicals

		no. 12	13
Acme 1 (1948) 226-228	77	*JHS* 62 (1942) 36 f.	88
5 (1952) 405-407	77	*Philologus* 107 (1963) 157-161	34
Acta Antiqua Academiae Scientiarum		*Rev. Phil.* 56 (1930) 248-256	57
Hungaricae 26 (1978) 433-456	12	*Rhein. Mus.* 9 (1854) 369-382	54
Aegyptus 27 (1947) 182, 183 f.	77	18 (1863) 563	54
*32 (1952) 45-53	69	19 (1864) 483-496	54
*33 (1953) 57-62, no. 25	92	*SCO* 29 (1979) 58-93	96
Amtliche Berichte aus den königlichen		*94-112	97
Kunstsammlungen 35.6 (1914)		*113-120	98
203-210	39	*31 (1981) 111-114	28
Anc. Soc. 9 (1978) 101-116	56	*115-117	81
Antik Tanulmányok (Studia Antiqua)		32 (1982) 235-238	14
22 (1975) 30-43	12	*36 (1986) 293-298	74
BASP 13 (1976) 177-179, no. 2	70	*298-305	75
*179 f., no. 3	16	*Sitzb. Heid. Akad. Wiss.*: see 3 *s.n.* Boll.	
* *BIFAO* 6 (1908) 61-63	61	*Studia Antiqua*: see *Antik Tanulmányok.*	
*76 (1976) 213-223	47	*Stud. Pap.* 6 (1967) 109-121	69
Bonner Jahrb. 168 (1968) 57-111:		*13 (1974) 83-88	84
*57-80, no. 1	49		

*Wiener Studien 100 (1987) 185-199   2 7

*ZPE 4 (1969) 187-191   6 6

   *5 (1970) 57-59   2 2

   *14 (1974) 71-73   5 2

   *16 (1975) 274   6 8

   *17 (1975) 25-27, no. 1   8 7

       *27-30, no. 2   1 0

       *30 f., no. 3   2 6

       *31-33, no. 4   3 1

   *19 (1975) 249-255   4 3

       *255-264   4 4

*22 (1976) 108   1 7

*24 (1977) 89 f.   4 1

25 (1977) 145-149   8 4

      153 f.   1 2

*30 (1978) 209 f.   6 2

*33 (1979) 261-278   7 2

37 (1980) 199 f.   5 6

*38 (1980) 261-264   9 5

*48 (1982) 149-170   3 2

*50 (1983) 147-154   3

*58 (1985) 93-95   9 3

72 (1988) 245-259   4 9

      279-286   5 6

      287-292   5 6

73 (1988) 61 f.   6 2

*74 (1988) 253-265   3 6

* * *

3. Other Publications

(Except for Betz, *Translation*, publications consisting only of translation are not taken up here).

*Antinoe (1965-1968). Missione Archeologica in Egitto dell'Università di Roma (Rome 1974), p. 121 f.   6 5

Audollent, *DT*, 38   5 4

Babelon, E., - Blanchet, J.-A., *Catalogue des bronzes antiques de la Bibliothèque Nationale* (Paris 1895), pp. 701-703, no. 2296   5 4

Betz, *Translation*:

   no. LXXXIII   2 9

   no. LXXXIV   4 0

   no. LXXXV: see Vol. I, p. xv on P. Harris 56

   no. LXXXVI   8 0

   no. LXXXVII   1 4

   no. LXXXVIII   1 1

   no. LXXXIX   1 3

   no. XC   9 2

   no. XCI   9

   no. XCII   6 3

   no. XCIII   1 0 0

   no. XCIV   9 4

   no. XCV   9 9

   no. XCVI   1 5

   no. XCVII   7 8

   no. XCVIII   7

   no. XCIX   3 3

   no. C   2 0

   no. CI   4 5

   no. CII   9 0

   no. CIII   7 3

   no. CIV   4

   no. CV   8 7

   no. CVI   1 0

   no. CVII   4 4

   no. CVIII   4 3

   no. CIX   5 6

   no. CX: see Vol. I, p. xvi on P.Wash. Univ. inv. 181+221

   no. CXI   7 0

versity of Michigan 1985); now
reworked as *P.Michigan XVI. A
Greek Love Charm from Egypt*
(P.Mich. 757), ASP 30, 1991 **48**
Mélanges Maspero II (MIFAO 67, 1934-
1937), pp. 206-212 **55**
Metzger, B.M., *Historical and Literary
Studies: Pagan, Jewish and Christian* (Leiden 1968),
pp. 104-110 **11**
Miscellanea Papyrologica (Papyrologica
Florentina VII, 1980),
pp. 169-172, no. 1 **73**
p. 176, no. 6 **42** Side B
*Omaggio al IV convegno dei classicisti
tenuto a Firenze dal 18 al 20 aprile
del 1911* (Florence 1911),
pp. 20-26, no. 5 **42** Side A
*Raccolta di scritti in onore di G.
Lumbroso* (Milan 1925),
p. 496 f. **60**

SEG VIII 574 **46**
SEG XXVI 1717 **47**
SEG XXVII 1243 **41**
*Studia Florentina Alexandro Ronconi
sexagenario oblata* (Rome 1970),
pp. 281-287 **24**
*Vogliano, A., Secondo rapporto degli
scavi condotti dalla missione
archeologica d'Egitto della R.
Università di Milano nella zona di
Medinet Madi* (Milan 1937),
pp. 49-51, nos. 15-16 **67**
Wessely, K., *Les plus anciens monuments du Christianisme écrits sur
papyrus* II (Patrologia Orientalis
18.3, Paris 1924),
p. 495 f., no. 13 **60**
Wessely, *Ephesia Grammata*,
no. 244 **54**
Wünsch, *DTA*, pp. 50-52 **54**

E. LOCATIONS

PLATES

Plate II: No. 58

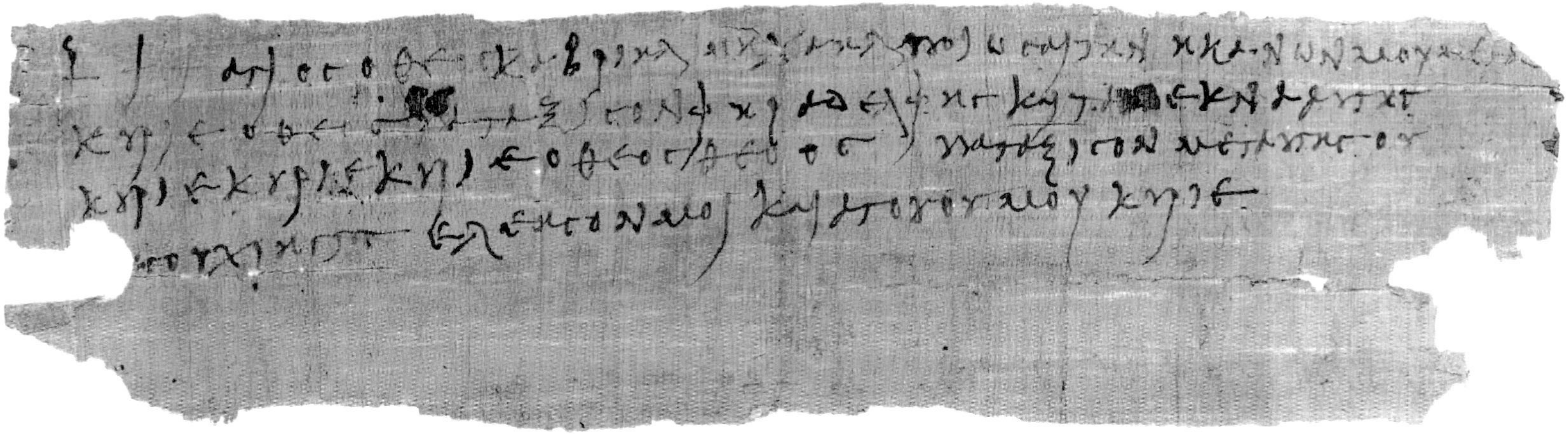

Plate III: No. 61 (reduced)

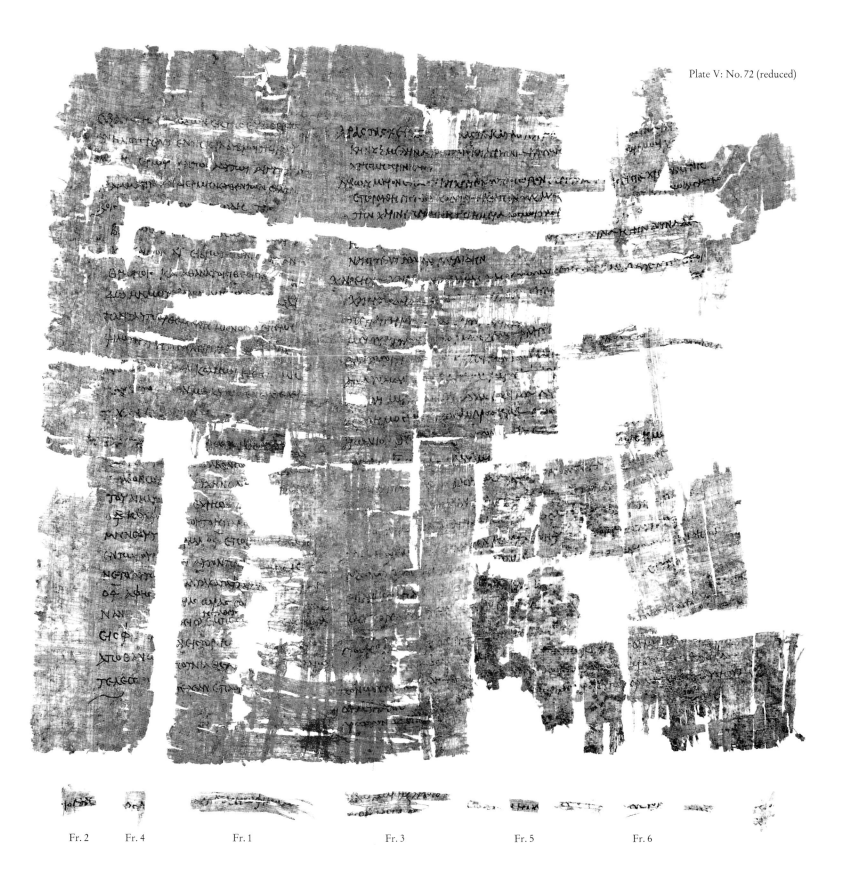

Fr. 2   Fr. 4   Fr. 1   Fr. 3   Fr. 5   Fr. 6

No. 83

No. 80
Plate VII

No. 85

No. 100, side ii

Plate VIII

Fr. A

Fr. B

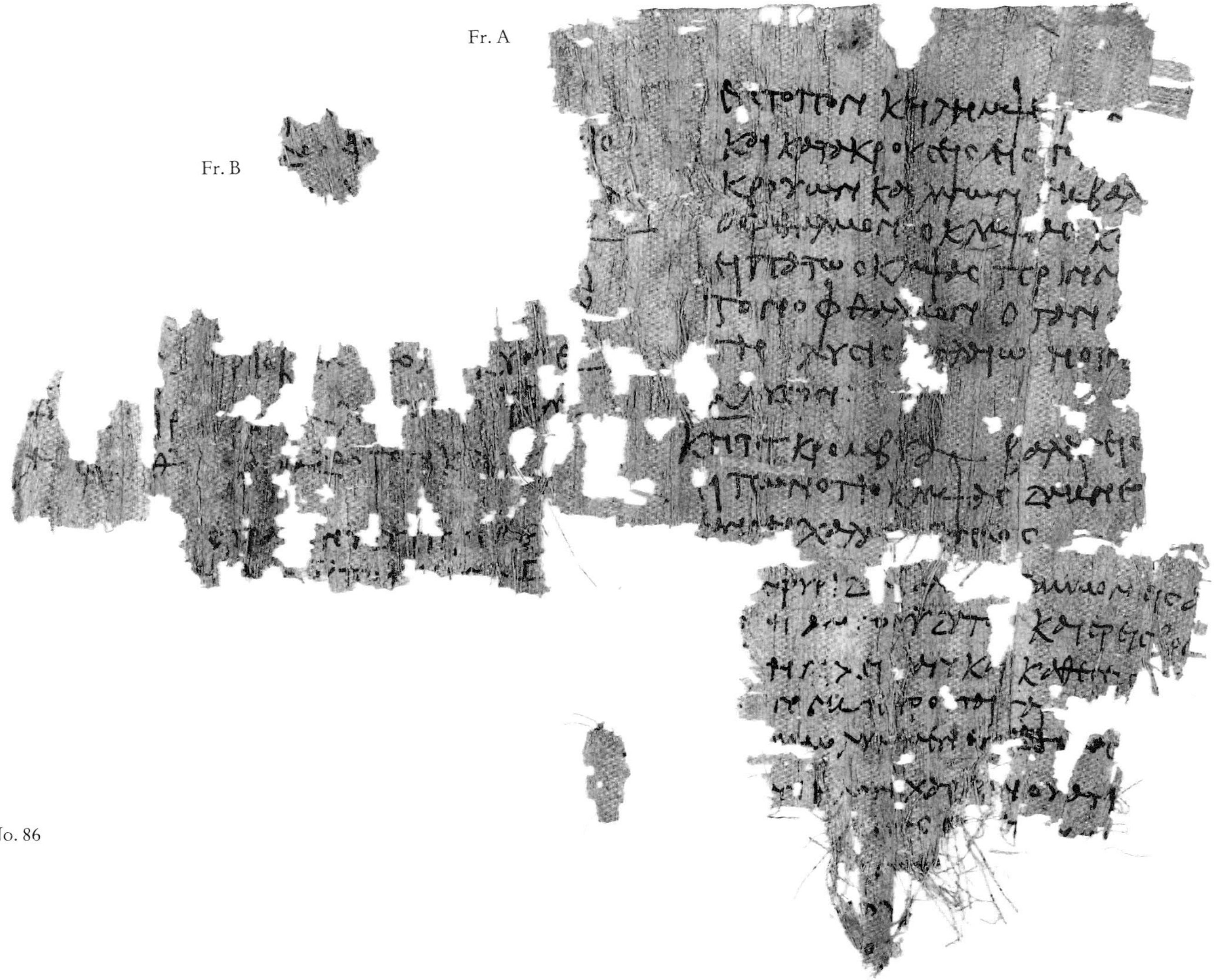

Plate IX: No. 86

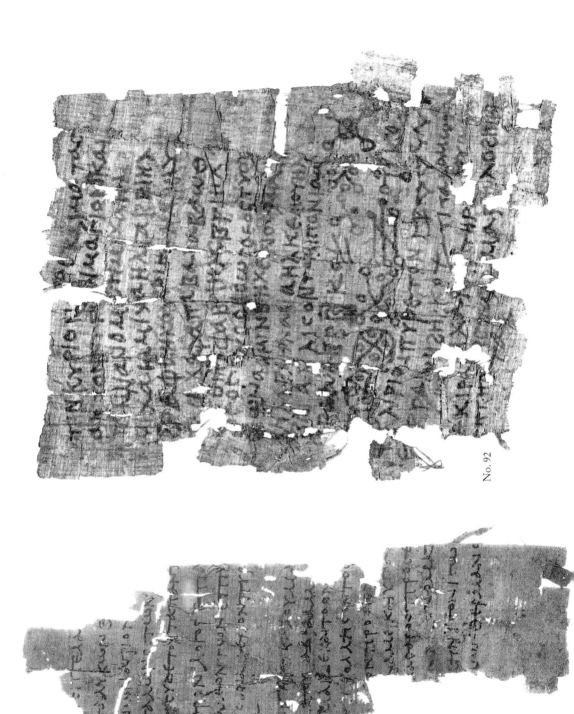

No. 92

No. 88
Plate X

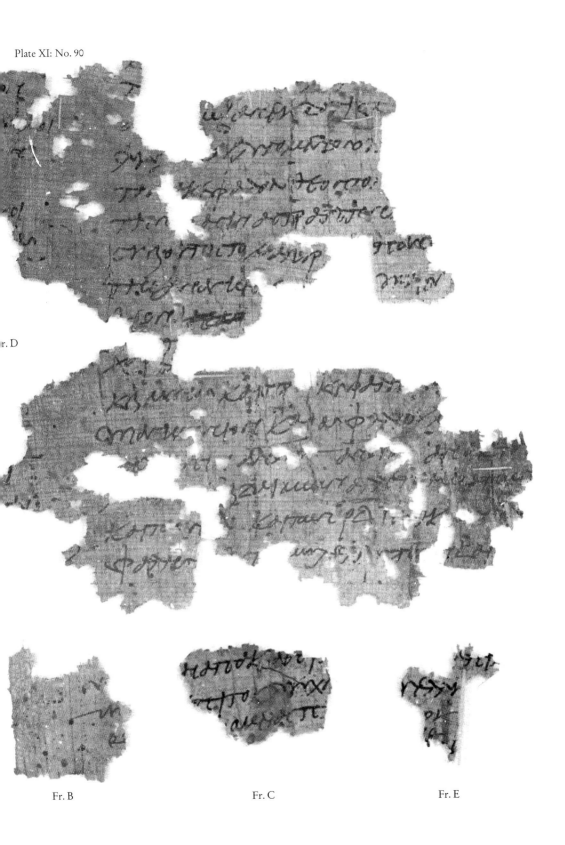

Fr. D

Fr. B   Fr. C   Fr. E

Side →

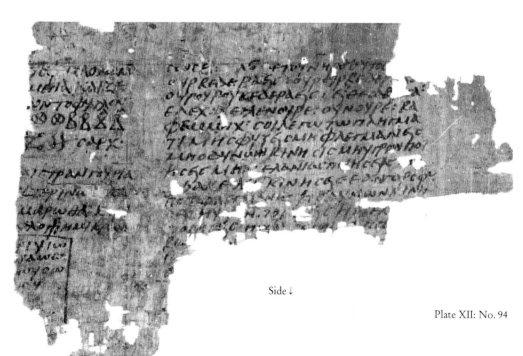

Side ↓

Plate XII: No. 94

recto

verso

Plate XIII: No. 99